CONTEMPORARY BRICS JOURNALISM

Contemporary BRICS Journalism: Non-Western Media in Transition is the first comparative study of professional journalists working in BRICS countries (Brazil, Russia, India, China, and South Africa). The book presents a range of insider perspectives, offering a valuable insight into the nature of journalism in these influential economies.

Contributors to this volume have conducted in-depth interviews with more than 700 journalists, from mainstream and online media, between 2012 and 2015. They present and analyse their findings here, revealing how BRICS journalism is envisioned, experienced, and practiced in the twenty-first century. Compelling evidence in the form of journalists' narratives reveals the impact of digital culture on modern reporting and the evolving dynamic between new media technology and traditional journalistic practice. Insightful comparisons are made between BRICS countries, highlighting the similarities and differences between them. Topics include professionalism, ethics and ideals, community journalism, technological developments in the newsroom, and the reporting of protest movements.

This book's ambitious analysis of journalistic landscapes across these non-Western nations will significantly broaden the scope of study and research in the field of journalism for students and teachers of communication, journalism, and media studies.

Svetlana Pasti is Docent of Journalism and Media Studies at the Faculty of Communication Sciences at the University of Tampere, Finland. She is the author of two monographs and more than 20 peer-reviewed chapters and articles in platforms including *The Global Journalist in the 21st Century*, *European Journal of Communication*, and *Nordicom Review*.

Jyotika Ramaprasad is Professor at the School of Communication, University of Miami, USA. Her research is focused on journalism studies and communication for social change. She has presented and published her work in various publications including *Journalism Quarterly*, *Journalism Studies*, *Gazette*, and *Mass Communication and Society*.

Internationalizing Media Studies
Series Editor: Daya Kishan Thussu, University of Westminster

www.routledge.com/Internationalizing-Media-Studies/book-series/IMS

Internationalizing Media Studies
Edited by Daya Kishan Thussu

Popular Media, Democracy and Development in Africa
Edited by Herman Wasserman

The Korean Wave: Korean Media Go Global
Edited by Youna Kim

Mapping BRICS Media
Edited by Kaarle Nordenstreng and Daya Kishan Thussu

Contemporary BRICS Journalism
Edited by Svetlana Pasti and Jyotika Ramaprasad

China's Media Go Global
Edited by Daya Kishan Thussu, Hugo De Burgh, Shi Anbin

CONTEMPORARY BRICS JOURNALISM

Non-Western Media in Transition

Edited by Svetlana Pasti and Jyotika Ramaprasad

LONDON AND NEW YORK

First published 2018
by Routledge
2 Park Square, Milton Park, Abingdon, Oxon OX14 4RN

and by Routledge
711 Third Avenue, New York, NY 10017

Routledge is an imprint of the Taylor & Francis Group, an informa business

© 2018 selection and editorial matter, Svetlana Pasti and Jyotika Ramaprasad; individual chapters, the contributors

The right of Svetlana Pasti and Jyotika Ramaprasad to be identified as the authors of the editorial material, and of the authors for their individual chapters, has been asserted in accordance with sections 77 and 78 of the Copyright, Designs and Patents Act 1988.

All rights reserved. No part of this book may be reprinted or reproduced or utilised in any form or by any electronic, mechanical, or other means, now known or hereafter invented, including photocopying and recording, or in any information storage or retrieval system, without permission in writing from the publishers.

Trademark notice: Product or corporate names may be trademarks or registered trademarks, and are used only for identification and explanation without intent to infringe.

British Library Cataloguing-in-Publication Data
A catalogue record for this book is available from the British Library

Library of Congress Cataloging-in-Publication Data
A catalog record for this title has been requested

ISBN: 978-1-138-21732-4 (hbk)
ISBN: 978-1-138-21733-1 (pbk)
ISBN: 978-1-315-44092-7 (ebk)

Typeset in Bembo
by Apex CoVantage, LLC

CONTENTS

Contributors *vii*
Foreword by Daya Kishan Thussu *xiii*
Acknowledgements *xv*

Introduction: why BRICS journalism matters 1
Svetlana Pasti and Jyotika Ramaprasad

PART I
Transitioning concepts and practices across BRICS 21

1 Professionalism: continuities and change 23
   Jyotika Ramaprasad, Svetlana Pasti, Fernando Oliveira Paulino, Ruiming Zhou, and Musawenkosi Ndlovu

2 Newsmaking: navigating digital territory 49
   Herman Wasserman, Jyotika Ramaprasad, Muniz Sodré, Maria Anikina, Ravindra Kumar Vemula, and Yu Xu

3 Ethics: ideals and realities 72
   Jyotika Ramaprasad, Deqiang Ji, Ruiming Zhou, Fernando Oliveira Paulino, Svetlana Pasti, Dmitry Gavra, Herman Wasserman, and Musawenkosi Ndlovu

vi Contents

4 Gender: towards equality? 104
   Nagamallika Gudipaty, Jyotika Ramaprasad, Svetlana Pasti,
   Cláudia Lago, Xianzhi Li, and Ylva Rodny-Gumede

5 Profession and practice: re-imagining the future of journalism 130
   Svetlana Pasti, Beatriz Becker, Nagamallika Gudipaty, Yu Xu, and
   Musawenkosi Ndlovu

PART II
Two-country comparisons of critical issues 157

6 Technological manifestations in the newsroom: India and Brazil 159
   Ravindra Kumar Vemula, Márcio Guerra, Christiane Paschoalino, and
   Layrha Silva Moura

7 Journalists and protest: Russia and China 173
   Dmitry Gavra, Dmitry Strovsky, and Dieer Liao

8 Community radio for the right to communicate:
   Brazil and South Africa 196
   Tanja Bosch, Raquel Paiva, and João Paulo Malerba

Appendix A: Data collection protocols *211*
Appendix B: Data collection and processing teams *220*
Appendix C: Tables for Brazil *222*
Appendix D: Tables for Russia *231*
Appendix E: Tables for India *239*
Appendix F: Tables for China *248*
Appendix G: Tables for South Africa *258*
Index *266*

CONTRIBUTORS

Maria Anikina is associate professor in the Department of Sociology of Mass Communications, Journalism Faculty, Lomonosov Moscow State University (Lomonosov MSU), Russia, where she teaches journalism theory, sociology, media sociology, and sociologic culture of journalists. Her current research examines acute trends in media consumption, new media users' behaviour, and the professional culture of journalists.

Beatriz Becker is associate professor in the graduate program in communication and culture and the Department of Languages and Expressions at the School of Communication, Federal University of Rio de Janeiro (UFRJ), Brazil. Becker has a Ph.D. in communication and culture from UFRJ. She is author of three books about television and TV news and leads the research group *Media, Audiovisual Journalism and Education*.

Tanja Bosch is senior lecturer in the Centre for Film and Media Studies at the University of Cape Town, South Africa, where she teaches media theory, qualitative research methods, and broadcast journalism. She completed her MA in communication for development studies while a Fulbright Scholar at Ohio University, where she also graduated with a Ph.D. in mass communication. Bosch publishes in the areas of community radio, talk radio and citizenship, health communication, youth and mobile media, and identity and social networking.

Leonardo Custódio is postdoctoral fellow at the Institute for Advanced Social Research (IASR), at the University of Tampere, Finland. He is the author of *Favela Media Activism: Counterpublics for Human Rights in Brazil* (forthcoming, Lexington Books). Custódio is also a member of the Laboratory for Community Media Studies (LECC) at the Federal University of Rio de Janeiro (UFRJ).

Dmitry Gavra is professor and chair of business communication and public relations in the School of Journalism and Mass Communications, St. Petersburg State University, Russia. His current areas of study and research are the sociology of journalism, business communications and business journalism, and public relations. His recent books (in Russian) are *Image of the State: Theory and Practice* (2010), *Theory of Communication Foundations* (2012), and *Image of the Territory in the Informational Society* (2013). He has published more than 120 articles in Russia, the United States, Germany, Sweden, Denmark, Brazil, and Turkey.

Nagamallika Gudipaty is associate professor in the Department of Communication, the English and Foreign Languages University, Hyderabad, India. Her current research interests are in political communication, journalism education, and journalism studies. She has published her research in *Media Asia* and *Journal of Media and Development*. Her recent contributions include a chapter each in *Health and the Media: Essays on the Effects of Mass Communication* (2016) (McFarland Books) and *Educational Policy Reforms: National Perspectives* (2017) (Bloomsbury).

Márcio Guerra is associate professor in the School of Communication at the Federal University of Juiz de Fora (UFJF) and a postdoctoral student at the Rio de Janeiro State University, Brazil. He has published two books, 13 book chapters, and several journal articles. He is coordinator of the Center for Research in Communication, Sport and Culture, accredited by Coordination for the Improvement of Higher Education Personnel.

Deqiang Ji has a Ph.D. and is associate professor of communication studies at the National Centre for Communication Invocation Studies at Communication University of China, Beijing, China. His research interests include political economy of communication, international communication, anti-corruption communication, and the intellectual history of communication studies in contemporary China. His most recent publications are the monograph *Digitizing China: The Political Economy of China's Digital Switchover* (in Chinese) and the China chapter in *The International History of Communication Studies* (co-edited by Peter Simonson and David W. Park, Routledge, 2016).

Cláudia Lago is a journalist and faculty member in the Department of Communications and Arts at the School of Communications and Arts of the University of São Paulo, Brazil. She holds a master's degree in social anthropology from Santa Catarina Federal University, 1995, and a Ph.D. in communication sciences from the University of São Paulo, 2003. She is president of the Brazilian Association of Journalism Researchers and vice-chair of the Journalism Research and Education Section of the International Association for Media and Communication Research (IAMCR).

Xianzhi Li is assistant professor in the School of Culture and Communication at Capital University of Economics and Business (CUEB), Beijing, China. She received a Ph.D. in communication from Tsinghua University in 2013. Prior to joining CUEB, she worked at Beijing Television for seven years, specializing in management and evaluation of television and network programs. She has published a number of academic articles on collective action in China. Some of her work has appeared in the *Global Media Journal* and *Modern Communication*.

Dieer Liao is a Ph.D. candidate in media studies at the School of Journalism and Communication, and a research assistant at the Israel Epstein Center for Global Media and Communication at Tsinghua University, China. He is currently (2016–2017) a visiting scholar at Duke University's Asian/Pacific Studies Institute. His research interests include transcultural communication, global communication, public diplomacy, political communication, and media and conflict.

João Paulo Malerba is a researcher at the Laboratory of Studies on Community Communication, and worked as a visiting teacher at the Rural Federal University of Rio de Janeiro, Brazil. He holds a Ph.D. in communication and culture from the Federal University of Rio de Janeiro with a sandwich Ph.D. period at the University of Westminster, UK. His current research investigates the new modes of community broadcasting within the context of convergence and of digitalization of communication. He has been studying community radio in Brazil and Latin America for more than ten years.

Layrha Silva Moura is an undergraduate student at the School of Communication at the Federal University of Juiz de Fora, Brazil, and a member of the BRICS researchers' group, who helped with data analysis.

Musawenkosi Ndlovu is senior lecturer in media studies at the University of Cape Town, South Africa, and a Mandela Mellon Fellow at the W.E.B. Du Bois Institute for African and African American Research, Harvard University, USA. He publishes in the areas of youth, media and politics, international communication, and South African media and culture.

Raquel Paiva is professor in the School of Communication at Federal University of Rio de Janeiro (UFRJ), Brazil, research fellow at the National Council for Scientific and Technological Development, and author of more than ten books in the field of community communication, including *The Common Spirit*. She is also a journalist and writer, and coordinator of the Laboratory of Community Communication and earlier of the National Institute for Studies in Community Communication.

Christiane Paschoalino is professor at the Machado Sobrinho College Foundation, Brazil, and also works as a substitute professor in the School of Communication at the Federal University of Juiz de Fora. She is a marketing specialist. She has published one book, book chapters, and several journal articles. She is also a member of the Center for Research in Communication, Sport and Culture, accredited by

Coordination for the Improvement of Higher Education Personnel. Her major research areas are journalism, culture, marketing, and sports.

Svetlana Pasti (formerly Juskevits) is docent of journalism and media studies at the Faculty of Communication Sciences at the University of Tampere, Finland. Her research focuses on journalists of Russia and other BRICS countries, especially in new online media. She is the author of two monographs and more than 20 peer-reviewed chapters and articles in various platforms including *The Global Journalist in the 21st Century*, *European Journal of Communication*, and *Nordicom Review*.

Fernando Oliveira Paulino is professor and dean at the University of Brasília (UnB), Brazil, and director of international affairs. He is also board member and chair of the Ethics, Right to Communicate, and Freedom of Expression Working Group in the Latin American Communication Researchers Association. Paulino was member of the Ethics Commission in the Journalists Union of Federal District (2001–2009), contributed to the updating of the Brazilian Journalistic Ethics Code (2007), was ombudsman in Brazilian public radio (2008–2012), and was one of the founders of the National Network of Brazilian Press Watchers (2005).

Jyotika Ramaprasad is professor in the School of Communication, University of Miami, Coral Gables, USA. Ramaprasad's research focuses on journalism studies, mostly profiles of journalists from countries in Asia and Africa, and on communication for social change. Her surveys of journalists in Asia and Africa have been published in *Gazette*, *The Harvard International Journal of Press/Politics*, and *Asian Journal of Communication*. Her work in communication for social change has been published in *Social Marketing Quarterly* and *Journal of Health and Mass Communication*.

Ylva Rodny-Gumede is associate professor and head of the Department of Journalism, Film and Television in the School of Communication at the University of Johannesburg, South Africa. Her current research concerns journalistic practices and models for journalism in post-colonial societies in the global South.

Muniz Sodré is professor emeritus at the Federal University of Rio de Janeiro, Brazil, research fellow at the National Council for Scientific and Technological Development, journalist, writer, and the author of more than 30 books in the fields of communication, Brazilian culture, and fiction. He is a visiting professor at several universities in Brazil and abroad. He belonged to the Economic and Social Council for the Presidency of the Republic (2003–2005) during the Lula government and was also president of the Brazilian National Library (2005–2010). He is a member of the Laboratory of Studies on Community Communication and Inpecc.

Dmitry Strovsky has a Ph.D. in political science and for many years worked as a teacher and then professor of the journalism faculty at the Ural Federal University in Yekaterinburg, Russia. He has written extensively in Russian and in English on issues concerning the historical and contemporary evolution of the Russian mass media and the relationship between politics and media. Currently Strovsky is a researcher and lecturer at Ariel University in Israel.

Daya Kishan Thussu is professor of international communication and co-director of India Media Centre at the University of Westminster in London, UK. Among his main publications are *Electronic Empires* (1998); *International Communication – Continuity and Change*, third edition (2014); *War and the Media: Reporting Conflict 24/7* (2003); *Media on the Move – Global Flow and Contra-flow* (2007); *News as Entertainment* (2007); *Internationalizing Media Studies* (2009); *Media and Terrorism: Global Perspectives* (2012) and *Communicating India's Soft Power: Buddha to Bollywood* (Palgrave, 2013). He is series editor for two Routledge book series: Internationalizing Media Studies and Advances in Internationalizing Media Studies.

Ravindra Kumar Vemula is associate professor, Department of Mass Communication & Journalism, the English and Foreign Languages University, Shillong, India. His research interests are in development communication, health communication with a special interest in HIV and AIDS, new media, and communication policy and analysis. He has published extensively in indexed international journals and books. He is the co-chair of the HIV & AIDS and Communication Working Group of the International Association for Media and Communication Research (IAMCR).

Herman Wasserman is professor of media studies and director of the Centre for Film and Media Studies, University of Cape Town, South Africa. He has published widely on media in post-apartheid South Africa, including the monograph *Tabloid Journalism in South Africa: True Story!* and several edited volumes on media, development, and democracy in Africa in the context of globalization. He is editor in chief of the journal *African Media Studies*.

Yu Xu is a Ph.D. student at the Annenberg School for Communication and Journalism, University of Southern California, USA. His current research interests include network theory and analysis, evolutionary and ecological processes in organizational communities, collective action and social movements, and journalism. Yu's work has been published in *Telematics and Informatics*, *International Journal of Communication*, *African Journalism Studies*, and *Digital Journalism*.

Ruiming Zhou is a Ph.D. candidate in the School of Journalism, Fudan University, China. Earlier, he spent three years as a journalist at *Guangzhou Daily*, one of the most renowned media outlets in China. In 2016, he held an appointment as honorary fellow in the Department of Communication Arts, University of Wisconsin-Madison. His doctoral dissertation focuses on journalism innovation in China, which reconsiders the process, features, and ideas of newsmaking in the current digital age.

FOREWORD

Daya Kishan Thussu

Journalism is facing many challenges, both as an industry and as a profession, with a declining readership for newspapers and increasing apathy towards television news, as more and more news consumers receive their information from online sources rather than so-called legacy media. Many studies – both academic and industry-based – are being conducted to delineate this unfolding process. However, relatively little academic research on the changing contours of journalism in major non-Western countries has so far been published, particularly in a comparative framework. The BRICS group – Brazil, Russia, India, China, and South Africa – is one such absence in international research on journalism, despite the fact that these large and diverse countries have some of the world's most dynamic and fast-growing media.

Since it was coined in 2001 by Jim O'Neill, then a Goldman Sachs executive, the BRIC acronym has continued to feature in international political discourses. South Africa was added to the group in 2011 on China's behest, to make the grouping more global by including the African continent – a key site for Chinese investment and influence. In operation as a formal group since 2006 and holding annual summits since 2009, the study of media in the BRICS countries, and journalism in particular, has been very limited. One key reason is the differences in media systems as well as the scale and scope of economic development within this group of nations.

At a time when newspaper circulation is steadily declining in mature Western markets, the growth of the newspaper industry is extremely impressive in countries such as India. China already hosts the world's largest Internet, and its blogging population and increasingly vociferous social media are influencing mainstream journalism. Driven by the mobile Internet, users for online content in India are expected to reach 600 million by 2020, according to industry estimates. Russian cyber-journalism too is expanding, as is the case in the other two BRICS nations,

Brazil and South Africa, as digital connectivity enables production, distribution, and consumption of online journalism.

Against this background, the present volume reports on the micro level of journalism in the BRICS nations, drawing on in-depth interviews with more than 700 journalists in BRICS countries, working in traditional media as well as online news outlets and operating in 20 cities, including national capitals and provincial cities to provide a rich, fulsome, and holistic picture.

In this ethnographic study of journalism practices in the BRICS countries, the authors provide insightful data about the challenges and opportunities that journalists face on a day-to-day basis. The editors deploy five distinctive themes to analyse the extensive data specifically collated for this book. These are journalistic professionalism, newsmaking in the digital age, the ethical dimension of journalism, gender imbalances in journalism, and changing journalistic practices.

In addition, the book also provides a comprehensive comparative framework for three key issues: technological change and its impact on journalism in two BRICS democracies, India and Brazil, a comparative analysis of journalists and protests in more controlled media environments of Russia and China, and the role of community radio for the right to communicate in Brazil and South Africa.

Contemporary BRICS Journalism: Non-Western Media in Transition is the first book-length study of evolving journalism practices in some of the world's biggest and fastest growing countries. Such studies contribute significantly to comparative media research and for further internationalization of media and communication as a field. The editors, Svetlana Pasti and Jyotika Ramaprasad, do an admirable job in synthesizing such extensive and diverse data in a comparative and collaborative project. Their endeavours will surely advance our understanding of international journalism.

ACKNOWLEDGEMENTS

This book owes its completion to our contributors and their national teams in the BRICS countries, all of whom have accompanied us at various times on this five-year-long journey to implement the study and then write the chapters of this book. We express our very deep gratitude to all of them. At the Tampere Research Centre for Journalism, Media and Communication at the University of Tampere, Finland, where the BRICS project was initiated and coordinated, we have benefited from the invaluable support of Kaarle Nordenstreng, Heikki Hellman, Katja Valaskivi, Virginia Mattila, Aila Helin, and Riitta Yrjönen. We are very grateful to the series editor Daya Kishan Thussu and the team at Routledge.

INTRODUCTION

Why BRICS journalism matters

Svetlana Pasti and Jyotika Ramaprasad

Contemporary BRICS Journalism: Non-Western Media in Transition is a sequel to *Mapping the BRICS Media* (Nordenstreng & Thussu, 2015), which focused on national media systems and thus covered journalists only as part of a larger system. Turning its attention from this macro-level analysis, the current volume presents micro-level, data-based, insider journalist–responders' views about the current state of BRICS journalism, both as envisioned and practiced in the second decade of the 21st century, using comparison as well as media systems contexts as frameworks to couch findings. In essence, *Contemporary BRICS Journalism: Non-Western Media in Transition* tells the cross-national story of BRICS journalism from the human perspective.

The book is the outcome of a five-year joint effort of more than 50 researchers from the BRICS nations (Brazil, Russia, India, China, and South Africa). Their collaboration became possible due to investment from a Western funding agency – the Academy of Finland – in a new research project on the BRICS media systems. This large media systems project included an empirical study of BRICS journalists, the first such comparative study in global journalism research, timely not only due to the expanding BRICS economies but also because of their increasing soft power that manifests, among other venues, in the exponentially growing news media in these countries. The empirical journalist study has led to two collaborative publications. The first, a special issue of *African Journalism Studies* (*AJS*) edited by Pasti and Ramaprasad (2015), is a collection of five articles taking a case study approach and providing an overview of journalists' views on several issues in each of the five BRICS countries respectively. The second, this book, takes a cross-national comparative approach to present these journalists' views in the context of their countries' post-colonial and post-communist history, as relevant, particularly in terms of the introduction of liberalization and privatization, and the new reality of digitization of their work and life.

Contemporary BRICS Journalism: Non-Western Media in Transition presents to the readers the still unknown BRICS journalists, who are not only agents of their professional worlds but also have some agency in the present time in the rise of BRICS. Every chapter is based on fresh empirical data contextualized in the local and national histories and situations, affording an understanding of the nature and dynamics of the changing, and sometimes of the stable conditions, in BRICS journalism. The book is based on the rich data of in-depth interviews with 729 BRICS journalists in 20 cities, representing different continents, cultures, and languages. It is thus an attempt to provide an ethnographic reading of journalism in the BRICS countries. It presents the data through the eyes of BRICS journalists, from their own subjective world. In essence, it is a narrative of their lived work experiences, privileged glimpses into the views of those in touch, on the ground, enduring or gaining from the real-life impact of political, economic, digital, and other upheavals on their profession and practice. It conveys these journalists' understandings of their profession and society, and also their anxieties and fears and their aspirations and hopes. This first book on BRICS journalists expands the boundaries of global media studies, moving non-Western journalists from the periphery into the centre and providing a wider lens for academics and their students to see perspectives they may not have encountered earlier. We hope that the book will serve as a window into the professional world of non-Western journalists and their own internal dynamics in this era of changing ideas and practices in journalism.

This introductory chapter provides the context for the study and details its method. It first clarifies that BRICS is not simply a group of emerging economies as defined by the West "but rather [an emerging] union" (Lukyanov, 2015, p. 2) that has an expanding, collaborative agenda aimed at controlling its own destiny, an agenda that goes beyond economic matters to encompass other spheres, including more recently the media. This media-related agenda of the BRICS countries gives greater currency to this book. The chapter then describes the empirical journalist study, providing details about its method and its comparative approach in presenting findings, as well as the committee approach it adopted to implement this cross-national study.

Clarifying BRICS

BRICS: not simply emerging economies

The close of the Cold War between the USSR and the United States towards the final years of the 1980s heralded the end of both the bipolar world and the era of superpowers. The Soviet Union ceased to exist as the world socialist system disintegrated, and the Warsaw Pact dissolved. Although the United States, as Yevgeny Primakov, Russia's foreign minister from 1996 to 1998, noted in 2002, is now the strongest country in the world in economic, military, and political aspects, this does not mean that it has become the sole defining power of the course of development of the world. The post-bipolar world has created conditions for the emergence of new, independent centres of economic and political influence (e.g., EU and China) as well as for an intense (albeit uneven) development of states that freed themselves from the constraints of the bipolar system. According to Primakov (2002), "The growth of interdependence in the world, the interdependence of the subjects of the world economy, world politics and international relations that generate qualitative changes in the development of mankind" indicates a move towards a multipolar world" (pp. 142–143).

A decade ago, Zakaria (2008) too predicted a post-American world, beginning in the final years of the 1980s, a world in which the "distribution of power is shifting, moving from American dominance", but defined more by the rise of the rest rather than the decline of America because "at the military and political level" we still live in a unipolar world (p. 2). Zakaria traces three major power shifts in the world historically. According to him, "The first [shift] was the rise of the Western world, around the 15th century. It produced the world as we know it now – science and technology, commerce and capitalism, the industrial and agricultural revolutions" (p. 2). The second shift was the rise of the United States in the 19th century: "Once it industrialized, it soon became the most powerful nation in the world" (p. 2). "The third great power shift of the modern age [was] the rise of the rest" as a result of the dramatic acceleration of the global economy (p. 2).

Today, BRICS, a group of non-Western countries, is the most impressive evidence of the rise of the rest. BRICS brings together five major emerging markets, comprising 43 per cent of the world's population and having a 30 per cent share of the world's GDP and a 17 per cent share in world trade. Over the past decade, the economies of the BRICS countries have expanded by a factor of more than 4.2 (BRICS Research, 2015). According to a recent survey by Bloomberg,

> The emerging economies will dominate the world by 2050 based on their projected Gross Domestic Product by Purchasing Power Parity (PPP). China and India have been predicted to become bigger than the United States, while Russia is forecast to become the number one economy in Europe.
>
> *(Russia Today, 2017, p. 1)*

Still, doubts about this economic strength have been expressed; particularly "after Brazil and Russia entered recession and growth in China slowed in recent years, Washington-based observers predicted the initiative's imminent demise" (Stuenkel, 2016, p. 1). In 2015, Western voices predicting the collapse of BRICS intensified when Goldman Sachs, after several years of losses, closed a fund that invested in BRICS countries. Information service Bloomberg suggested that this was "the end of the BRICS era" (Zhigalkin, 2015, p. 1). In 2016, the *Financial Times* (2016) indicated that the BRICS concept was dead and would be replaced by TICKS, a new group of emerging markets comprising Taiwan, India, China, and South Korea, in which investors were showing interest. O'Neill (2016), who coined the term BRIC in November 2001 in an interview he gave to the BBC, however, points out that "the Brics countries collectively are bigger today even in the most optimistic scenario I thought 15 years ago, and it's primarily because of China". O'Neill (as cited in Stuenkel, 2016) also indicates that, "The suggestion that the BRICS importance was overstated is simply naïve. The size of the original four BRICs economies, taken together, is roughly consistent with the projections I made all those years ago" (p. 3).

At the same time, the narrow view of BRICS as only a set of emerging economies or promising investment markets is an insufficient description of the BRICS phenomenon today and of its potential in the near future. Georgy Toloraya, executive director of the Russian national committee on BRICS research, recounts that, "The forerunner to BRICS was actually a strategic axis: Russia-China" (Toloraya, 2015a, p. 2). In 1997, China and Russia issued a joint declaration on a multipolar world and the formation of a new international order, which challenged America's status as global hegemon (Tsygankov, 2009, pp. 7–8). At about the same time, about twenty years ago, Primakov envisioned a strategic grouping of Russia, India, and China (RIC), which came to be known as Primakov's Triangle. This triangle "gradually become [sic] more institutionalized and began to take on new members. Today, the BRICS forum is a reality in world politics" (Gvosdev, 2015). Thus, as Sakwa (2015) indicates, what was to become the BRICS association was far more than an invention of Goldman Sachs business analyst Jim O'Neil, who in November 2001 published a research paper where the BRIC acronym appeared for the first time. As Sakwa (2015) explains,

> The BRICS association is a neo-revisionist body, aspiration to a greater voice and the achievement of more equitable relations, rather than a revisionist force planning revolutionary change. Thus, the establishment of the BRICS group is a way of distancing itself from responsibility for the maintenance of the Western order, but they are not suggesting that there is a need to articulate an alternative. The key issue for them is to broaden the basis of global governance.
>
> *(pp. 2–3)*

Pointing to its political dimension, Toloraya (2015a) describes BRICS as "the first intercivilizational project for elaborating international and global social norms" (p. 1). He argues that

> The move towards establishing interstate association is largely a response to global economic imbalance and political chaos in the post-bipolar world from the largest – but dependent from [sic] the global centers of decision-making – countries. The reality forced BRICS members to establish a mechanism for promoting their interests, where they could participate in making decisions that are important for them.
>
> *(Toloraya, 2015a, pp. 1–2)*

Other evidence of the multidimensional nature of BRICS is present. For example, in the post–Cold War era, the BRICS topic has emerged as a new type of specialization in such disciplines as history and political science (Sakwa, 2015). The BRICS theme has gradually become popular in a broad spectrum of disciplines; panels on BRICS have become an integral part of the main conferences also in communication research (IAMCR, ICA) and Central and East European studies (ICCEES). Research projects on BRICS have been initiated in universities and new publications on the BRICS dynamics are on the rise (Grane, 2015; Grincheva & Lu, 2016; Stuenkel, 2015; Vahalik & Staniskova, 2016).

Western press accounts have not given enough credence to BRICS either. Their reports either define BRICS simply as a group that meets internationally or tend to focus on the economic and political differences among member states, suggesting that these divisions make BRICS a coalition that lacks the consolidation required for it to be a strategic bloc (Marakhovsky, 2015). For years, "Western newspapers have depicted the BRICS grouping . . . as either nonsensical or threatening" (Stuenkel, 2016, p. 1). But according to Lukyanov (2015), head of the Council on Foreign and Defense Policy of the Russian Federation, BRICS has not come together as a threat to the West: "Nobody is seriously defying the West" (p. 2). Lukyanov (2015) notes that "there is a gradual process of the West losing its monopoly in the world and it is accompanied by the same gradual process of emerging the countries [sic] which can theoretically fulfill the functions of [alternative institutions]" (pp. 2–3). As Lukyanov further explains, "BRICS are fundamentally non-Western, but that does not imply that they are anti-Western" (p. 1); and "The BRICS is a collective 'non-West', not the 'anti-West', but non-Western nonetheless" (p. 3). Toloraya (2015a) too suggests that while "BRICS is an alternative to the 'west-oriented' platform for discussing geopolitical evolution" and is "based largely on political will", it should not be simplified nor presented as "anti-western" because, for BRICS, "Western states represent the main source of technology and investment, as well as a trading area" and they "consider Euro-Atlantic values as an example to follow (adopted, of course, to local conditions)" (p. 2).

Lukyanov (2015) calls BRICS "a process – not even an organization, but rather a sort of union that is emerging, along with its gradual development" (p. 2), "a club that brings together countries that have common interests" (p. 3). No formal criteria for entry into the coalition exist, and countries wanting to be included must have full sovereignty in these two components: "capability to conduct independent policy [and] non-involvement in any alliances, which impose certain restrictions" and "sufficient economic potential in order to implement independent policy" (Lukyanov, 2015, p. 3). In Lukyanov's opinion, "there are few countries in the world that meet these criteria" (p. 3); "the rest of the countries either don't have full sovereignty or if they have – like European countries – their sovereignty is restricted to a point by certain circumstances" (p. 3).

Alexander Lukin, director, Center for East Asia/SCO Research, MGIMO University, Moscow, sees the role of BRICS as a reformer for a more equitable world order. According to him, the BRICS countries, given their full sovereignty, are able to avoid becoming the objects of global governance of the West, led by the West's belief that the Western model is an advanced model of social structure and should be naturally desired by the people of all countries. Lukin regrets that the West is governed by its powerful ideology of democracy rather than realism that prevents the West from addressing problems pragmatically (Lukin, 2016). Lukyanov (2015) considers the "influence of the BRICS [as] another sign of the gradual weakening of the West's influence in the world. . . . The West is aware of its own weakness and is concerned that there will be alternative institutions" (p. 2). For Stuenkel (2016),

> A world with BRICS leadership may, in the end, be more democratic than the previous world order. Allowing greater levels of genuine dialogue and a broader spread of knowledge, this will help us find more innovative and effective ways to address global challenges.
>
> *(p. 5)*

BRICS' initiatives to build a multipolar world: economic and other cooperative action

Sakwa (2015, p. 3) sees the emergence of BRICS as "a growing maturity to the international system", but he notes that

> This is not adequately reflected in the institutions of international governance. The international system has become more pluralistic, yet the dominant institutions still reflect the predominance of the West. In other words, there is a tension between 'globalisation', the technocratic and technological shrinking of global space and intensification of financial, trade and informational flows, accompanied by what Keohane and Nye called inter-dependence, and 'globalism', the rise of the US to global dominance during the Second World War, and its institutionalisation in the Bretton Woods and Atlantic security systems thereafter.
>
> *(Sakwa, 2015, p. 3)*

Sakwa (2015, p. 4) suggests that "the emergence of the BRICS reflects attempts to make the international system more pluralistic, if not yet fully multipolar". In its attempts to build this more pluralistic or alternative geopolitical architecture for the world, BRICS' initiatives span a spectrum of fields apart from the economic. In 2009, the first BRICS summit held in Russia declared as its common goal the reform of international financial institutions to achieve a larger voice and representation of developing countries in these institutions through an open, transparent, and merit-based selection process. However, attempts to change the Bretton-Woods system of monetary government, operating since 1945 under American leadership, failed, and the International Monetary Fund (IMF) and World Bank remain the instruments for dictating policy to emerging economies (Toloraya, 2015c).

In continuing its efforts, in 2015, BRICS initiated the New Development Bank (NDB) and a reserve currency pool (the BRICS Contingent Reserve Arrangement) to provide mutual financial support within BRICS and to other developing countries, not only as additions to the existing global institutions, but also as "steps to assert greater control over future geopolitical developments" (Lukyanov, 2015, p. 1). Lukyanov (2015) states that these alternative international institutions will "develop further and increase their financial influence and presence" and partake in "the creation of additional opportunities" (p. 3).

Among BRICS' other financial initiatives was establishing an alternative credit rating agency led by BRICS (the BRICS Credit Rating Agency) to challenge the monopoly of the West, an idea that emerged during the 2015 BRICS summit in Ufa; BRICS "started engaging financial experts on a business model for the new rating agency as well as what methodology it would adopt" (Mutize & Gossel, 2017, pp. 1–2). The BRICS countries are dissatisfied with their ratings from the big Western credit rating agencies – Standard & Poor's and Moody's. These two and Fitch "control more than 80% of the world's ratings business" (Mutize & Gossel, 2017, p. 1). Critics of these big three Western credit rating agencies "claim that the frequent downgrades of developing countries are unjust and serve Western political interests" (Mutize & Gossel, 2017, p. 1).

Among other initiatives was India's selection in 2016, during its chairship, of the following theme, "Building Responsive, Inclusive and Collective Solutions", for the 8th BRICS Summit (http://brics2016.gov.in/content/innerpage/about-usphp.php). The aim of this focus was to improve and institutionalize cooperation, to implement the decisions taken in previous summits, to integrate current cooperation mechanisms, to create new cooperation mechanisms, and to continue existing mechanisms. In particular, India held the People's Forum, to

> look into the policies of the BRICS governments and their institutions to present the voices from struggles and movements across the BRICS countries and promote people to people contact, a form of interaction which still remains unexplored between the civil societies of the countries. With participation from progressive trade unions, social movements, academia and civil societies from various BRICS countries, the forum took a critical look at the reported inclination of BRICS governments to neo-liberalism and corporate globalization.
>
> (Chakraborty, 2016, p. 1)

India also hosted the first meeting of the BRICS Joint Working Group on Counter Terrorism on September 14, 2016, in New Delhi, attended by delegations from all BRICS countries. The meeting discussed various issues related to terrorism including domestic perspectives and assessments of threat scenarios and cooperation among BRICS on capacity building, information and technology sharing, countering online radicalization as well as cooperation in multilateral forums such as the United Nations and the Financial Action Task Force (Ministry of External Affairs, 2016).

In sum, it may be said that today BRICS is developing in two directions: 1) consolidating its position in the system of international relations, and 2) broadening and intensifying collaboration among BRICS countries in several fields of mutual interest, including security, ecology, space research, transport, health, education, and cultural cooperation, and conducting "joint research, drawing leading Western specialists" (Toloraya, 2015b, p. 50).

BRICS' initiatives to build a multipolar world: international communication

Apart from the above initiatives, the BRICS coalition has also acted on its desire to play a greater role in international communication; its various member countries held events to highlight issues, which then became BRICS' interests and sometimes even attracted the interest of countries outside the coalition. The first milestone in this move was China's implementation of World Media Summits (WMS). China organized the first WMS in 2009 with the theme "Cooperation, Action, Win-Win and Development"; the most recent WMS (the third) was held in 2016 in Doha, Qatar, hosted by the Al Jazeera Media Network, a WMS presidium member, with the theme "The Future of News & News Organizations" (WMS, 2016). WMS has grown over the years and become a multilateral coordination mechanism for global media organizations, including leading Western media corporations (Li, 2014). In 2013, it "set up the Global Awards for Excellence in order to recognize and encourage the world media community to contribute to good journalism, uphold social responsibility and set professional examples" (WMS, 2015, p. 1). WMS represents BRICS' wish to legitimize globally their values and attitudes to freedom of the press and freedom of expression that until recently were mostly delivered by such Western organizations as Freedom House, Reporters Without Borders, and World Audit.

The second milestone was the Civic Forum BRICS, organized by Russia on the eve of the BRICS Summit in July 2015, the year of the Russian Federation Presidency (BRICS official website of Russia's Presidency in BRICS, 2015). This is an important undertaking for the BRICS countries where civil society is weak and, in fact, BRICS' governments have an uneasy relationship with civil society and media freedom, and where there are problems with the observance of human rights. Three BRICS countries – Russia, India, and Brazil – have placed seventh, ninth, and tenth respectively on the list of the 20 most dangerous countries for journalists (CPJ, 2016). Russia and China are tightening state control over their media, Internet, and civil society (Agora, 2016; Yang, 2016). These countries adopted new laws preventing the financing of any civil organizations from abroad. In Russia, the law has already come into force resulting in the closure of many scientific and cultural NGOs and the rejection of funding under threat of closure (Dzhibladze, 2013). In China, a similar draft law is under discussion and may soon become reality. In India, civil society organizations are also in difficulty with the government (Doane, 2016), and a similar situation exists in South Africa (Joseph, 2015). At the same time, there is some concern among BRICS governments about the quality of life in their societies as articulated in their joint strategic plan for the long-term development of BRICS (BRICS Think Tank Council, 2015).

The third milestone was the first meeting of the BRICS communication ministers held in Moscow in 2015 with the support of the Russian Ministry of Telecom and Mass Communications within the Ufa declaration, adopted at the 7th BRICS Summit in 2015. For the first time, "infocommunication market players from five countries presented their vision of global software market demonopolisation, participation of international community in management of critical Internet infrastructure and expanding of collaboration in spheres of telecom and IT between BRICS countries" (Minsvyaz, 2015, p. 1). In 2016, India held the 8th BRICS Summit in Goa and the Second BRICS Communication Ministers Meeting and a communication conference in Bengaluru. The event focused on drawing up a course of action for creating new frameworks of cooperation and collaboration among BRICS countries including improving collaboration in the field of digital economy, future communications, and mobile technology, among others (ANI, 2016).

BRICS' initiatives to build a multipolar world: media

According to Congjun Li, president of *Xinhua News Agency* and executive chairperson of the first BRICS Media Summit, although the BRICS countries "have acquired formidable economic strength", "their soft power remains weak" (2014, p. 2). He suggests that BRICS increase the influence of their media organizations and have their media play a bigger role to make their voices heard through the world (Li, 2014). He recommends the following four-point strategy: 1) strengthen intra-BRICS media cooperation and have the media coordinate their voice so as to safeguard BRICS' interests, 2) enhance intra-BRICS media exchanges "to learn the strategy and narrative technique to win the respect of the world and to find effective ways to project the national image in an objective and ample manner" (p. 2), 3) use WMS to enhance mutual trust and clear up misunderstanding among BRICS media and thus promote cooperation, and 4) "jointly confront the challenges presented by new media and new technologies through their cooperation projects" (p. 3). All this, it is expected, will help BRICS media to "do more in international communication, constantly strengthen their ability to have their voices heard internationally, and help improve the BRICS mechanism, so as to win the understanding and support of the world for BRICS cooperation and development" (Li, 2014, p. 3).

In support of this strategy, in November 2015 Russia opened a BRICS school for young journalists, hosting more than 20 delegates from leading BRICS media outlets, including Xinhua News Agency (China), Press Trust of India (India), *Folha de S. Paulo* (Brazil), and the South African Broadcasting Corporation (South Africa). The training focused on information cooperation, national multicultural and multidenominational influences on journalism, and reporting on social media (BRICS.ru, 2015).

In December of the same year, Beijing organized the first BRICS Media Summit. Leaders from 25 media groups from BRICS attended the event hosted by *Xinhua*. Co-organizers of the summit, representatives from five countries, held a meeting and agreed to further promote media exchanges among the BRICS countries. This included establishing each of the following: a liaison office for the BRICS Media Summit, the BRICS Media Foundation, the BRICS Media Journalism Awards, a BRICS photo exhibition and training and exchange programmes for BRICS journalists, and a coordination mechanism for BRICS' joint media coverage of the G20 Summit. Cai Mingzhao, the president of China's Xinhua News Agency and executive chair of the first BRICS Media Summit, noted the already occurring multidimensional inter-BRICS activities covering political, economic, financial, trade, social, and cultural sectors, and correspondingly, the increasing role of media and journalists to help develop these activities. In particular, he said, "The media, as a carrier of information communication and messenger for cultural exchanges, play an irreplaceable role in deepening cooperation among these countries" (*Xinhuanet*, 2015, p. 1).

The BRICS journalist study

The impetus for the study

The expansion of the BRICS repertoire of initiatives starting with the economic and the political, moving through civil society, and now touching upon the media, are all attempts to add value to their grouping. This pathway and the immense transitions witnessed, initiated, and experienced along the way, as pertinent in terms of their timeline, were the springboard for the macro-level BRICS media systems project (BRICS project) and the micro-level BRICS empirical journalist study. The project and the study were launched in 2012 on a wave of popularity of the BRICS theme in public debate and international relations, but also in an atmosphere of Western criticism of and lack of faith in BRICS as a viable union with the argument that BRICS is an artificial coalition of countries with highly disparate political, economic, and cultural conditions. Time will tell what correctly predicts the viability of BRICS, Western pessimism or BRICS enthusiasm, but it was in the context of these contrasting approaches and BRICS' own struggle for recognition but also its popularity that the BRICS journalism study took seed, almost prescient in its focus ahead of the media and communication initiatives of BRICS itself, but keenly cognizant of a world in which the media are indispensable and, very importantly, privatizing and digitalizing.

The transitions occurring in the BRICS countries create paradoxical situations that still need to be resolved. On the one hand, the BRICS nations are growing economies, moving in the logic of global liberalization, and becoming increasingly digital. On the other hand, the role of the state with its deep tradition of regulation is traditionally strong here and further enhanced by the creation of the alliance of BRICS countries, negotiating and adopting a common strategy in international affairs and creating multidisciplinary cooperation within BRICS. BRICS encapsulates both the forces of change and the forces of maintaining the status quo, and the news media are no exception to this paradoxical situation, creating additional reasons for the empirical study. Media liberalization and their adoption of new technologies is spawning a growth of private news media, which portends increasing freedom from government, but such media are also subject to corporate control and the pursuit of profit. Similarly, while online news allows an alternative to mainstream discourse that is influenced by traditional spaces of power, the Internet also allows opportunities for authoritarian monitoring and control (both political and social) of cyberspace.

In the journalism profession, the transition to large-scale (though not complete) privatization means more freedom for journalists to practice the profession, to investigate, to pursue news, but it also creates a greater likelihood of corruption and ethical malpractice in the pursuit of money at both the organizational level and the level of the individual journalist. The expansion of news media that privatization launched also means far more employment opportunities for women but no guarantee that a corporate structure and the societal values embedded in this structure will allow women to climb the ladder and break the glass ceiling. The forces of liberalization apart, the transition to digitization means, for the journalist, the loss of the agenda-setting monopoly that was the privilege of traditional media; today, the agenda is beginning to emerge independently from sources such as social media and new forms of alternative Internet-based media, including blogs. The loss of monopoly over the profession also means that journalism is no longer the province of journalists alone; new specialists from the field of technology (software engineers) and art (web designers) as well as narrow profile experts from different disciplines have arrived, as has digital news. They bring new audiences to the media, audiences that skilled marketers work to keep and increase.

Journalistic practice, in turn, is in the process of transition from the traditional elite forms of mainstream media, traditional genres, and one-way flow of communication to new digital multimedia platforms, which integrate the audience as a source of information and/or as authors. Also, journalism is moving from hired work to freelancers and to entrepreneurship, and journalists today work simultaneously for both local media and global information networks. Paradoxes do not allow for easy answers. The book provides journalists' views about the impact of these transitions on their profession and their daily practice, from newsmaking to feminization. Our journalist respondents recognize these paradoxes and provide critiques that include both the beneficial and detrimental impact of these transitions as they reflect on these matters

Also, paradoxically and symptomatically, international journalism research does not thus far have studies that focus on BRICS, putting these countries on the periphery of attention of contemporary world journalism history. Even recent global comparative projects, such as Weaver and Willnat's (2012) *The Global Journalist for the 21st Century* (GJ) and the first phase of the study by Hanitzsch et al.'s

(2012) *Worlds of Journalism Study* (WJS) did not include journalists from all the BRICS countries. Both GJ and WJS included only three countries from BRICS, namely, Brazil, Russia, and China (Pasti, Ramaprasad, & Ndlovu (2015). The recent second phase of the WJS (www.worldsofjournalism.org) has collected data from all five BRICS countries, and thus it can be expected that soon publications from this study will provide BRICS journalism data. For now, this book fills the gap in international comparative research about BRICS journalists.

The study's method

The study's approach was qualitative, its method semi-structured in-depth interviews, and its design cross-sectional (journalists were interviewed once). Data were collected between December 2012 and January 2015, using a questionnaire but allowing for probes (Appendix A). Sampling decisions specified convenience sampling for the selection of cities, news organizations, and journalists (including snowball sampling at this level) but within certain parameters: in each country, four cities – two major and two provincial – and news organizations that represented the following characteristics: 1) traditional and online, 2) national and regional, 3) newspaper, magazine, radio, television, and online, 4) private, mixed, and state (government owns more than 50 per cent of direct or indirect assets), as applicable, and 5) quality (influential in public life) and popular (large audience). Despite the use of a convenience sample, effort was directed towards getting a good representation of journalists from various ranks, genders, and ages (actual and professional age). Additionally, the sampling frame specified 24 news outlets in each capital city and 12 in each provincial city, two journalists from each outlet, and an even division between journalists from traditional and online news outlets. Thus, in each country 144 journalists would be interviewed (96 in capital cities, 48 in provincial cities; 72 from traditional media, 72 from online media) yielding a total of 720 journalists from the five BRICS countries.

The sampling plan was not always realized due to local circumstances of differential growth in online news, accessibility to and willingness of news outlets and journalists to participate, and other factors. Further, samples were localized to reflect critical indigenous factors. For example, in selecting news organizations, the Brazilian team defined quality news vehicles as those having the highest impact on the political agenda, whereas the South African team defined them as community media. Also, for example, in some cities of South Africa, China, and India, purely online news outlets were small in number or non-existent and thus news portals and online versions of traditional news media were included. The final sample included 729 journalists because South Africa included 150 journalists, China 146, India 145, and Brazil and Russia 144 each. It had 487 metro and 242 provincial city journalists, and 484 offline and 245 online journalists. The sample BRICS cities are depicted on national maps in respective appendices (C–G).

The interviews were conducted face-to-face (with the exception of those in Kolkata and Pune in India, in which some interviews were conducted by phone), in a setting (office or café) preferred by the interviewee but ensuring privacy, by national researchers and also trained research assistants, mostly students of journalism and mass communication (Appendix B). The questionnaire was administered in a language the interviewee was comfortable with (Portuguese, Russian, English, Bengali, Marathi, Hindi, Telugu, Urdu, or Chinese). On average, interviews lasted 45 minutes. All interviews were taped, transcribed, and analysed by authors or trained coders in consultation with authors to obtain counts for those questions that allowed such analyses, as well as to identify commonalities and individual opinions. In essence, coding was quantitative and descriptive. Central elements of the results are presented in country tables in the BRICS order from Appendix C to G.

Specifically, the questionnaire (Appendix A) included questions on demography; working conditions; impact of new technology including social media, of economic changes, and of (the increasing number of) female colleagues; organizational structures and professional solidarity; government control of (news) media content and of new technology as well as self-censorship of certain content in the interest of the nation and its public; professional values; ethical dilemmas and the exchange of news for some benefit; and the future of journalism. While the questionnaire provided the overall data framework, it allowed for detailed probes into several aspects of journalists' work to elicit nuanced beliefs and opinions that are more likely to provide a micro-level view, that of the ant traversing complicated territory rather than that of the bird soaring high above and missing the details. This method of scrutiny also provided a view of journalism as it is both envisioned and practiced, the normative ideal and actual reality. Naturally, the lines of questioning using probes differed for each interview, allowing the journalists to spend more or less time and to reflect or not on questions that were particularly relevant locally or to the journalist. This added depth and relevance to the information, but naturally resulted in data that were sometimes, but not totally, topically dissimilar or differently nuanced across the interviews in the five countries.

The study's comparative approach to findings

While a case study approach was used to collect data within each country, the analysis expanded beyond case studies to a structural and analytical comparative approach. The most obvious level of comparison was across the five countries; these countries' media are different in many ways even though the countries have come together as a coalition. Beyond this obvious level of cross-country comparison are those between online and traditional news media, salient in an age when the Internet has changed the dynamics of this profession and the character of its output. The sample's inclusion of both capital and provincial cities provides yet another level of potential comparison. Additional comparisons could be made among journalists within a country and between the BRICS coalition and the West. From among the following potential comparisons, 1) journalists; 2) traditional versus online news media; 3) cities; 4) BRICS countries; and 5) BRICS versus the West, it is the comparisons among BRICS countries that are prominent in the book, followed at times by comparisons at the organization and city levels, though these are not always made with structural formality. Naturally, differences by journalists come through as various differing views are quoted or presented, and sometimes reference is made to differences with the West. Where applicable, the book includes system-level information to validate the comparisons and to explain comparative findings.

The study's use of a committee approach to implement the research

The book is the work of a geographically dispersed group of scholars, whose work was facilitated by face-to-face and virtual meetings and communication (requiring considerable coordinating efforts), but ultimately tied to a single intellectual endeavour. To achieve this aim, we developed "a *committee approach*, in which an interdisciplinary and multicultural team of individuals who have expert knowledge on the cultures, languages and research field in question jointly develop the research tools" (Hanitzsch, 2008, p. 101). In our study, the committee approach helped to create a matrix of collaboration among team members that crossed five boundaries: 1) country: Brazil, Russia, India, China, and South Africa; 2) language: Portuguese, Russian, English, Bengali, Marathi, Hindi, Telugu, Urdu, and Chinese; 3) historical context: post-colonial, post-communist; 4) researcher seniority: senior scholars, doctoral students; and 5) writing styles: various academic homes.

Our implementation of the committee approach included systematic communication with each other (via email, phone, Skype, and Facebook) and a series of annual seminars starting with Tampere in 2012, and followed by Dublin (2013), Hyderabad (2014), Montreal and Rio (2015), and finally London and Leicester (2016). Available members of all national teams met in person and together formulated the research approach and method (qualitative, in-depth, semi-structured interviews), the research tools (interview and sampling protocols), and the strategy and the tactics of the study (time period, training interviewers, translations where necessary); and planned joint conference panels and publications. These virtual and in-person meetings and communication allowed us to develop a true partnership engaging cultural sensitivity, patience, and understanding that in turn enabled mutuality, reciprocity, and responsiveness. We became the 'BRICS family' as we worked together for the past five years.

Our collaborators are well known researchers in the field of media, journalism, and communication, who sometimes brought along their younger colleagues with experience in related fields in the BRICS countries. The project provided us with a unique opportunity to dialogue among ourselves, representatives of non-Western cultures, as we conducted the research and prepared joint conference presentations and publications. Our conversations helped our attempt to interpret our results within local, non-Western contexts, to add the national and local, both historical and current, to the empirical evidence from respondent journalists. In this area of work, in recent years, the critique of Euro-American centrism in communication theories has led "to a call for Afrocentric/Asiacentric approaches to research, and the emergence of geocultural theories" (Wang, 2014, p. 373). Our authors come from the BRICS countries; they have knowledge and insight into their countries and have thus provided a richness that comes from their indigenous perspectives that are non-Western voices in a field dominated by Western authors. In essence, our approach was to present in this book the polyphony of the voices of non-Western scholars who accomplished this study and are experts in their subject. We wanted to contribute to the decolonization and de-Westernization of journalism research in this field that is still dominated by the views of Western academics and a universal normative approach.

The book in outline

The book consists of two parts and eight thematic chapters. The first part of the book 'Transitioning concepts and practices across BRICS' includes five themes that are important to all BRICS countries, and includes all five countries' data in each chapter. The second part of the book 'Two-country comparisons of critical issues' focuses on three selected topics that are critical to transitioning media systems and two countries where this topic is very salient.

Part 1: transitioning concepts and practices across BRICS

In Part 1, Chapter 1 focuses on *professionalism* as it is articulated by journalist-respondents in terms of its various definitions and dimensions, and includes journalists' own self-appraisals of their professionalism. This explication apart, the chapter also provides journalists' reading of their functions and the value of union membership to them. For context, the chapter draws on the literature explicating professionalism in general but also where available on literature from the BRICS countries. It touches on the attempt of professions in general to close or maintain boundaries and how, in the case of the journalism profession, digital media are presenting challenges to this endeavour.

The next chapter, Chapter 2, presents as background for the empirical data the intricacies of the changes that are occurring with the digitization of the field of communication. It then focuses specifically on journalists' views about the impact of technological developments in the BRICS countries on *newsmaking*, particularly in terms of their use of social media in journalistic practice. The chapter also presents journalists' views on government control of content and the organizational hierarchies in traditional and online news media outlets.

Chapter 3 provides journalists' narratives about the ethical dilemmas they encounter in their daily practice. In particular, it focuses on the phenomenon of paid news, i.e., news exchanged (or suppressed) for money or benefit and other related corrupt practices such as advertorials that are passed off as news. The contextual narrative provides some of the local within-BRICS structural factors that shape the journalism realities within which journalists make decisions about *ethical practice*.

Chapter 4 explores the *feminization* of journalism in BRICS. After drawing historical parallels across the BRICS nations, the chapter presents journalists' narratives about the growth, progress, and obstacles to feminization in news media organizations.

The final chapter in this section, Chapter 5, presents BRICS journalists' views on their *working conditions*, their sources of (dis)satisfaction, and the *future of their profession*. It also includes these journalists' opinions about changes needed in the socio-political conditions of their countries in order for journalism to fully accomplish its functions and tasks.

Part 2: two-country comparisons of critical issues

The first chapter in Part 2, Chapter 6, addresses the concerns of journalists within the context of the vast *technological changes* that are taking place in the news media of India and Brazil. In so doing, the chapter presents the voices of journalists telling what technological changes (innovations) have occurred in the past few years in the newsroom and how these changes have influenced their practices, the quality of journalism, and their personal stories.

Chapter 7, the next chapter in this section, presents *how journalists in Russia and China view protests*, particularly given that some journalists have themselves become professionally involved in protests. Both Russia and China have witnessed protests on a wide range of socio-political and economic issues, and these protests have become, without exaggeration, a new phenomenon of everyday life in these countries.

Finally, Chapter 8 explores the development of *community radio* in South Africa and Brazil, the two BRICS countries with a very strong tradition of community radio. The chapter outlines the unique historical and political factors giving rise to the development of community radio in each of the countries, and provides some comparative reflections on the role played by community radio in the present day.

References

African Journalism Studies (AJS). (2015). Special issue: The BRICS journalist: Profession and practice in the age of digital media. *3*(36). Routledge.

Agora. (2016). *Svoboda interneta 2015: torzhestvo tsenzury. Nepravitelstvennyi doklad* [Internet freedom: A celebration of censorship. Non-governmental report]. Retrieved from https://rublacklist.net/14661/

ANI. (2016, November 10). Second BRICS communication ministers meeting to begin in Bengaluru today. *The New Indian Express*. Retrieved from www.newindianexpress.com/nation/2016/nov/10/second-brics-communication-ministers-meeting-to-begin-in-bengaluru-today-1537033.html

BRICS official website of Russia's Presidency in BRICS. (2015). Civil BRICS Forum opens in Moscow. Retrieved from http://en.brics2015.ru/news/20150630/216249.html

BRICS project. *Media systems in flux: The challenge of the BRICS countries*. Retrieved from http://uta.fi/cmt/tutkimus/BRICS.html

BRICS Research. (2015). National Committee for BRICS Research (NSR): Moscow, Russia.

BRICS.ru (2015, November 17). *BRICS school of young journalists opens in Moscow*. Retrieved from http://en.brics2015.ru/allnews/20151117/678566-print.html

BTTC (BRICS Think Tank Council). (2015). *Towards a long-term strategy for BRICS*. Brasilia: DF-Brazil. Retrieved from www.nkibrics.ru/ckeditor_assets/attachments/55cca926627 26921aa020000/na_puti_k_dolgosrochnoy_strategii_stran_briks_angl.pdf?1439476006

Chakraborty, M. (2016). *Civil society meets before BRICS 2016 in India: Organisations and individuals critical of BRICS policies*. Media India Group (MIG). Retrieved from http://mediaindia.eu/social-vibes/civil-society-meets-before-brics-2016-in-india/

CPJ (Committee to Protect Journalists). (2016). *1211 journalists killed since 1992*. Retrieved from https://cpj.org/killed/

Doane, D. (2016, September 7). The Indian government has shut the door on NGOs. *The Guardian*. Retrieved from www.theguardian.com/global-development-professionals-network/2016/sep/07/the-indian-government-has-shut-the-door-on-ngos

Dzhibladze, Y. (2013). *Trends in civil society in Russia*. London: Chatham House. Retrieved from www.chathamhouse.org

Financial Times. (2016, January 28). The BRICS are dead: Long live the ticks. Retrieved from www.ft.com/content/b1756028-c355-11e5-808f-8231cd71622e

Grane, R. (2015). *Building bridges among the BRICs*. London: Palgrave.

Grincheva, N., & Lu, J. (2016). BRICS summit diplomacy: Constructing national identities through Russian and Chinese media coverage of the fifth BRICS summit in Durban, South Africa. *Global Media and Communication, 12*(1), 25–47.

Gvosdev, N. K. (2015, June 30). The Ufa 2015 summit is a testament to the late Yevgeny Primakov's lasting geopolitical vision. *The National Interest*. Retrieved from http://nationalinterest.org/feature/how-yevgeny-primakovs-legacy-lives-13220

Hanitzsch, T. (2008). Comparing journalism across cultural boundaries: State of the art, strategies, problems, and solutions. In M. Löffelholz & D. H. Weaver (Eds.), *Global journalism research: theories, methods, findings, future* (pp. 93–105). Malden-Oxford-Carlton: Wiley-Blackwell Publishing.

Hanitzsch, T., Seethaler, J., Skewes, E. A., Anikina, M., Berganza, R., Cangöz, I., Coman, M., Hamada, B., Hanusch, F., Karadjov, C. D., Mellado, C., Moreira, S. V., Mwesige, P. G., Lee, P., Reich, P. Z., Noor, D. V., & Yuen, K. V. (2012). Worlds of journalism: Journalistic cultures, professional autonomy and perceived influences across 18 nations. In D. H. Weaver & L. Willnat (Eds.), *The global journalist in the 21st century* (pp. 473–494). New York, NY: Routledge.

Joseph, N. (2015). NGOs: Under fire, under surveillance. *Index on Censorship, 44*(3), 80–82.

Keohane, R. O., & Nye, J. (1989). *Power and interdependence* (2nd ed.). New York: Harper Collins Publishers.

Li, C. (2014, July 14). BRICS news organizations can play a bigger role in int'l communication. *China Daily Latin America*. Retrieved from http://usa.chinadaily.com.cn/world/2014-07/14/content_17756276.htm

Lukin, A. V. (2016). Novaya Mezhdunarodnaya Ideokratiya i Rossia [New international ideocracy and Russia]. *Comparative Politics, 1*(22), 41–57. Retrieved from www.comparativepolitics.org/jour/article/view/386

Lukyanov, F. (2015, July 10). The BRICS may be non-Western but they are not anti-Western. Interview. *Russia Direct*. Retrieved from www.russia-direct.org/qa/brics-may-be-non-western-they-are-not-anti-western

Marakhovsky, E. (2015). *BRICS in the world information environment. International Affairs*. Special issue: BRICS Russia Ufa 2015. Moscow: Ministry of Foreign Affairs of the Russian Federation.

Ministry of External Affairs. Government of India. (2016, September 14). *First meeting of the BRICS joint working group on counter terrorism*. Retrieved from www.mea.gov.in/

press-releases.htm?dtl/27400/First_Meeting_of_the_BRICS_Joint_Working_Group_on_Counter_Terrorism_September_14_2016

Minsvyaz [Ministry of Telecom and Mass Communication of the Russian Federation]. (2015, October 22). *The first ever meeting of BRICS ICT minister was launched.* Retrieved from http://minsvyaz.ru/en/events/34185/

Mutize, M., & Gossel, S. (2017, February 7). BRICS wants to set up an alternative rating agency: Why it may not work. *The Conversation.* Retrieved from https://theconversation.com/brics-wants-to-set-up-an-alternative-rating-agency-why-it-may-not-work-72382

Nordenstreng, K., & Thussu, D. K. (Eds.). (2015). *Mapping BRICS media.* London: Routledge.

O'Neill, J. (2016, October 14). *Brics 'grew more than I thought'.* Interview to BBC news. Retrieved from www.bbc.com/news/business-37655987

Pasti, S., & Ramaprasad, J. (2015). Editorial: The BRICS journalist within the changing dynamics of the early 21st century. *African Journalism Studies.* Special issue: The BRICS journalist: Profession and practice in the age of digital media. Routledge, *3*(36), 1–7.

Pasti, S., Ramaprasad, J., & Ndlovu, M. (2015). BRICS journalists in global research. In K. Nordenstreng & D. K. Thussu (Eds.), *Mapping BRICS media* (pp. 205–227). London: Routledge.

Primakov, E. (2002). *The world after 11 September.* Moscow: Myslj.

RT (Russia Today). (2017, February 13). Russia gets top notch grade in emerging markets survey. Retrieved from www.rt.com/business/377172-russia-economy-emerging-countries/

Sakwa, R. (2015, August 3–8). BRICS and the end of greater Europe. Paper presented at the IX World Congress of ICCEES in Makuhari, Japan.

Stuenkel, O. (2015). *The BRICS and the future of global order.* London and Lanham, MD: Lexington Books.

Stuenkel, O. (2016, October 18). Why the BRICS coalition still matters. *The Conversation.* Retrieved from https://theconversation.com/why-the-brics-coalition-still-matters-67202

Toloraya, G. (2015a, September 9). BRICS: Future checkpoints. *Russian View (RV).* Retrieved from www.russianview.com/article?id=141&lang=en

Toloraya, G. (2015b). *BRICS looks to the future, international affairs.* Special issue: BRICS Russia Ufa 2015. Moscow: Ministry of Foreign Affairs of the Russian Federation, 45–56.

Toloraya, G. (2015c, July 15). The BRICS continue to transform into a viable Western alternative. *Russia Direct.* Retrieved from www.russia-direct.org/opinion/brics-continue-transform-viable-western-alternative

Tsygankov, A. (2009). What is Russia to us? Westernisers and slavophiles, in Russian Foreign policy. *Russie Nei Visions, 45,* 7–8.

Vahalik, B., & Staniskova, M. (2016). Key factors of foreign trade competitiveness: Comparison of the EU and BRICS by factor and cluster analysis. *Society and Economy, 38*(3), 295–317.

Wang, G. (2014). Culture, paradigm, and communication theory: A matter of boundary or commensurability? *Communication Theory, 24,* 373–393.

Weaver, D. H., & Willnat, L. (Eds.). (2012). *The global journalist in the 21st century.* New York, NY: Routledge.

WMS (World Media Summit). (2015, January 27). *WMS global awards for excellence 2014 presented.* Retrieved from www.worldmediasummit.org/media/wms_news_media/2015/0127/2501.html

WMS. (World Media Summit) (2016, February 29). *The 3rd world media summit to be held in March in Doha.* Retrieved from www.wmsdoha2016.com/

Xinhuanet. (2015, December 1). *First BRICS media summit convenes presidium meeting.* Retrieved from http://news.xinhuanet.com/english/2015-12/01/c_134872391.htm

Yang, F. (2016). Rethinking China's Internet censorship: The practice of recoding and the politics of visibility. *New Media & Society, 18*(7), 1364–1381.

Zakaria, F. (2008, May 12). The rise of the rest. *Blog.* Retrieved from https://fareedzakaria.com/2008/05/12/the-rise-of-the-rest/

Zhigalkin, Y. (2015, November 10). Ischeznovenie "kirpichikov" [Disappearance of brics]. *Radio Svoboda.* Retrieved from www.svoboda.org/a/27356147.html

PART I
Transitioning concepts and practices across BRICS

1
PROFESSIONALISM

Continuities and change

Jyotika Ramaprasad, Svetlana Pasti, Fernando Oliveira Paulino, Ruiming Zhou, and Musawenkosi Ndlovu

Profession, professionalism, and professionalization: historical interpretations

If any term exemplifies that the meaning of words lies in their use, it is the word 'professionalism'. It encapsulates the attempt to distinguish occupations from professions, it references a certain cluster of traits, which in turn may differ by time and space, it is normative but also operational, it implies power but also hegemony, it is empowering and exploitative, it is a good thing and not. The term is used cursorily or deterministically. When applied to journalism, these same ambiguities about professionalism persist.

For several decades now, sociologists have attempted to provide an explication of profession, professionalization, and professionalism in an attempt to separate professions from 'mere' occupations. Their evolving discussion may be grouped into two approaches: the administrative structural-functionalist 'traits' approach and the critical 'power' approach.

Summarizing from a historical review of the traits approach to defining *professions*, Larson (1977) suggested that for social scientists, "professions are occupations with power and prestige" (p. x) because professionals have 1) specialized knowledge based on specific training (cognitive dimension) that fulfils societal needs, 2) are devoted to public service (normative dimension) and not material goals, and 3) are rated advantageously (evaluative dimension) in terms of autonomy and privilege in comparison to occupations; these together provide them with prestige and the public trust to self-regulate (Cogan, 1953; Millerson, 1964, as cited in Larson, 1977). Further, professions have schools, associations, and codes of ethics. For a considerable length of time (and continuing to date), the definition of *professionalism* too used this reductionist traits approach: expertise, altruism, public service, ethical standards, collegial control, and so on.

In Parsons' (1939) functionalist approach, professions are institutional frameworks in which important social functions are enacted, which in turn serve the social order, and along with other social forces or structures (such as the economy) bring equilibrium to society. In this traits/functionalist view, occupations organize themselves over a period of time through a process of *professionalization* to provide a public service and to enact functions. Scholars, however, acknowledge today that the polysemy, the nuance, and the changing nature of the concept of professionalism (and therefore of profession and professionalization) cannot be subjected to such explication (Martimianakis, Maniate, & Hodges, 2009). Today, they consider this a time-wasting exercise and suggest that, instead of seeking such precision, a focus on the discourse of professionalism would yield greater understanding (Evetts, 2013).

The critical approach to this exercise in the explication of 'profession' does not have a benign view of professions, professionalism, and professionalization. According to Hughes (1963), professionals "profess to know better than others the nature of certain matters" (p. 656); they "do not merely serve; they define the very wants which they serve" (Hughes, 1970, p. 153). For Freidson (1989), professionals exert control over three critical aspects: 1) recruitment, claiming that they recruit only those who resist the abuse of privilege and then they hone the recruits' altruism through socialization, 2) training, determined by members and conducted in higher education institutions, and 3) the work they do, depending on the profession and the clientele. Through such control, they create market shelters (or even market closures) earning advantages through 'knowledge monopolies' and 'gatekeeping' (Brint, 1993). Freidson, however, also suggests that occupational control of work is necessary because practitioners alone can understand the complexities of the work they do (Freidson, 2001, as cited in Evetts, 2013), thus defending professions in face of more serious critiques such as Larson's (1977) that invoke hegemony (Brint, 1993). For Larson, professions engage in "a collective assertion of special social status and . . . a collective process of upward social mobility", creating a "structured inequality" (1997, pp. xvii–xviii), functioning as an effective form of social and ideological control, and defining particular social realities for the public. Professionalism as a mechanism of control is omnipresent in organizations that exhibit a hierarchical structure, work standardization, and external regulation, aka 'organizational professionalism'; it is in their recruitment campaigns and mission statements, in their training manuals, and in their managerial literature.[1] In this critical approach, professionalization (or the professional project) is the mechanism through which professions as institutions maintain their privileged status.

Journalism professionalism

Journalism began its professionalization project in the early part of the 20th century, gradually adding traits such as objectivity to the definition of journalistic professionalism (Beam, 1990). Studies of journalism professionalism followed; in these, scholars (Johnstone, Slawski, & Bowman, 1972–1973; McLeod & Hawley, 1964; Weaver & Willnat, 2012) employed as measures a priori traits mostly and journalists' lived experience sometimes (Beam, 1990). However, even though journalists may share some traits, e.g., subscribing to the normative ideal of providing a public service to the cause of democracy or social justice and having ethical codes and standards of practice (Singer, 2003), they do not have to undergo training in journalism, and their autonomy (and that of the institution of journalism) is not universal and is particularly challenged under the organizational professionalism of corporate control. Thus, the traits approach does not provide support to the claim that journalism is a profession. At the same time, journalists do "consider themselves professionals [in terms of] loyalty to the ideals [and to] shared norms" of the profession (Singer, 2007, p. 81).

Moving away from the traits approach allows for an assessment of where power is asserted by affirming professionalism in journalism. While Beam (1990) defines power more broadly including journalistic control of resources, he indicates that this control is based on 'expertise'. At the individual level, journalists' claim to expertise and to upholding related standards such as objectivity makes them believe that they are singularly outfitted to produce knowledge for the public. Losing some of this power with the advent of digital technology and of citizen journalism has been a difficult experience for journalists (Deuze, 2005; Lewis, 2012; Singer, 2003). At the level of the institution, journalists' entire occupational ideology serves to legitimize their position in the world (Deuze, 2005). Deuze suggests that the professionalization of the institution of journalism was (and continues to be) an "ideological development" that sought to maintain a dominant sense of what journalism is or should be (p. 444). It is on this dominant ideology that "most newsmakers base their professional perceptions and praxis" (p. 445). Deuze (2005) defines ideology as "a system of beliefs characteristic of a particular group" (p. 445) and identifies five elements of ideology: public service, objectivity, autonomy, immediacy, and ethics. From his study of how these vary under different circumstances, he concludes that "any definition of journalism as a profession working truthfully, operating as a watchdog for the good of society as a whole and enabling citizens to be self-governing" is both naïve and one dimensional (p. 458).

Glasser (1992) makes a somewhat similar point; he suggests that there can be no universal or objective knowledge that re-presents the world as it really is. Thus, trying to build a lasting foundation for truth is "a self-deceptive effort to eternalize the normal discourse of the day" (Rorty, 1979, as cited in Glasser, 1992, p. 132).

In sum, the literature suggests that while practitioners and others may consider journalism to be a profession, and possibly the sole legitimate authority on a daily, and more recently an immediate, record of the world, it does not appear to meet all the criteria of a profession in terms of both required or suggested traits and the belief system it is founded on.

Journalism professionalism in BRICS: a historical view

In Brazil, a journalistic press was banned during the colonial period (1500–1808). After 1808, when this industry got a start as businesses began to print books and newspapers, it was as an elite institution mainly because of the high illiteracy in the country. Even when radio and television appeared, the mass media kept this elite bias in choosing those they would accept as journalists (Santanna, 2006). To this day, Brazil places a very high value on a degree in journalism as part of its professional ideology.[2]

In the Soviet Union, and current day Russia, journalism education meant something other than a degree. In the pre-Soviet times, major writers used the national tradition of literary criticism to publish critical opinions about societal matters. During the Soviet times, this tradition of social criticism became the driving force in the education of students in journalism so that they could implement the role of social organizers. The education stressed *masterstvo*, such mastery of the profession that a journalist could take an article from conception to completion single handedly using different genres such as *feuilleton* (critical, analytic, in-depth articles), reviews, and stories. *Masterstvo* implied excellence and professionalism in journalism. The Soviet school of journalism laid down the maxim that the quality of writing was more important than the audience and the topic (Korkonosenko, 1998).

Although all the journalistic genres were subdivided into the informational and the publicist during Soviet times, this distinction was irrelevant because "every [piece of writing] brought a publicistic component" irrespective of the type of media (Bogdanov & Vyazemsky, 1971, pp. 259–260). *Publitsistika* is defined as "the literature on . . . public-political questions", which includes both factual (informational) materials so that readers can draw their own conclusions and materials that have "different reasoning, summarising, proposing these or those conclusions" (Bogdanov & Vyazemsky, 1971, pp. 677–678). The professionalism of Soviet journalists was measured by the level of development of his/her publicist skills. Even in the present time, *publitsistika* is highly valued and considered "one of the highest stages of journalistic creativity co-related with bright literary talent and a citizen's position", i.e., articulating and defending one's position on important issues (Vinogradova, 2000, p. 45).

In the early 1990s when journalism experienced de-Sovietization after the collapse of communism and the resultant political and economic liberalization of the media and labour market, in Russia, a strong professional identity was not present in journalism. Journalism as a party-political service died overnight and was reborn as an open market practice with new practitioners flooding journalism. That initial period of post-Soviet journalism was marked by a lack of consensual understanding about the profession. In this time of increasing commercialization, the media began to earn money by using questionable tactics such as fomenting conflict between competitors during elections, misrepresentation, and manipulation of public opinion in the information wars between oligarchs (Pasti, 2004; Simonov, 1998; Zassoursky, 2004).

Today, the choice for Russian journalists is between adopting a political stance and creating an economic advantage for themselves, with consequences for professionalism. The political choice leads to protesting the lack of journalistic freedom and ends with the departure of the journalist from unfree media, or from the profession, or even from the country. The economic choice leads to loyalty to unfree media and a pragmatic decision to stay in journalism to earn a living.

The idea of professionalism in India is an amalgam of influences, needs, and expectations. Journalism in pre-independent India (before 1947) was essentially nationalist in character, playing a role in the fight for freedom from British colonialism. This professional ideology of criticism continued into post-independent India at least in the print media. Guaranteed a free press, print media journalists engaged in critical debates on national and international matters (Thussu, 2005). According to Eapen (1969), after independence, journalists believed their professional role was "informing, educating and guiding the linguistic, religious or regional community within which their papers circulate" (p. 173). More recently, the respected newspaper *The Hindu* outlined truth telling, freedom, justice, humaneness, and social good as the principles of responsible and ethical journalism (*The Hindu*, 2003). Unlike print media, broadcast media were government institutions and were thus drafted into the task of nation building with programming that facilitated social change, agricultural extension work, and such. This idea of journalism as a resource to drive development was not limited to broadcast media; in the form of development journalism, it also became the expectation from print media (Aggarwala, 1979).

Today, however, with the advent of privatization in India and the consequent explosive growth of media, the entire news business is more market driven, though government radio and television still maintain the professional ideology of enabling social change. The market-based media system has led to the demise of unions and associations, which were strong during the time of a left-leaning ideology in the early years of the nation. These recent events further complicate ideas of an already multifaceted concept of professionalism in India.

In post-1949 China, news work was conducted under the guidelines of the Party-state and was essentially an act of propaganda, similar to the practice in the Soviet Union. After the Party's adoption of the policy of reform and opening up (*Gaige Kaifang*), in 1978, news work and therefore news itself changed. Students of journalism were exposed to Western ideas of journalism through textbooks and academic conferences. After the early 1990s, these students who had become reporters and editors by this time began to apply Western ideas to their practice. For example, CBS' *60 Minutes* was their model when planning a new news programme. This modelling was not simply about the rhetoric and storytelling techniques, but more importantly about adopting Western professional ideology. Since that time, journalists in China increasingly speak about objectivity, the fourth estate, making news stories rather than Xinhua-style articles, etc. Thus, the Western definition of professionalism in journalism has become a part of Chinese journalists' ideas.

It is difficult to find a South Africa–centric or exclusively South African prescriptive and/or descriptive scholarly definition of journalism professionalism (or of professionalism in general). Instead, generic and Western definitions of journalism are available largely as a result of the country's colonial history and its impact on both local intellectual traditions and higher education curriculum. Despite the absence of abstract scholarly theorization and conceptualization of journalism professionalism as a set of definitions, what is expected of journalism 'professionals' is evident in the critique of practice. For example, normative critiques, available in abundance, indicate "dropping journalism standards", "shallow journalism", "tabloidization of journalism", etc. (Claassen, 1996; Claassen, 2001; Krüger, 2004; Wasserman, 2010). Further, it is assumed that journalism 'professionalism' is learned through academic training, experience, and newsroom practice (De Beer & Stein, 2002; Tsedu, Wrottley, & Clay, 2002). Still, a peculiar brand of journalism practice did exist in South Africa and was exemplified in *Drum*, a consumer/lifestyle magazine, which in the 1950s had a strong political stance. Within it emerged a group of black journalists whose feature-type short stories challenged the apartheid government and vividly captured day-to-day township life at the time (Hadland, 2005).

In the early '90s post-democracy, as South Africa joined a globalized world, which the 1989 fall of the Berlin Wall symbolized, for the South African people, the triumph of capitalism, South African media began to speak the language of the market. Alternative media disappeared, and mainstream media gradually moved to the liberal centre to cater to post-apartheid, multiracial audiences. The market orientation required that media search for new audiences; they found these in the consumers of tabloids and indigenous language media, both of which rose in number. This shift was accompanied by a decline in hard news and investigative journalism, and a rise in human-interest journalism. The human-interest stories as well as stories that came from the now smaller hard news and investigative journalism segments relentlessly focused on government failures, maladministration, and corruption. This in turn put post-apartheid South African journalism right in the middle of a professional debate about the role of journalism in a developing democracy. Should the role be to engage in developmental journalism or to act as a watchdog?

Studying BRICS journalists' explications of journalistic professionalism

Evetts (2013) suggests that to understand professionalism as a concept, a focus on the *polysemic discourse of professionalism* is necessary. As applied to journalism, both Deuze (2005) and Glasser (1992) suggest 'research in practice' as *the* method to study journalistic professionalism and journalism itself, an approach somewhat similar to the lived experiences approach to journalism studies. For Deuze, a true understanding of how occupational ideology gets operationalized in actual work emerges only from seeing how journalists in different work scenarios negotiate these core values. Glasser advocates for a pedagogy of practice ('knowledge in practice') because knowledge is socially constructed and culturally bound; he suggests that we need to ask "what we can learn from a careful examination of artistry . . . the competence by which practitioners actually handle . . . practice" (Schön, 1987, as cited in Glasser, 1992, p. 139).

The BRICS study partially simulated the research-in-practice method; it replaced observation with in-depth interviews to understand, through the BRICS journalists' narratives, the polysemy of professionalism and how these journalists negotiate the core values of their occupational ideology and operationalize them in everyday practice (Deuze, 2005).

The BRICS study

Towards the above-mentioned purpose, journalists were asked to discuss who they considered to be a professional journalist, whether they self-appraised as professionals, why they became journalists, what were journalism's functions in the public sphere, and how much they participated in unions/associations, the last particularly included because of the role unions/associations played in some BRICS countries in the past. These questions may not exhaust all the ways in which professionalism is defined in various parts of the world, but they capture some of its main aspects.

Findings

Journalistic professionalism and self-appraisal: the traits approach

It is evident from the responses that BRICS journalists employed a traits approach to defining a professional journalist. In Brazil, among traditional media respondents, 85 per cent had a journalism degree, and curiously, even in online media – supposedly a freer platform for independent and diverse journalism – 74 per cent held a journalism degree. This is explained by the fact that education was among the qualities that rose to the top in the Brazilian definition of professionalism. Included in the group of qualities defining professionalism were technical expertise such as being "competent, with good knowledge about the subject", independence, and adherence to moral-ethical values, such as honesty and sincerity. For technical expertise, a few traditional media journalists (4 per cent) mentioned that journalists should be able to multitask across platforms, i.e., they should possess the ability to write, edit, produce, and verify stories for both online and traditional media. For moral-ethical values, most journalists viewed "dishonesty and lack of character" as well as corruption negatively; 61 per cent disapproved of writing news in exchange for money or services, 17 per cent would approve if this was done officially through a contract and presented as a piece of advertising, and 9 per cent approved or were ambiguously neutral about this practice.

The emphasis placed on moral-ethical values by Brazilian journalists is critical in face of the violence that plagues journalism in Brazil and that could put journalists' integrity at risk. The lack of security and necessary conditions for work creates at least two professional challenges for Brazilian journalists: a) producing news without fear of collateral effects against the journalist or his/her family, and b) practicing a journalism that provides the annunciation of different ideas, so important for democracy and for society. According to the Committee to Protect Journalists (CPJ), Brazil has the 11th highest number of journalist murders in the world that go unpunished (CPJ, 2015). Still, Brazilian news media have played a significant role in the democratization of the country in the last 30 years, giving visibility to corruption cases, and have been a channel for helping and guiding the audience, which contacts them first (before contacting state institutions such as the police or local governments) to know their rights and be informed about various public policies (ANDI, 2007). Most respondent journalists in Brazil believed that they had achieved the status of a professional as a result of their degree in journalism, their skills to select and report the news, and their respect for ethics and journalistic principles.

Russian journalists' model of professionalism primarily included four criteria: a high level of education that fostered erudite, well-bred, broad-minded journalists, who had a command of the language and an analytical mind; technical expertise that included excellent skills in news gathering and analysis of information, ability to write stories based on information, curiosity, and willingness to get first-hand sources, competence in the subject, ability to use new digital technology, and communication and management skills (sociability); adherence to the moral-ethical principles of honesty and sincerity; and adherence to the norms of journalism practice, including objectivity, checking sources, not distorting facts, and not engaging in 'copy-paste', i.e., using other people's work as their own.

Education, always an important requirement for journalists in the Soviet Union, is in the post-Soviet era reflected in such criteria of professionalism as writing timely stories based on facts. The emphasis on moral ethical principles derives from the current situation characterized by a lack of honest journalism and widespread corruption in the profession and in society.

In Russia, self-appraisals reflected the high ideals set to achieve professionalism. Even journalists who had advanced to become chief editors set a high standard for themselves: "No, I am far from professional. You should always strive for something more". Other experienced journalists agreed: "In our profession, you cannot consider [that you have] attained perfection. When you start to think that everything is fine, it's time to retire; our work requires continuous learning and self-improvement". But younger, beginning journalists, who did not have a journalism education, considered themselves professionals based on their honesty and their aversion to writing custom articles and engaging in propaganda.

Among Indian journalists, in general, professionalism meant a serious work ethic and a sincere dedication to the profession. Specifically, Indian journalists' criteria for professionalism fell into five categories: technical expertise defined in terms of knowledge of events/subject matter; adherence to a moral-ethical value system (given considerable salience in these narratives); adherence to the norms of journalism practice; a nose for news (ability to judge what is newsworthy as well as having the personal traits of inquisitiveness, curiosity, and attentiveness); and responsibility to society that would manifest as responsible reporting, i.e., a commitment to social betterment and an ear-to-the-ground judgment to implement self-censorship for sensitive or sensational issues.

In these narratives about professionalism, the traits of honesty, integrity, and truthfulness surfaced repeatedly as ethical values, and these translated into the normative practices of independence, objectivity and balance, lack of bias, and accurate reporting that is thoroughly fact-checked because "every word is sacrosanct". For Indian respondents, an unprofessional journalist "inserts personal speculation about problems, human tragedy, etc." into a story or "is incompetent and ignorant about the subject". The emphasis on moral ethical values might be a reaction to current conditions of journalism where owners, hand in hand with politicians, and politician-owners themselves interfere with newsmaking and have created the phenomenon of paid news (positive news coverage for money) (Athique, 2012). In these circumstances, when the power elite such as politicians and business owners are viewed with suspicion by the public, often the journalist is regarded as the moral interlocutor on behalf of the citizen. Thus, morality and social responsibility still continue to be qualities a professional journalist is expected to have.

The idea of responsibility in the Indian context derives from an expectation, post-independence, that the media, including news media, practice development journalism to assist the government in development efforts that lagged under colonialism (Aggarwala, 1979). In fact, this expectation was encoded in codes of ethics for journalists (www.presscouncil.nic.in/Content/62_1_PrinciplesEthics.aspx).

In India, most respondents self-appraised as professionals because they believed they followed the mandates of the profession and the ethics of journalism, maintaining their journalistic sensibilities and their integrity. Metro journalists who expressed doubts about their professionalism indicated reasons such as pressure from higher authorities and their own personal traits, both of which could introduce bias in stories; however, they also said that management was even less professional than they were. These journalists often had to spin a story to satisfy business and political interests: "I am a senior journalist but there are people above me, so the news will be changed according to their convenience". Narratives about personal traits that hampered their professionalism included "there are areas that I need to work on" and "as I have strong opinions, it becomes a task to keep my personal biases away from the story I am writing". A metro online journalist believed that "very few journalists are doing their work professionally" and that "fake journalism is taking over".

Chinese journalists' concept of professionalism included technical skills in terms of interviewing and writing expertise, ability to interact socially, and knowledge of and competence in the subject; ethical conduct, i.e., valuing ethics in general and in journalism practice in particular and not engaging in mercenary activities that threaten the integrity of journalism and are condemnable (most journalists considered working for profit unprofessional); adherence to the norm of objectivity; and a nose for news, i.e., the ability to judge the news value of an event or issue as well as having curiosity, a quality valued very highly. Chinese journalists regard professionalism mainly in terms of their capacity to discover and publish news. While one would consider this as an integral part of the profession itself, in China it takes on added importance. It is actually a representation of an improvised journalistic practice, wherein journalists have to struggle with social control inside and outside the newsroom. In particular, journalists in China employ various tactics to ferret out news in face of the Party's attempts to dominate news production. Most journalists indicated that they were still traversing the rather long route in their struggle to be professional and thus few of them considered themselves professionals.

In South Africa, all respondent journalists shared an understanding of the distinctive characteristics of a professional journalist. These included: moral-ethical values such as staying away from corrupt practices, the hallmark of highly ethical journalists, and adherence to norms of practice such as independence from vested interest(s), whether government or organized business, including corporations that employed them, as well as lack of bias. Specifically, these journalists considered any form of bribery and any conflict of interest that could lead to framing a story differently or selecting a story to meet some outside agenda as corrupt practices; and their definition of lack of bias particularly referenced crafting stories to fully represent all possible pertinent viewpoints and facts in a story. In the words of a journalist: "Get your facts straight. . . . It's the stuff that you learn in your first year that will never ever change. [For me], it's . . . a thing of respect". Respondents noted that acts of corruption were few and far between. While journalists frowned upon paid news, they also pointed out that low wages could make bribes attractive if journalists continued to be underpaid. Possibly the high importance placed on lack of bias and shunning outside agendas is a reflection of the needs of a post-apartheid South Africa that wants to divest itself of past practices of reflecting the perspectives of the Afrikaaner media and other dominant power groups.

South African respondent journalists attributed high professionalism to themselves; it was a badge of honour for them to never be corrupt, biased, or influenced by vested interests. They could not foresee a time and space where and when they could ever consider being unethical. This professional orientation however led to ethical dilemmas and created a moral 'crisis' for many in their professional work, specifically when their stories were subjected to editorial reframing or they were told they could not pursue certain stories because of moral, commercial, or political reasons.

Journalistic professionalism: the power approach

The critical discourse about power as it relates to professionalism is different from the power journalists may experience from the symbiotic relationship between them and their elite sources or even from performing functions such as informing the public or assisting with social change. Power of profession in critical terms is instead related to a monopoly or legitimacy perception on part of the journalists that keeps 'non-journalists' out, considering them unskilled and their work illegitimate due to the lack of institutional checks and balances. In this study, journalists were not directly queried about whether they had sole legitimacy to produce news or whether they self-referenced feelings of power, but their responses, particularly about online news, were searched for any assignation of such power to themselves.

In Brazil, traditional media, especially print media, continue to have more credibility than online media. While 58 per cent of Brazilian readers trust newspapers, only 27 per cent trust the content published on electronic sites, blogs, and social media (Presidência da República, 2015). More importantly, in this study, some journalists said that the information they provide had greater credibility than that from social networks:

> I think journalism today can't live without social networks. But I think that, at the same time, people need to be very careful with this because what's there is not always the truth; this is what's really going on. Now, the challenge for journalists [is to check the] information, because it's not enough for you to get information that's out there and believe that to be true, because you have different types of people there: from hyper intelligent, educated, and honest people to nasty and dishonest people. It's a fuzzy set; there are various opinions, various demands, and therefore information checking is essential.

In Russian journalists' reflections on questions about the essence of their profession, young journalists both in traditional and online media made a claim to power. In St. Petersburg, an interviewee who founded a journalistic startup provided his explanation of the fundamental difference he saw between journalists and bloggers:

> We have twenty popular bloggers in the country who write texts and many people read them. They are not journalists because they have no access to information. A journalist is someone whom people call asking for help to write an article on their problem, to whom somebody provides documents opening [the door for] a potential investigation. [A journalist] meets with different politicians and has the right to talk to them and not to believe them.

Comparing the profession in Soviet times, as described to her by senior colleagues, with the current situation, a young female journalist from a popular newspaper criticized the major trend to serve the interests of readers because she thought this lowered the status of journalists. In particular, she noted that the Internet has strengthened interaction between journalists and the audience, making them equals, when in fact the journalist should be superior to the reader:

If earlier, in their relations, the journalist was at the top and a reader at the bottom, now it is vice versa. Journalists seek to serve the interests of readers. . . . In principle, journalism should orient to the interests of readers, but [there is] no need to serve them because it implies serving the lower interests of the majority. That is, journalism falls to the level of the average man in the street. This is a bad thing. Journalism, in my opinion, should on the contrary educate the man in the street. Now this enlightening function is unfortunately losing [ground]; the profession is sliding simply to a banal serving of the majority. This is a minus.

In India, a Kolkata journalist indicated that there was no "I am better than you" kind of attitude on his part towards online journalists. Very rarely did respondent journalists in India express a hegemonic position in terms of claiming exclusive legitimacy to provide information or interpret social reality. The few who did were mostly print media journalists who considered online news questionable. According to one Kolkata respondent, online media have "less accountability, less script, less quote-checking, less barrier on words used. Traditional media have more guidelines". Some Pune respondents pointed out that the somewhat instantaneous nature of online news kept online journalists from engaging in the thorough checking that is possible for print news. While acknowledging audience reliance on digital platforms of news and of news sharing, one Pune journalist indicated that the audience "is dependent on [print media] for reliable and authentic news because the news that comes in other media . . . may not be authentic. . . . [The audience] can cross check things from newspapers". In fact, one Pune journalist felt that print was even more authentic than television news, and another implied that print requires a different and more demanding type of "capability" than television or online news does.

More directly, one Pune journalist said, "If you ask me, I do not believe in citizen journalism. Because [their writing is] just random thoughts" and further that they "cannot be trusted at all. Because they will have bias", while no one will doubt a trained journalist because the audience "will trust [that the journalist is] checking everything and . . . following all the journalistic rules and ethics". A journalist in Kolkata voiced a somewhat similar sentiment and indicated that the audience had sustained respect for trained journalists, and while he acknowledged that citizen journalists could do well, he said this would happen if they were given training and guidance: "Every neighbourhood can have a journalist now because of social media. . . . The respect that a journalist would get as someone who could write and publish news has not diminished. With some guidance, some professional attitude, the newcomers will do well for themselves".

A very few respondent journalists did express opinions about the power of journalism, some indirectly, others more directly. A Hyderabad journalist, discussing various views about what media are and what they can do in terms of impacting "society's thinking" and "the public's mind" concluded: "All in all, I would say that media shape a society". A Pune journalist's reason for becoming a journalist was, "Out of curiosity, for knowledge; it is a different kind of power. We have a means to publish something, so people keep coming to us – 'please print this and that for us'. That is the power, I think". Another Pune journalist decried the loss of power thus: "Now that anyone can be a journalist, no one is scared of journalists. Earlier police persons or anyone else used to be scared of journalists. This is in a way good". Such a justification of power implied that journalists 'do good'. In the words of a journalist from Pune, "Like I told you earlier, we express our own viewpoints in this profession and we can bring a lot of change. This power is there in media, which can be used to do some good work".

In China, hegemonic thinking about journalism had a slightly different take. Since the mid-1990s, a figurative territorial dispute in terms of defining news has been occurring in China. From that time on, China's media have undergone continuous commercialization wherein dozens of media outlets have become market-oriented and financially self-supported. Thus, the hegemony of Party-advocated propaganda and of social control on newsrooms is being impaired day by day, year by year. Journalists in market-oriented media have adopted the news paradigm in place of the propaganda paradigm using the pretext of audience preference from marketing feedback as the reason to do this. In other words, these journalists have started constructing a professional ideology within a market-oriented media instead of using the Party-state ideology, and are trying to demonstrate that they are presenting news as different from the propaganda that is coming from the so-called Party-controlled media. A Chinese investigative reporter said journalists in Party media show "their loyalty to the Party and governments for which they are doing propaganda, while [we] are making news".

Closer to the matter at hand, the issue of defining news territory extends, as in other countries above, to online versus traditional news media. After 1998, online media grew rapidly in China. These media integrated and disseminated news much faster than did traditional media and delivered information in a vivid and lively way, but seldom devoted themselves to fundamental newsmaking norms such as fact-checking that are applied widely in traditional media. Thus, traditional journalists criticized their colleagues in online media as doing unprofessional news work at that time. A senior manager of a magazine in Shanghai said,

> Online journalists are much more hard-working indeed. Well, I cannot say anything other than that they are hard-working. They are absolutely less professional than we, the traditional journalists, are, although they do technology-oriented jobs. In comparison, traditional media journalists do their jobs with low-level technology, but their news coverage uses far more professional criteria.

A reporter from a newspaper in Guangzhou discussed the accuracy of online news:

> To a large extent, new media are now pursuing speed, while fact-checking and further tracing of a news event is unfortunately ignored. They operate on

a fast track. In contrast, traditional news media [have] an extreme emphasis on fact-checking, accuracy, and general quality of our news products.

Around 2000, the State Council, in an attempt to ensure that online media are not legitimized, prescribed how these media could 'make' news: only by editing, integrating, and forwarding what traditional media have already produced. Many traditional media journalists in this study believed that their work was much more serious, formal, and critical, because they had "better qualifications for covering news, including reporting and writing skills", while online journalists "cannot do more than re-editing and integrating produced news articles". Later, in the 2010s, when domestic social media flourished in China, citizens produced more and more fragmented and informal news articles independently. Thus, journalists as well as citizens in new media considered traditional media journalists as not promoting open participation to promote the public good. An online news journalist indicated that online media responds to audience needs besides reporting news:

> If you work in traditional media, you are working for the media institution itself, but if you work in new media, you are not only working for that media institution but also for your audiences. You should consider and evaluate their tastes and opinions, because you are performing a service.

A reporter at a radio station in Beijing said that new media were a symbol of the future orientation of the media industry: "New media integrate various forms such as texts, pictures, audio, and video, so it is able to grow comprehensively to attract audiences".

This contestation over who has jurisdiction over news reveals the struggle of journalists against the Party and the disagreement between traditional and online journalists. To date, no one group has established its hegemony since the mid-1990s, and thus this jurisdictional contestation in China is likely to continue in the coming decades. It does, however, lead to a diversity of journalistic ideology, indicating that the Party-state ideology is definitely undermined.

In South Africa, the power discourse was of a slightly different nature. One journalist, for example, said that it was due to the presence of journalists that people were informed, "because people would not know or be informed if there were no journalists". Another said, "I think in some instances we think we are a whole lot more influential than we really are and in other cases we really are. I think certain columnists are highly influential and I think certain titles are highly influential". This influence, a journalist indicated, could have an impact in real life, but not always:

> There are instances where you scoop a story and some things get done and you welcome things like that. . . . I mean there's development happening for those people there which should have happened anyway. So, if something gets done, that's great. But there are instances where you write a story but still the system doesn't change.

Summary: traits and power approaches

The global spread of Western journalism's occupational ideology and ideas about professionalism was evident particularly in the mention of some of the norms of journalistic practice, i.e., objectivity and balance, as respondent journalists discussed the idea of professionalism. Other values these journalists mentioned are generally accepted as principles of journalism (fact-checking, accuracy, and independence from elite influence) or as qualities of a good journalist (nose for news, i.e., curiosity, attentiveness, ability to tell what is newsworthy, and technical skills; newsmaking skills; and competence in the subject matter and in digital technology). In this age of (presumed) digitalization, it is interesting that digital skills were not often noted among required traits of journalistic professionalism and in fact were absent in the responses of journalists in some countries. This may be an indication of the lack of deep penetration of digitalization, but it could also mean that these journalists did not believe that such skills were critical to the practice of journalism. Journalists' pluralistic orientation to professionalism across countries was also evident. In Brazil and Russia, education was highly valued; in India, high value was placed on responsibility towards society. In South Africa, the emphasis was on moral values such as honesty, sincerity, and integrity, with specifics such as staying away from corrupt practices, and in China the focus on avoiding mercenary activities added to the divergent views on professionalism in the BRICS countries.

The BRICS' journalists who self-evaluated as professionals believed that they met the standards they had articulated. In general, those who expressed uncertainty or refrained from calling themselves professionals had set themselves high goals and, in their self-appraisal, indicated that they had yet to meet the goal, that the goal may even be out of reach, or that they were working hard on keeping their strongly held biases out of their newsmaking work. In India, those who self-assessed as not being professional believed that they were kept from this by pressure from supervisors, who in turn, they indicated, were even less professional.

The power of profession that ascribes singular legitimacy to journalists to tell 'important' stories did emerge in some journalists' responses but these were mostly in reaction to online news and, for India, particularly in comparison with print news. The deficits of online news as compared with print news, as outlined by the Indian print journalists, were lack of authenticity, lack of thoroughness, and possibly a greater trust in print media on part of the audience. In China, the offline hegemony over online was a continuation of the territorial dispute over legitimate newsmaking between market-oriented and Party-state journalists.

Joining journalism for journalism's functions?

Included in some explications of journalistic professionalism is the idea of the public service orientation of the profession, sometimes defined in terms of creating and sustaining a democracy but also in terms of an orientation that supports the nation state in its endeavours either to develop the country or to promote it.

In Brazil, 60 per cent of respondents cited "providing information" as the main role of the news media in the public sphere. This must be "quality" information that promotes "social transformation", and denounces corruption, abuses, and mistakes made by the state and the public so as to actively help ordinary citizens. For the most part, it was passion that motivated traditional media journalists in Brazil to join the profession, passion not just for providing information but also for some sort of activism: "I have a passion for information and for life. I want to improve the world with the way I am". Other reasons for becoming journalists were "writing well since childhood", "was aware of [the need for this] talent for journalism", and "contributing to the school or the neighbourhood newspaper".

According to Russian journalists, journalism's functions were to provide information, report the news, educate and entertain, investigate, analyse, and provide objective coverage. In Petrozavodsk, some journalists considered it important to express the views of various groups and to form public opinion:

> Public service is the most important thing . . . [whether providing a] forum for discussions [or] for the expression of different opinions. Now journalism does not do this; [it is] less professional than in Soviet times, despite the fact that [at that time] there was ideological oppression.

A St. Petersburg journalist's figurative answer was, "First be Sherlock Holmes, a journalist who investigates; second be Charlie Chaplin, a journalist who makes the show; and third be a person at confession, a journalist who shares his innermost thoughts". In Moscow, online journalists indicated that a journalist should be a moderator between government and society. In the traditional media in St. Petersburg and Yekaterinburg and in online media in Petrozavodsk, journalists believed that they should help people to find and access information, fight for justice, and serve society. For many, journalism was simply a job to make an income.

One Russian journalist "saw in . . . childhood the newspaper *Leninist Sparks*, where notes from children were printed. . . . I thought why can't I also [do this]?" In the words of a St. Petersburg respondent: "From . . . childhood, I was publishing articles in our city newspaper for teenagers". Many who came to journalism in the beginning of the post-Soviet period shared the following sentiment: "It was the second half of [the] 1980s: *Perestroika, Glasnost*. For me, during that period, journalism was very important as a tool for social and political changes. And I decided to take part in it". Journalists in Russia appeared to be drawn to journalism from a young age, but they also entered the profession due to family tradition and to get a good income.

For journalists in the Indian metros of Delhi and Hyderabad, the functions of journalism were "[making] people aware of their own rights and duties, [interpreting] the rules of the land, and [enabling the] audience to think critically", but these journalists also clearly distinguished these normative functions from the reality of their daily practice. Most metro journalists were critical of the news media for their failure to play a watchdog role in the public sphere: "The media is a maimed watchdog; it's aging and losing its edge"; "we . . . left the [watchdog] role long back"; and "[a] dog respects and is faithful to the master [alone] . . . , but here the story [is reversed]. The media doesn't take care of the country or respect and honor the public in any way, but always [looks after] its own benefits".

In Kolkata, journalists mentioned the following functions: to report the truth and to tell stories in an objective and fair manner. They shared with journalists from Pune the belief that they had the "duty to inform the public" on matters of societal concern, such as ensuring justice, removing inequality, resolving issues for the common people, and raising important questions, as well as the duty to recognize unsung heroes. For the Kolkata and Pune journalists, the role of news in the public sphere was to voice public opinion as well as to shape it: "You cannot actually separate society and journalism. Whatever is there in society gets reflected in news, and whatever is there in news forms the public view and opinion". For these provincial city journalists, journalism was critical to the functioning of democracy: "[It] is supposed to play the role of checks and balances"; therefore, "whatever ongoing state of affairs is there to which [the] public is not having any access, news media should report it". Pune journalists also mentioned entertainment as a function; one Pune journalist summed up functions thus: "empowerment, education, entertainment".

In the Indian metros, most traditional media journalists entered the field intentionally (because they were "good writers"). Online professionals however did so more by accident and some of them were not sure they would continue in the field given their youth and their original intention to join other fields such as film and advertising. Most provincial city journalists entered the profession due to their interest in journalism, because "it's not boring, it's not traditional, it's developing day by day, it's entertaining, it's challenging, [and] it's fast", and because they wanted, "to become a pillar of society, to be a voice for the people, for the common man". Two journalists in Kolkata and more in Pune joined the profession by chance; the Pune journalists indicated that they then recognized the interesting nature and promise of this profession and stayed with it.

Chinese journalists considered disseminating information to be a fundamental function of journalism followed by providing an objective picture of the world/day. Other functions these journalists mentioned were interpreting new laws, explicating societal problems, educating and enlightening the public, and even searching for solutions (constructive criticism). These journalists' views about the news media's role in the public sphere paralleled the above: information dissemination came first qualified by such criteria as loyalty to facts, discovery of truth, recording transitional China objectively, and ensuring the public's right to know. Interpretation came next, important in such a rapidly transforming country to explain to audiences how the government operates and how a public policy is formulated and implemented. In general, however, Chinese journalists were more concerned with their performance as defined by their ideas about professionalism, i.e., knowledge, objectivity, and competence, than with interpretation even if they subscribed to a journalism of interpretive discourse. In addition to providing a marketplace of information and an interpretive space, the discursive orientations of Chinese journalists included, as in the past (Pan & Lu, 2003), the Party-state tradition of being a mouthpiece for the Party and the people.

In China, most interviewees were eager to pursue journalism as a career. Some believed that journalism would bring public good to society, and that to engrave everyday into history was an exciting way to watch a China that is on a rapid path to transformation. Others reported that as journalists they could concern themselves with and discuss the critical issues that arose in this quickly changing society, and journalism provided them with the platform to be critics of their country and its society just like the traditional Chinese intellectuals of the past. And still others indicated that it was their dream profession since their childhood and that being a reporter would definitely bring honour and fame to them. A small number of young people turned to journalism because they did not get their first choice of subject in the nationwide enrolment system used in China. Nevertheless, most respondent journalists shared this in common: to follow the ideal media institutions and models of the late 1990s and early 2000s such as the renowned example of the *Southern Metropolis Daily*. This daily's coverage of the case of a young citizen who lost his life in custody under the Custody and Repatriation administrative procedure led to the abolition of this procedure in 2003.

In newly democratic South Africa, journalists indicated that the news media's role in the public sphere included the watchdog role, i.e., holding those in public office fully accountable to citizens, as well as the social responsibility and developmental roles, i.e., educating the public about critical issues. Most South African respondent journalists said they had good writing skills or a "desire to join journalism", a reason that they considered loftier than "family tradition". The journalists expressed a deep love for their profession; many could not imagine themselves elsewhere. This intense desire and a positive orientation towards freedom and professionalism are likely the reasons for the equally high number of journalists willing to stay in the profession despite the financial difficulties of South African news media institutions.

Summary: reasons and functions

For journalists in all five BRICS countries, information dissemination, interpretation, and public service were the main functions of journalism. The particularities lay more in the specific type of public service: in Brazil, denouncing corruption to actively help citizens; in Russia, investigation; in India, engaging in social justice; in China, helping with understanding the rapidly transforming country; and in South Africa, developing a critical consciousness among the public.

Many journalists from across the BRICS countries said that journalism was their passion, their childhood dream, that they had always wanted to be a journalist, and that they would continue in this profession. In Brazil, a reason to join the profession was engaging in activism through journalism; in Russia, the new post-Soviet political environment was an incentive; in China, there was a desire to participate in recording the history of this rapidly transitioning country, addressing issues this transformation raised, and the hope to be critics in the vein of the Chinese intellectuals of the past. In general, for the BRICS journalists, journalism's allure lay in multiple factors: excitement and challenge, fame and honour, opportunity to use a talent for writing, contributing to society, and so on.

Union and association membership

A final and in some cases vanishing aspect of 'professional' journalism is membership in unions/associations.

Brazil has 31 regional unions that comprise a National Federation of Journalists (FENAJ). Despite this, among Brazilian respondents in the BRICS study, just 19 per cent were part of a union; those who were not indicated "lack of initiative on my part", or "it's a mistake, but unfortunately I'm not associated" as reasons for non-membership. Further, some considered unions to be "a business" or a "political party" without the requisite values and efficacy to promote the rights of journalists. Besides, in Brazil, jobs for journalists include that of a press advisory and it is for this reason that journalists sometimes stay away from union activities. A significant number of journalists are employed outside newsrooms with most of them working in communication and media public relations (FENAJ, 2014).

With the exception of journalists in Petrozavodsk, most Russian journalists did not belong to a union because they did not see any meaning in such organizations; particularly the younger generation saw unions as a useless legacy of Soviet journalism. In Petrozavodsk, half of the journalists in both traditional and online media were members of the regional union of journalists. Over the years, this union has earned the reputation of being a defender of the rights and freedoms of journalists, has served as the centre for vocational training of local journalists, and has been the organizer of international professional contacts and exchanges with the neighbouring countries of northern Europe.

In Indian metros, while all journalists expressed a need for trade unions/associations none belonged to one; reasons were: they did not have information on the process of becoming members, they did not have the requisite number of years of experience, "no one [had] the time", and "owners [would] never allow" it. Unions were valued because they provide "a sense of security", and may "address our grievances [because there will be] someone who . . . can present my case, . . . someone who will raise [an issue]". Journalists in India are mostly employed on a rolling contract basis that they consider permanent employment, but the risk of being terminated is perennially present; as one journalist said, they were "temporarily permanent" or "permanently temporary". Associations were not considered to be of much help or relevance because "juniors are ignored" and "it is more for networking and free drinks". Online media journalists did not consider unions/associations because of their small fraternity; "if it grows, who knows, maybe we can one day create an online journalists' association".

In Kolkata, very few journalists were association members, partly because association policy did not accord them membership due to their particular circumstance, be it type of job or years of service. At the same time, some of these journalists did not perceive a need for in-house unions/associations because "the outside-media-house or inter-media organizations are very strong". In Pune, in contrast, a majority of the journalists were members of a union of journalists. In both Kolkata and Pune, in-house unions/associations were rare or non-existent partly because these "permanently temporary" journalists are not allowed to form unions or stage agitations; additionally, in Pune, journalists considered media houses' "corporate culture" and "policies" as barriers. And still further, government radio, the only news radio permitted in India, does not allow employees to have unions. Journalists in both cities expressed similar reasons for valuing unions/associations; a few mentioned workers' rights and negotiation with employers, but most spoke appreciatively of activities that improved their work-related expertise and performance, or provided an opportunity to socialize, network, or engage with the journalistic community. In Pune, a couple of journalists were concerned about security and the increasing physical attacks on journalists, which their union was addressing, and a group of women journalists were working informally to include sensitive coverage of gender issues.

Despite the fact that more than half of all respondents confirmed that a primary organization of journalists existed in their media outlet, union membership was not high in China in general and in Guangzhou too where collective action by industrial workers occurs frequently. Low membership was particularly true for online journalists. Journalists themselves were confused about membership, about whether they can join of their own free will or need to receive notification to do so.

A large majority of South African journalists were not unionized even though interviewees complained about pay and job security. Freelancers were, however, increasingly joining the South African Freelancers Association (Safrea). Safrea "expanded its member base by 27 per cent in 2014. Considering that, conservatively, around 596 employees in the media sector lost their jobs, it is not surprising that Safrea's membership numbers swelled considerably" (Nevill, 2015, p. 1). Reasons for lack of union membership among permanent employees included the rather young age of the journalists, lack of need to join trade unions, the alliance between the unions and the ruling African National Congress (ANC), which would technically put journalists in 'alliance' with the government and thus compromise their independence (none of the interviewees were members of a political party), and the fact that South African courts deal with labour issues far more effectively than do trade unions.

Summary: unions

Union/association membership was not large in the BRICS countries often for similar reasons: lack of time, lack of information, barriers such as years of experience, and uncertainty about the benefits of membership. In Brazil, journalists were concerned that journalist unions also included public relations personnel, while in Russia, journalists saw unions as a Soviet legacy. In India, journalists saw benefits in terms of security of jobs, but employers often banned unions, while in China and South Africa, journalists were concerned about union alliance with the ruling party.

Discussion and conclusions

The summaries presented after each topical section clearly indicate heterogeneity in the views of the BRICS journalists about the dimensions that comprise the construct of professionalism, but they also indicate some similarities. The commonalities, in brief, were as follows. Passion for journalism was the common denominator reason across countries for joining the profession. From inside the profession, journalists commonly referenced technical expertise, moral-ethical values, and adherence to norms of journalism as indicators of professionalism. Interestingly, while "independence" was mentioned by journalists in some countries, it was not as salient in the journalists' narratives as some of the other indicators were, even in a long-standing democracy such as India. Measuring themselves against the shared and other indicators that were particular to their country, in all countries except South Africa, at minimum, some interviewees believed that they had yet to reach the status of a professional. Irrespective of their self-appraisal, these journalists shared the opinion that a major function of journalism is information provision and interpretation. Union membership was sporadic in all five countries due to shared barriers such as lack of time and insufficient number of years in the profession.

Some of these commonalities may be explained by factors such as the undergird of journalism practice that is more or less globally present today, the spread of democracy, which has led to better conditions for journalism practice, and the global visibility of journalistic norms that has facilitated their diffusion though not necessarily their universal acceptance (Waisbord, 2013). The question arises whether these somewhat shared indicators and manifestations of professionalism provide a BRICS journalistic coalition, an identity in the explication of professionalism that separates BRICS journalists as a group. One factor that seems salient enough and sufficiently different from the Western discourse on professionalism is the idea of a moral dimension to journalistic professionalism, a unique perspective shared by journalists in Brazil, Russia, and India. Moral values such as honesty, sincerity, and integrity, commonly voiced as indicators of professionalism in Brazil, Russia, and India, are not often found in Western discussions of professionalism. They are also not part of the US ethics codes for example, which focus more on guiding day-to-day decision making in the actual reporting of news (SPJ Code of Ethics, 2014). But it is a matter of judgment whether this comes close to suggesting even a partial BRICS journalistic professional identity.

While it might be tempting to look for and see a BRICS personality of professionalism, and despite some commonalities among BRICS narratives, it appears that professionalism is so imbued with local values that only broad strokes of similarity may be seen. For example, technical expertise comprised some similar items across countries but also some dissimilar items. The differences, or more appropriately the specificities, in the explication of professionalism by respondent journalists may be explained instead by the historical-politico-economic-socio-cultural context of each country and its ramifications for journalism. In Russia, journalists in the past were an intellectual class, erudite and learned, and the remnant of this status is seen in the primacy of education as an indicator of professionalism. Some unique indicators of professionalism also emerged by country. In China, for example, although a number of journalists have today become more independent from the Party-state than they were in earlier times, they still regard journalistic professionalism more in terms *other* than autonomy. In India, the perceived role of journalism as a partner in the country's development post-independence, the encoding of this in codes of ethics, and the value placed on community have led journalists to include social responsibility in their construct of professionalism. This idea of responsibility to community, society, nation is frequently indicated by journalists of the South. In this study, however, only Indian journalists articulated this function; Brazil's community orientation and South Africa's value of ubuntu, i.e., communitarianism, did not surface as much.

Further, while the public service function was in general important among BRICS journalists, it too had particularities defined by local conditions: fighting corruption in Brazil, advocating for social justice in India, and developing critical consciousness in post-apartheid South Africa. China's rapid societal transition has journalists place primacy on recording and interpreting these changes for the public.

Even self-perceptions of professionalism and their reasons differed somewhat. In India, changing ownership patterns in traditional media, resulting in pressures to include and exclude, to slant and source in particular ways, have impacted journalists' self-perception; they feel forced into acting in unprofessional ways. In Russia and China, there was an expression of humility; in Russia, self-perception of professionalism came from the criteria journalists imposed on themselves subjectively – a standard one always aimed for but never reached, while in China, journalists felt the road to professionalism was long and they were still on the path. In South Africa, humility was replaced by genuine pride in self-perceptions of professionalism; journalists' main criterion was never succumbing to corruption, and they felt they had won this battle and were true professionals.

As one Indian journalist said, "'professional' journalist is a loaded title". It is also a normative concept in terms of its descriptors and expected functions at the very least, and thus aspirational and rarely fully achievable. And even though in its macro level normative form it may share broad strokes of similarity across nations, at the micro level even the norms are contested, fragmented, and local, partly because the same words may have different meanings in the local context (Waisbord, 2013). Furthermore, what Evetts (2013) says about professions is also true of the work of professionals: "The operational definition of profession can be highly pragmatic" (p. 781).

In face of this local/national reproduction of journalists' professional identities, theorizing about journalistic professionalism in general is difficult and theorizing about it for the BRICS countries as a group is even more difficult. All that can be said is that there is the local in the global meaning of professionalism and the borders of both the local and the global meaning are fuzzy, permeable, and changing.

So, has the professionalization project for journalism succeeded in its "boundary work" (Gieryn, 1983), keeping others out and claiming a unique expert knowledge? Journalism's boundaries have always been porous, despite attempts by governments and the profession to the contrary; today, in the digital age, this permeability is more than ever evident, and journalism's knowledge claim is more about an expertise of technique rather than a body of knowledge. In general, this is also true of BRICS journalism. Other questions about the hegemony of professionalism do, however, remain: are journalists asserting a special status and using an occupational ideology to control others and define a particular social reality?

In this study, some characteristics of the dominant ideology of journalism, "a system of beliefs" as defined by Deuze (2005, p. 445) that serves to legitimize the occupation and its position in the world, emerged with different emphases in the five countries – the normative ideas of public service, of objectivity, and of ethics (though not so much of autonomy and immediacy) – and to that extent indirectly indicated a belief in these journalists about the quality of their storytelling. A direct hegemonic view also emerged in the narratives of some journalists, but only sporadically; these few journalists did suggest they had a special status and claimed to be the sole arbiters of an authentic and reliable view of the world as compared with online/citizen journalists. In general, with a few exceptions in India, BRICS journalists in this study defined professionalism more as residing in the person rather than in the person's relationship with societal institutions in terms of power relations. It is possible that these narratives did not appear because the in-depth interview protocol did not directly address these questions; more complete answers in the form of BRICS journalists', not scholars', narratives about journalistic hegemony will therefore have to await another study.

In summary and conclusion, it may be said that in their narratives about professionalism, BRICS journalists in this study continued to employ a traits approach but every now and then they also provided glimpses into their view of the power of the profession, mostly as a contestation with online journalists' credibility. At the same time, because the in-depth interview method elicited some detailed responses, the telling of the traits was not entirely reductionist; it was woven with examples and context that provided a somewhat nuanced view. Apart from traits and power, the voices of journalists also pointed out the continuities and changes in professionalism, the changes wrought by digital technologies and market-based media, and the continuities maintained in the basic tenets of journalism, ethical and otherwise, but also adapted to local BRICS countries' historical and current conditions, the political, the economic, the cultural, and so on. The discourse of these journalists was largely normative and therefore critical of any divergence from the norms, but it was also sprinkled with the actualities and realities of their lived experience. Thus, essentially, it may be affirmed that to some extent this study provides a polysemic reading of professionalism as concept but particularly as practice with regard to the BRICS journalists.

Notes

1 Evetts (2013) contrasts organizational professionalism with occupational professionalism, which incorporates collegial authority, trust from employers and clients, autonomy, discretionary judgment, training, occupational identity, and codes of ethics monitored by professional associations.
2 Brazil has a large number of colleges of communication, 549 courses in social communication including journalism courses, more than 40 post-graduate programmes in communication, and growing registrations for communication courses in public and private institutions reaching 186,000 in 2012, almost 1/1000 inhabitants.

References

Aggarwala, N. K. (1979). What is development news? *Journal of Communication, 29*(2), 180–185.
ANDI. (2007). *Midia e Políticas Públicas de Comunicação*. Brasília: ANDI. Retrieved from www.andi.org.br/file/50190/download?token=OxqpRlmc
Athique, A. (2012). *Indian media*. Cambridge: Polity Press.
Beam, R. A. (1990). Journalism professionalism as an organizational-level concept. *Journalism and Communication Monographs, 121*(June 1), 1–43.
Bogdanov, N. G., & Vyazemsky, B. A. (1971). *Spravochnik zhurnalista* (The handbook of a journalist). Leningrad: Lenizdat.
Brint, S. (1993). Eliot Freidson's contribution to the sociology of professions. *Work and Occupations, 20*(3), 259–278.
Claassen, G. (1996). News as vaudeville: The dramatic image, news diffusion and the demise of cultural literacy through show business. *South African Theatre Journal, 10*(2), 101–116.
Claassen, G. (2001). Exploring a model for training journalism students. *Ecquid Novi, 22*(1), 3–24.
Cogan, M. (1953). Toward a definition of profession. *Harvard Educational Review, 23*, 33–50.
CPJ (Committee to Protect Journalists). (2015). Retrieved from https://cpj.org/reports/americas/brazil/
De Beer, A. S., & Stein, E. (2002). Sanef's '2002 South African national journalism skills audit'. *Ecquid Novi, 23*(1), 11–86.
Deuze, M. (2005). What is journalism? Professional identity and ideology of journalists reconsidered. *Journalism, 6*(4), 442–464.
Eapen, K. E. (1969). *Journalism as a profession in India: Two states and two cities*. Unpublished doctoral dissertation, University of Wisconsin, Madison.
Evetts, J. (2013). Professionalism: Value and ideology. *Current Sociology, 61*(5–6), 778–796.
FENAJ. (2014). *FENAJ pede que Sindicatos respondam pesquisa sobre jornalistas em assessoria de imprensa*. Retrieved from www.fenaj.org.br/materia.php?id=4228Or/
Freidson, E. (1989). Theory and the professions. *Indiana Law Journal, 64*(3), 423–432.
Freidson, E. (2001). *Professionalism, the third logic: On the practice of knowledge*. Chicago, IL: University of Chicago Press.

Gieryn, T. F. (1983). Boundary-work and the demarcation of science from non-science: Strains and interests in professional ideologies of scientists. *American Sociological Review*, *48*(6), 781–795.

Glasser, T. L. (1992). Professionalism and the derision of diversity: The case of the education of journalists. *Journal of Communication*, *42*(2), 131–140.

Hadland, A. (2005). *Changing the fourth estate: Essays on South African journalism*. Cape Town: HSRC press. Retrieved from www.hsrcpress.ac.za/product.php?productid=2092

Hughes, E. C. (1963). Professions. *Daedalus*, *92*(4), 655–668.

Hughes, E. C. (1970). Teaching as fieldwork. *The American Sociologist*, *5*(1), 13–18.

Johnstone, J. W. C., Slawski, E. J., & Bowman, W. W. (1972–1973). The professional values of American newsmen. *The Public Opinion Quarterly*, *36*(4), 522–540.

Korkonosenko, S. G. (1998). Sotsiologiya zhurnalistiki v sisteme teorii zhurnalistiki [Sociology of journalism in the system of journalism theory]. In S. G. Korkonosenko (Ed.), *Sotsiologiya zhurnalistiki. Ocherki metodologii i praktiki* (Sociology of journalism: Essays of methodology and practice) (pp. 25–60). Moscow: Gendal'f.

Krüger, F. (2004). *Black, white and grey: Ethics in South African journalism*. Cape Town: Juta and Company Ltd.

Larson, M. S. (1977). *The rise of professionalism*. Los Angeles, CA: University of California Press.

Lewis, S. (2012). The tension between professional control and open participation: Journalism and its boundaries. *Information, Communication & Society*, *15*(6), 836–866.

Martimianakis, M. A., Maniate, J. M., & Hodges, B. D. (2009). Sociological interpretations of professionalism. *Medical Education*, *43*(9), 829–837.

McLeod, J. M., & Hawley, S. E., Jr. (1964). Professionalization among newsmen. *Journalism & Mass Communication Quarterly*, *41*(4), 529–577.

Millerson, G. (1964). *The qualifying associations*. London: Routledge & Kegan Paul.

Nevill, G. (2015). *Media job blood-letting*. Retrieved from http://themediaonline.co.za/2015/04/media-job-blood-letting/

Pan, Z., & Lu, Y. (2003). Localizing professionalism: Discourse practices in China's media reforms. In C. C. Lee (Ed.), *Chinese media, global contexts* (pp. 215-236). London, UK: Routledge.

Parsons, T. (1939). The professions and social structure. *Social Forces*, *17*(4), 457–467.

Pasti, S. (2004). *Rossiiskiy zhurnalist v kontekste peremen. Media Sankt-Peterburga* [A Russian journalist in context of change: Media of St. Petersburg]. Tampere: Tampere University Press. Retrieved from www.uta.fi/cmt/yhteystiedot/henkilokunta/svetlanapasti/publications/pastinkirja.pdf. In English, Juskevits, S. (2002). *Professional roles of Russian journalists at the end of the 1990s: A case study of St. Petersburg media* (Unpublished licentiate thesis). Tampere: University of Tampere. Retrieved from http://tampub.uta.fi/bitstream/handle/10024/76288/lisuri00006.pdf?sequence=1

Presidência da República. (2015). Retrieved from www.secom.gov.br/atuacao/pesquisa/lista-de-pesquisas-quantitativas-e-qualitativas-de-contratos-atuais/pesquisa-brasileira-de-midia-pbm-2015.pdf

Rorty, R. (1979). Transcendental arguments, self-reference, and pragmatism. In P. Bieri, R. P. Horstmann, & L. Kruger (Eds.), *Transcendental arguments and science: Essays in epistemology* (pp. 77–103). Netherlands: Springer Science & Business Media.

Santanna, F. (2006). *Mídia das fontes: o difusor do jornalismo corporativo*. Covilhã: BOCC. Retrieved from www.bocc.ubi.pt/pag/santanna-francisco-midia-fontes.pdf

Schön, D. (1987). *Educating the reflective practitioner: Toward a new design for teaching and learning in the professions*. San Francisco, CA: Jossey-Bass, Inc., Publishers.

Simonov, A. K. (1998). Minimal'nye eticheskie trebovaniya k professional'nomu zhurnalistu (Minimal ethical requirements for a professional journalist). *Proceedings of the St. Petersburg Public Human Rights Organisation, 'Citizen's Control', Problemy zhurnalistskoi etiki v teorii i praktike smi post-kommunisticheskoi Rossii* (The problems of journalistic ethics in theory and practice of media of post-communist Russia) (pp. 73–128). St. Petersburg.

Singer, J. B. (2003). Who are these guys? The online challenge to the notion of journalistic professionalism. *Journalism*, *4*(2), 139–163.

Singer, J. B. (2007). Contested autonomy. *Journalism Studies*, *8*(1), 79–95.

SPJ Code of Ethics. (2014, September). Society of Professional Journalists. Retrieved from www.spj.org/ethicscode.asp

The Hindu. (2003). *The Hindu*, special editorial, August 27.

Thussu, D. K. (2005). Adapting to globalization: The changing contours of journalism in India. In H. de Burgh (Ed.), *Making journalists: Diverse models, global issues* (pp. 127–141). London, New York: Routledge.

Tsedu, M., Wrottley, S., & Clay, P. (2002). Sanef's 2002 South African national journalism skills audit: An introduction. *Ecquid Novi*, *23*(1), 5–10.

Vinogradova, S. M. (2000). Slagaemye zhurnalistskoi professii (The components of journalistic profession). In S. G. Korkonosenko (Ed.), *Osnovy tvorcheskoi deyatel'nosti zhurnalista* (The foundations of journalistic creativity) (pp. 7–58). St Petersburg: Society Knowledge.

Waisbord, S. (2013). *Reinventing professionalism: Journalism and news in global perspective*. Malden, MA: Polity Press.

Wasserman, H. (2010). *Tabloid journalism in South Africa: True story*. Bloomington and Indianapolis: Indiana University Press.

Weaver, D. H., & Willnat, L. (2012). Journalists in the 21st century: Conclusions. In D. H. Weaver & L. Willnat (Eds.), *The global journalist in the 21st century* (pp. 529–551). New York: Routledge.

Zassoursky, I. (2004). *Media and power in post-Soviet Russia*. Armonk, NY: M. E. Sharpe.

2
NEWSMAKING
Navigating digital territory

Herman Wasserman,[1] *Jyotika Ramaprasad, Muniz Sodré,*[2] *Maria Anikina, Ravindra Kumar Vemula, and Yu Xu*

Introduction

Newsmaking practices around the world have changed significantly in past years, mostly as a result of the rise of new digital technologies. These have enabled greater citizen participation at the same time as they have generated from Silicon Valley an interest in newsmaking as a strategic tool for profit making. For example, Apple is contracting news curators for a new kind of service, which is to recommend information directed towards iPhone and iPad users. Among these initiatives, *Apple News* combines curating with smartphone information sharing; *Flipboard* software democratizes curating, allowing the user to create digital magazines (there are already around 100,000 of these); and *Scoop* enables article recommendation (containerized embedded articles), blogs, videos, news, and reports. All of this guides publics directly to informative material, disconnecting them from traditional publication centralizers such as mainstream news organizations.

On the user front, the ability of these initiatives to generate content, co-produce journalism, and interact more directly with journalists has created opportunities for journalistic production to be more transparent, more closely linked with audiences, and more responsive to citizens' news agendas. In other words, the news is moving away from its old markets, and the traditional press could be losing its agenda-setting power. The question then becomes: what are the implications of these changes for journalism as a specific and professional activity?

It is commonly thought that journalism is a communicative process, with a scope much wider than pure and simple information, capable of mobilizing various types of discourse. Journalism's modern conceptual centrality is based upon the production of news, a specific form of rounding up of and communicating information. The conventional discursive strategy of news as a genre of communication is to claim objectivity, mostly within a free-market context, as opposed to other rhetorical strategies that can contribute to the construction of an event.

In broader terms, news is in fact an early form of 'attention economy' that is now frequently being used to characterize the contemporary media. And, thus, news as opinion becomes a commercial product whose market identity is set from the middle of the 19th century, at the point of transition from *publicism* or "opinion journalism" to commercial journalism. It is during this process that meaningful factual reports or actual facts (the 'events') appear which are given the name *notícias* in Brazil; news, for the North Americans; *événement*, for the French; *suceso*, for the Spanish; and so on.

Although news is presented as 'factual', as representing a journalistic *happening*, it is at the same time an intellectual elaboration by journalists rather than a socio-historic fact. For the purposes of understanding the news, the distinction established by Maurice Mouillaud is useful: "The hypothesis that we sustain is that the event is the shadow projected by a concept constructed by the information system, the concept of fact" (Mouillaud, 2002, p. 51). If this shadow is not projected, the news is a factoid, a North American neologism to describe something which seems, but does not constitute, a fact (Sodré, 2009).

News, typically, is a report of something that was or will be registered in the storyline of the everyday relations of a determined historic reality. Ted Turner, founder of the first dedicated news television channel, CNN (*Cable News Network*), claims to have shifted, in the era of globalization, events from the past tense ("it happened") to "something that is happening" (Sodré, 2009, p. 24)

Until recently, the press has been in a privileged position to determine the version of those events that count as 'news', as expressed in the famous slogan coined in 1896 by the North American editor for *The New York Times*, generally thought of as the most influential newspaper in the world, bringing its readers "All the news that's fit to print". Historically, the decision about what was 'fit' to be classified as news was defined by the journalist as a professional arbiter. It has also been guaranteed by a type of text – clear and concise – honed within the ideological structure of the information system, where reality is assumed to be transparent and able to be rendered in the form of factual news.

But what is becoming more and more evident in the day-to-day running of media corporations is that 'journalism' is no longer an exclusive category within the traditional methods of communication. The construction of the event is now not exclusively the domain of professional journalism, as Arquembourg (2002, p. 10) correctly points out: "The events are certainly the fruit of the work of the collective; they also interweave the participation of actors and a public which is not just a mass of information consumers".

Journalists now are just one of the many categories of actors mobilized to determine the facts and then transform them into news. Their audiences have also changed. One should think primarily of the audience as a *public*, which can be considered as a particular sphere of ideas in which individuals who are particularly switched on to what becomes visible in the *scene* of a *public space* take a stance or commit to some collective cause. Unlike an audience, therefore, the public is constituted, albeit provisionally, of a collective subject and may diffract or diversify around different experiences. Therefore, there are many different publics. In the context of Brazilian news, for example, young people, well-off people, politicians, and slum dwellers make up clear examples of that, as do the experiences of the poor majority in South Africa who continue to be marginalized by most of the mainstream news channels (Wasserman, Bosch, & Chuma, 2016).

In the past, the credibility of the press came primarily from the place of privilege that the journalist occupied as a mediator between the scene of the event and global society, the position of a witness. To be a witness is to watch an event and, as a consequence, have direct access to what is produced. The fact of being *present at the place* gives the witness moral rights and the right to communicate. *Histor* (from which the word *history* is derived) is how the ancient Greeks described a witness: someone who, having watched a fact, has the right to tell the story.

The effects of the simultaneousness and ubiquity of electronic communication alter the space–time coordinates of information, thus reducing the 'moral rights' of the witness, but increasing the 'right to communicate' amplified by new technologies. From this, a new standard in *agenda setting* arises, more segmented and diversified. Equally, there arises a new kind of relationship between the audiences and the knowledge of reality; that which now is considered 'true' is merely one of the possibilities of each reported event.

Other factors also impinge on newsmaking in the BRICS countries, among which is the freedom journalists (including citizen journalists and bloggers) have to produce news without fear. While they use different methodologies, and there is controversy about reliability of their ratings, the two major surveyors of press freedom around the world, Reporters Sans Frontières and Freedom House, rate the level of press freedom in BRICS as low, but they also indicate significant differences among the countries, with China as having the least freedom, South Africa on the other end of the spectrum, and Brazil, Russia, and India in the middle (Sparks, 2015). These differences in the level of press freedom illustrate that the BRICS countries represent a heterogeneous context for news production. Their respective economies vary greatly in size, and their political systems vary in their ideological foundations, with consequently little coherence in the relationship between the media and political power (Sparks, 2015).

The BRICS countries are all marked by high levels of violent social conflict (Sparks, 2015). China stands out as the country with the highest level of imprisonment of journalists (Sparks, 2015). Brazil, Russia, and India are also dangerous places for journalists to work, judging by the number of work-related deaths recorded by the Committee to Protect Journalists (CPJ) (Sparks, 2015). China again differs from the other BRICS countries in that the threats to journalists there come mostly from the state, via its legal system, in order to silence 'troublesome' voices. In Russia, India, and Brazil, attacks on journalists are common but mostly extra-legal, while in South Africa the dangers remain mostly at the level of threats (Sparks, 2015).

The BRICS context: new alternatives in the newsmaking landscape

While both journalistic freedom and violence towards journalists impact newsmaking, it is digital transformation that is of particular interest to this chapter. One of the challenges arising from this development is how to keep various co-producers of journalism ethically accountable for their production, as well as how to make journalism economically sustainable, when newsmaking is no longer the scarce skill it used to be and traditional advertising models have been turned upside down, with the result that many print publications have met their demise.

In some regions of the Global South, however, print media are still alive and well, in contrast to their northern counterparts. As emerging economies, some of the countries in these regions still need to develop their online media infrastructure, and enable more equitable access to the Internet than is currently available. The ubiquity of social media, reliant on stable network connections, availability of hardware, digital media literacy, etc., cannot be assumed to be as self-evident in the BRICS countries as it is in the countries of the North where more favourable conditions exist in this regard. Still, BRICS countries have seen a strong growth in the number of Internet users; in India; for example, the projected growth in Internet users is seen to be the highest in the world (Thussu, 2015).

Notwithstanding current issues of access and availability, users in these countries often also display creativity in circumventing economic and political constraints in order to use digital media platforms to disseminate political news, engage in activism, and spread information. An example of this creative adoption and adaptation of technology is for instance the 'please call me' service invented in South Africa, which allows users who have depleted their airtime to contact another user with the request that they call them back (Mapumulo, 2016). Trends also show that users increasingly access social media through mobile phones to engage with and try to impact the mainstream news agenda.

Brazil is recognized internationally as the largest media market in South America. In their day-to-day news production, Brazilian journalists are already being affected by digital technology. It is widely understood in the Brazilian professional context that journalistic information has come to occupy a strategic position and has attracted attention from Silicon Valley. News circulation in Brazil by means of smartphone sharing is growing. According to the *Reuters Digital News Report* (Reuters Institute for the Study of Journalism, 2016), Brazilians are internationally those who most consume news online (72 per cent of the population) and those who most comment on the news on social networks (47 per cent).

Anonymous bloggers today are transforming the electronic space available to Brazilian news consumers into a bridge to the world. As well as this, segmentation and diversification are moving in the direction of a 'civic' or community communication. A few examples of how new technologies have affected the journalistic landscape in Brazil are outlets, such as *Mídia Ninja, Agência Pública, Coletivo*

Papo Reto, and *Coletivo Mariachi*, that present themselves as an alternative to traditional media and are the work of a collaborative network of media activists. This journalistic landscape has its roots in the media and cultural circuit known as *Fora do Eixo*; the circuit achieved nationwide fame during the massive demonstrations that took place in major Brazilian cities in June 2013, against the increase in bus fares and the FIFA Confederations Cup. During marches and rallies, *Mídia Ninja* would produce live coverage of the protests, relying upon, among other instruments, cell phone cameras. *Mídia Ninja* has a news website and participates in social media; it describes their project and goals in the following terms (free translation): "Our agenda lies where the social struggle, and the articulation of cultural, political, economic and environmental transformations are expressed. The internet changed journalism and we are part of this transformation" (https://ninja.oximity.com/partner/ninja/about). More than 355,900 people have liked 'Ninja' (*Mídia Ninja*'s profile) on Facebook.

Agência Pública is a non-profit independent news website that focuses on investigative journalism, producing articles that are mainly centred on "the impact of mega sports events; torture and violence (committed) by State agents; mega investments in the Amazon (forest/region); urban crisis; and companies and violations of human rights" (http://apublica.org/quem-somos/#sobre). *Pública* operates as a news agency and all its articles, stories, and reports are freely reproduced by a network of more than 60 media outlets, under the creative commons licence, as *Pública* itself explains on its website (http://apublica.org/quem-somos/#sobre). Since its creation in 2011, *Agência Pública* has won journalism awards such as the Petrobras Journalism Award, in 2015, for an article about the transposition of the São Francisco River. The organization is funded by institutions such as the Ford Foundation, the Omidyar Network, and the Open Society Foundations, but also by crowdfunding initiatives. More than 100,000 people have liked *Agência Pública* on Facebook.

According to a study by the Getúlio Vargas Foundation (FGV), published in 2015, Brazil has 154 million smartphones (http://exame.abril.com.br/tecnologia/noticias/numero-de-smartphones-supera-o-de-computadores-no-brasil). This phenomenon may have helped in the birth of new media outlets such as *Coletivo Papo Reto* and *Coletivo Mariachi*. The first one, which was the subject of an article in *The New York Times* (Shaer, 2015), was created by the youth of one of the most famous *favela* complexes of Rio de Janeiro, Complexo do Alemão, in 2014, in order to report and produce news about the area that they live in, one that they considered not to be appropriately covered by traditional media outlets.

As Matthew Shaer from *The New York Times* pointed out,

> Within weeks, Papo Reto had become a kind of signal tower for the community. Members of the collective received [material on] police raids and bullet-riddled vehicles from Alemão's residents via . . . WhatsApp. Papo Reto disseminated the [material via] social media.
>
> *(Shaer, 2015, p. 78)*

The Facebook profile of *Coletivo Papo Reto* has been liked by more than 15,800 people; they promote their presence on YouTube and Instagram in their profile description as well.

Coletivo Mariachi was created by the photographer and webmaster Silnei L. Andrade, the journalist Claudia Severo, and the Mexican filmmaker Luis Carlos Landingo, in June 2013, with the goals of (free translation): "informing the public of the abuses committed by State agents during the demonstrations, about the representation of street resistance and to expose the lying, manipulative narratives of the big media and of government-related blogs" (www.youtube.com/watch?v=cJ0vM_lSfro). *Mariachi*'s Facebook profile, which describes itself as a news website, has been liked by more than 62,000 people.

The new technologies have also helped initiate online magazines produced by different segments of the country, such as *Revista Maçaneta*, a seasonal magazine that approaches issues related to gender and sexuality (more than 1,400 likes on Facebook) and a vast number of politics-oriented and left-leaning blogs, such as *Diário do Centro do Mundo* (more than 167,000 likes on Facebook) and *Pragmatismo Político* (more than 840,000 likes on Facebook), or even the weekly magazine *Revista Fórum* that started its life as a printed vehicle in Porto Alegre but operates exclusively online at this moment. In its Facebook profile, the magazine describes itself as (free translation): "a magazine that has in its DNA the strength of the movements and the certainty that a better world is created from the multiplicity of voices" (www.facebook.com/forumrevista/info/?tab=page_info). More than 489,000 people have liked *Revista Fórum* on Facebook.

It is clear then that information about events in Brazil is presented to a variety of publics across an increasingly varied set of platforms beyond traditional media. The different ways in which information is presented across this diversity of platforms may reveal different configurations of forces (hegemonic or counter-hegemonic) in society, rather than the temporary focus on one occurrence, which more often than not has formed the central approach to news reporting in the conventional Brazilian press.

According to a survey published by the consultancy company comScore, *Future Focus Brazil 2015*, Brazilians spend significant amounts of time on social networks. They spend 650 hours a month on social networks, with Facebook being the most used. Recent research (Reuters Institute for the Study of Journalism, 2016), comparing data from 26 countries, indicated that 72 per cent of Brazilian Internet users access news from online platforms, 70 per cent of users have accessed news through social networks, 47 per cent of users share news by social networks or email, and 44 per cent have commented on news using social media tools.

In Russia, the transformation of journalistic practices has been taking place rapidly as a result of the growth of Internet penetration. The development of online media, both news and other, in Russia is gradually transforming the professional journalistic culture and changing the way journalists work with information (Anikina, Dobek-Ostrowska, & Nygren, 2013). This communicative space provides journalists with new professional tools and channels of expression such as the blogosphere. This has led to a juridical response by the State, with a so-called "law on bloggers" published in 2014, which requires the authors of Internet sources (websites, blogs, etc.) with an audience of more than 3,000 users per day to officially register at *Roskomnadzor* (the federal service for supervision of communications, information technology, and mass media) (*Vzglyad Delovaya Gazeta*, 2014).

Since the early 2000s, traditional media have not only increasingly moved online, but are now also supplemented by the space of social networks. Russian journalists make very high use of social media; social networks are both the channel for interpersonal communication and a mechanism of professional activity (Anikina, Dobek-Ostrowska, & Nygren, 2013).

The daily Internet audience in 2015 in Russia comprised 53 per cent of Russian citizens, with an annual increase of 8 per cent (Rozhnova, Borisova, & Zolotukhina, 2015). This has led to a change in news consumption practices, with 41 per cent of Russians now getting their news from the Internet. Further, for active groups of Russian society, social media have become a sphere for public discussion in different segments of social life, gathering at times diverse participants in the conversations, and also at times replacing offline discussions (Volkov & Goncharov, 2014).

India has witnessed rapid and unprecedented changes in society, economy, and polity largely due to major technological leaps in the last few decades. In general, technology has made the life of Indian journalists relatively easy. Computerization in the workplace, unlimited access to the Internet, provision of smartphones, and ease of news operations have led to changes in the practices of newsmaking. These technological changes have impacted the Indian media system because of their direct effect on media production practices and consumption patterns. Both the Internet and mobile phones have enabled convergence of media platforms, which in turn has led to an upsurge in India in traditional, non-conventional, as well as experimental media platforms. Convergence in media platforms has led most traditional news channels and newspapers to have a web presence. Websites, which earlier merely hosted 'shovelware', i.e., news already published or telecast in traditional media, have now taken the lead in breaking news (Rana, 2010).

In China, the number of social media users has been growing explosively in the past few years. In this BRICS study's Chinese sample, the two most widely used social media applications among Chinese journalists were WeChat and Sina Weibo, with a penetration rate of 99 per cent and 75 per cent respectively. WeChat literally refers to "micro message" in Chinese. It is an instant messaging app developed by the Tencent company. Sina Weibo, initiated by Sina Corporation, is the biggest Chinese-language microblog service product in China. It functions similarly to Twitter.

Journalism as an occupation in South Africa has come under similar pressures as in many other parts of the world, with declining circulation figures for mainstream print media (although tabloid newspapers aimed at a working-class black audience seem to largely resist this trend). On the other hand, the South African media have also seen major shifts in recent years due to the increased adoption of new technologies by media users, and integration of these technologies into mainstream journalism practices. Although still a fairly new (post-2000) phenomenon in South Africa, online journalism has shown strong growth in recent years (Ndlovu, 2015). Most newspapers now follow a digital-first strategy, and user-generated content on social media is increasingly making its way to mainstream news sites and then reported in traditional media. Perceptions that online journalism has lower prestige than traditional media are changing with the rise of news sites that offer content not found in either traditional outlets such as newspapers or radio, or even in mainstream news platforms like *News24*. Examples of these new outlets are *The Daily Maverick*, which publishes investigative journalism and analysis, the *Rand Daily Mail*, which provides think pieces and commentary, and *Groundup* with its investigative, community-oriented stories (Ndlovu, 2015).

The rise of online media in South Africa has provided new platforms for alternative voices – particularly from the youth – to emerge. In some cases, for example the recent student protests, mainstream media – including online news outlets – found it difficult to break new stories and often found themselves trying to catch up with information posted on Twitter or Facebook (Jacobs & Wasserman, 2015).

While the changes in the media landscape have been significant and often disconcerting for journalists working in traditional media, the growth of this online space is promising for a new generation of journalists that has to take South African journalism into the future. This is particularly true given the ruling party's proposal that the self-regulatory appeal system of the Press Council be replaced by a statutory Media Appeals Tribunal, as well as the proposed Protection of State Information Bill, passed by Parliament and awaiting the president's signature. These are seen as indications of a narrowing public sphere and a shrinking space for democratic debate in the media. Further, many media houses have undergone staff retrenchments, juniorization, and cutbacks partly as a result of the global economic downturn and partly as a result of the changing business model of media. These developments have particularly impacted the print media. The real growth and energy in South African journalism seem to be in online media; the emergence of several independent online news and analysis sites in recent years is testimony to this.

The BRICS study

Within the context of the many changes in newsmaking, particularly the introduction of digitalization, this chapter presents BRICS journalists' views about new technology particularly as it relates to the practice of journalism. It explores journalists' reported use of social media in their practice both as source and for audience feedback. Further, it includes journalists' opinions about whether certain content should not be covered, particularly if it is content that could aid an enemy, and about government control of the Internet and of political and entertainment content. Finally, it presents the different types of hierarchies in newsrooms with the aim to clarify how newsroom structures may have changed under digitalization of media organizations and journalistic work.

Findings

Social media: new tool for journalists

In the BRICS study, overall more than 70 per cent of respondent journalists in Brazil used social networks and gave a positive assessment of the possibilities that the tool provides to the profession. For them, Facebook is an extension of their work; it is used to promote their work, to search for sources and primary information, and to obtain feedback: "Social networks give a greater voice to the public. They feel integrated into the media". Most of the respondents indicated that, in their personal life, they used social networks sparingly because extensive use could generate a lot of exposure, meaning that too many details of their private lives could be seen by others. Respondents also noted the danger of false information due to "excessive freedom" and the need for surveillance of information supplied by the user:

> I think journalism today can't live without social networks. But I think that, at the same time, people need to be very careful with this because what's there is not always the truth. . . . Now, the challenge for the journalist [has] greatly [increased] with the [need to check] information, because it's not enough for you to get information that's out there and believe that to be true, because you have different types of people there: from hyper intelligent, educated, and honest people to nasty and dishonest people. It's a fuzzy set, there are various opinions, various demands, and therefore information checking is essential. So, today, I think that social networks do not live without journalism and journalism can't live without social networks.

Some respondents argued for stronger regulation to meet the challenges of the virtual world; for example, one said:

> I think that in our country we live this democratization of information, involving freedom, involving abuses, and we don't have solid legislation to deal with it. So, the problem is not the control of material, but the lack of legislation. Nowadays, if you slander someone on social networks, are you going to pay for it? How? In what way? We don't have a justice [system] that is prepared, which is fast enough to handle it. So, I think the problem is not control, but regulation.

In Russia, some professionals saw social networks as having particular importance in specific locales. A St. Petersburg journalist indicated that "Facebook is mainly for a Moscow audience". Others had some concerns. For one interviewee, the management of social media could be an issue: "I witnessed yesterday that online editors reached an agreement about who would break news first"; essentially, different online news media agree on which outlet will break the news first on which social media site. Some others pointed to the manipulative power of social media; according to a Moscow respondent, "There are attempts to influence the audience and manipulate them through social media; I see this as a negative issue".

Russian respondents did not consider social media a serious competitor for professional media yet; as one journalist said, "Until professional journalists come to social media, [social media] would not be competitors of online media". Another indicated that he did "not think that social networks can supplant the traditional media". Further, he indicated that

> Social networks are used for communication. . . . Therefore, I do not consider either *VKontakte* or *Odnoklassniki* traditional media. Well, maybe, they could serve as a source of information exchange and for exchange of some links. They are fast and convenient, such as Twitter. I take it as a news feed, where I can find the links, but no more, because these media certainly do not replace traditional ones.

The respondent journalists saw online media as part of the mass media system, while they considered social media, which they used for a variety of reasons, as an additional space for the professional and civic activity of journalists.

In India, with most media outlets extending their operations online, social media such as Facebook and Twitter have become an invaluable resource for many journalists from both traditional and online news media. They are a major source of information and a channel of news dissemination for these journalists in their professional and personal lives. According to a television journalist in Hyderabad, "Social media makes it easier for you to contact people, gives you updates about events, and also helps you contact your sources. If not for social media, [we] journalists cannot survive"; they have become "a crucial source" for online media journalists not just for stories but also as a "feedback mechanism". For most journalists, personal and professional lines blur as they "post stories on Facebook pages, ask opinions from audience, which actually is our marketing technique. . . . We constantly share things on our official Facebook page and our personal page". Further, online media offer a freedom and instantaneity that traditional media do not; in the words of a print media journalist in Delhi, "There are no gate-keeping systems; so, the feedback is instant and a lot more cruel in my opinion. It is like facing reality. It helps keep a check and creates accountability".

Most respondent journalists in Pune used social media platforms or friendship groups, WhatsApp (a phone-based social networking application), and Twitter (that provided news "from all over the world" and is "the biggest source of breaking news these days"), both for work and in their personal lives. Print newspapers expanded their readership, and journalists received audience reactions and comments through such use. Journalists also appreciated getting direct quotes from celebrities through their Twitter updates. The line between use of social media for personal and professional reasons blurred with each influencing the other for almost all Pune journalists. Unlike Pune journalists, traditional media journalists in Kolkata did not depend much on social media for sourcing news and sharing information. On the other hand, these journalists more strongly perceived social media as a channel to improve readership and spread news among people not reached otherwise, those, "people [who] are talking less and using [the] Internet more".

Both the Internet as well as social media have had a tremendous impact on the professional work of journalists and news organizations in India specifically with regard to the sourcing of news. An increasing dependence on online sources for news and opinions is evident, also enabling the use of "ordinary citizens' voices . . . in polls and human interest stories". Journalists who rely on the Internet as a news source are slowly replacing those who chase stories and sources in the field. In general, work in the media has become much easier in some respects with the increasing use of online quotes and tweets or with using discussion- or studio-based programmes that can receive instant feedback.

Chinese journalists in the BRICS study agreed that social media increased the efficiency of their work by accelerating the dissemination of information and developing social networks and social capital. Respondents differed in the way they used Weibo and WeChat. One group of journalists primarily used Weibo for professional purposes. Sina Weibo encourages identity verification, and many respondents acknowledged that they were verified users of the service. Their real identities were displayed in their profiles. Consequently, their Weibo accounts usually attracted a lot of followers, contributing to the accumulation of their online social capital. For their personal needs, these journalists used WeChat in part because social networks on WeChat were mainly composed of relatives, close friends, and acquaintances rather than strangers. A group of respondents however indicated that they owned anonymous accounts on Weibo solely for personal purposes. To communicate with colleagues, contact potential interviewees, gather information resources, disseminate news and information, and collect feedback from audiences, they used the WeChat platform. Thus, for the most part, journalists separated their professional from their personal social media sites.

Those who did not make such a separation had their own strategies, such as restricting access to some of their online content. As one respondent in Shanghai said, "I categorize my social contacts on WeChat and Weibo into different groups to keep a balance between my professional and private life. Some of my posts are only visible to a specific group of audiences".

In South Africa, social media are starting to influence journalists' everyday lives and work practices, with large percentages of journalists around the country, working in both traditional and new media, reporting that they used especially Facebook and Twitter regularly. Online journalists reported that social media, especially Twitter, was a threat to their position as journalists as it enabled people to remain abreast of the news without having to consume formal, online media.

For this reason, most mainstream online news sites also have Twitter accounts from where they can direct users back to their sites (Ndlovu, 2015).

Government control: mostly anathema for journalists

According to most respondent journalists in Brazil, freedom of expression must be defended; these journalists were not willing to accept the curtailment of information after their experience during the long period of military dictatorship, which was characterized by such curtailment and considerable censorship. Today, Brazil is a democracy; it does not have a sworn enemy and its media freely broadcast programmes and themes related to entertainment and politics, though the latter is regulated mainly during election periods. Given this situation, some respondent journalists had simple answers to questions of control: "there's no need for control" or "we don't have enemies". Essentially, some Brazilian journalists defended the freedom to talk about anything in answer to a question about control over coverage that may help the enemy. Others analysed the social role of their outlet or considered "competing" media an enemy. For instance, *O Globo* (from Rio de Janeiro) could be assessed as an "enemy" to "Folha de São Paulo" (from São Paulo). But, in general, the respondent journalists agreed that "What is true, what is news, what is of interest to society must be published. The more democratic, the better. And if it is democratic, it does not exist against the interest of the country as a nation".

Apart from the refrain, "You should write about everything, there are no taboos", some journalists indicated that

> it's necessary to develop actions and strategies to assist citizens to identify, in the universe of available information, the 'good information'. And this will only occur with the strengthening of educational processes . . . in all social spaces, formal and informal.

About 60 per cent of the journalists were against both the blocking of the Internet and the control of political and/or entertainment materials, indicating their defence of the freedom of expression that the news media had won. Only a minority of respondents believed that such control must prevail. The majority's belief was that this control should rest on the shoulders of society, the public, the professional community, or the journalist. For the control of entertainment materials, one sentiment was:

> In this case, I think the case doesn't have to be as much as [for] political affairs because entertainment doesn't have the same weight as politics. But, of course, you have to have a certain attention not to trivialize the kind of information that you are going to pass on.

Another respondent indicated that "it's a controversial issue. I think there should be a board of ethics, which does not have state interference, but [is composed] of representatives of various segments of society".

Russian journalists, traditional and online, shared the belief that they should cover diverse issues and depict reality but also that they should not support social/political groups and parties. Many also rejected the idea that political content should be controlled or censored. In particular, online journalists expressed more opposition to the control of entertainment and political materials than traditional news media journalists.

While journalists working in traditional news media were more willing to accept control than online journalists were, those traditional media respondents who had extensive professional experience also cautioned against control. One journalist from St. Petersburg said,

> I believe there is nothing to hide. We have hidden a lot of things. It is not the time to muffle. If we had not muffled the things *then* and would have demonstrated socialism and socialist countries (we had a lot of bad things, a lot of good things), probably 1991 would not have happened. It is necessary to show what is good and what is bad.

Furthermore, online journalists felt less strongly about the defence of national interests than did their traditional media counterparts, and they demonstrated a greater openness to alternative viewpoints. A few journalists had reservations about the question of whether journalists should not cover stories that play into the hands of their country's enemies. One journalist found the question "strange" and then elaborated,

> Journalists should cover the topics that play into the hand of his or her country's citizens. And the journalists should not be preoccupied by how the enemies, if they exist, would use this. Journalists should just be concerned about making life in their country better.

Another respondent, also focusing on the social mission of journalism, said, "Journalists should cover the topics which are important for society and for the city without regard to what this means for enemies or friends".

In Moscow and St. Petersburg, journalists more clearly expressed their negative attitudes towards the control of political information in mass media than in Yekaterinburg and Petrozavodsk. One possible explanation for this difference could be the formal status of the cities as the first and the second capitals of Russia, in geographical proximity to the state powers. Responses of Yekaterinburg journalists working for traditional and new media were strikingly different from those in other cities. In Yekaterinburg, support for control of political content was stronger than in any of the other three cities. It was furthermore interesting that this question provoked less detailed responses than other questions linked to control. This situation to a certain extent mirrors previously noted reactions to opinion polls in Russia where respondents were hesitant to provide frank and detailed answers to so-called 'sensitive questions' (Klimov, 2006).

Journalists' responses reflect the wider debates taking place in Russia about Internet access and control. For instance, the theme of Internet pornography was raised by several interviewees. Some journalists advocated the idea of parental control of the Internet to keep children from exposure to pornography. A journalist said, "Everyone should solve the problem on the personal level and look into his own family". Another indicated that "it is possible and necessary to block Internet access *only* for minors". Sometimes, according to respondents, limits on the Internet are needed "in terms of pornography distribution and child pornography".

Several responses pointed to how media laws were being implemented. For example, the *Law of The Russian Federation No. 2124–1 on Mass Media*, dated December 27, 1991 (with amendments in the latest edition dated December 30, 2015), formally provides journalists with a range of rights and contains norms to coordinate interactions in the information sphere. But the formal liberal character of this document is not reflected in the daily practice of journalists. As one of the respondents in Petrozavodsk remarked, "If the law on mass media works, there would not be the need to control. If the Charter of Broadcasters[3] was implemented! Simply, it is necessary to follow the existing law".

Many respondents offered responsibility as an alternative to control and restrictions; in the words of a respondent from Petrozavodsk, "Freedom implies responsibility". The diverse forms of control that were voiced included moral responsibility: "I think the Internet should be controlled but there is no need to restrict access. . . . Censorship should be moral in nature".

In a democracy like India, any external control or censorship is always strongly contested by the media (Kohli-Khandekar, 2008). In India, film is the only visual media that has a censor and certification board, the *Central Board of Film Certification (CBFC)*. Recent debates on Internet control have led India's Supreme Court to strike down Section 66A of the Information Technology Act, 2000, which "allowed arrests for posting offensive content on social media sites . . . because it affected Indian citizens' right to free speech" (Choudhury & Mahapatra, 2015).

Most Delhi and Hyderabad respondents did not believe in government or political party control of the media; they indicated that the larger the government controls on media, the harder it would be to work democratically. Instead, they suggested self-regulation. Some of these journalists however felt that there ought to be some government control for "security reasons", in the "interest of communal harmony", or for other sensitive issues. As one journalist said, "Freedom of thought and communication is essential in a democracy, but in cases of terrorism, crime, and sex there ought to be some control".

A majority of journalists fiercely opposed any control of the Internet, saying that "there should be no control as their work and profession depended on it". One respondent indicated that the Internet "is the only singular free medium left for us. You are trying to limit somebody. Where is the freedom then?" Journalists in New Delhi opposed government tracking of mobile phones. One journalist, however, indicated that scrutiny is needed in the issuance of SIM cards: "During the crime beat, I have often encountered cases wherein lack of proper control on documentation of IDs leads to misuse, crime, and incidents of terror". With regard to control of entertainment content, journalists in Hyderabad felt that this was the responsibility of society and the public. A few journalists both in Delhi and Hyderabad felt programme content should be monitored by professionals: "Some subjects need to be approached with caution, be [treated] more sensitively, and need to be regulated. But it brings us back to the same question about who will regulate".

A minority of respondents in Pune was comfortable with considerable government control of media, but in general in both Kolkata and Pune answers to questions about government control trended in the direction of little or less control, with some journalists positing the absolutist position of no control. Government control of the media in general, of particular topics, and of new communication technology in particular was generally anathema to these respondent journalists, but they were willing to accept control of content such as pornography, rape incidents, and religious sentiment. They were also willing to accept control of content that invaded people's privacy or defamed people, threatened national security, enabled terrorism (mostly related to mobile use), and inflamed communal tensions.

Journalists in Pune mostly held the opinion that the government should not control political affairs content in the media. They perceived government control in this matter to be anti-democratic and a threat to freedom of the press, "because then whosoever is the government in control will be the one to dictate the terms, and then there would be no sense to calling this a democracy, right?" One journalist indicated that government control would be legitimate only to minimize communal tension. More journalists, though still only a small number, were willing to have government control entertainment content; soft porn and indecent portrayal of women were also concerns for some journalists. On the other hand, some journalists believed that the media should exercise self-control rather than be controlled by government.

Except two, all other Kolkata journalists felt that the government should not control political affairs content in the media. In this, they were similar to Pune journalists. They valued their freedom of speech and believed that editorial policies are already in place for news media to self-regulate. In fact, their expectation or hope was that "Media should highlight the success and failure of the government, and if they highlight [failure, the] government should not take any decision against the media". Like Pune journalists, some Kolkata journalists were concerned about the impact of adult content in media on children and wanted government control over such content. Others felt that it was not the government's job to regulate media.

In general, in India, journalists were against government control of political content but were more accepting of control over entertainment, particularly soft porn and indecent portrayals of women. Journalists' views about government control of the media in general or of certain subjects as well as of new technologies ranged from the absolutist "no" and "yes" positions to more nuanced answers about accepting control for certain topics such as pornography and offering reasons for control in general such as stopping terrorism or communal agitations.

In China, only 30 per cent of the respondents agreed with the statement that "journalists should not cover subjects that play into the hands of our country's enemies", and this percentage was about the same for both traditional media and online journalists. These journalists mainly perceived their roles as mouthpieces for the party and the government. In their perspective, journalists should safeguard national interests and be in sync with the standpoints of the government. It was also risky for these journalists and their news agencies to report otherwise because they would definitely be severely punished by the propaganda departments.

Those who disagreed with the statement basically asserted that the responsibility of journalists was to report all the important facts. For example, they believed that if China's enemies told the truth, journalists had no reason to avoid reporting on this. Some respondents emphasized the importance of the people's right to know. As one journalist in Guangzhou said, "Chinese citizens should know the reasons why they [the enemies] are against our country. Everyone has the right to know all the truth".

About one quarter of the journalists in both media types agreed that on no occasion was it necessary to block or control the Internet. Journalists in Beijing seemed to be more conservative; they were less likely to support no regulation of the Internet. There was consensus among Chinese journalists that it was necessary to block or control websites producing violent and pornographic content because they believed that exposure to such content would inevitably have a negative influence on the youth. When asked for the reasons why they supported blocking or controlling online information about content that was not violent or pornographic, some journalists pointed out that most Chinese citizens were not sufficiently competent to tell apart authentic from inauthentic content.

Most of the Chinese respondent journalists had divergent views about control of political materials in media; however, there were some who either refused to answer the question or said they did not know. "Don't know" responses are very common in surveys of political attitudes and values in China (Lei, 2011). Those who considered it unnecessary to control political content in media emphasized freedom of press or speech. They agreed that journalists' responsibility was to "protect the interest of the general public, rather than the interest of the bureaucratic privileged class". Some respondents' opposition to such control was conditional. They argued that control should be avoided if news reports did not threaten national security. In contrast, some pointed out that a lack of control would lead to social instability; they believed that the state and the professional community should play an active role in the control process, providing instructions about what topics should be or should not be covered.

Compared with media control of political materials, Chinese journalists were more inclined to consider control of entertainment as unnecessary. However, their point of view was premised on whether the coverage invaded personal privacy. Some respondents criticized the paparazzi for spreading too much gossip; one journalist in Beijing said, "The paparazzi have already gone too far.

Too much attention has been paid to private lives of celebrities, which is quite annoying".

In South Africa, against the background of new threats to freedom of expression such as the ruling party's attempts to change the self-regulatory system for media complaints to a statutory one with a proposed Media Appeals Tribunal, as well as the passing of the Protection of State Information Bill which is widely seen to have a chilling effect on uncovering corruption, the vast majority of respondents said that they were against any measures that would control the media, whether that is to block the Internet for whatever reason, to control media content for political reasons, or to control entertainment media for social reasons. Interestingly, whereas some journalists working for traditional media could foresee some exceptions where control of the media might be justified, those working in online media unanimously rejected any form of external control. This says something not only about the libertarian ethos of digital media, but also about the younger generation (the majority of young journalists work in digital media) that is adamant not to repeat the mistakes of the past.

Reporting structures: horizontal networked model in digital media

Hierarchy in Brazil is seen as a form of work organization, and is much more present in traditional than in online news media due to the larger number of employees in the former. In media outlets that have a professional hierarchy, its structure is as follows: editor in chief, management, editorial board members, and news chief, with some peculiarities in the case of multinational companies.

Online media journalists pointed out that they did not have a hierarchy because this allowed for greater freedom in their work. In addition, online media had fewer respondents who had bosses, so answers such as "[hierarchy] does not affect [us]" were more common. Some answers from online journalists also highlighted the different pros and cons of a hierarchical structure: "I believe that [hierarchy] facilitates in parts, but it can make it difficult when we are obliged to meet the interests of the owner of the newspaper", and "Sometimes it helps, because several heads discussing a matter can be better for the end result. Sometimes it creates confusion, because of the disagreement about a decision".

In one case, a hierarchy did not officially exist, but to systematize and organize the work, the journalists nominated a 'boss':

> In terms of wages and organization, there's no hierarchy. The three journalists have the same wage, comply with the same time [requirements], and occupy the same hierarchy. As it's very strange to work like this – because you need to have guidelines, an orientation – we adopted one of the journalists as a boss, because he has been on radio for longer and knows the organization better. But that's our thing; it's not in the radio's timetable.

Very few respondents said that their relationship with their boss affected their work negatively. Most of the respondents (on average, 70 per cent in traditional and online media) indicated that they had friendly and harmonious relations with their bosses. These journalists also indicated relationships of friendly equality, of a work environment that was comparable to a family, and of bosses who had become great friends. Most respondents (on average, 60 per cent) claimed satisfaction with their relationship with their boss. For these respondents, the existence of a boss facilitated their work because it indicated to whom they should report in case of any problems, difficulty, or the need for feedback.

Most respondents from online journalism who did not have a hierarchical structure in their newsrooms or media claimed that this absence "makes no difference"; but sometimes it does "hamper the work", because they do not have someone to report to: "We always need someone who is ahead, in a more objective way, to determine or define some types of situation".

In Russia, on the topic of their relationship with their editorial offices, journalists gave very emotional reactions (interviewers often noted that respondents were 'smiling' or 'laughing'). The relationship was sometimes presented in terms of a partnership or fellowship and described as democratic, normal, working, good, and excellent; journalists often made use of metaphors and images like 'family', 'stairs', 'tsar circles', and 'religion'. For example, a St. Petersburg journalist said, "I could say sincerely that we are almost one family in a good sense"; and another said, "I would say that the boss is the *tsar* but I say this with sympathy. . . . The tsar is kind, understands everything".

Journalists representing big media holdings that had regional departments had an interesting take on the matter of their various bosses. A St. Petersburg journalist working in a media company located in different countries differentiated among different types of authorities:

> I think that a Moscow boss is more important in terms of current working issues, and a boss from Prague is probably more meaningful because our American authorities are sitting there. The main head is American and he is located in Prague.

Some journalists mentioned formal relationships with superiors where they had to make an appointment to see their superiors.

In India, most of the journalist respondents working in traditional media in Hyderabad and New Delhi reported a standard hierarchical structure in their organization, whereas those working in online media outlets had skeletal staff, with a non-standard informal structure. A few journalists said that it was easier to work within a hierarchy as "there is camaraderie with a sense of partnership and equality" even in a hierarchical workplace. Because the new media outlets were mostly run by young people, the sense of camaraderie was high among them in comparison with those who worked in the traditional media, where the age range spanned the spectrum from the young to the older, and where older people held senior positions.

Similar views of journalistic hierarchy were found in Pune, where all newspapers had similar, rather straightforward and simple, staff hierarchies starting with editors at the city or edition level, followed by assistant editors or chief reporters and then, in order, reporters working on individual beats; some had correspondents above reporters. Only large, established media houses had finer differentiation in staff categories with prefixes like 'senior', 'junior', 'sub', 'deputy', 'chief', 'special', or 'principal'. Most television news channels had bureau chiefs, who supervised a staff comprising reporters, anchors, and camerapersons, and also liaised with head offices for coordinating work. The staff structure for online journalists was comparatively 'flat' with all online reporters reporting to a senior level editor directly. A somewhat similar scenario was present in the one news radio channel in the sample.

Most Pune journalists reported a friendly, helpful, and open environment in their workplace. They felt free to discuss their work and valued the guidance they received from their seniors. They cherished the free exchange of ideas and believed that the feedback improved their work. In fact, they appreciated the hierarchical structure because it created a clear division of work ('channelized' the work) and thus coordination; as one journalist said, "Hierarchy does influence, but it influences in a positive way".

The organizational structures in Kolkata seemed to be spread out horizontally with divisions within the media house, as well as vertically. The work in the television media houses was mostly divided between 'input' and 'output' divisions. The input division, headed by an 'input head' or 'chief reporter', was responsible for sourcing news and included reporters from all beats. The output division, headed by an 'output head' or 'chief editor' was responsible for editing and included different editors for different beats. Newspapers had four or more levels, including editor, news editor, chief reporter, reporter, and a few levels in between with some variations from organization to organization. Similar to Pune media houses, big banners had many levels in the organizational hierarchy.

A very few of the Pune journalists did not have a good relationship with their boss and mentioned its impact: "If the nature of your relationship is like that, then you don't feel free to work and thus cannot cover out of the way topics". On the whole, however, an open work environment and ability to discuss work freely with their seniors and colleagues was crucial to the functioning of journalists in Pune. In the words of a female journalist, "I am the only female employee. . . . So, as a girl, he understands me a lot; he helps me a lot; he guides me a lot. I am happy with him being my boss and guiding me".

The value Kolkata journalists placed on a friendly and open environment in their offices is reflected in a journalist's comment: "I really look forward to going to the office and that is because of the people there". While all the television journalists found their newsroom culture to be friendly and good, some newspaper journalists indicated that they worked in a more formal structure: "There is definitely, a very definitive line of hierarchy, and you are . . . encouraged to . . . abide by it". But formality in newsroom culture was not a problem for many; it provided them with better coordination and communication. Similarly, some journalists did not see supervisory-level influence on their work as negative: "Whatever our seniors decide, we do that. That's affecting us, not in a bad way always". Two journalists did mention the negative influence of editorial pressure on their freedom to work.

Like Pune journalists, most journalists in Kolkata had a good and friendly relationship with their bosses and also saw their supervisors' guidance as resulting in good work: "When you fail to get [a story, they] always help you to move on, . . . to achieve another news [story]", and "When you have someone to appreciate or influence your work, you will automatically work well". With the exception of two respondents, journalists in Kolkata felt free to discuss and debate their work with their superiors if necessary.

In general, in India, a formal hierarchical structure was present in all traditional media outlets and journalists found the structure useful; there was also, for the most part, an easy camaraderie and a nurturing relationship present between superiors and their juniors. Given the newness and small size of online ventures, online news journalists experienced more loosely held horizontal structures.

In China, online media differed from mainstream media in their newsroom hierarchies. While the grassroots online media adopted a networked model of organization, i.e., one that was not hierarchical but maintained through flexible networks, the governance structures of the traditional media were all hierarchical, with different levels of authority and power. Most respondents reported that it was hard to evaluate whether the hierarchical structure in their newsroom helped or complicated their work. Ideally, according to them, this hierarchy should help to increase the efficiency of their work.

Most Chinese journalists maintained a formal relationship with their superiors, showing respect for them and meeting their requirements, but some reported that the nature of this relationship was based more on equality, friendship, and a cooperative partnership. The relationship had a positive impact on their daily work; for example, one journalist described his superiors as "both teachers and friends". However, this type of relationship was less likely to be formed with editors-in-chief than with the heads of their own editorial departments.

In South Africa, journalists generally reported a high degree of collegiality among staff working in the newsroom, with a flat hierarchy and open relationships. A slight difference was observed between the working environment of journalists in the private media and those working for the public broadcaster. Editorial hierarchies seemed to be stricter at the latter workplace. The increased commercial pressures on the news media had also impacted working conditions, and editors had to put more pressure on journalists to deliver work. One senior journalist remarked on this heightened pressure as follows:

> Now, it's a tighter ship that we are running; we must work harder, produce more, and not waste time because I could be doing a story whilst I am sitting here. There is a whole lot coming from the top now. . . . I think it all goes back to the resources; we have about 15 people who have left – subs and journalists –

and that means more work for those who are there. The editor needs to then make sure everyone is there, everyone is pulling their weight, and so on.

Interviewees working for the SABC remarked on the collegiality in the newsroom among journalists, but pointed out that editors did wield their authority from time to time. One of them articulated it as follows:

> Our staff, we love each other, even if we don't hang out as friends over the weekend or go out for coffee and things like that; some of us do but not all of us do. When there is a staff crisis, we stand together and it's because we have a common 'enemy' called the editor. Like, for instance, [a colleague] and I, I will give him a heads-up if I feel something is coming his way that is unfair. So, the staff has that kind of a relationship where we have each other's backs. The relationship between hierarchy, is not that fabulous; it's a personality thing.

This relationship was seen to affect work at the SABC, as there was "no room for debate" with the editor regarding ideas for news stories, and journalists had to follow orders on what to report. Journalists were also instructed not to report on matters concerning the SABC's controversial chief operating officer (Hlaudi Motsoeneng, who was found to have been dishonest about his qualifications), although their counterparts at the SABC's radio stations were "a lot freer". In some cases, SABC journalists reported on a "positive" relationship with colleagues and indicated that everyone is treated equally. This was especially the case with journalists working for the SABC in the Eastern Cape, which has a smaller editorial office and where relationships between journalists were more relaxed.

Journalists working for newspapers also generally reported that the hierarchy in their newsrooms was more relaxed, but that some degree of editorial authority over junior reporters was necessary for editorial decisions to be made. One newspaper journalist reflected on this situation thus:

> I wouldn't say it's democratic because ultimately the bosses need to take the decisions; you certainly can't do whatever you like. I think the majority of editors I've worked with are open to us differing with them and occasionally we persuade them that [we] are right. If you fail to persuade them, you pretty much have to do what they ask you to do.

Conclusion

The aim of this chapter was to contribute to widening the discussion on journalism in the BRICS countries, in essence to chart how these journalists view the current dynamics of newsmaking in terms of social media use, control of the Internet by government, and differences in the structure of traditional and online news media workplaces.

As mentioned earlier in this chapter, significant differences exist between the levels of press freedom in the BRICS countries. In general, however, journalists valued freedom from government control for political and entertainment news, even if in some cases they reported an understanding of the context and history from which such controls derived. They were particularly protective of the Internet, and where in a few countries some journalists felt government control was acceptable, it was for limited reasons such as protection from terrorism and pornography.

Although the nature of the organizational structures and hierarchies differed across the BRICS countries, in general, new media platforms also provided new forms of editorial organization, with flatter hierarchies and looser editorial relationships, than traditional news media. Most journalists characterized their immediate working environment as collegial, and their relationship with their bosses as friendly and at times nurturing. Chinese journalists reported working in a more formal hierarchy than their counterparts in other BRICS countries, but still found this environment friendly and conducive to their work. It may be surmised from the answers of journalists that journalistic hierarchies fulfil an ambivalent function – as an environment that provides a home and a sense of security, but also a structure that sometimes imposes limits on journalistic work in terms of story selection and writing.

Across the BRICS countries, the common denominator seems to be the rise of online media, particularly social media, as the dominant journalistic form and platform of the future. While traditional media still play an agenda-setting role in these countries, and are in several instances subjected to governmental interference and control, the online news media, in the view of respondent journalists, provide alternative outlets for especially the youth and the marginalized to voice their opinions and disseminate news. With their capacity to spread information across borders, these new media hold the potential to play a role in intra-BRICS communication and representation in the future.

Notes

1 Acknowledgement: the South African sections of this chapter drew on interview data gathered by Ndlovu.
2 Vanessa Ferreira contributed to this article.
3 This Charter of Broadcasters was signed in 1999 by six television channels as a self-regulative document for Russian broadcasters. See www.presscouncil.ru/index.php/teoriya-i-praktika/dokumenty/756-khartiya-teleradioveshchatelej.

References

Anikina, M., Dobek-Ostrowska, B., & Nygren, G. (Eds.). (2013). *Journalists in three media systems: Polish, Russian and Swedish journalists about values and ideals, daily practice and the future*. Moscow: Journalism Faculty.

Arquembourg, J. (2002, July–August). Le mythe de Pandore revisité. *Dossiersde l'Audiovisuel, 104*, p. 10.

Choudhury, A., & Mahapatra, D. (2015, March 24). Supreme Court strikes down Section 66A of IT Act which allowed arrests for objectionable content online. *Times of*

India. Retrieved from http://timesofindia.indiatimes.com/india/Supreme-Court-strikes-down-Section-66A-of-IT-Act-which-allowed-arrests-for-objectionable-content-online/articleshow/46672244.cms

Jacobs, S., & Wasserman, H. (2015, November 25). The day mainstream media became old in South Africa. *Washington Post*. Retrieved from www.washingtonpost.com/news/monkey-cage/wp/2015/11/25/the-day-mainstream-media-became-old-in-south-africa/

Klimov, I. (2006). Vypiski iz knigi S. Sadmena i N. Bredberna "Kak pravil'no zadavat' voprosy . . ." (Extracts from the book by S. Sadman and N. Bradburn "How to ask questions. . ."). *Sotsialjnaya realjnostj* (Social reality), *9*, 113–127. Retrieved from http://corp.fom.ru/uploads/socreal/post-170.pdf

Kohli-Khandekar, V. (2008). *The Indian media business*. New Delhi: Sage Publications.

Law of the Russian Federation. N 2124-1 (1991) (in version from 30.12.2015). On Mass Media. Retrieved from http://www.consultant.ru/cons/cgi/online.cgi?req=doc&base=LAW&n=191737&rnd=280370.3127632256#0

Lei, Y. W. (2011). The political consequences of the rise of the Internet: Political beliefs and practices of Chinese neitizens. *Political Communication*, *28*(3), 291–322.

Mapumulo, Z. (2016, May 1). Please call me inventor: It wasn't only about money. *City Press*. Retrieved from http://city-press.news24.com/News/please-call-me-inventor-it-wasnt-only-about-money-20160501

Mouillaud, M. (2002). *O jornal: da forma ao sentido*. Brasilia: UnB.

Ndlovu, M. (2015). What is the state of South African journalism? *African Journalism Studies*, *36*(3), 114–138.

Rana, P. (2010). *Supplement journalism in India*. New Delhi: Pentagon Press.

Reuters Institute for the Study of Journalism. (2016). *Digital News Report 2016*. Retrieved from www.digitalnewsreport.org/

Rozhnova, A., Borisova, S., & Zolotukhina, T. (2015). *Internet in Russia: Penetration dynamics*. Fond Obshchestvennogo Mnenia (FOM). Retrieved from http://fom.ru/SMI-i-internet/12369

Shaer, M. (2015, February 18). The media doesn't care what happens here. *The New York Times*. Retrieved from www.nytimes.com/2015/02/22/magazine/the-media-doesnt-care-what-happens-here.html?_r=0

Sodré, M. (2009). *A narração do fato*. Rio de Janeiro: Vozes.

Sparks, C. (2015). How coherent is the BRICS grouping? In K. Nordenstreng & D. K. Thussu (Eds.), *Mapping BRICS media* (pp. 42–65). London: Routledge.

Thussu, D. K. (2015). Digital BRICS: Building a NWICO 2.0? In K. Nordenstreng & D. K. Thussu (Eds.), *Mapping BRICS media* (pp. 242–263). London: Routledge.

Volkov, D., & Goncharov, S. (2014). *Potentsial grazhdanskogo uchastiya v reshenii sotsial'nykh problem* [The potential of civil participation in social problems solution]. Retrieved from www.levada.ru/old/sites/default/files/potencial_grazhdanskogo_uchastiya_0.pdf

Vzglyad Delovaya Gazeta (View business newspaper). (2014, August 1). *The act on the bloggers entered into force in Russia*. Retrieved from www.vz.ru/news/2014/8/1/698285.html

Wasserman, H., Bosch, T., & Chuma, W. (2016, January 22). Voices of the poor are missing in South Africa. *The Conversation*. Retrieved from https://theconversation.com/voices-of-the-poor-are-missing-from-south-africas-media-53068

3
ETHICS

Ideals and realities

Jyotika Ramaprasad, Deqiang Ji, Ruiming Zhou, Fernando Oliveira Paulino, Svetlana Pasti, Dmitry Gavra, Herman Wasserman, and Musawenkosi Ndlovu

Introduction

Against the background of the neo-liberal turn of the global economy, the rising role of capital and capital-dominated markets in journalism has been widely recognized. It is manifested in the profit-driven ambition of news media across the globe (McChesney, 2004; Philo & Miller, 2001; Ward, 2013). Meanwhile, regulatory bodies, irrespective of whether they are public institutions, professional associations that self-regulate, or the state, have been losing power or even retreating from the central position of regulation in the name of guaranteeing freedom, or of 'deregulation', a key phrase in post-1980 media theories and policies (Barbrook, 1988; Toffler, 1980; Tunstall, 1986).

As a result of these forces, the practice of ethics in the profession of journalism has been challenged. The phone-hacking scandal at Rupert Murdoch's *News of the World* is a typical example of the use of questionable practices.[1] Examples also exist in developing countries, where the general level of corruption in journalism, particularly in emerging economies exemplified by BRICS, is relatively high (Kruckeberg & Tsetsura, 2003; Ristow, 2010; World Democracy Audit, 2017). Reasons could be the immature system of regulation, the underdeveloped self-regulation mechanisms and discipline of associations, and the great space for power rent-seeking, a form of corruption that manifests as the pursuit of self-interest by using public power, especially by referencing people who hold public positions.

This chapter provides an empirical map of some ethical challenges that today's journalists in the countries of the BRICS coalition perceive and experience, and of how they deal with them in their daily practice. Among the many controversial reporting practices that have been the subject of study, the issue of paid news has emerged recently as being of critical importance. In Weaver and Wilhoit's first study, exchange of money between source and reporter was included as a controversial practice, but it focused on the journalist paying the source money for confidential information (Weaver & Wilhoit, 1986). Of interest to the BRICS study was the practice of a journalist accepting money or benefits from a source to write a positive article. Such journalistic practice is called paid news in some countries. While this is not the nomenclature for the practice across the world, it is used in this chapter for the sake of consistency and because it clearly indicates some sort of payment in exchange for news, and is applicable to both personal and institutional corruption.

To set the stage for this empirical exercise, the chapter presents for each of the BRICS countries a) legal definitions of corruption in general, b) those sections of journalism codes of ethics that exemplify how legal definitions of corruption are translated into guidelines for journalistic practice, and c) the milieu in which journalists engage with issues of ethics, i.e., the current politico-economic context in which news media in these countries operate, particularly the predominance of the market logic and deregulation in journalism, but also the socio-cultural environ, where relevant. The chapter concludes with a time and space analysis of the topic, addressing issues such as shifts, if any, in journalism practice from allegiance to an ethical idealism to a practice that is laced with corruption, and how these ideas of idealism and corruption may have different meanings across the BRICS countries.

The BRICS context

Defining corruption in the BRICS countries

No matter how complicated in the real world, in legal parlance corruption is clearly defined in BRICS. In Brazil, government officials who engage in corrupt practices are subject to criminal, civil, and administrative sanctions. Since 1988, when the constitution was passed, Brazil has experienced an important period of regulation in terms of corruption and information access laws (Brazilian Chamber of Deputies). These laws established the possibility for citizens to propose judicial action against corruption and to defend public administration. The Brazilian Law Against Corruption (#12.813/2013) was approved in 2013; it covers conflicts of interest. It made possible federal intervention in states that do not follow transparency and accountability principles. To guarantee implementation, the law provides the possibility of punishing enterprises that engage in bribery with public servants. Further, the Brazilian Information Access Law (#12.527/2011) of 2011 allows journalists and non-journalists to ask questions to federal and regional governments, chambers, and judicial institutions, and to receive answers within 30 days. This law is a particularly useful tool for journalists and others whose main job requires data. Finally, the 1965 Brazilian Law #4.898 covers the abuse of authority by public officials with possible punishment in the form of civil, criminal, and administrative sanctions.

In Russia, the Russian federal law (No. 273-FZ) *On Combating Corruption* (2008) defines corruption as

> abuse of public office, giving or receiving bribes, abuse of powers, commercial graft or other illegitimate use by an individual of his/her official status against legal interests of society and the State to receive private gain in the form of money, values, other property or services involving property, and other property rights for himself/herself or for third parties, or illegal provision of such a benefit to the said individual by other individuals.

In India, the legal framework relating to corruption and corrupt practices includes a web of legislations and government regulations. The 1860 Indian Penal Code, particularly Sections 161 to 165A, dealt with corruption among public servants. This code made it a crime for public servants to accept a gratification or a valuable, other than legal remuneration, for an official act and to use their public office for illegal gain; it also considered influencing a public servant to be a crime. In 1988, sections 161 to 165A of the penal code were repealed by and included in the Prevention of Corruption Act (India: The Prevention of Corruption Act, 1988; *A Comparative View of Anti-Corruption Laws of India*, 2016). In 2014, "President Pranab Mukherjee of India signed into law landmark legislation aimed at combating corruption by creating an anti-graft ombudsman with broad powers to prosecute all offending politicians, ministers, and senior civil servants, including the Prime Minister of the country" (*India: New Anti-Corruption Law*, 2014).

In China, while a variety of anti-corruption laws and regulations exist, two statutes are of primary importance in terms of controlling authority: the Criminal Law of the People's Republic of China (Criminal Law) (adopted 1979, updated several times, most recently in 2015) and the Anti Unfair Competition Law of the People's Republic of China (AUCL), 1993. Further, while the AUCL addresses only commercial bribery, the Criminal Law recognizes two forms of bribery, based on the identity of the bribe recipient: "official bribery" (offering a bribe to a state functionary) and "commercial bribery" (offering a bribe to a representative of a private enterprise or institution) (Yang et al., 2014). The "Criminal Law prohibits giving and receiving money or property – including cash, items and proprietary interests – to obtain an undue benefit" (GAN Business Anti-Corruption Portal, 2016). Essentially, in China, "according to Chinese official terminology, the core element of the definition of corruption . . . is the notion of the use of public authority and public resources for private interests" (He, 2000, p. 244).

In South Africa, according to the Prevention and Combating of Corrupt Activities Act (#12),

> any person who, directly or indirectly accepts or agrees to accept any gratification from any other person; or gives or agrees or offers to give any gratification to any other person; in order to act, personally or by influencing

another person to so act, in a manner designed to achieve an unjustified result, is guilty of the offence of corruption.

(Act 12, 2004)

It is clear from these definitions that despite any differences that may exist within the BRICS countries in political setting, economic environment, and cultural tradition, their definitions of corruption are quite similar. Whether mentioned overtly or not, the focus of these anti-corruption laws is in principle to criminalize the use of public power for personal gain. Journalism's codes of ethics are also more or less similar across BRICS in their condemnation of using journalism's power for organizational or individual advantage.

Codes of ethics in the BRICS countries

Autonomy is a key characteristic of occupations that consider themselves professions. To maintain this independence and keep other institutions from encroaching on this freedom, professions, including the journalism profession, institute self-regulation in the form of codes of ethics for their members. Codes of ethics are not legally binding but carry (or at least expect to carry) moral force. These codes differ by country because they "are rooted in the socio-cultural milieu of a society" (Ramaprasad, Liu, & Garrison, 2012, p. 98). Within the dynamics of this country milieu and with a focus on the critical ethical issues particular to journalism, various in-country media associations and individual media, including in BRICS countries, formulate ethics codes.

In Brazil, Article 6 of the current code of ethics indicates that it is a journalist's duty to "combat and denounce all ways of corruption, especially when they are practiced with the purpose to control information" (FENAJ, 2014). The Brazilian code also does not allow journalists to make use of their position as journalists to obtain personal advantage, and it obliges journalists to disseminate accurate information. Furthermore, different from other countries' ethics codes, the Brazilian journalists' code (last updated in 2007) recognizes press advisor initiatives as a legitimate place to practice journalism. In other words, the press advisor is noted as a journalist and thus journalistic production also occurs outside media companies.

In Russia, ethical codes exist at both national and regional levels and by internal rules introduced by editorial offices. In post-Soviet Russia, in February 1994, 27 journalists signed the Moscow Charter of Journalists (an ethics code), thus leading a new claim for self-regulation of the professional community. They strove to create ethical journalism in Moscow with voluntary obedience to the rules and control of conduct among its signatories. In April 1994, the Congress of Journalists adopted the "Code of Ethics of a Russian Journalist" taking as a basis the Moscow Charter, and made observance of the code obligatory for every member of the Union of Journalists of Russia. Because it followed similar documents from democratic countries, the code did not cater to domestic circumstances, and journalists found it hard to implement the guidelines. For instance, a ban on leadership in political parties eliminated many talented publicists[2] from membership in the union (Avraamov, 1999). Moreover, as it was adopted without wide discussion with practitioners (only 60 delegates were in the Congress), the code turned into an idle declaration rather than a driving tool for everyday usage.

According to the 1994 Russian journalism ethics code,

> A journalist considers malevolent distortion of facts, slander, the obtaining of payment for the dissemination of false or hiding of truthful information under any conditions as a grave professional misdemeanor. On the whole a journalist should not take, either directly or indirectly, any kind of compensation or reward from third persons for publishing any kind of material or opinion.
>
> *(Code of Professional Ethics of Russian Journalist, 1994)*

In India, the press is privately owned and guided by the Press Council of India's (PCI) Code of Ethics (Press Council of India, 2015). PCI's concern with the abuse of power is evident in its statements, including the following: "The power of the press has prompted the public men through the ages to try to cultivate and curry its favours through overt, and more often than not, covert means" (Press Council of India, 2010a, p. 80). In face of this possibility, the council advises journalists to not exchange their journalism for financial benefits of cash or kind, and particularly cautions them to guard against such acts during elections. Its expectations for journalists are well reflected in the following statement (Press Council of India, 2010a):

> Ultimately the strength of the moral fabric of the press itself shall decide whether or not to be swayed by the inducements and enticements thrown in its way by those in power. The media persons must realise that the burden of [whatever] favours and facilities they receive, whether they are showered on them by the public or the private organisations or the individuals in authority, is [ultimately] borne by the people.
>
> *(p. 80)*

According to the *Code of Ethics* of the All-India Newspaper Editors' Conference (2007), "there is nothing so unworthy as the acceptance or demand of a bribe or inducement for the exercise by a journalist of his power to give or deny publicity to news or comments".

India's state owned broadcasters, *All India Radio* and *Doordarshan*, under *Prasar Bharati*, the broadcasting arm of the government of India regulated in turn by the Ministry of Information and Broadcasting, have their own code of ethics. Private broadcasters on the other hand are self-regulatory, with independent bodies such as the Indian Broadcasting Foundation (IBF) and the Broadcasting Content Complaints Council (BCCC) framing regulations based on the 'Programme Code' prescribed under the (now amended) Cable Television Networks (Regulation) Act, 1995, and the rules thereunder (The Cable Television Networks [Regulation]

Act, 1995). Specifically, the code of ethics for these private broadcasters' news sections were promulgated by the News Broadcasters Association (2008), which includes the News Broadcasting Standards Authority; this authority administers the code of ethics. Journalistic codes of ethics for both state and independent broadcasters focus on issues similar to those for the press, in particular alerting broadcasters to the fact that they are public trustees of the airwaves and thus neutrality is essential in their coverage.

In China, the official All China Journalists Association announced the first formal code of journalistic ethics, the Code of Professional Ethics for Chinese Media Workers, in 1991 (Lo, Chan, & Pan, 2005); this code was amended for a third time in 2009 and currently it forms "the guideline of professionalism and ethics for Chinese journalists" (news.xinhuanet.com, 2014). China also has a Self-discipline Convention for China's Internet Industry since 2005, and a Self-discipline Convention for Mobile Phone Media (news.xinhuanet.com, 2014). A news.xinhuanet.com (2014) report also indicates that "Special operations aimed to crack down on blackmail journalism and fake news are being carried out to purify the environment for journalism". In accordance with the definition of corruption in China, journalists are prohibited from reporting in exchange for payment. Further, journalists are required to separate news reporting from business activities such as advertising and donations (*Several Rules on Prohibiting Paid News*, 2014).

In South Africa, under apartheid, the law rather than ethical principles formed the yardstick for adjudicating journalistic conduct. This situation changed when apartheid-era laws affecting the media were scrapped as part of the democratization process. Some laws remained, however, which later provided much cause for concern among the media – for instance Section 205 of the Criminal Procedure Act, which allows a judge or a magistrate to summon journalists to give testimony about an alleged offense. Still, the oppressive legal environment of apartheid gave way to a system of self-regulation in the democratic era, with a Press Council and ombudsman established to hear complaints by the public against the printed media, and an independent judicial tribunal, the Broadcasting Complaints Commission (BCCSA), established by the National Association of Broadcasters (NAB), to adjudicate complaints against broadcasters that are members of the NAB. The South African Press Council's Code of Ethics and Conduct for South African Print and Online Media states (Section 2.2) that "The media shall not accept a bribe, gift or any other benefit where this is intended or likely to influence coverage" (www.presscouncil.org.za/ContentPage?code=PRESSCODE). The Broadcasting Complaints Commission's code for Broadcasting Service Licensees does not however contain reference to such conflicts of interest (http://bccsa.co.za/wp-content/uploads/2015/12/BCCSA_Broadcasting_Code_NEW.pdf).

Advent of market logic and deregulation in the BRICS countries

Apart from the legal and moral force respectively of corruption laws and journalism ethics codes, news media also encounter politico-economic factors as they participate in their daily news production routines. In recent times, the logic of capital has gained remarkable spread and primacy globally, and the BRICS countries and their institution of journalism are no exception to this phenomenon.

The Brazilian media sector has considerable economic strength, a characteristic that has been developing since the 1960s in the context of lack of a regulatory body and hence lack of a consistent regulatory framework and communication policy. In general, the private media system has benefited from this absence of regulation and has become powerful. Private television and radio are unfettered and thus able to generate considerable revenue and political influence. Even though private newspapers do not share this economic strength, they have benefited from the growth in the consumer market between 2003 and 2014, when, different from some other countries, the number of newspaper readers in print and digital versions rose in Brazil (Associacao Nacional De Jornais, n.d.).

The lack of a regulatory body to guarantee pluralism and diversity has led to media concentration in Brazil. For example, of the more than 500 television channels on air, around 80 per cent are linked to the major communication conglomerates. In fact, the state was directly responsible for stimulating the formation of networks by creating partnerships between large national media and political/economic groups. Around a third of the members of the National Congress have some kind of connection to television and radio broadcasters, and a large number of companies are controlled directly or indirectly by political interests (Paulino & Silva, 2013). Strong political parallelism is thus present in Brazil. In legal terms, the constitution determines important principles like freedom of expression and a system of equality for public, private, and state channels. However, these principles are not enacted into specific laws, and whatever laws on media regulation exist have not been updated. The Brazilian Telecommunication Code, for example law #4117/1962, has been regulating broadcasting for the past 54 years.

After three decades of post-Soviet transformation, the Russian media have been identified as "a statist commercialized model" (Vartanova, 2012, p. 139). The definition clearly addresses their hybrid character, including paradoxes of political economy of the Russian media. One of them is the media market. On the one hand, the Russian media are ranked tenth in the world by economic indicators (Pankin, 2010), operating at the intersection of state and business interests. Media have grown into a mass industry of entertainment, information, and advertising. On the other hand, the Russian government acknowledges the non-market character of media – the overwhelming majority of the regional and local newspapers exist owing to various subsidies and administrative resources (*Russian Periodical Press Market 2009: Condition, Trends, Prospects*, 2010).

The second paradox is a marriage of liberalism and authoritarianism in the Russian media system. On the one hand, the media reveal the same logic of commercialization, concentration, and convergence as in the West (Terzis, 2008), moving to homogenization of media systems and the triumph of the liberal model, as classified by Hallin and Mancini (2004). The analysis of its structure and trends represented in terms of media economy and technology

(Vartanova & Smirnov, 2010) implicitly suggests a perspective of its gradual convergence with Western models whereby "Russia is no longer such a special case" (Nordenstreng, 2010). On the other hand, the so-called market liberalism of the Russian media successfully coexists with the authoritarian approach of the government: "instrumentalization of media" (Zassoursky, 2004) as well as "market authoritarianism" (Shevtsova, 2005). The trend of the last decade is for a proportional decrease in the commercial capital share and an increase in the state capital and mixed (state and commercial) capital shares. The dependence of the media on the state increases in two ways: through state ownership and through regular subsides – both buying the loyalty of the media (Pasti & Nordenstreng, 2013).

Since the liberalization of the Indian economy in the early 1990s, Indian news media have grown in number, commercialized, and become concentrated (Bhattacharjee, Wang, & Banerjee, 2016; Painter, 2013; Singh, 2014; Telecommunication Regulatory Authority of India, 2013). The immense growth of Indian media in contrast to the Anglo-American trend of decline has been fuelled in part by policies that liberalized foreign investment in India. A market logic now pervades the Indian news media. Accompanying this is the considerable integration of companies to form conglomerates fuelled by a lack of regulatory policy for horizontal or vertical integration or cross media ownership (Kumar, 2015).

In 1992, the Chinese media underwent a major transformation. The Chinese state, while retaining political control, actively introduced market mechanisms into its news media system, in a move to make the media financially independent (Zhao, 2000). It was recognized that "the media were not only the Party's mouthpiece, but also had commodity values" (Bai, 2005, p. 5). Thus, commercialization occurred at the behest of China's communist party, but the media were still state owned in continuance of the past ownership practice. In a next step, the party endorsed conglomeration first for economic reasons of sustainability of media outlets, but later as state policy that included both market and political considerations (Zhao, 2000, 2004). As a result of these changes, the Chinese news system is "becoming a platform for profit-making, while speaking in the voice of the ruling Party-elite" (Zhao, 2004, p. 205). In essence, "fusion of the Party state and market power has created a media system that serves the interests of the country's political and economic elite" (Zhao, 2004, p. 179).

South Africa's (re)integration into the market-oriented global political economy after 1994, post-fall of the Berlin Wall, and its adoption of neo-liberal policies, produced a highly commercialised media market. In this market, even the country's public service broadcaster, the SABC, draws more than 80 per cent of its revenue from the private market, through advertising. In fact, almost all mainstream print, digital, satellite/broadcast media, except those that relate to the SABC, are in private hands, whether they are pro- or anti-government. Some attempts have been made to balance the commercial dominance, for instance through the awarding of community broadcasting licences and the establishment of the Media Development and Diversity Agency, funded by the fiscus (the basket of revenue collected by the national treasury) and a levy on private media, with the aim of supporting small and community media outlets.

The BRICS study

The in-depth interview questions on journalistic ethics focused on paid news, but cast a wider net by also asking journalists to speak to the ethical dilemmas they may have encountered in their daily work. To gather responses on paid news, journalists were asked whether they had engaged in writing articles for money or services, whether this practice was prevalent in their country, and how this practice relates to professionalism. For data on ethical dilemmas, journalists were asked to describe work-related situations in which they had faced difficult moral choices; often these ethical dilemmas are the focal point of ethical debates among journalists. Journalists were also probed when necessary to discuss unwritten rules that regulate the relationship among journalists in the newsroom in particular and in the profession in general.

Findings

Paid news: news (and even non-news and disguised news) for cash and benefit

The ideal for news media in a society is that they should be independent from other powers that may drive them to serve their interests rather than the interests of the public, no matter how hard it is for the media to survive economically and how difficult it is to be neutral. The roots of this ideal are Anglo-American; this ideal defines corruption in journalism as lack of independence of the profession of journalism from politics, the market, and other potentially harmful sources of influence. Reporting for money or services is thus simply unacceptable in this definition of an ideal news media and thus also unacceptable in terms of journalism ethics. Many controversial journalistic practices fall under the umbrella of paid news, including extortion to suppress news, all done in exchange for benefit (cash, gifts, introduction to the power elite, advertising packages, etc.) to the media organization or journalist.

The Press Council of India has defined paid news as "Any news or analysis appearing in any media (Print and Electronic) for a price in cash or kind as consideration" (Press Council of India, 2010b, p. 4). Respondents from Kolkata and Pune further explained the cash or in-kind considerations referenced in this definition; paid news could mean accepting money mostly (but sometimes gifts) for writing favourable articles. Delhi and Hyderabad journalists provided similar definitions of paid news: "Paid news may also be indirect as *no* one pays you a bribe, but they will sponsor trips, you get gifts from PR professionals, lobbyists, etc."; in sum, there is a "fine line between PR and paid news, [a line] which most channels cross for money".

Paid news could also mean writing favourable articles for large advertisers; in the words of one Indian journalist: "You give me an advertising package of Rs. 10 lakhs, then we will publish your four or five articles in our newspapers, complimentary". In this case, the loyalty of the media is provided in exchange for advertising revenue. According to Russian journalists, such paid news may also take a subtler form: the news media organization develops special relations with the advertisers and businesses who regularly buy advertising in their outlet and then never reports negatively on them. Advertorials when they are unmarked, while not directly paid news, are yet another practice that exchanges money for what appears to be news. They are a sort of advertisement that provides information about a product or service in the style of an objective journalistic article or an editorial, and they are often not labelled as an advertorial. They are inherently deceptive and thus an ethical transgression. Advertorials do harm to audiences, especially the poor and poorly educated, who are not fully media literate and cannot thus differentiate advertisements from the news. These audiences are in essence deceived by the conspiracy of both the advertisers and the media.

Further, sometimes the pay in paid news is introduction to powerful people rather than bribes, which are considered criminal. One Indian metro city journalist indicated that the pay may be in the form of being "in the good books of politicians". Here the journalist is seeking the patronage of influential people, and sometimes of powerful institutions.

A particularly extreme form of paid news (more accurately, non-news) is extortion to hide a story, i.e., exchanging silence for a benefit. Newspersons often discover irresponsible, even illegitimate actions, on part of a person or organization/corporation, actions that definitely jeopardize the public interest and that could have far-reaching social influence. An unethical newsperson might make a monetary deal with this person/organization to suppress news that could expose this irresponsible action. While the reputation of the person/organization is saved, the public interest is unfortunately damaged. A Russian journalist explained this type of practice as it manifests in relation to corporations that have money and may have something to hide:

> This is a very simple scheme. When a company has money, journalists start . . . investigating, searching for secrets, crises, mistakes, problems, etc. Finally, they prepare a negative report. Positive features of the company disappear. Then, they start blackmailing: "either you pay us or I'll publish the results of my investigation as honest material". Often companies pay or buy advertising space [that they do not need].

Brazil

A majority of journalists from both traditional and online news media reported that they refused to participate in paid news. Still, according to some Brazilian journalists (25 per cent of online news journalists and 17 per cent of traditional media journalists), paid news was prevalent in Brazil. Thus, practice reportedly was not always synchronized with the ethical norms of journalism.

A majority (63 per cent from online and 60 per cent from traditional media) condemned the practice of writing texts for money or services. Traditional media journalists called it "advertising and not journalism" and said that it "goes totally against . . . professional ethics policy. People who do this are the worst of journalism". Online media journalists felt the same way, calling paid news "unprofessional [and indicative of the] lack of ethics in a profession". One online journalist said, "Personally, I think this is unacceptable, but unfortunately there are people and press organs that [do] this. But, thank God, Brazil is still a free country; even with paid material you can work freely". Essentially, this journalist recognized that paid news exists, but also that, at the same time, there is the freedom to talk about this practice, and thus to discuss ways to try to avoid it. In the words of another journalist, "the journalist can be excellent in [her/his] profession, but he/she is unethical when he/she accepts to do paid/puff pieces/articles".

Russia

In Russia, journalists acknowledged their participation in paid news, sometimes using financial reasons to justify engaging in a practice that does not accord with ethical norms. Almost every fourth Russian respondent (22 per cent) said that in the past year they had written articles, in the commercial or political interest of clients, for money or services. Yekaterinburg, the most distant region from Moscow, had the largest percentage of journalists – almost every second journalist (48 per cent) – who produced paid articles. Figures for other cities were as follows: Moscow, 10 per cent; St. Petersburg, 15 per cent; and Petrozavodsk, 36 per cent. In Russia, then, journalists openly acknowledged that their reporting practices were in some measure asynchronous with ethical norms.

Journalists' narratives indicated that journalists and media organizations engaged in paid news for economic reasons. For example, journalists in the provincial cities said that paid news was justifiable in face of low wages and high prices for child support and housing. In Petrozavodsk, a female traditional media journalist said,

> For us, mostly, reasons are economic ones. Provincial journalists have very poor living conditions. Imagine, the journalist doesn't have enough money to pay for housing, nothing to feed the baby. I know journalists who have stepped on this slippery slope in this situation.

One young male online journalist from Yekaterinburg perceived exchanging positive articles for advertising as a natural way to earn money. He said,

> What is my attitude to paid journalism? I should say, positive. It's the way to get profit, to gain money. We also want to eat good food, to drive good cars,

> to have modern mobile phones, a warm country house. All of us need money. How can we get money? The answer is clear – by advertising. White or black. Or grey. If we speak about paid journalism – here it is. When somebody . . . says he needs a positive article about [him/herself] and [his/her] company, we answer, "OK, here is the price – you pay, we write". It's only business. Of course, I tolerate it. All of us use it.

Paid news was also done for political reasons: "It's disgusting and nasty to write the interview sometimes for the future mayor before the elections: you are inventing questions for him and you are answering them yourself. It's all unpleasant, but it is an opportunity to make money".

Some journalists even perceived the ideological orientation of the media as a particular kind of political corruption because the ideology slants coverage in someone's interest and does not provide the full truth. If the media disorients the people in this manner, it is unethical:

> You know perfectly well that all socio-political mass media of Russia are in a certain way ideologically marked. You can't write in the project *Slon.Ru* material on . . . how good Stalin was. You never publish this article there: "10 reasons that Stalin was the best ruler of Russia". The ideological policy of *Slon.Ru* will not allow it; there will never be such material. And the magazine *Odnako* would never publish an article about the fact that Russia should give up in the Crimea. They are ideologically marked [publications].

Further, supervisors were part of the paid news phenomenon as indicated by a Moscow journalist:

> When I worked on the TV channel "Russia", in parallel, I led a lifestyle column in *The Chief* magazine; there the salary was very small. And once our chief-editor said, "There is a customer and we want to put him on the cover as the main interviewee of the issue. This will a biased article". When he told me the payment, I cheered up . . . and I naturally agreed.

One journalist said, "If you work somewhere in media, you have to accept rules of the game", i.e., informal rules regulating the behaviour of journalists. In this context, one online journalist explained that "it is a false stereotype" to think of a journalist as "a free professional, a man of honour, intended to give the people the truth". Thus, even if a journalist does not approve of paid journalism, s/he must do it because of the editorial expectation to do so. A female journalist from traditional media in Yekaterinburg spoke of this expectation; she said, "corruption is inevitable" because her "media's advertising department has a contract with" companies and she "has to write complimentary articles about them for extra money. And there's no way out".

When paid articles are written to obtain the support or even patronage of an influential person or institution, the practice has its downside too. A young male online journalist from Yekaterinburg explained:

> When you communicate with an influential or useful person and have a 'silent contract' [with the person] that you will help each other, finally you become dependent and you can't write anything negative about this person. It's not direct corruption in my point of view; nobody gives me money, but we help each other. I'm now trying to get out of this situation, but it's a complicated process. It's inevitable. We live in the world where you have to pay for everything.

Journalists also write favourable articles about their sources to create a positive image of them and thus to build a special relationship with them. In St. Petersburg, an experienced male journalist in traditional media said, "I've never produced articles with positive information for money. But often I do it to support my sources". In this case, money is not exchanged; rather positive coverage is bartered for the potential supply of exclusive information from sources to journalists.

Respondent journalists were more or less evenly split in their opinion about paid news; half had a negative opinion, while the other half said it did not conflict with professionalism. Yekaterinburg had the largest percentage of journalists (66 per cent) who did not find the practice of writing articles for money or services to be unethical. Comparative percentages in the other Russian cities were as follows: Moscow, 32 per cent; St. Petersburg, 59 per cent; and Petrozavodsk, 56 per cent. Journalists who had a negative attitude towards paid articles believed that corruption and professionalism are incompatible. A young male journalist from online media said that only an "honest journalist" is "a real journalist", one who never produces paid materials. He added that "if a professional gets money or other benefits for [writing news articles], he's not a journalist; he's a professional writer of paid materials". In Moscow, an old male journalist from traditional media noted that "a journalist can't be a cynic. He still needs sincerity and honesty if he wants to deliver a message to the audience". Those who write corrupt articles and even become quite successful in the profession, in his opinion, sooner or later become cynics. Thus, they are not true journalists. In Petrozavodsk, a female journalist from online media agreed completely:

> The question is: who is a professional? If a person is able to tell a story in an interesting way, it's enough to produce a good paid article. But when we speak about the professional, (s)he should know the journalists' ethics code. And not only know, but implement it in everyday professional activities. Such a person is a real professional. And (s)he'll never produce paid materials.

India

When it came to the personal practice of paid news, with the exception of one journalist in Kolkata, those Kolkata and Pune journalists who answered the question said that they did not engage in paid news. In the metro cities of Delhi and Hyderabad too, no journalist said that s/he engaged in paid news. Thus, respondents reportedly mostly engaged with and followed the ethics of journalistic practice, synchronizing action with norms. One traditional media journalist said,

People used to offer me money and gifts for their product promotions, but I never took any money or gifts. During the time of a product launch, these people offer me a good amount of money to write a special article about the product; it's really a big dilemma for me.

Indian journalists acknowledged that paid news was prevalent in India: "[Paid news] is common practice in almost all news outlets today as it is easy and fast news". These journalists also pointed out that business reporting beats are a more fertile ground for paid news to germinate and grow because these journalists have access to business houses. "Paid news", they further indicated, is also "rampant . . . during elections when [journalists] are supposed to give opinions as per the managements' perspectives and political ideologies". In Kolkata too, many respondents pointed to elections as the time of heightened prevalence of paid news. According to a Pune respondent, the Election Commission's definition restricted covering a politician from only one party.

Respondent journalists in Pune and Kolkata indicated that paid news occurred at both the organizational and individual level. In the former, editors/publishers entered into a deal with the payee but journalists had to write the stories. In the latter, individual journalists themselves cut the deal and then wrote positive stories. A few respondents believed that paid news was an organization level phenomenon alone, negotiated by management, and that journalists were unaware of which among their stories was paid for: "Some reporter is given an assignment but that is already paid news. Reporters are not necessarily aware of that". Other respondents believed that it was journalists who approached politicians to negotiate an exchange of money or other benefits for publishing stories. In Delhi and Hyderabad too, similar sentiments prevailed. In the words of a journalist, paid news depends "on the owners and occurs at the level of management". These journalists considered themselves bound by the rules of ethical practice, but they believed that management did not follow these rules, given that the media are often owned by political parties or profit-making entrepreneurs. They indicated the pressure they experienced to go against ethical norms: "[The organization] had started doing paid news. . . . We used to feel that it is against the ethics of journalism, but due to pressure from management we had to do it".

Further, respondent journalists expressed disdain for paid news. Most provincial city respondents felt that the practice of paid news is negatively related to professionalism in journalism and is distasteful. Paid news they believe compromises the integrity of stories, because stories should be unbiased and objective; paid news also violates the ethics of journalism. A similar sentiment was found in the metros: paid news "reduces newsworthiness and professionalism and erodes the concept of journalism by compromising what news stands for". At an individual level, "paid news degrades a person who is involved and shakes the faith of the audience. The journalists simply do their job, but yes, this affects their professionalism negatively". One metro journalist stated, "Paid news and corruption go hand in hand and their influence over the media is undeniably huge". Another called it "a malaise which has no remedy, and it has got internalized". And yet another journalist indicated that "paid news has a major impact in the way it shapes beliefs and attitudes and builds public opinion. Such practices can hide reality and convey news selectively based on media's perspective".

According to Kolkata and Pune respondents, when paid news takes the form of suppressing stories through extortion from sources that have something to hide, the media, is 'controlled' and "one can say it misguides the society. . . . It makes society look in the other direction". These respondents believed that such paid news harms the journalist because the audience could lose trust/confidence in the journalist. Respondents also expressed disdain for advertorials. When money is exchanged to provide what appears to be news but is advertising, it is "commercialism in a package of editorial stuff; [it] is a breach of trust actually [because] what is news is news and what is advertising is advertising". A journalist added that rules and regulations dictate that advertising is a revenue source; when ads are published, they should be clearly indicated and formatted as such and not as news.

China

In China, in traditional and online media in all cities, with two exceptions – traditional media journalists in Beijing and Guangzhou – more than 50 per cent of the respondents said they had produced articles for money and other consideration. Thus, in this regard, respondents acknowledged clearly that their practice was not synchronized with ethical norms of journalism. In Beijing, Shanghai, and Guangzhou, a larger per cent of traditional media respondents than those working for online media indicated that they produced paid news reports, while in Wuhan the opposite was the case.

At the same time, almost half of the interviewees in Beijing and a third of the respondents in the other cities said that corruption in journalism is not acceptable. And, all interviewees exhibited solidarity in their opinion that advertorials were outside the firewall of journalistic professionalism. In China, advertorials usually take the form of a special page (*zhuanban*) or a regular radio/TV programme and are not labelled as advertisements. For the interviewees, it was not worthy of a journalist to place an advertorial on a page identified as a news page. Some journalists remarked that it may be reasonable to use advertorials because they offer some information or a public service, but they still found them hard to accept because they are used to increase private assets. The journalists' narratives indicated that advertorials would be accepted only if this was necessary for the commercial survival of the outlet.

Further, nearly all interviewees explicitly stated that extortion was the antithesis of journalistic professionalism. These journalists indicated that while extortion was not rare in China's journalistic practices, it was more likely to be found among those in the frontline of daily news production, i.e., middle-level desk managers, as well as among financial reporters; these personnel had the might to turn the newsroom into a corrupt space. Many Chinese corporations operate on the stock market but the market is not always in their favour in China's incompletely free-market economy system. In this situation, financial reporters can uncover the truth, but they can also bury stories about mistakes and corruption. According to interviewees, extortion is not the business of journalists, and it is pointless to debate whether it makes sense morally once the extortion is revealed. Instead, these journalists believed that courts should take upon themselves the duty to discipline such illegal behaviour.

Despite respondent journalists' criticism of advertorials and extortion, they (as noted earlier) engaged in the practice of paid news; in addition, respondents were generally accepting of envelope journalism. According to a journalist from Beijing, while "corruption is an unhealthy problem in the news industry . . . it is common to give some money to journalists to cover transportation costs". This reimbursement is usually put in an envelope and called the 'red package' or 'red envelope' (*Hongbao*). The money (about 100 to 500 RMB or about 15 to 75 USD) is often used to cover the cost of a round trip between the newsroom and the location of a news event, and sometimes includes a worktime meal. Most respondent journalists considered journalistic professionalism as an ideal prototype in the Chinese context, in which *Hongbao*, also understood to be a tool to sustain the relationship between journalists and various sources and organizations, is common. In most cases, these journalists accepted *Hongbao* as they did not want to indicate to sources that they did not care about building a relationship with them, but group pressure was also a factor; they did not want to be an exception to their peers. Thus, they stated that *Hongbao* is inevitable despite their identity as professional journalists.

Support for this cultural interpretation of "some money" is found in Chinese journalists' answers to the question about how satisfied they were with their income. Most journalists (80 per cent) indicated that they were satisfied. Piecemeal, *Hongbao* piles up so that it becomes an invisible section of journalists' income, one that is not spoken about. It constitutes an indispensable part of most journalists' earnings, particularly for journalists who rate their salaries as unsatisfactory.

While it may be understood that media organizations are responsible for the total cost of their journalists' reporting work, it is also widely believed by both the press and the public in China that receiving such money is not a violation of the ethical code and even of the law. In China, "some money" builds relationships between journalists and various organizations, so that journalism can cover a variety of topics: the political, economic, social, and cultural. The money provides mutual benefits – to the media as well as to organizations in finance, education, sports, etc. Sources use this Chinese-style reimbursement to start or to maintain contact with a reporter. Within this Chinese culture of reciprocity, the source (either an authority, a firm, or an individual) exerts external social control in an imperceptible way.

Not all respondent journalists, however, believed that professionalism and *Hongbao* were compatible. Respondents from Caixin Media emphasized that *Hongbao* is not allowed by their code of ethics. These reporters from one of the most renowned and respected media outlets in China indicated that *Hongbao* is without doubt contradictory to the notion of journalistic professionalism.

Overall, however, the Chinese journalists' narratives indicated that both idealism as a set of normative claims for journalists and journalism to adopt and corruption as a set of localized interpretations put into practice coexist in the workplace. In China, this 'ethical parallelism', i.e., accepting the idealism of ethical norms but engaging in some practices that contradict the ideal, as seen in the local interpretation of *Hongbao*, may also be used to understand findings about paid news. Locally, journalists' stance against corruption but at the same time their production of paid news may not be as contradictory as it may seem from the Anglo-American journalism ethics perspective. In the Chinese context, this is ethical parallelism, wherein the local understanding is that this is simply a way to establish a relationship and earn some money.

South Africa

In South Africa, bribery of journalists, or so-called 'brown envelope journalism', was not found to be a widespread phenomenon, unlike the case in many other African countries (see for instance Lodamo & Skjerdal, 2009). In all sample cities, journalists indicated that they had not accepted money for articles. If the two interviewees who misunderstood the question to mean earning a freelance income are discounted, not a single journalist in these cities indicated that they had taken money for providing articles or services.

In Port Elizabeth, the smallest city in this study, located in the poorest province in the country, a majority of journalists (52 per cent) said they did not know whether the practice of paid news was prevalent in South Africa; only a small percentage (8 per cent) said it was. This was also the only city where respondents (16 per cent) indicated that they knew colleagues who had written articles for money or services. Responses of journalists in Durban were somewhat similar to those found in Port Elizabeth; a small percentage (16 per cent) thought that the practice of paid news was prevalent in South Africa, but the majority (80 per cent) said they did not know. One journalist here said,

> No, we aren't allowed to do that. You must get permission; when I joined here I was given a declaration form to declare my business interest, business interests of my wife, which property I own, and those things are monitored from time to time. And if I get a present that is worth more than R300, I must declare it in the office. That happens a lot here . . . and then there will be an auction where they auction off all the freebies we have received.

A small percentage (36 per cent in Cape Town) said that low levels of pay may make bribes attractive.

Journalists reported awareness of the ethical proscription of conflicts of interest and bribery, and indicated that routines and processes were in place to counter such unethical practices. The notion of journalistic professionalism, which includes adherence to ethical codes and the avoidance of corrupt practices, resonated through journalists' responses to questions about bribery and conflicts of interest. Across the sample cities, journalists overwhelmingly thought that corrupt practices cannot be combined with the notion of journalistic professionalism. All the journalists interviewed were of the opinion that "a venal journalist is not a journalist". Thus, in South Africa, journalists' narratives indicated that their beliefs and practice were, to a large extent, in line with the ethical norms of journalism.

Ethical Dilemmas

In voicing their ethical dilemmas, journalists sometimes included concerns related to the corruption of journalists and organizations in their pursuit of money and gain. They also, however, spoke of a wide range of ethical conundrums they faced in their regular practice of journalism, some that articulated anguish for their subjects and their audiences, and others that questioned their own professionalism or narrated their experience of conflict between various positions.

Brazil

In Brazil, traditional and online media journalists faced similar ethical dilemmas; these were: "difference between my position and the editorial position", "questions about my objectivity", "conflicts between the public interest and the interest of my social group", "contradiction between urgency and professionalism", "choice between profitability and freedom of expression", "bribes", and such. One journalist spoke of the "difficulties in separating what is news and what is an ad". Another mentioned that he had doubts about whether to publish or not a "story about suicide". Ethical dilemmas of journalists were also connected with "economic, political, social, and even family pressures", owing to difficult life conditions and low income.

Respondents also discussed directly or indirectly the reporter–consultant relationship. Many journalists work as press advisors; in fact, sometimes, journalists work part-time in a media channel and part-time as a communication consultant. Only one respondent evaluated this kind of practice positively. Altogether, 63 per cent of online news journalists and 60 per cent of traditional media respondents assessed the practice negatively, and 13 per cent of online journalists and 33 per cent of traditional media journalists considered the practice "normal", i.e., acceptable, "if made in an official form, through contract or by the publicity department". These latter respondents emphasized that the reader should be made aware that they are being exposed to a journalism that is biased.

Brazilian journalists spoke of unwritten rules in their work, particularly the one that said that journalists cannot oppose the owner. In all but Rio de Janeiro, journalists (2 per cent in Brasília, 4 per cent in Vitória, and 4 per cent in Juiz de Fora) mentioned the unspoken rule that "you cannot go against the owner of the company". This unwritten rule for journalists to watch over their companies' interests is an integral part of professionalism in the Brazilian media system.

Russia

Some respondents reported that they had not experienced ethical dilemmas because the understanding of ethical issues and conduct in their media organization was in tune with their individual moral principles. One young online journalist in Yekaterinburg said that she (like a few other journalists) only works in media that are not contrary to her moral and religious views: "I worked always in the media where nothing conflicted with my values. Here all of us are like-minded people". Her colleague, a young journalist, recalled a time when she received moral support from her boss in a difficult situation:

> When I worked in the programme 'History in details', I needed to shoot a piece about the reserve-museum. One of the story subjects was supposed to be the founder of this museum. He was very old and ill. But we were told to shoot him. When we came [to the site], we came to know that he recently had a heart attack. . . . I thought about this and abandoned the interview, and convinced my boss.

Sometimes journalists' understanding of their own unethical behaviour for the sake of sensationalism and newspaper ratings came after many years of journalistic work. One journalist recalled the following:

> I was editor of the first St. Petersburg tabloid newspaper. We had really bad [unethical] situations where we had caused people great disappointments. By pure thoughts, we just wanted to open this niche [sensationalism], in the early '90s, when everything seemed so new and fresh. It seemed to us that this is freedom of speech and so on. One day we published one photo which almost brought a woman to suicide.

Ethical dilemmas could also be associated with investigative journalism and the practice of hiding one's journalistic identity. One online journalist said in this regard: "I had to go, not as a journalist but as an aunt, to attend a parents' meeting, to see how it is. This . . . requires a certain artistry. It is unpleasant because it is cheating".

The top three unwritten rules journalists mentioned were not stealing themes and sources from their colleagues; not quarrelling with, betraying, or denigrating colleagues; and not lying in their stories. Unwritten rules also included "mutual aid to colleagues", "verification of information", "protection of sources of information", "objectivity", and "not to show dead bodies close up". The self-regulation of Russian journalists was thus based on having the same rules of conduct for each other, for their sources, and their audiences. These rules governed their conduct and reflected the journalists' perceptions of the most important qualities of a decent person: do not betray, do not steal, and do help.

India

In Kolkata and Pune, the majority of respondents said they had not faced ethical dilemmas in their work. From among those who did, some felt they were forced into a certain style of reporting. A journalist gave the example of covering a calamity: "You feel this is not the way to report it, but due to the competition you are forced to do that". Another journalist mentioned the dilemma in having to make a decision about an attractive offer of a fellowship from an international organization accompanied by a cheque in exchange for publishing ten positive stories. Others described their discomfort with working for a newspaper owned by a politician or with being forced to cover political news in favour of a particular political party or the government: "When dengue spread very badly, it was the government's responsibility to control that. [But] because my television channel was pro-government . . . I was not able to cover that news [despite the fact that I am a health reporter]". Another journalist expressed a similar sentiment, feeling forced to share only positive government-related content, despite the opposite being true at times. The words of one journalist summed up well an organizational culture that creates ethical dilemmas for journalists: "We have been told: when you enter the office, your ideology is like a shoe. You have to [take it off] and enter the temple. Once you leave [the temple], you can put your [shoe] back [on]".

A provincial city journalist reported a slightly different type of dilemma, one faced when covering situations where a person is in difficulty. The dilemma is whether to cover the story or to instead immediately go to help the subject of the story: "There are instances where I did not know whether I should write the story or help the person first. There have been cases where I have ended up helping the person. . . . Therefore, my story didn't stand".

In Delhi and Hyderabad, most journalists from both online and traditional media reported that they faced ethical dilemmas in the course of their duties, both within and outside their organization. Organizational pressure appeared to be a major source of ethical dilemmas. The mismatch between the expectations of journalists and management, although accepted as an inevitable part of the process, created concern among journalists about objectivity. An online journalist from Delhi had to choose between a firm's focus on making profits and journalists' freedom of speech. One journalist said, "I have experienced ethical dilemmas when I am bound to change the angle of a story to fit in with the channel's ideology or management's understanding of things". Some journalists, while sure that "ethical dilemmas emerge when you are not clear about your ethics" and certain in their belief that "when you know what you will do and what not, it becomes easy", recognized that "there is a pressure from upwards to tweak a little something there". Apart from these "pressures and threats from outside", these metro journalists also faced ethical conflicts within themselves: "Many a time I have faced internal contradictions between speed and quality while delivering a segment". About this, one journalist said, "We have a sense of urgency that overtakes professionalism".

China

Only a minority of Chinese interviewees reported ethical dilemmas in their work. These dilemmas were related to social control inside and outside the newsroom and the uncertainty about whether their reporting of societal problems resulted in any positive change.

Social control in the newsroom generally came from supervisors, subverting factual reporting to the interests of the organization. A reporter may cover her story based on what she has seen and heard, but an editor, even a desk manager, may ask her to revise the draft to fit into a pre-set news frame, which by often being sensational and thus having audience appeal, meets the news outlets' need to garner large audiences. Social control from outside the newsroom comes in the form of informal instructions from publicity departments and the Office of the Central Leading Group for Cyberspace Affairs (*wangxinban*) of the Party. These offices may instruct the news media that a particular story should not be published. Because journalists have no way to predict when such an instruction may arrive, they live with considerable uncertainty about their newsmaking. Journalists also are on the receiving end of social control from advertisers, who expect the news media to protect their commercial enterprise; advertisers' power comes from the fact that they can easily withdraw their advertising.

A somewhat different type of dilemma arises from journalists' own expectations of making a difference in society; they report societal problems but are never sure whether solutions will be found and implemented. Journalists tell stories about citizens' lives that are tragic to a degree they had never imagined, but they are sceptical about whether their reports result in a solution because tragic life occurrences are widespread in China. Some interviewees indicated that they often felt trapped in this struggle. Interviewees complained that there are a lot of citizens in China who do not regard journalism as an autonomous field that provides a public service, and therefore they think that it cannot be a way to find solutions to their problems.

South Africa

In Cape Town, 98 per cent of respondents could not recall any situation which required them to make a moral choice. In Johannesburg, this figure was 60 per cent. The only significant ethical dilemma that journalists in Johannesburg experienced had to do with internal relations in the newsroom. Among these journalists, 18 per cent reported a "mismatch between my position and the position of the editorial". In Port Elizabeth, 44 per cent said that they had faced moral choices. Again, these choices pertained mostly to editorial decisions made in the newsroom setting. In Durban, while most respondents (96 per cent) said they had faced moral choices, they did not provide much indication about what these choices entailed. Given the contested nature of media ethics in South Africa, and the debates surrounding the self-regulatory system, it is somewhat surprising that more journalists did not see moral controversies reflected in their own professional lives.

South African newspapers are full of stories exposing corruption because, to a large extent, South African journalists see themselves as fighters of corruption. At times, this position creates moral dilemmas for journalists. A specific case in point is when the police want journalists to share their files or expose their sources:

> A couple of years ago, when I was doing a series of stories for my previous employer, I faced an ethical dilemma being a part of a team which had exposed alleged corruption and wrongdoing. The story was done and published. We suddenly had people asking to share information with them because they wanted to [pursue] criminal charges. This caused me the ethical dilemma. On the one hand, I am a law-abiding citizen and I want to help [the law] to succeed in its attempts to fight crime and wrongdoing. Thus, my law-abiding citizenship side was saying I should give them my files. But on the other side, I collected that information from my sources as a journalist and not as a police informer. I never told my sources that I was talking to them on behalf of the police and whatever they were telling me I was going to give it to the police. They thought they were talking to a journalist whose interest was that I was going to publish it and not pass it onto the police. So, if they hear that what they told me when they took me into their confidence, sat down with me and gave me this information for story purposes only, how would they feel if they hear that after telling my story I played the role of a police informant? [That] I then crossed the fence to the other side, played a police informer, and gave the information to the police. I was just not comfortable.

This response points to the awareness among South African journalists that, although they may be forced by law to surrender information to the police, and although such pressure is exerted upon them from time to time, this practice is frowned upon and is likely to fall foul of the Press Council's Code of Conduct in terms of independence and avoiding conflicts of interest. The public interest is at the centre of this code and its application by journalists.

Towards a contextual and multifaceted understanding of journalistic ethics in BRICS countries

BRICS journalists mentioned various ethical issues they faced in their daily practice of journalism ranging from self-doubts about the impact of their work in solving social issues and their ability to be objective, through worry about making the decision to put pressure (or not) on vulnerable persons to be their story subjects, to concern about the influence of the profit-making goals of their media organization and conflicted feelings about their own pursuit of money and connections in exchange for their pen. Brazilian journalists were concerned about the influence of owners on content and about journalists also acting as press advisors, while Russian journalists included in their examples of dilemmas the use of impersonation to get a story. In India, journalists spoke of the choice between covering a story when the subject was in a difficult situation and helping the subject, and also of sometimes having to choose between speed and quality. In China, journalists particularly mentioned pressure from censorship. South African journalists articulated their anguish when law enforcement agencies wanted information that was provided in confidence by sources, but a majority of them did not report having to make any major ethical decisions recently. In general, in all five countries, the primary and common dilemma journalists experienced was the pressure they felt from the politico-economic entanglements of their media outlet.

It appears that commercialization, privatization, and concentration as well as resulting alliances between the media and power elites in the political and economic spheres, sometimes in an atmosphere of underdeveloped accountability mechanisms and absence of fully functioning democratic institutions and also of a fully developed civil society, were at the root of some of the ethical issues in BRICS journalism.

The Russian case provides a clear example of how market forces work their impact on news media. Here, the market in general and the media market in particular are both marked by a lack of transparency (Vartanova & Smirnov, 2010). 'Informal intermediators' – people, firms, and organizations facilitating informal relationships between bureaucratic officials and private business – mushroomed in the late 1990s and the early 2000s. Such intermediation became a stable feature of the economic environment, and the informal contacts led, in turn, to a selective enforcement of the formal law (Paneyakh, 2008, cited in Olimpieva & Pachenkov, 2013). Respondents in the Olimpieva and Pachenkov (2013) study "believed that people employed in intermediary firms are closely related (by kinship or friendship) to state officials" (p. 1374). In fact, according to them, "the state officials themselves establish these (intermediary) firms in order to get additional 'informal' payments" (p. 1374). According to Resnyanskaya (2007), at the other end, "business elites bartered the loyalty and information support of their owned media for financial and economic preferences from the state" (p. 5).

India, which has a strong tradition of a free press, written into the constitution and rather fiercely guarded for the most part since Indian independence in 1947, provides another example of the impact of a predominantly commercial logic in the news media industry. In early 20th-century pre-independent India, the press had emerged as a tool to fight oppressive colonial rule. Thus, post-independence, the news media were hailed as the 'fourth pillar' of the Constitution of India, a testimony to the responsible role that the media were accorded in the world's largest democracy. Since the last couple of decades, however, there has been a rapid slide in this idealism due to pressures arising from commercialization. With the advent of the market logic in journalism in India, the free press tradition is wearing thin; capital and profit occupy prime positions, in turn impacting ownership that is increasingly concentrated and sometimes in the hands of politicians, overtly or covertly.

Brazil, China, and South Africa have experienced somewhat similar scenarios to those in Russia and India. It is then reasonable to suggest that the politico-economic complicity that marked the marketization of journalism, one in which profit seeking by media businesses became the norm and political intrusion became possible, created favourable conditions for media organizations and individual journalists to engage in ethically controversial reporting and editorial practices. An arena in which these politico-economic intrusions played out with implications for journalistic ethics was paid news.

In essence, respondent journalists from the BRICS countries interpreted paid news in many different ways, not just as writing for money and but also as bartering news articles and sometimes even suppressing news to form alliances with business/advertisers/government and even sources, to gain some cash, in-kind, or soft advantage. The definition included disguised forms of paid news that are not easy to detect, such as that which rewards advertisers with coverage or seeks influence in return for coverage. Ethical issues in journalism in the real world, particularly paid news and its various manifestations, are more complicated than a definition, however. Contrary to the clearly stated legal and ethical principles, in all five BRICS countries, about the practice of journalism and the use of the power of profession to gain personal favour, the picture on the ground, as narrated in the interviews, was more complicated: the issues were multifaceted and rooted in local political, economic, and socio-cultural circumstances.

While acknowledging the importance of the legal and ethical codes, most respondents admitted that a certain level of journalistic corruption, particularly the phenomenon of paid news, did exist in practice. Either they engaged in corrupt practices themselves or they reported the prevalence of these practices in the journalism of their country. Where journalists indicated that their organizations and supervisors either arranged to procure paid news or were directly engaged in it, some reported willing collusion, others that they could not escape the practice. Journalists believed that the level of corruption in their organization depended on the management's complicity in it, and further that the level may be higher in business reporting beats because businesses had the resources to pay for stories. When a journalist made a personal decision to write a paid article, it was most often motivated by money and sometimes by other types of benefits; in this scenario, paid news was seen simply as a transaction and sometimes as a way to compensate for low salaries.

Specifically, Russian and Chinese respondent journalists acknowledged that they engaged in writing articles for money, and so did Brazilian journalists but to a much smaller extent. Indian and South African respondents said they did not do paid news but acknowledged – Indian journalists much more so than South African journalists – that it was prevalent in their countries. Thus, ethical practice of sample journalists in India and South Africa was reportedly in synchrony with the ethical norm. In South Africa, on the whole, journalists reported a high sense of ethical awareness; they perceived themselves as very ethical and as upholding professional standards of journalism. Among them, there was widespread and outright rejection of payment for coverage and other forms of corruption, and their position on excluding any form of corruption from professional journalism was very clear. These findings seem to bear out the renewed emphasis on media ethics in the post-apartheid era in South Africa. Journalists in South Africa on the whole seem to be very aware of their ethical responsibilities and of the importance of self-regulation in face of renewed threats to impose stronger statutory regulation.

The empirical data for South Africa, and for India in particular, however, gives one pause; only one journalist in India and not a single journalist in South Africa directly acknowledged doing paid news. It could be concluded that, at least among sample journalists, practice matched the code of ethical conduct, but whether reported idealism and self-perception match reality is of course a different question. It is possible that respondents provided socially desirable answers, and in the case of India sometimes they did not answer the question (9 of 49 journalists in Kolkata and Pune), leaving open the possibility that at least some of the missing values were related to not wanting to acknowledge unethical practice. Further, Indian and to some extent South African journalists' responses about the prevalence of paid news among colleagues in face of their own reported avoidance of the practice also point to a third-person effect, i.e., a perception that others are more likely to be influenced by a communication, or in this case, to engage in a practice, than themselves (Davison, 1983). This is an 'ethical asynchrony' ascribed to peers and colleagues, pointing to a gap between normative idealism and the corrupt practice of their colleagues.

In India, paid news became so highly prevalent at the time of elections that the Election Commission of India had to step in. The commission created a structure of district-level committees to control paid news (*Election Commission Issues Guidelines*, 2014), and media houses were punished for engaging in this practice. In India, the free press tradition had instilled in journalists an understanding of ethical journalism practice; however, today, and particularly after the advent of the Internet, media content has deviated from ethical standards due to profit seeking and owner pressures (Ghosh, 2014). The politico-economic milieu of India, and the value change that has accompanied globalization in terms of materialism, have played a part in this change. Journalists subscribe to the norms of ethical journalism or at least affirm belief in them, but they do not always operate by these norms, particularly when it comes to the various forms of paid news or non-news, either due to pressure from superiors, or their own greed or need (journalists in India are not always well paid and work under contract rather than in permanent jobs). Thus, according to Narayanan (2015), Indian news media seem to have failed in their attempt to self-regulate. Noted journalist Panneerselvan has, however, indicated that a majority of the working journalists in India are ethical, and the few exceptions cloud the name of the entire fraternity in the eyes of the public (Narayanan, 2015).

In general, widespread corruption in a profession lowers the threshold of resistibility and leads to a general tolerance of such practice. In other words, corruption becomes commonplace, and moral authority resides in only those few who remain incorruptible. This is likely the case in Russia. Previous studies carried out in the first few post-Soviet decades (1990s–2000s) found that journalists' engagement in the practice of writing paid articles, termed in journalistic slang as *zakazuha* (ordered publications) and *dzhinsa* (paid article), in the political and commercial interests of their clients, was widespread (Pasti, 2004, 2010; Zassoursky, 2004). Empirical studies in the 1990s revealed that the condition of "the withdrawal of government authority in many spheres and the absence of control over this withdrawal created favourable conditions for the flourishing of corruption" (Levin & Satarov, 2000, pp. 116–117). At the same time, some Russian journalists in the BRICS study articulated what may be called an internal code of conduct, which included the following ethical principles: not to steal topics and sources from colleagues, not to betray colleagues, not to lie in their publications, i.e., to be honest with the reader, and to protect sources. These unwritten rules seemed to unite both idealists and pragmatists and provided a measure of self-regulation, based on having the same rules of conduct for each other, for their sources, and their audiences. For Russian journalists, a non-corrupt article is one that is honest, and written in the public interest, not in the interest of business or politics.

At the same time, in all five countries, there were respondents who articulated their opposition to paid news, considering it totally unprofessional. In India and South Africa, the sentiment that doing paid news was unprofessional practice was substantial but, at minimum, some journalists in all countries expressed a similar sentiment. Such opposition to paid news was articulated in strong language; paid news was "venal" and a "malaise", and persons who did this were not worthy of being called journalists. Indian respondent journalists condemned paid news and argued that it is anathema to professional journalism to provide articles for money. For the most part, they felt similarly strongly about advertorials and extortion to suppress news. In China too, the sentiment against extortion and advertorials was strong; these were considered unacceptable practices even when paid news was openly acknowledged and practiced.

China presents an interesting case. The notion of ethics in Chinese journalism practice is ambiguous arguably because of the complex interplay of the state, market, and society in shaping the nature of journalism in this transitional society. In other words, ethics is a multidimensional, even contested, system of philosophical concepts that has disciplinary impact on Chinese journalists. The interpretive model, 'ethical parallelism', describes the multiple understandings of ethics in Chinese journalism. It may be said that a majority of China's journalists are not likely to categorize the making of money in the practice of journalism as negative; in fact, it seems that most of them would use the practice of paid news as they do their job.

Ethical parallelism encompasses two dimensions in China. On the one hand, the market-driven process of professionalization for Chinese journalism, and certainly the three-decade-long introduction of Western mainstream journalism and communication theories, provoked a new set of notions for journalists and journalism to call for an autonomous position (by identifying themselves as information disseminators and public opinion influencers, and their profession as independent) in an Information and Communications Technology (ICT)-led development environment and an increasingly differentiated society. Journalists from both traditional and online media accepted this 'professional idealism', despite a history in which professionalism was substituted by a Marxist class struggle theory-based instrumentalism. On the other hand, many respondents also admitted that receiving money, particularly *Hongbao*, was also ethically right and had become a routine in their daily life.

Central to this dilemma is an ethical narrative emerging from the deeply rooted cultural tradition in China and the distinctive ways in which Chinese society is organized, a narrative that is different from the one that provides definitions of corruption in other parts of the world. In short, both idealism and realism (based in a localized concept of corruption) exist in Chinese journalism in parallel. This might help to understand the seemingly contradictory finding of a negative attitude towards corrupt behaviour among half of the respondent journalists from China as well as the engagement of more than half of these journalists in the production of paid news.

The question about what is considered ideally ethical journalism in China may not be easy to answer given the presence of ethical parallelism. Future researchers should engage actively with the dynamics of Chinese society, a society in rapid transition, characterized by an unevenness and disparity that has destroyed pre-reform China's system of ethics, which was a stabilizing influence on society. It was a society in which people felt less exploited and believed they received more justice, despite extreme poverty and the underdeveloped economic situation in the narrow sense of economic growth.

Hongbao is also common in other countries of the world, including India and possibly South Africa (to a much smaller degree), where several local names are used for the practice, but in the English language it is more commonly known as brown envelope journalism or simply envelope journalism because money or some other enticement is handed, usually in an envelope, to journalists on a reporting mission (Skjerdal, 2010). Some scholars argue that this practice should not be judged in terms of universal ethics but should be open to local understandings, including that gift giving is a cultural tradition in some countries and it is offensive to not accept the gift and, as already mentioned above, that the wages are insufficient to provide a living (Skjerdal, 2010).

To provide a more nuanced interpretation of the findings, we conclude by offering the following.

BRICS journalists in this study provided varied responses to the question about paid news. There was recognition among many journalists that paid news was unprofessional. Journalists' narratives about practice indicated ethical synchrony, ethical asynchrony, and ethical parallelism between norms and actions. For the most part, journalists reported that they followed norms. When norms about paid news were contradicted in practice, journalists indicated a willing and knowing subversion of these guidelines on part of their organization/themselves for the sake of gain and sometimes to compensate for poor wages, or they believed (in China) that paid news was not a departure from culturally situated norms in which relationships were important and the exchange of money was a way to maintain these relationships between source and journalist.

For China, a simplified and essentialized notion of journalism ethics is not suitable to advance understanding of ethics practice. In China's case, the reason is based in the socio-cultural milieu within China and its impact on journalistic practice. In other BRICS countries, where journalists do not receive adequate compensation, this notion of lack of fit of an essential ethic to the on-the-ground circumstances may also help to understand practice. In many of these newly emerging economies, even if pay is adequate, living standards are only now improving; people have made do for decades and the opportunity to enjoy material benefits for the first time, to catch-up, to make up for a backlog of deficit, may offset any qualms about exchanging money for their writing. In a previous research study on journalism ethics in India, accepting cash and some types of in-kind gifts including alcohol from sources were normatively rated between unacceptable and very unacceptable and were practiced rarely or never (Colaco & Ramaprasad, 2008). For taking complimentary tickets/passes for sports/other events from sources, the corresponding means were 2.85 (for acceptability of the practice) and 2.30 (for reported actual practice), where 3.0 stood respectively for "unsure" (for acceptability) and "sometimes" (for practice). Thus, some forms of envelope journalism are found acceptable in India too.

It may be said that, in general, in the BRICS countries, an ethical dualism prevails, albeit to differing extents, in which the idealism of an independent, transparent, responsible, and professional journalism does exist, but is accompanied by a real-world practice that deviates from this idealism. We must clarify the lines between theory and practice in the same time–space. In fact, journalists often "argue that media ethicists do not refer to the experiential and practical elements of the journalistic profession in their day-to-day ethical decision making. Instead, ethicists get bogged down by 'high' theory for which there are few practical reference points" (Rao & Lee, 2005, p. 100).

Corruption is not only a legal, ethical, and moral concept, but is also culturally situated. Journalists in all five BRICS countries believed in the idealism of non-corrupt or even anti-corrupt journalism, but also provided reasons for the presence of corruption in journalism. Their narratives did not present a standard conceptualization of corruption across the five countries, but instead offered a multi-layered interpretation within distinctive political and cultural traditions.

Notes

1 The *News of the World*, a newspaper published in the United Kingdom from 1843 to 2011, had a reputation for exposing VIPs' drug use, criminal acts, and sexual peccadilloes. It met its demise in part due to allegations that it hacked into mobile phones of crime victims, celebrities, and politicians. More information about the phone hacking scandal can be found at www.bbc.co.uk/news/uk-14070733.
2 *Publitsistika* is "the literature on the public-political questions. The publicist materials state not only facts owing to which a reader draws conclusions him/herself, but they also include different reasoning, summarising, proposing these or those conclusions" (Bogdanov & Vyazemsky, 1971, pp. 677–678). In the present time, *publitsistika* is highly valued and considered "one of the highest stages of journalistic creativity co-related with bright literary talent and a citizen's position" (Vinogradova, 2000, p. 45).

References

A comparative view of anti-corruption laws of India: A legal, regulatory, tax and strategic perspective. (2016). Retrieved from www.nishithdesai.com/fileadmin/user_upload/pdfs/Research%20Papers/A_Comparative_View_of_Anti-Corruption_Laws_of_India.pdf

Act 12. (2004). Prevention and Combating of Corrupt Activities Act South Africa. *An overview of anti-bribery and anti-corruption laws in Southern Africa.* Retrieved from www.nortonrosefulbright.com/knowledge/publications/137789/an-overview-of-anti-bribery-and-anti-corruption-laws-in-southern-africa

All-India Newspaper Editors' Conference. (2007). *Code of ethics.* Retrieved from www.unesco.org/fileadmin/MULTIMEDIA/HQ/CI/4.%20India%20AINEC%20code%20of%20ethics.pdf

Associacao Nacional De Jornais (ANJ) (n.d.). Retrieved from www.anj.org.br/maiores-jornais-do-brasil/

Avraamov, D. S. (1999). *Professional'naya etika zhurnalista* [The professional ethics of a journalist]. Moskva: MSU.

Bai, R. (2005). Media commercialization, entertainment, and the party-state: The political economy of contemporary Chinese television entertainment culture. *Global Media Journal, 4*(6), 1–54. Retrieved from http://s3.amazonaws.com/academia.edu.documents/35899537/Journal_article_-_Media_Commercialization__Entertainment__and_the_Party-State.pdf?AWSAccessKeyId=AKIAIWOWYYGZ2Y53UL3A&Expires=1488676865&Signature=IU7f9q%2ByxpnmOoX7JCgblZjcET8%3D&response-content-disposition=inline%3B%20filename%3DJournal_article_Media_Commercialization.pdf

Barbrook, R. (1988). *American theories of media deregulation.* Retrieved from www.imaginaryfutures.net/2007/01/19/american-theories-of-media-deregulation-by-richard-barbrook/

Bhattacharjee, A., Wang, L., & Banerjee, T. (2016, January). Media ownership and concentration in India. In E. M. Noam & The International Media Concentration Collaboration (Eds.), *Who owns the world's media? Media concentration and ownership around the world* (pp. 772–800). New York, NY: Oxford Scholarship Online.

Bogdanov, N. G., & Vyazemsky, B. A. (1971). *Spravochnik zhurnalista* [The handbook of a journalist]. Leningrad: Lenizdat.

Brazilian Information Access Law (#12.527/2011). (2011). Retrieved from http://repositorio.unb.br/bitstream/10482/17909/2/2015_LumaPolettiDutra.pdf

Brazilian Law (#4.898). (1965). Retrieved from www.planalto.gov.br/ccivil_03/leis/L4898.htm

Brazilian Law Against Corruption (#12.813/2013). (2013). Retrieved from http://www2.camara.leg.br/legin/fed/lei/2013/lei-12813-16-maio-2013-776005-norma-pl.html

Code of professional ethics of Russian journalist. (1994). Retrieved from http://ethicnet.uta.fi/russia/code_of_professional_ethics_of_russian_journalist

Colaco, B., & Ramaprasad, J. (2008). Receptions and rejections: Professional ethics of Indian journalists. Paper presented at the International Association for Media and Communication Research Annual Congress, Stockholm, Sweden.

Davison, W. P. (1983). The third-person effect in communication. *Public Opinion Quarterly, 47*(1), 1–15.

Election Commission issues guidelines to monitor news during Assembly elections in Haryana. (2014). Retrieved from www.dnaindia.com/india/report-election-commission-issues-guidelines-to-monitor-paid-news-during-assembly-elections-in-haryana-2014468

FENAJ. (2014). Retrieved from http://fenaj.org.br/wp-content/uploads/2014/06/04-codigo_de_etica_dos_jornalistas_brasileiros.pdf

GAN Business Anti-Corruption Portal. (2016, May). *Anti-Corruption Legislation.* Retrieved from www.business-anti-corruption.com/anti-corruption-legislation/china

Ghosh, J. (2014). Ethics of Indian news media: Aberrations and future challenges. *Global Media Journal-Indian Edition, 5*(2), 1–10. Retrieved from www.caluniv.ac.in/global-mdia-journal/ARTICLE-GMJ-DEC%202014/ARTICLE-%203.pdf

Hallin, D., & Mancini, P. (2004). *Comparing media systems: Three models of media and politics.* Cambridge, UK: Cambridge University Press.

He, Z. (2000). Corruption and anti-corruption in reform China. *Communist and Post-Communist Studies, 33*, 243–270.

India: New Anti-Corruption Law. (2014). Retrieved from www.loc.gov/law/foreign-news/article/india-new-anti-corruption-law/

India: The Prevention of Corruption Act, 1988. Retrieved from www.oecd.org/site/adboecdanti-corruptioninitiative/46814376.pdf

Kruckeberg, D., & Tsetsura, K. (2003). *A composite index by country of variables related to the likelihood of the existence of 'cash for news coverage'.* Retrieved from www.instituteforpr.org/files/uploads/Bribery_Index_2003.pdfwww.instituteforpr.org/wp-content/uploads/Bribery_Index_20031.pdf

Kumar, S. (2015). Five reasons why media monopolies flourish in India. *Scroll.in.* Retrieved from http://scroll.in/a/694139

Levin, M., & Satarov, G. (2000). Corruption and institutions in Russia. *European Journal of Political Economy, 16*(1), 113–132.

Lo, V. H., Chan, J. M., & Pan, Z. (2005). Ethical attitudes and perceived practice: A comparative study of journalists in China, Hong Kong and Taiwan. *Asian Journal of Communication, 15*(2), 154–172.

Lodamo, B., & Skjerdal, T. S. (2009). Freebies and brown envelopes in Ethiopian journalism. *Ecquid Novi: African Journalism Studies, 30*(2), 134–154.

McChesney, R. W. (2004). *The problem of the media: U.S. communication politics in the twenty-first century.* New York: Monthly Review Press.

Narayanan, N. (2015, March 19). Five ethical problems that plague Indian journalism. *Scroll.in.* Retrieved from http://scroll.in/article/714570/five-ethical-problems-that-plague-indian-journalism

News Broadcasters Association (2008, April). *Code of Ethics & Broadcasting Standards.* Retrieved from http://www.nbanewdelhi.com/assets/uploads/pdf/code_of_ethics_english.pdf
- news.xinhuanet.com. (2014). *Chinese journalism development report.* Retrieved from http://en.theorychina.org/chinatoday_2483/whitebooks/201504/t20150407_321169.shtml

Nordenstreng, K. (2010). The Russian media system: Something special? In E. Vartanova (Ed.), *Content, channels and audiences in the new millennium: Interaction and interrelations* (pp. 183–186). Moscow: Faculty of Journalism, Moscow State University. Retrieved from www.uta.fi/jour/henkilokunta/nordenstreng/Russian_Media_System.pdf

Olimpieva, I., & Pachenkov, O. (2013). Corrupt intermediaries in post-socialist Russia: Mutations of economic institutions. *Europe-Asia Studies, 65*(7), 1364–1376.

Painter, J. (Ed.). (2013). *India's media boom: The good news and the bad.* Oxford, UK: Reuters Institute for the Study of Journalism.

Paneyakh, E. (2008). *Pravila igry dlya russkogo predprinimatelya* [The rules of the game for the Russian entrepreneur]. Moscow: Kolibri.

Pankin, A. (2010, May 25). Democracy is dangerous for the media. *The Moscow Times.*

Pasti, S. (2004). *Rossiiskiy zhurnalist v kontekste peremen. Media Sankt-Peterburga* [A Russian journalist in context of change: Media of St. Petersburg]. Tampere: Tampere University Press. Retrieved from www.uta.fi/cmt/yhteystiedot/henkilokunta/svetlanapasti/publications/pastinkirja.pdf

Pasti, S. (2010). A new generation of journalists. In A. Rosenholm, K. Nordenstreng, & E. Trubina (Eds.), *Russian mass media and changing values* (pp. 57–75). London: Routledge.

Pasti, S., & Nordenstreng, K. (2013). Paradoxes of journalistic profession: Case of Russia in the context of the BRICS countries. In E. Vartanova (Ed.), *World of media 2012 yearbook of Russian media and journalism studies* (pp. 243–268). Moscow: Media Mir.

Paulino, F. O., & Silva, L. M. (2013). *Comunicação Pública em Debate: Ouvidoria e Rádio.* Brasília: Editora UnB, 17–21. Retrieved from http://repositorio.unb.br/bitstream/10482/14774/3/Livro_ComunicacaoPublicaDebate.pdf

Philo, G., & Miller, D. (2001). *Market killing: What the free market does and what social scientists can do about it.* Essex: Pearson Education Limited.

Press Council of India. (2010a). *Norms of Journalistic Conduct.* Retrieved from http://presscouncil.nic.in/OldWebsite/NORMS-2010.pdf

Press Council of India. (2010b). *Report on paid news.* Retrieved from http://presscouncil.nic.in/OldWebsite/CouncilReport.pdf

Press Council of India. (2015, March). *Principles and Ethics.* Retrieved from http://presscouncil.nic.in/Content/62_1_PrinciplesEthics.aspx

Ramaprasad, J., Liu, Y., & Garrison, B. (2012). Ethical use of new technologies: Where do Indian journalists stand? *Asian Journal of Communication, 22*(1), 98–114.

Rao, S., & Lee, S. T. (2005). Globalizing media ethics? An assessment of universal ethics among international political journalists. *Journal of Mass Media Ethics, 20*, 99–120.

Resnyanskaya, L. (Ed.). (2007). *SMI n politika* [Mass media and politics]. Moscow: Aspekt Press.

Ristow, B. (2010). *Cash for coverage: Bribery of journalists around the world.* Retrieved from Institution National Endowment for Democracy. www.cima.ned.org/resource/cash-for-coverage-bribery-of-journalists-around-the-world/

Russian Federal Law (No. 273-FZ). (2008). *On combating corruption.* Retrieved from http://www.rusfintrade.ru/files/article/2816/20170517_3.pdf

Russian Periodical Press Market 2009: Condition, Trends, Prospects. (2010). Moscow: Federal Agency for the Press and Mass Communication of the Russian Federation. Retrieved from www.fapmc.ru

Several rules on prohibiting paid news. (2014). Retrieved from http://press.gapp.gov.cn/reporter/contents/250/205920.html

Shevtsova, L. (2005). *Putin's Russia.* Revised and expanded edition. Washington, DC: Carnegie Endowment for International Piece.

Singh, D. V. (2014, November). Media concentration and diversity in media: Study of Indian media ownership patterns in the context of diversity debate. *Mass Media – A Communication Research Journal, 3*(31), 13–18. Delhi, India.

Skjerdal, T. S. (2010). Research on brown envelope journalism in the African media. *African Communication Research, 3*(3), 367–406.

Telecommunication Regulatory Authority of India. (2013, February 15). Consultation paper on issues relating to media ownership, No. 01/2013. New Delhi.

Terzis, G. (Ed.). (2008). *European media governance: National and regional dimensions.* Bristol, UK: Intellect Books.

The Cable Television Networks (Regulation) Act, 1995. (1995). Retrieved from http://delhi.gov.in/wps/wcm/connect/DOIT_EXCISE/excise/notified+areas/notified+areas1. For amended act, see http://www.trai.gov.in/sites/default/files/Cable_TV_Amendment_Act_2011_final.pdf

Toffler, A. (1980). *The third wave.* New York: William Morrow.

Tunstall, J. (1986). *Communications deregulation: The unleashing of America's communications industry.* Oxford: Basil Blackwell.

Vartanova, E. (2012). Russian media model in post-Soviet dynamics. In D. Hallin & P. Mancini (Eds.), *Comparing media systems beyond the Western world* (pp. 119–142). Cambridge, UK: Cambridge University Press.

Vartanova, E., & Smirnov, S. (2010). Contemporary structure of the Russian media industry. In A. Rosenholm, K. Nordenstreng, & E. Trubina (Eds.), *Russian mass media and changing values* (pp. 21–40). London: Routledge.

Vinogradova, S. M. (2000). Slagaemye zhurnalistskoi professii (Components of the journalistic profession). In S. G. Korkonosenko (Ed.), *Osnovy Tvorcheskoi Deyatelnosti Zhurnalista* [The foundations of journalistic creativity.] (pp. 7–58). St. Petersburg: Obshchestvo 'Znanie' Sankt-Peterburga i Leningradskoi oblasti.

Ward, S. J. A. (2013). *Global media ethics: Problems and perspectives.* Malden, MA: Blackwell Publishing Ltd.

Weaver, D. H., & Wilhoit, G. C. (1986). *The American journalist: A portrait of news people and their work.* Bloomington: Indiana University Press.

World Democracy Audit. (2017). Retrieved from www.worldaudit.org/democracy.htm. Society Knowledge .

Yang, W., Shi, E., Peterson, T. P., Park, R. (2014, January). Understanding China's Approach to Anticorruption. Retrieved from https://www.mmlawus.com/newsitem/pdf/Corporate_Counsel_China_article_8740033177497.pdf

Zassoursky, I. (2004). *Media and power in post-Soviet Russia.* Armonk, NY: M. E. Sharpe.

Zhao, Y. (2000). From commercialization to conglomeration: The transformation of the Chinese press within the orbit of the party state. *Journal of Communication, 50,* 3–26.

Zhao, Y. (2004). *The state, the market, and media control in China: Who owns the media,* 179–212. Retrieved from www.sfu.ca/cmns/faculty/zhao_y/B10%20Zhao%20179-212%202004.pdf

4
GENDER

Towards equality?

Nagamallika Gudipaty, Jyotika Ramaprasad, Svetlana Pasti, Cláudia Lago, Xianzhi Li, and Ylva Rodny-Gumede

Women in the news media: historical parallels in BRICS

Globally, the term 'feminization' of journalism has been in vogue for more than half a century (Devraj, 2010) although it was a struggle for women journalists across the world to find their feet and stand up for themselves in a field that was clearly associated with the masculine in terms of power and status in society (Djerf-Pierre, 2007). A few women pioneers defied the social order and joined the profession very early in the history of journalism in various parts of the world including in the BRICS nations, paving the way for the entry of women into the hitherto male bastion.

In Brazil, until the first half of the 20th century, journalism was practiced not only by journalism professionals, but also by writers and artists such as the dramatist Nelson Rodrigues. In her research on the trajectories of Brazilian female writers of the 19th century, Muzarte (2003) found many feminists who were pioneer journalists or founders of newspapers and journals: "[These feminists] had a sizable share of responsibility in the fundamental role of awakening the Brazilian women's consciousness. There was Josefina Álvares de Azevedo (Recife, 1851 as cited in Muzarte, 2003), journalist and dramatist, whose fight for suffragism was outstanding". Muzarte (2003) explains the difficulty in limiting the pioneers to one profession alone, given the vast variety of fields they contributed to:

> The number of women in the nineteenth century who were writing in books or journals is huge, and their acting field was enormous; they lived in several regions of Brazil, belonged to more than one social class, were Aryans or Africans . . . , in a way that if I were to speak of the women in the nineteenth century press, I would be restraining myself to a region or city, or to one journal and to a determined time.

(p. 225)

This group did not even include the women who wrote for magazines, an important sphere of action, even though what they wrote was in conformity with the female ideals of that time.

It was only in the 20th century that journalism reinforced itself as a profession in Brazil. The mainstream press at the time was staffed exclusively by men, and any women who worked in these offices in the beginning of the century were mostly cleaners, secretaries, or telephone operators. The exception was women's magazines, especially feminist journals, which employed women as journalists. A pre-eminent example is that of the writer, dramatist, journalist, cartoonist, translator, and feminist Patrícia Galvão (1910–1962), known as Pagu, whose work and actions inspire Brazilian feminists even today.

With time, expressly from the 1950s onwards, women began to get space in newsrooms. Regina Helena de Paiva Ramos, in a book on Brazilian female journalists (2010), wrote stories about women such as Carmen da Silva, Judith Patarra, Lyba Fridman, and more than 50 other women, who helped to change Brazilian journalism, fighting against prejudices in and out of newsrooms. These women faced countless adversities; they were restricted to writing features and other soft stories and faced impediments to becoming reporters, due to the prejudices present against women journalists. Until the '70s, journalism was considered an 'unsuitable' profession for females because of the atmosphere of bohemia, considered inappropriate for women, surrounding the profession. Only in the late '70s and '80s the participation of females in the press built momentum, with leading positions being occupied by women, until journalism became, in the subsequent decades, a predominantly female profession. The rise of women in the profession is related to the modernization of newsrooms as well as to the requirement of a degree to enter into professional journalism practice, which gradually allowed the entry of journalists trained in universities.

In Russia, journalism appeared as a masculine occupation since the Tsar Peter the Great started the first Russian newspaper, *Vedomosti* (the oldest Russian word meaning Gazette), in 1702 and became its editor. But soon, Ekaterina II, empress of Russia, 1729–1796, established a magazine, *Vsiakaiavsiachina* (Sundries), in 1769, and began to write for it. She also started another magazine, *Sobesednik Liubitelei Rossiiskogo Slova* (the Colloquist of Russian Word-Lovers), between 1783 and 1784. Her example inspired other educated women to engage in journalism.

In Tsarist Russia, between 1901 and 1916, more than 850 women were active in journalism (Farris, 2001). Until the October socialist revolution of 1917, there was only one female in the Union of Journalists among 460 members. In 1927, females accounted for 7 per cent and in 1929 for 10 per cent. In the 1960s, women comprised 25 per cent of the local press; in the 1970s, they comprised 35 per cent of the various media, and by the beginning of the 1990s, they accounted for 37 per cent of this group (Svitich, 2000). The feminization of journalism has intensified since the fall of communism and the collapse of the Soviet Union in 1991, and with the start of the liberalization of the media and of the labour market, when the Communist Party and the state stopped the total supervision of media and their personnel policies.

In the 19th century, journalism in India was male dominated, although a few women journalists, especially those working in the Indian language press, played significant roles in the freedom movement. Hemant Kumari Chaudhurani (born in 1868) became the editor of a Hindi magazine called *Sugrahini*, and Mokshoday-ani published the first issue of a Bengali magazine, *Banga Mahila*, in 1870, which stood up for women's rights and pledged it would fight for women's causes (South Asian Research Centre for Advertisement, Journalism & Cartoons [SARCAJC], n.d.). In the 1930s, the years preceding Indian independence, Homai Vyarawalla, the first woman photojournalist in India, covered some memorable moments in India's struggle for independence and in the immediate post-independence period (Tiwari, 2014). Immediately after India's independence in 1947, there was not much progress in terms of the number of women who entered the profession, either on the desk or as reporters in both English and regional daily newspapers. Several papers did not have a single woman. All India Radio, the state radio, did have a few women from the '40s onwards, but these women worked as newsreaders and professional artists. In the '50s and '60s, a few pioneering women such as Prabha Dutt and Usha Rai made a mark despite their trepidation about surviving the harsh working conditions. It was only during the '80s, when the state-run national television broadcaster Doordarshan came into being, that more women joined the profession as newscasters and anchors (Bhardwaj, 2014).

In Chinese feudal society, women were constrained by societal prejudices and were not allowed to be educated. They were unable to fight for their rights under this system, leaving the profession of journalism completely devoid of females. It was only by the end of the 19th century, after the Reform Movement of 1898, that there was a presence of females in the profession. This Reform Movement, with its charter of 'reforming politics' and 'reforming law', was the first profound social transformation initiative and led to the first enlightenment movement in modern China. It was at this time that thoughts about women's liberation and gender equality began to be formed, leading to the women's liberation movement. In modern China, the growth of women in journalism was spurred by this liberation movement. This period proved positive for Chinese women; during this time, the first women's newspaper came into being and the first female journalist joined the profession (Song, 2003). Soon, more than 40 women's newspapers were established with about ten women journalists present in the profession (Fang, 1987). Although small in number, these women journalists had an important influence on the history of women in journalism in China, writing against the propaganda of patriotic ideology and about democratic revolution, women's liberation, and so on.

Women in South Africa have historically been excluded from the education and employment opportunities provided to men. The situation was no different in the news media for women of all colours (Rodny-Gumede, 2012). Things have, however, come a long way since the '80s, when women began to take an active part in journalism. In accordance with the strict racial hierarchies of the day, there were few coloured people in newsrooms and none were black Africans (Rossouw, 2005). Rossouw (2005), a female journalist, talks about the time when she first started out in the profession in the 1980s. At the time, she was one of few female journalists and the only female journalist of colour in the newsroom. While race might have been the overarching reason for unjust policies, double injustice was often done to women in the newsroom, as well as in other sectors of society, through patriarchal and sexist attitudes that prevented women of all colours from the same job opportunities as men (South African Truth and Reconciliation Commission, 1998).

Women in the news media: current situation

As the journalism histories of the BRICS countries have witnessed, the last couple of decades have seen a shift in the presence of women in media and journalism, as in other professions and public life in general, due to socio-political and economic changes such as higher levels of education, urbanization, and economic liberalization, rather than any particular move towards gender equality. The post '90s period witnessed a new social order in Brazil and Russia and economic liberalization in India. Similarly, modern China embraced capitalism in the '70s, and South Africa changed dramatically following its democratic elections in 1994. Such sweeping changes in the BRICS nations' economies not only increased the influence of media in public life but also brought changes within the media industry itself. Moreover, they helped to begin the process of feminization of media (if feminization simply means an increase in number of women in the profession), leading to an increase in the number of women in training schools and especially in the broadcast and online media, in a pattern that resembled the global trend of an increasing number of women in the workforce (Standing, 1999).

In the book, *The Global Journalist*, Weaver and Willnat (2012) indicate that the average proportion of woman journalists across the 29 countries and territories included in the 2012 edition "was 41 per cent, an increase from 33 per cent reported as an average in the first edition of *The Global Journalist* in 1998" (Weaver & Willnat, 2012, p. 530). Several studies indicate the trend of increased participation of women in news organizations in the BRICS nations too. For instance, female and male journalists are almost equal in number at around 50 per cent in South Africa (Byerly, 2013), but they exceed the number of male journalists in Brazil (63 per cent) (Mick & Lima, 2013), China (53 per cent) (Zhang & Su, 2012), and Russia (60 per cent) (Pasti, Chernysh, & Svitich, 2012). In India, although the number of women journalists is on the increase, it is very difficult to arrive at a definite number, given the rapid growth of the regional language media. A study by the International Women's Media Foundation (IWMF) (2011a) found that women's representation had doubled to 25 per cent of the workforce across companies surveyed in India from that of Gallagher's 1995 study, which placed the number at 12 per cent. Even with this progress, men still dominated by a 4:1 ratio. However, Byerly's (2013) study indicated that female journalists formed 18 per cent of the journalist population in India.

In a 2012 study, Mick and Lima (2013) found that Brazilian journalists as a professional category were mostly female, young, and white. Only 23.7 per cent of the journalists were of African origin, although 50.7 per cent of the Brazilian population consists of people of Afro descent (Mick & Lima, 2013). Most were up to 30 years of age (59 per cent) and female (63 per cent). The study further indicated that journalism was a popular programme in universities and in higher education courses (graduation being made mandatory to practice the profession, from 1969 to 2009[1]), particularly among young women (Mick & Lima, 2013). The increase in the number of women journalists in Brazil is attributed to their higher levels of education compared to men.

Urbanization in Russia brought changes in the gender structure of journalists. The economic crisis of 2008–2009 in Russia led to large-scale feminization of journalism as more women than men opted to be journalists. Female journalists were twice as numerous as male journalists in small cities, while in mid-sized and big cities, their number was almost equal.[2] This shows that small city journalism is feminizing faster than big city journalism. Perhaps, feminization has to do with the higher educational qualifications and the longer life expectancy of females in Russia (Pasti, Chernysh, & Svitich, 2012). A Union of Russian Journalists 2010 study of the regional press found that in the provinces, the typical editor in chief was female, aged 45 to 60, with higher education in the humanities, and with journalistic experience of ten to 20 years (Kasytin, 2010).

Women journalists in India too tend to be well educated, with university degrees or post-graduate degrees, as well as professional qualifications such as diplomas in journalism and/or mass communication. According to the International Federation of Journalists (IFJ), women armed with university degrees and technological knowhow, and who are adept at working for long hours at the desk, had become successful in the field in recent years; this coincided with the arrival and growth of online and social media, including a number of news and current affairs webzines (IFJ, 2009). Today, women are found in every type of journalism, ranging from entertainment and lifestyle to political, economic, and business, and even sports news (IFJ, 2009). However, unlike the trend in Russia, in India, women are more likely to be found in urban and regional centres like Delhi, Kolkata, Hyderabad, and Pune than in rural centres as almost all news organizations are located in large cities with a large number of employees. In smaller semi-urban towns, generally an organization will have just the reporting staff or stringers who send news to the regional centres, made possible by extensive digitization of news media operations. This optimizes establishment costs for news organizations.

Zhang, Zhang, and Lin (2014) indicate that women made up 51.5 per cent of Chinese journalists, while men constituted 48.5 per cent; the average age of these journalists was 32 years. A study of the living conditions of Chinese online journalists confirmed the finding of a larger presence of women in online media (59.5 per cent women and 40.5 per cent men) (Zhou, Xie, & Kou, 2014). The study also indicated that it is young people (average age of 29.1 years) who are joining the profession. According to a survey by the Chinese Universities Media

Alliance, Communication University of China, the proportion of male to female students is 36:64 (IPIN, 2015). This large gender gap in education also results in more women journalists.

Similar to other BRICS nations, in South Africa too there was an increase in the number of females who were joining journalism schools (Nordenstreng, 2009). South Africa boasts of having reached a gender parity of 50/50 in its journalistic workforce as well as in arts, culture, and gender equality reporting. Made and Morna (2009) found that women journalists dominated financial/economic and business reporting and comprised 40 per cent of sports reporters.

Digitization as a factor in feminization of the journalism profession

The rise of computerization and Internet technologies also created greater opportunities to empower women and transform gender relations (Green & Adam, 1999). Though initially computer and Internet technologies were deemed a masculine domain due to their "American military-industrial-academic complex" (Van Zoonen, 2002, p. 10), later, these technologies began to be used for peaceful forms of communication and experimentation, and were thus seen as feminine domains too. Haraway and Randolph (1997) suggested that "new ICTs in essence are feminine media and this new technology forms a basis for a society where women are potentially liberated and they are more suited for a life in the digital era" (p. 43).

Digitization has also changed the form of journalism and created new opportunities for women in most Western nations. Thus, once a male bastion, journalism now has an increased presence of women, though limited to certain classes and subcultures (IFJ, 2009). In India, for example, the software boom increased the number of women working as journalists, although they are still in the minority (IFJ, 2009). Working from home, remote editing, and mobile communication have reduced the need to work onsite, allowing women to reinvent themselves by writing columns or blogs online (Franks, 2013a). The structural hierarchy present in a traditional newsroom is absent in a networked organization as it builds an ethic of "community, consensus and communication", all central features of femininity (Jenkins, 1999, p. 236).

Equality illusion?

Despite the factors that have led to an increase in the number of women in the profession, lack of gender equality still manifests in terms of fewer women in senior positions and the pay gap between male and female journalists (Franks, 2013b; Griffin, 2014) in most countries.

As the IWMF (2011a) report on the status of women in the news media indicated, women held only 26 per cent of the governing and 27 per cent of the top management jobs. The report further stated that women represented only a third

(33 per cent) of the full-time journalism workforce in 522 companies. This is definitely an improvement over the situation described in Gallagher's pioneering 1995 international study, conducted in 239 nations, which showed that women occupied an average of only 12 per cent of the top management positions (Gallagher and von Euler, 1995). Gallagher and von Euler pointed out that the term 'feminization' was something of a red herring: "Even if the lower ranks of media organizations accommodate a growing number of women, there is no evidence that the upper echelons of the media have become 'feminized'" (p. 1). This perhaps remains true even today to a large extent, though there are variations within different regions of the world. IWMF (2011a) findings indicate that there is a higher representation of women in governance and top management within both Eastern Europe (33 per cent and 43 per cent respectively) and Nordic Europe (36 per cent and 37 per cent respectively) compared to other regions. In Lithuania, for example, women dominate the reporting ranks of junior and senior professional levels (79 per cent and 71 per cent respectively), and their representation is nearing parity in the middle and top management ranks (IWMF, 2011a). In some individual nations in the Asia and Oceania region too, women outnumber men at that level, despite the fact that for the region as a whole only 13 per cent of the senior management is female.

With the exception of Russia, where women were in a particularly strong position, nearing parity in top management and holding around a third of governance positions (IWMF, 2011b, p. 14), the BRICS countries exemplify the smaller representation of women in senior management positions. In Brazil, although women are a majority in the profession, only 8.7 per cent of them have incomes higher than ten minimum wages (2,700 USD approximately) as against 17.8 per cent of men (Mick & Lima, 2013). As the highest wages are paid to those in management positions, one can surmise that, although they form only 36 per cent of the journalistic workforce, males occupy most of these positions. According to Neves (2013), "in high level positions, the gap in pay between men and women is still quite large: in 2010, women earned the equivalent of 63.8 per cent of the men's wages" (p. 410).

In India, the well-established and strong media landscape is full of female journalists. Yet, while the advantage of class, caste, and higher education has seen some women climb to the top rungs of the profession, the majority of women journalists today are still concentrated in the middle and lower rungs of the profession. In one study, more than half of the respondents (53.33 per cent), of a total of 138, estimated that women comprised less than 10 per cent of top level management in positions such as board members, executives, chief financial officers (CFOs), and general managers (IFJ, 2015). Also, while more men are found in full-time contract positions, large numbers of women in the country are moving or being pushed into freelance jobs.

In China, a 2013 survey of women journalists in Shanghai found that while 94 per cent had a bachelor's or higher degree, very few (9 per cent) had moved into the executive and management levels (Female Journalist Work Committee of Shanghai Journalists Association [FJWCSJA], 2014).

In South Africa, there is an increase in the number of women journalists at the entry and middle level, but they are underrepresented in senior positions; for instance, Daniels (2014) found that only 12 out of 43 South African editors were female. A South African National Editors' Forum (SANEF) audit of gender equity and work relations for women in the news media showed that racism and sexism abound in South Africa (SANEF, 2006). Rabe (2006) argues that despite a constitution built on human rights such as anti-racism and anti-sexism, the data from the SANEF 2006 study indicates that discriminatory practice, structural inequalities, prejudices, patriarchy, and sexism are prevalent in South African newsrooms. Further, affirmative action policies of news organizations also do not remove the imbalances in salary structures or sexism at the workplace; there are several obstacles for most women to advance in their careers (Daniels, 2014; Made & Morna, 2009) as they face problems in balancing their professional life with family commitments. The glass ceiling for women exists in terms of managerial decision-making roles, equal pay, and lack of women-friendly organizations including access to childcare, and government policies that may be poor in monitoring the implementation of its pro-women policies in most organizations.

Studies of Western media reveal that one of the main reasons for gender imbalance, especially in senior positions, is the nature of responsibilities that women confront. Family commitments and other responsibilities far outweigh career choices in the long run for women. Often women find themselves juggling both responsibilities or giving up the profession because the requirements of exacting positions such as news reporter and senior editor, with daily deadlines and short delivery intervals, are difficult for most to meet (Franks, 2013b; Wihbey, 2015). The executive editor of *The Miami Herald*, Aminda Marqués Gonzalez, articulated the situation well:

> Journalism is hard work, with irregular and intense hours [and] women still do the bulk of childrearing and day-to-day maintenance of the home. . . . [Most of] the women in my peer group who had kids . . . quit.
> *(Griffin, 2014, http://niemanreports.org/articles/where-are-the-women/)*

The question then arises: are we living in a world of 'equality illusion' (Banyard, 2010, as cited in Cerqueira, Cabecinhas, & Magalhães, 2016)? Is feminization merely reflected in numbers and not in the quality of engagement of women in the profession? Will women in traditional organizational structures continue to face the glass ceiling?

Gendered women

Despite the larger presence of women as professional writers and presenters of news in the field of journalism, they continue to be marked as the 'other'; as 'different' from their male colleagues (Chambers, Steiner, & Fleming, 2005). Male journalists are considered neutral and professional, while females are 'gendered' as their work is defined and judged by their femininity (Chambers et al., 2005). The term, 'female journalist' itself seems pejorative to some, as it is a label that clings automatically to media workers who happen to be female, despite their insistence on being identified only as journalists (Sneha, 2012). Vigil (2016) argues:

> As a writer who happens to be a woman, the value of my writing and the content of my work should not be dictated by the fact that I am a woman. No one ever precedes word [sic] 'journalist' with 'male' like they do 'female'. They're just journalists.

Yet, it appears that sexism and prejudices are normalized through everyday practices in most organizations to such an extent that they are accepted even by women journalists (Steiner, 2012). A recent study of the role of gender in journalist–politician interactions among Russian and Swedish journalists concluded that "gender appears to the journalists as a significant factor in their interaction with politicians" (Voronova, 2014, p. 163). In particular, the Russian case showed that "light coquetry" to elicit information was approved not only by male bosses and colleagues but also by females; in fact, "A political editor in Moscow said that all [journalistic] pools, in the offices of the president and prime minister, mainly consist of girls" (Voronova, 2014, p. 161).

In South Africa, inequality or gender imbalance is apparent in the nature of work assigned, work conditions, and the attitude of the industry (Made & Morna, 2009; Rabe, 2006). Affirmative action policies of media organizations may give women access to jobs but do not remove preconceived notions about what women should or should not do within the realm of their profession. This points to a gap between the statistics confirming gender equality in the newsroom on the one hand and what research tells us about women's experiences in the newsroom on the other (Rodny-Gumede, 2012, 2015).

The BRICS study

While the literature indicates an increase in the number of women in the news media in recent times, the situation at the ground level in terms of gender equality and neutrality in media organizations, especially in new economies such as the BRICS nations, has yet to be established empirically. This chapter focuses on the issue of feminization of journalism in the BRICS nations, in terms of its status and influence on the profession, as articulated by journalists. Journalists in the BRICS study were interviewed to ascertain whether the ratio of male to female journalists had changed in their media outlets in the past five to ten years, and whether gender / increase in female journalists had influenced pay, assignments, and opportunities in the organization, as well as the career of respondent journalists, to any significant degree.

Findings

Increasing number of female journalists

The interviewees in this study indicated an increase in the number of female journalists in the last five to ten years in the various media outlets. In Russia, the economic crisis of 2008–2009 led to a large-scale feminization of journalism as more women than men opted for the profession. Further, the growing disinterest in the profession among men contributed to this trend. Young male journalists did not perceive journalism as a promising profession for themselves mostly because of the imbalance between the level of salaries and the demands of the work. The desirable occupations for them were media management and business: "We strive to get a job in media management with media products or in business. There you can earn. And if you are employed in a mere craft you get such a ridiculous salary". A St. Petersburg female journalist corroborated this: "Men prefer to join public relations and marketing because they have to provide for their family. Many male political and economic commentators have left their jobs". This journalist, however, also indicated other reasons for the reduction in the number of men in journalism: "Our online media does not have men at all as we write a lot about statistics and monitor different databases; it is hard work and requires concentration and men are not interested". In a St. Petersburg online media outlet, a female journalist said,

> They run away from [the media outlet] very quickly and say that they cannot work at such a tempo. Among the correspondents, we have more women.... Although the commercial department is headed by a male, all the employees working under him are females.

In India, in the two metro sample cities, although the total number of employees in online media was ten or fewer, the majority were women. A female journalist in India said, "Over the years, the media industry has been flooded with women taking up odd media jobs. There are some camera women as well in the industry, which was not the norm a few years ago". Unlike a few years ago, young women from the urban milieu or those who migrated from rural areas to cities, to pursue higher education, were ready to take up jobs with irregular working hours and in places far away from home. A young female journalist indicated that "In the earlier days, parents did not consider [journalism to be] a fit profession for girls, but now they are okay and happy that their daughters have taken up journalism". This is despite the view of male respondents that it is not easy for women to work in the field. As one male respondent said, "Journalism is not a very easy field, and it requires a lot of mettle and is a little risky". The past limited presence of women in the journalistic workplace was reportedly due to certain social barriers: long hours, late shifts, and safety concerns, and covering beats such as crime, which meant visiting the crime scene and being around the police who may not always use appropriate language.

More recently, some journalism organizations in India have created an enabling environment for women to enter journalism, including a greater acceptance by men. Women in turn have been inspired to enter the profession due to the presence of prominent female journalists as role models. Some media outlets like Delhi's NDTV and Hyderabad's CVR Health television channel have encouraged more participation by women. One male journalist from NDTV said, "[Ours] is a woman friendly organisation". A Hyderabad journalist said, "When I first started working in this company, there were only five female staff, but now there are 50 [out of a total of 400 employees]". Another said, "[The increase in number] is healthy competition, which is a good sign. It reflects on the growth of journalism".

In China, in all the media outlets surveyed, there was a clear sense that the ratio of female to male journalists had grown substantially. In South Africa too, interviewees indicated that there was an increase in the number of female journalists, but the news media are still very male dominated. Still, a female newspaper journalist said, "There are probably more opportunities for women in news media today than twenty years ago".

Glass ceiling

The perception of male and female interviewees was that gender in general did not matter in the profession; in the words of an Indian male journalist, "I feel that gender is no longer so important in journalism now; it is only the kind of work you end up doing" that is important. The BRICS data tell a different story. Across all BRICS nations, women were found mostly at the entry levels, while men dominated the senior and management positions. In Russia, the man is at the top of the pyramid and there is a top–down flow of communication, while typically the woman is at the centre and everything revolves around her; this provides for an interesting dynamic. In the words of a female journalist,

> I [a woman] can drink coffee with a reporter, and sometimes scold, and sometimes praise, bypassing the chief of the department. That is, the woman is in the centre of the circle and around her it is as if the planets revolve . . . and for men, it is a strict hierarchy.

Still, the dominance of men in managerial positions is clear. A Russian journalist summed up the situation thus: "But let's put it this way; if the bulk of working journalists are women, males still occupy managerial positions more often". A male journalist in India said, "The share of female numbers is growing, not so much in top management but much more at the junior level". A female Indian journalist indicated that "Men dominate at the higher positions, but at the newsroom level it is more or less equal participation".

In China, the respondents unanimously indicated that although women journalists were far more numerous than male journalists were, the majority of leaders in their own news agencies were men. On the whole, while only a small proportion of respondents in China believed that there were gender differences in professional skills, reference was made to the traditionally accepted role of women. Commenting on these traditional values, a male respondent in Wuhan said, "Chinese culture values men's work done outside the home, while women's work centres around the home". A female respondent from online media added:

> Chinese society is dominated by men. With regard to gender roles, Chinese culture emphasizes that men should take on more responsibilities at work. At the same time, women are supposed to spend more time in managing their families, including maintaining a healthy marriage and raising children.

Having a child was particularly responsible for the fact that in China women journalists in the middle- or high-level positions still account for a small proportion of the total workforce as compared with those in entry-level positions. A female journalist said, "Once a woman decides to give birth to a child, it's hard for her to be fully engaged in work because raising a child takes a considerable amount of time and energy". A male journalist concurred, "Women are certainly more hard-working before giving birth to children than the men, but after that, it changes". In South Africa too, a female journalist voiced a similar sentiment:

> Women still struggle to advance in their careers and often have to let go of their aspirations to advance early in their careers. . . . South African women, despite help at home, often [do] what other women around the world do; juggle family commitments with a work life. The fact remains that women simply cannot put in the same number of hours as their male colleagues.

Thus, in South Africa, while "The number of female journalists has certainly grown, we still do not see women advancing to more senior positions. . . . This is a serious problem". The majority of female journalists overwhelmingly stated that more female journalists in the newsroom did not necessarily translate into women having more power in the newsroom or increased influence over news agendas, as there were no women in senior positions. In the words of a South African female journalist, "Gender equality in the newsroom does not necessarily mean that women wield more power".

Some male journalists too expressed concern about the glass ceiling for women and voiced their unease about the growing inequality and the cases of male chauvinism in the profession. A senior Russian male journalist said,

> Men have the advantage, of course, in Russia, although I am an opponent of this. My wife is a very successful journalist. I've always found it very frustrating when she talked about the facts of male chauvinism in the profession. I think that in the provinces it is bad, because they are more traditional, while St. Petersburg is more a European city. I remember in the early '90s, we were at a lake in the Pskov region, when my wife sat behind the wheel. The local

guys applauded with a mixture of amazement and ostentatious admiration but that really riled me, to be honest.

Expressing a different sentiment, a female Chinese radio journalist indicated that women could assist in creating gender parity: "In our broadcasting station, competent female employees could use their powerful personal abilities to make up for the gender gap, and the director of our department is a great example".

Interestingly, women were often blamed for the lack of equality in positions held by the two genders. For example, some male respondents in India thought that women's tendency to impose limits on themselves made them lag behind in their careers, and a few women agreed with this assessment. According to a male journalist, women sometimes impacted men's salaries too because of their willingness to work for less:

> Men and women have equal opportunities to grow in any company. It all comes down to who will seize it, but somehow women are ready to take up work for lesser salary and this reduces the market value as a whole. It affects pay, assignments, and opportunities.

In South Africa too, a majority of respondents argued that women are bad at seizing opportunities for mentorships and career advancement, and have to learn to create opportunities themselves to break through the glass ceiling. One South African female journalist presented the rise in number of women journalists within the economic context:

> The push to increase the pool of female reporters has also coincided with the financial downturn and the crises that many media houses find themselves in. We see cost cutting exercises everywhere and the truth is many newspapers are laying off staff and definitely do not hire anymore.

Gendering journalistic roles

Women in journalism had other issues to contend with, too. In Brazil, the response to the question about whether there was a difference in the status of men and women in the newsroom usually received a tautological answer: gender does not matter, as there are many women in the newsroom. In South Africa too, a majority of the journalists thought that gender did not matter in journalism. This sentiment was common in some of the other countries too. This suggests that there was no prejudice or imbalance in the number of women journalists or in the kind of work they were assigned. In reality, despite the increasing number of female journalists in newsrooms, the positions and functions that were deemed inherently 'female' or 'male' were clear in all BRICS countries. Women were considered more suitable for certain kinds of assignments or limited to carrying out certain tasks due to their gender. A naturalization of roles attributed to females was reported across all BRICS nations.

According to a Brazilian journalist, a woman is better on television, as "it works with image, and beauty is a female attribute". A male respondent said,

> On TV . . . women have more advantages. TV works with image, and it is nicer to watch a beautiful woman than to watch a beautiful man. A beautiful woman on TV is much more pleasant, much more newsworthy. I would not say prejudice, but there is a preference for women.

In India too, the increased presence of women in television was attributed to their looks. One male journalist turned the tables and said that the increased presence of women in television was "because they think they can come on camera".

Both male and female journalists believed that women were better at getting sources to talk, though not always due to ability and skill. For example, in Russia, respondents' narratives indicated that interactions between male journalists and male politicians can sometimes cause hostility, which can be a disadvantage for male journalists. Further, they indicated that politicians do not feel free in their comments when talking to male journalists, but are more forthcoming when interviewed by a woman. One respondent said, "Gender helps. I do believe that women have a specific set of benefits; there is the possibility to use their gender, including for establishing contacts with sources. Some sources find it easier to talk to a woman". A young male newspaper journalist added, "When they [male sources] see a pretty clever girl, they immediately begin to spread their peacock feathers". Male sources often perceive male journalists as competitors and try to throw their intellectual weight around. In China, when it came to collecting political news, female journalists were thought to be more suitable because, as one journalist said, "Since most political officials in China are male, they are inclined to answer questions put forward by female journalists". A female Chinese journalist provided the other side of the coin: "women interviewers, who normally have better relationship potential, may have an advantage over men" in getting information from sources. In India too, women journalists believed that they were being sent to charm and get the required information:

> I've seen people, basically bosses from other media outlets, send female journalists with the cameraman to shoot and the person on screen to cover the news or to gain information to write an article/story in the newspaper. The reason behind this could be anything. Maybe because the girl can get information easier than a male by showing her girl charm.

Other reasons for gendering roles were also expressed. A Brazilian male interviewee indicated that the station editor preferred men in debate programmes and women in television news, as "this will render the programme more gentle". A female Brazilian manager reinforced gendered roles thus:

> Men, on the other hand, are capable of doing certain things better in journalism, such as investigative work, which does not mean that women cannot do

this. Men have an attitude with reports that is interesting and that I do not identify in most of the women. Men tend to have more initiative, to investigate deeper. But I believe that in my team and since I entered the labour market, I do not remember having suffered any kind of gender discrimination.

One Chinese male journalist from a newspaper voiced a similar sentiment, "Men may be more suitable to be investigative reporters".

Other beats too were considered better or worse for women; traditional perceptions were also present among female journalists on gendered specializations in the newsroom. A young female journalist from online media in Russia said,

It is clear that a journalist specializing on crime topics should be a man, and perhaps an old and experienced man. Women may be more rigorous and can spend more time on the details of companies, which is a necessary requirement in dealing with the economy.

A male Chinese journalist indicated that "it is kind of like a tradition that most sports reporters are men". A young female respondent from online media in Beijing, referring more to opportunity than skill, said, "From my personal point of view, technology occupies the main position in the new media industry, and men in this area have relatively more space and better opportunities for development". Still, women also felt they could handle better some parts of the job. A young female journalist from China believed that, "Women could usually get a better handle on things when a greater sensitivity is required to communicate with people, like writing a feature".

Reference was also made by both females and males to male physical strength as an asset that enabled them to more adequately perform the job or particular parts of the job. In China, a female journalist said, "better physical strength enables male journalists to be better qualified to collect breaking news and conduct investigative reports. And it is unlikely for them to encounter any kind of sexual harassment". Another female Chinese respondent said, "After reaching a certain age, women usually become less focused due to their duty to the family; thus, men are more suitable for going on business trips". A female Indian journalist too articulated a similar view: "Management thinks that male journalists are a big support in our media outlet. It is true. They can go anywhere and they work under any circumstances". A male journalist in India said, "Male journalists have more access in collecting news and reporting. They can work for twenty-four hours and in any kind of situation. With that in mind, management takes the decision [to employ more men than women]".

In a very typical gendering of roles, women were considered as the ones who should cover stories about women's issues. For example, in South Africa, there were a few male journalists who argued that women journalists are better suited to cover certain types of stories, in particular stories on sexual violence perpetrated against women. The female journalists, however, believed they could cover all kinds of stories.

South African interviewees also indicated that both male and female journalists cover more or less the same beats. But, as Rodny-Gumede (2015) has indicated, there are gender differences in how beats are covered and interpreted by female journalists vis-à-vis their male counterparts. One female journalist's words exemplify this:

> In an ideal world, we would put issues of gender, gender equity, and the status of women higher on the agenda. If we look at the South African transition, women have got a raw deal. Women, especially black women, are still facing the brunt of poverty, social exclusion, racism, and HIV/AIDS.

As such, an increase in number of female journalists seems to have done little to change power dynamics, including the influence that female journalists have in the newsroom and the editorial control they have even over their own beats.

At the same time, the gendering of roles sometimes led women to cover stories that were disregarded earlier, demonstrating how female journalists articulate their own role in society. A female Brazilian journalist said,

> In general, it is highly tiered. The boss is a man. This is always the same, so much so that if you notice, we tend to have higher consideration for news regarding women, that which values them, complaints about rape, violence. We tend to be highly directed to that, as my female employee and I have already gone through complicated situations. I consider myself an activist in the matter of gender. I consider we have greater freedom to articulate what we want and direct our work to what we consider more interesting. We take these struggles seriously. The issue of being a woman has already affected me several times.

In India, an increase in the number of beats was an interesting outcome of the larger female presence. Women expanded the range and nature of stories covered: "There [are] issues which . . . male journalists do not write on; they [i.e., women] are writing [about these issues]". In South Africa, a majority of the female journalists interviewed said that they would like to change the proportion of certain kinds of stories [and] "bring slightly different angles to the stories". In this regard, female journalists emphasized that "there is a need to strengthen coverage of women and children and the concerns of these groups".

Beats apart, in India, women expressed solidarity with each other. When the co-worker was a woman, it influenced the ability of women to bond; many women mentioned simply "feeling better" having other women around, where previously they might have been excluded from the old boys' club: "It's like you go out with a female colleague and it makes things a little bit different, definitely it does. We can share information with each other and we can have fun also".

Sexist attitudes

The interviews with BRICS journalists also uncovered some sexist narratives. In many sample organizations across the study, there was a consistency in the implied sexist attitudes of male journalists towards females. In Russia, a few interviewees attributed the rise in number of female journalists to what they called women's 'manipulative side'. A male journalist said, "By being soft spoken they have a sense of control over what they speak. They move up the ladder easily while males are the ones left behind. I always felt that there is discrimination against men". A male Russian journalist said women lacked solidarity, and suggested that men have an advantage over women, owing to their solidarity with each other, a "plus" when working in the media:

> I remember when I was looking for work in the editorial office, the first and foremost requirement was that applicants should be boys. Even at the press service, the main condition was that [the applicant should be] a young man and not a girl. The press service is mostly staffed by women, but although the press service is headed by a woman, she was not going to work with women. This is also how the party "Women of Russia" works when it comes to choosing women: the majority are women, but they do not support each other, and it played a big role. And I enjoyed [this lack of solidarity among women], yes.

In fact, some Russian interviewees even voiced an advantage in their physiology and the perception that men were fairer and more logical:

> Being a man helped me in finding the job [of a journalist]. Even if it was the job of iron casting, it would be the same. Because the employer is sure that it is better to take a man. The man will not go on maternity leave, will not fall ill very often, i.e., it is solely physiology. Men pay more attention to males and trust them, and in principle, they are deemed to be better and fairer than women, solely by virtue of their own thoughts and by logic.

Russian journalists exhibited other sexist attitudes too. An online journalist said,

> In general, journalism is probably a woman's profession . . . because society believes that a man is someone who earns a lot, and in journalism you won't make much money. . . . And, if you are employed in a mere craft, you get such a ridiculous salary. Journalism is a craft and it seems to me that it is the girl who should be doing it because she will marry. Firstly, the husband's pay would be additional; secondly, if the girl is married, she can easily change jobs.

In South Africa too, sexist attitudes prevail in the newsroom and male colleagues often take a condescending view of their female colleagues. A female journalist said,

Sexist attitudes abound and there is little one can do to change the attitudes of male colleagues. This might not be condoned and I know that we have a clear sexual harassment policy; this does not stop some of our male colleagues though.

Similarly, another journalist said, "Unfortunately it is still the case that men often take a condescending view towards suggestions made by their female colleagues. Not all men are the same, but generally this is still the case".

Women as assets to the profession

On a positive note, respondent journalists acknowledged the capabilities of women as journalists. In Brazil, women journalists were considered more efficient and harder working than men, despite the preference for men in certain journalistic jobs. One male respondent said, "As women are more flexible and supple, they are able to handle many things at the same time". In Russia, some males mentioned that due to the diligence of women there are more women in journalism. In the opinion of a Soviet generation journalist working in a newspaper, "It is easy to work in journalism today as access to sources is very easy. But women are more careful and more meticulous than men, who tend to make more mistakes". In St. Petersburg, a senior female journalist indicated, "As an editor, I would like to hire guys. However, I think that the degree of responsibility is greater in women. [The editor] can be tough and task oriented with men, but they are lazy; women are more disciplined".

In India, women's presence also challenged men to work harder and to produce better content. As one journalist in Kolkata said about women journalists,

> They are competing with the male journalists [and] the competition will improve both the performance of the male and female journalists. Most interestingly, the gender diversity resulted in coverage of events and issues that had not earlier been considered as story material. . . . It has added value to our perception; it has given a new angle. . . . Previously . . . when I started my career, [the media were] highly dominated by men [who would] decide what women will like. Actually, we never used to ask any woman if she really liked [the] content . . . we generate. . . . [Now] we ask them, really will [this] work for women, what they think, how we can generate better content.

Many journalists in India preferred working with women. A newspaper manager indicated that "women are better journalists than men and they go to any limits to get a story. I, as a manager, prefer to work with women journalists". An Indian male journalist said, "[Our organization] has almost all female staff and our boss actually believes that females work very effectively". Women were also considered to be superior administrators, as one Indian female online journalist indicated: "In fact, I think working with women is far better than working with men because . . . I think men are much ruder. If you are reporting to a woman, then it is like . . . they are very open". Women were considered to be kinder. A male Indian journalist indicated that "Where a male journalist would come out as insensitive, a woman can handle the same situation with ease".

Indian journalists mentioned several admirable characteristics of women as professionals: "[They] have greater patience that results in better stories particularly in political coverage", "the girls are more sincere in doing their assignments and they are more punctual in their work", "[they] like being professional and doing things on time". At times, though, their work efficiency was attributed to personal rather than professional reasons. "They have to finish work and go home", explained one male journalist, though not everybody agreed with that view. And sometimes there was a patronizing tone evident in comments of this nature: "They are more sincere and they are working like their male counterparts . . . and they are very humble, very full of respect".

In China too, women's efficiency was noted. A Chinese female journalist working in a television channel indicated, "I think women work better in media. Normally men pay more attention to the final result, while women care more about the entire process, including some minor details. That is the biggest difference between the genders".

In South Africa, the views varied on what would actually change should more women come into leadership positions. A female journalist said,

> On the one hand, there is a perception that if women were to hold more power things would change. Basically, women would be more sympathetic to their female colleagues. On the other hand, though, there are no guarantees; women can also be each other's worst enemies and I have worked with female colleagues who have been my seniors who quite frankly have changed very little, and leaned quite heavily on their male counterparts. Not sure it would make a substantial difference unless coupled with broader societal transformation.

Concern about men leaving the profession

Questions about the impact of the increase in number of female journalists on the organizational workforce elicited some interesting responses. Most responses in Brazil and Russia indicated a growing concern for the decreasing number of male journalists and how it would affect news organizations.

In Brazil, the perception that emerged in some of the interviews was that the increased female presence was creating a problem for the smaller number of male journalists. One male journalist said, "The presence of males has already decreased in communication courses; now I believe there are more women in the newsroom". Another said that "There should be more men. The newsrooms have started to worry about having a male–female balance". A male respondent said,

> I believe that prejudice exists in reverse compared to other professions. In Brazil, it is a problem for a man to be a journalist as 80 per cent of the newsrooms are women; it is only natural that they reach management positions.

In Russia, there were media outlets where all the journalists were women. Interestingly, both female and male respondents were concerned about the fewer number of men in newsrooms. For instance, for radio programmes, it was hard to find good and suitable male voices. Apart from the marketing and public relations jobs they favoured, men also opted to enter the teaching profession. A young male journalist from online media said,

> With more females joining the industry, men now opt for teaching as there are not enough men in the teaching profession. This makes entry into the teaching profession easy for men. [Even males who] have a weaker performance [in entrance examinations results] than females [will] be employed as faculty because there are not enough men in the profession.

Pay and career advancement opportunities

In Brazil, the BRICS data indicated a difference in income levels between men and women in journalism. In Russia, as outlined above, some men believed that journalism did not offer good salaries and therefore was not a profession for men. They found the profession suitable for women because when women get married, theirs would be a supplemental income to that of their husband.

In India, the perception of most interviewed journalists in Delhi and Hyderabad was that work and pay was fair and non-discriminatory. All online journalists and a majority of traditional media journalists believed that not much difference existed in the work environment and that pay scales were decided according to work assignments. According to an Indian male journalist, "Whoever works hard and achieves good results will be appreciated". An Indian female journalist indicated, "Rising in one's career depends totally on how you handle yourself. It has nothing to do with gender". Kolkata and Pune journalists believed that women were not being discriminated against with respect to covering major stories and were rewarded accordingly: "Women have started looking for big stories. The number of beats has also increased. That is why women are now given more salaries, respectful treatment, and encouragement". However, subtle references to discrimination were made; according to an Indian female journalist, "It is easier for men to progress in this field. From a career point of view, I firmly believe that females have lesser opportunities to grow although the work is the same for both".

In China, 49 per cent of the respondents indicated that gender had no effect on work or career in the profession. They said it was leadership skills and the quality of work rather than gender that determined whether a journalist would be promoted or not. Among those who believed that gender mattered, the majority thought that it was easier for a man to rise in his career within journalism, while a few argued that the females possessed this advantage. As one female journalist said, "It is easier for a man to rise in this field as they are preferred for most jobs in media". In South Africa, interviewees were all in agreement that, despite increased gender equality, women still struggle to advance in their careers. All the interviewees also stated that women earn less than men.

Sometimes, it was not a question of advancement but simply of entry into certain aspects of journalism. A young female journalist from Petrozavodsk said, "My friends working in Moscow say that a girl finds it much more difficult to break into television as boys are preferred".

Conclusion

UNESCO has termed gender equality as a fundamental human right (IFJ, 2009). Its reflection in the profession of journalism is mixed. First, the literature indicates that, due to the dramatic political and economic changes in these countries, all BRICS nations have witnessed a phenomenal growth in the number of female journalists, sometimes reaching parity and sometimes exceeding the number of male colleagues. In all but India, there were more women than men in the profession in the past two decades. However, global statistics indicate that this growth has stagnated (Global Media Monitoring Project Report, 2015) in the last few years. This is perhaps due to the global economic downturn, which affected all sectors and was not gender specific.

Second, the literature also indicates that, over the last decade, more and more young women enrolled in higher education; this increase was also seen in journalism training schools across the BRICS nations. As a result, a majority of women journalists are young and educated. The BRICS study found that in Russia and Brazil, the concern was that the number of men in journalism had diminished in the last decade, and that this had created problems. In Russia, the lack of male voices for radio as well as the appearance of media outlets staffed entirely by women were concerns. In Brazil too, there was concern about the gender imbalance (fewer males) in the newsrooms.

Third, irrespective of numbers, the BRICS study's respondent journalists indicated that decision-making powers continued to be with males in all BRICS countries, because males were in senior positions while most women were in entry- or mid-level positions. This reported glass ceiling finding of the BRICS study is in line with the IWMF (2011a) finding that though men are a minority in the workplace, they are often managers. Not much appears to have changed in the past decade and more if one compares the status today with that in the early 2000s as reported in the UNESCO reports on women journalists and the UN expert committee findings (Joseph, 2002). The predominant reason interviewees mentioned for this lack of change related to societal limitations women face such as responsibilities in marriage, raising a family, and lack of ability to report for night duty or be on call 24/7. Exacting duties at work coupled with family responsibilities result in women giving up their professional aspirations. These societal limitations are seldom contested as they are supported by the conservatism of national cultures.

Fourth, though at first glance both male and female journalists articulated their role in society as aligned with the liberal conceptualization of equality, where gender does not influence pay, growth in career, or particular role orientations, there was an underlying normative role for the women in this profession. In this way, women's increasing role in the labour markets is reflected but also limited in journalism. As Banyard (2010) argues, there is only an illusion of equality among men and women journalists because differences crop up in various ways. For instance, in India and China, while there was an emphasis on performance over gender, societal limitations were also mentioned. In Brazil and South Africa, the hierarchical organizational structure, with men in managerial positions, vested them with power in decision making. In Russia too, there was a certain preference for men over women as they are deemed physiologically superior and more logical thinkers. In turn, women journalists argued that they expanded the repertoire of stories by covering underreported topics such as women's issues and/or writing stories using a different angle. As Rodny-Gumede (2015) has indicated, while male and female journalists acknowledge that more has to be done to factor in the concerns of the poor and marginalized communities often neglected in coverage as well as in conceptualizations of the audience, female journalists put a strong emphasis on serving women and children in particular.

Fifth, many respondents across all BRICS nations agreed that women are more hardworking and efficient than men are, and adhere to deadlines. Men believed that women undersell and limit themselves in various ways, although women are better journalists than they are. Some women projected their own limitations by saying that men are better at chasing investigative and crime stories. As a result, women journalists remain ghettoized in the area of 'pink journalism', reporting on topics specifically targeted towards women, often including subjects of gender and parenting. Vigil (2016) found that men write almost 90 per cent of the articles on international politics and economics, while women write the majority of the articles about family and style. However, Pasti, Chernysh, and Svitich (2012) found that this was not the case in Russia, where females dominate in practically all fields of coverage, except for sports, computer and high tech issues, gardening, and politics, in which fields near parity existed between male and female journalists. And further, they found that even in covering topics regarded as male, such as repairs and construction, female journalists were increasing in number.

Sixth, despite expressions of equality at the workplace, sexist narratives emerged. Women were preferred as television anchors for their beauty and were perceived as good at interviewing men due to their charm. Respondent journalists indicated that politicians are more responsive to female than to male interviewers on television. Women were employed for political reporting as femininity could be used as a weapon to gather news from reluctant sources. In an interview on the topic, Ammu Joseph, Indian journalist, author, and media watcher, sums up this aspect best: "Women's visibility in television news has been recognized worldwide as a fairly complex phenomenon which involves a number of factors, not all of them related to professional values" (Devraj, 2010). Using a blatant sexist narrative, some male journalists said that women put their femininity to use at the workplace to climb up the career ladder in a sort of reverse discrimination. To sum up, traditional views persisted on gender relations and gender roles within the profession: a man holds a higher position in the hierarchy having a higher income and more power, while a woman must be attractive and a conscientious worker.

Seventh, there was a perception that if women were placed in higher managerial positions, they would be better managers than men would as they are more sensitive to the needs of the people in the organization, would bring about changes in content to deal with more sensitive issues, and help improve the performance of the company with their sincerity and commitment.

While the BRICS data indicated considerable similarity among BRICS nations with regard to most matters related to gender parity, in the area of pay and career advancement there were differences. In Brazil, China, and South Africa, male and female wages were reportedly different. In India, however, journalists stated that pay depended on performance and not gender. As far as rising in the profession was concerned, though a majority of the journalists insisted that being female did not affect their careers, a minority expressed disagreement and pointed out both management's preference for male over female employees as well as the ease with which men could climb the professional ladder compared to women.

The final word is that there is universality in the progress, concerns, and issues that women journalists face irrespective of nationality, race, and medium. The time now is simply to convert thoughts of gender parity into actions of equality.

Notes

1 Although no longer mandatory from that date onwards, companies tend to hire professionals with a degree in the field.
2 Small cities have less than 200,000 inhabitants, middle-sized cities have 200,000 to 999,000 inhabitants, and big cities have a million and over population.

References

Banyard, K. (2010). *The gender illusion: The truth about women and men*. London: Faber and Faber.
Bhardwaj, D. (2014, November 3). *Status of working women journalists in India, a study of Delhi NCR*. Retrieved from http://shodhganga.inflibnet.ac.in/bitstream/10603/29333/4/13%20chapter%205.pdf
Byerly, C. M. (2013). Factors affecting the status of women journalists: A structural analysis. In C. M. Byerly (Ed.), *The Palgrave international handbook of women and journalism* (pp. 11–26). New York: Palgrave, Macmillan.
Cerqueira, C., Cabecinhas, R., & Magalhães, S, I. (2016). Gender and media: where do we stand today? In C. Cerqueira, R. Cabecinhas, & S. I. Magalhães (Eds.), Gender in focus: (new) trends in media (pp. 5–11). Braga: CECS.
Chambers, D., Steiner, L., & Fleming, C. (2005). *Women and journalism*. London and New York: Routledge, Taylor and Francis e-publication.
Daniels, G. (2014). *State of the newsroom: Disruptions accelerated*. JHB: Wits Journalism, University of Witwatersrand.

Devraj, R. (2010, March 4). *Q & A: More women journalists doesn't mean more gender awareness*. Reprint. Inter Press Service. Retrieved from www.ipsnews.net/2010/03/qa-more-women-journalists-doesnrsquot-mean-more-gender-awareness/

Djerf-Pierre, M. (2007). The gender of journalism: The structure and logic of the field in the twentieth century. *Nordicom Review: Jubilee Issue*, 81–104. Retrieved from www.nordicom.gu.se/sites/default/files/kapitel-pdf/248_248_djerf-pierre1.pdf

Fang, H. Q. (1987). Research about women journalists in modern China. *Chinese Journalist*, 6, 19–21.

Farris, J. P. (2001). Appendix: Checklist of women journalists in Imperial Russia. In B. T. Norton & J. M. Gheith (Eds.), *An improper profession: Women, gender, and journalism in late Imperial Russia* (pp. 281–310). Durham & London: Duke University Press.

FJWCSJA (Female Journalist Work Committee of Shanghai Journalists Association). (2014). The survey report of Shanghai women journalists in 2013. *Journalism Review*, 31(3), 35–42.

Franks, S. (2013a, November 13). Hard evidence: Is there still a gender bias in journalism? *The Conversation*. Retrieved from http://theconversation.com/hard-evidence-is-there-still-a-gender-bias-in-journalism-19789

Franks, S. (2013b). *Women and journalism*. London and New York: I. B. Tauris & Co. Ltd. in association with Reuters Institute for the Study of Journalism. Retrieved from www.ibtauris.com/reuters

Gallagher, M., & von Euler, M. (1995). *An unfinished story: Gender patterns in media employment*. Reports and Papers on Mass Communication, 110. UNESCO Publishing. Retrieved from http://unesdoc.unesco.org/images/0010/001016/101613eb.pdf

GMMP (Global Media Monitoring Project Report). (2015). *Who makes the news?* Retrieved from http://cdn.agilitycms.com/who-makes-the-news/Imported/reports_2015/global/gmmp_global_report_en.pdf

Green, E., & Adam, A. (1999). Editorial comment. *Information Communication and Society*, 2(4), v–vii.

Griffin, A. (2014, September 11). Where are the women? Why we need more female newsroom leaders. *Nieman reports*. Retrieved from http://niemanreports.org/articles/where-are-the-women/

Haraway, D., & Randolph, L. M. (1997). *Modest_witness@second_millenium: FemaleMan©_meets_oncoMouse™: Feminism and technoscience*. New York: Routledge.

IWMF (International Women's Media Foundation). (2011a). *Global report on the status of women in the news media*. Washington, DC, USA. Retrieved from www.iwmf.org/wp-content/uploads/2013/09/IWMF-Global-Report.pdf

IWMF (International Women's Media Foundation). (2011b). *Global report on the status of women in the news media*. Washington, DC, USA. Retrieved from www.iwmf.org/wp-content/uploads/2013/09/IWMF-Global-Report-Summary.pdf

IFJ (International Federation of Journalists). (2009). *Getting the balance right: Gender equality in journalism*. Brussels, Belgium. Retrieved from http://portal.unesco.org/ci/en/files/28397/12435929903gender_booklet_en.pdf/gender_booklet_en.pdf

IFJ (International Federation of Journalists). (2015, March). *Country report: Media and gender in India*. Part of the IFJ Media and Gender in Asia-Pacific Research Project "Research Study on Media and Gender in Asia-Pacific". Retrieved from www.ifj.org/uploads/media/INDIA.pdf

IPIN. 爱拼网. (2015). *The ratio of male and female students in Chinese universities in 2015*. Retrieved from www.ipin.com/school/ranking.do?rankingType=meizhi

Jenkins, H. (1999). The work of theory in the age of digital transformation. In T. Miller & R. Stam (Eds.), *A companion to film theory* (pp. 234–261). Malden, MA: Blackwell.

Joseph, A. (2002). *Working, watching and waiting: Women and issues of access, employment and decision-making in the media in India*. United Nations Division for the Advancement of Women (DAW), Expert Group Meeting on "Participation and access of women to the media, and the impact of media on, and its use as an instrument for the advancement and empowerment of women". Beirut, Lebanon, 12 to 15 November 2002. EGM/MEDIA/2002/EP.4/Rev.1. Retrieved from www.un.org/womenwatch/daw/egm/media2002/reports/EP4Joseph.PDF

Kasytin, V. (2010). Zhurnalistika i mediarynok. Regionaljnaya pechatj [Journalism and market: Regional press]. Paper presented at the International Conference Magazines and New Media Culture in Russia, Faculty of Journalism, Moscow State University, Moscow.

Made, P., & Morna, C. L. (2009). *Glass ceilings: Women and men in Southern Africa media*. Johannesburg: Gender links for equality and justice. Retrieved from http://genderlinks.org.za/programme-web-menu/publications/glass-ceilings-women-and-men-in-southern-african-media-2009-08-04/

Mick, J., & Lima, S. (2013). *Perfil do jornalista Brasileiro*. Florianópolis: Editora Insular.

Muzarte, Z. L. (2003). Uma espiada na imprensa das mulheres no século XIX. *Revista Estudos Feministas, 11*(Junho 1), 225–233.

Neves, M. A. (2013). Anotações sobre Trabalho e Gênero. *Cadernos de Pesquisa, São Paulo, 43*(149, maio/ago), 404–421.

Nordenstreng, K. (2009). Soul-searching at the crossroads of European journalism education. In G. Terzis (Ed.), *European journalism education* (pp. 513–515). Bristol: Intellect Publishers.

Pasti, S., Chernysh, M., & Svitich, L. (2012). The Russian journalists and their profession. In D. H. Weaver & L. Willnat (Eds.), *The global journalist in the 21st century* (pp. 267–282). New York: Routledge.

Rabe, L. (2006). Glass ceiling, concrete ceiling. *Rhodes Journalism Review, 26*, 20–21.

Ramos, R. H. P. (2010). *Mulheres jornalistas, a grande invasão*. São Paulo: Imprensa Oficial.

Rodny-Gumede, Y. (2012). Race, class and gender and the transformation of the South African news media. *Journal of Gender and Religion in Africa, 18*, 159–176.

Rodny-Gumede, Y. (2015). Gender and public discourse formation in South Africa: Male and female journalists' influence on news agendas. *Communicatio: South African Journal for Communication Theory and Research, 41*(2), 206–219.

Rossouw, R. (2005). The media and transformation. In A. Hadland (Ed.), *Changing the fourth estate, essays on South African journalism* (pp. 221–227). Cape Town: HSRC Press.

SANEF (South African National Editor's Forum). (2006). *The glass ceiling and beyond: Realities, challenges and strategies for South African media*. Retrieved from www.sanef.org.za

SARCAJC (South Asian Research Centre for Advertisement, Journalism & Cartoons). (n.d.). *Women journalists during British Raj*. Retrieved from www.sarcajc.com/Women_Jounalists_during_Bri.html

Sneha. (2012). *The gender of journalism*. Retrieved from www.newslaundry.com/2012/03/29/the-gender-of-journalism/

Song, S. H. (2003). The characteristics and traditions of the women journalists in the modern Chinese history. *Journalism & Communication, 3*, 41–47.

South African Truth and Reconciliation Commission. (1998). Final report of the Truth and Reconciliation Commission of South Africa. Volume 4, Chapter Six, Institutional Hearing on the Media. Cape Town: Juta.

Standing, G. (1999). Global feminization through flexible labor: A theme revisited. *World Development, 27*(3), 583–602. Pergamon. Retrieved from PII: S0305-750X(98)00151-X

Steiner, L. (2012). Failed theories: Explaining gender difference in journalism. *The Review of Communication, 12*(July 3), 201–223.

Svitich, L. G. (2000). *Fenomen Zhurnalizma*. Moskva: MGU, IKAR.
Tiwari, N. (2014, December 8). Do you know who is India's first female photo journalist? *The Better India*. Retrieved from www.thebetterindia.com/13969/homai-vyarawalla-india-first-female-photo-journalist/
Van Zoonen, L. (2002). Gendering the Internet: Claims, controversies and cultures. *European Journal of Communication, 17*(1), 5–23.
Vigil, L. H. (2016, February 3). The woeful state of women in journalism. *Ms Magazine Blog*. Retrieved from http://msmagazine.com/blog/2016/02/03/the-woeful-state-of-women-in-journalism/
Voronova, L. (2014). 'Send pretty girls to the White House': The role of gender in journalists-politicians' interactions. *Journal for Communication Studies, 7*(2/14), 145–171. ESSACHESS.
Weaver, D. H., & Willnat, L. (2012). Journalists in the 21st century: Conclusions. In D. H. Weaver & L. Willnat (Eds.), *The global journalist in the 21st century* (pp. 529–551). New York: Routledge.
Wihbey, J. (2015, June 5). *Gender disparities and journalism: Research perspectives*. Retrieved from http://journalistsresource.org/studies/society/news-media/female-journalists-media-sexism-emerging-trends
Zhang, H. Z., & Su, L. S. (2012). Chinese media and journalists in transition. In D. H. Weaver & L. Willnat (Eds.), *The global journalist in the 21st century* (pp. 9–12). New York: Routledge.
Zhang, Z. A., Zhang, J. J., & Lin, G. C. (2014). Chinese journalists survey under the new media environment. *Contemporary Communications, 29*(3), 4–8.
Zhou, B. H., Xie, X. Y., & Kou, Z. H. (2014). The investigation report on Chinese new media journalists' living situation. *Journalism Review, 31*(3), 42–48.

5
PROFESSION AND PRACTICE
Re-imagining the future of journalism

Svetlana Pasti, Beatriz Becker, Nagamallika Gudipaty, Yu Xu, and Musawenkosi Ndlovu

Introduction

Journalism as a profession and as practice is undergoing a fundamental change in terms of power, technology, economy, and identity. Traditional media – in the past, bastions of the journalistic profession, owning the exclusive rights to information, the only employers of journalists – are today forced to share the space with innovative forms of journalism, which spontaneously and autonomously but also strategically, organized by social movements and groups, emerge on the Internet and collect readership. This is not least due to the fact that click-availability of information and communication in cyberspace has become common. Journalism is no longer the exclusive domain of traditional media; it is also a voluntary agency comprising individuals, subcultural groups, non-governmental organizations, amateurs, and professional startups, which work with distinct types of platforms, business models, and targeted audiences. Moreover, the state and business, greater today than ever in the past, directly inform society about their work through their own websites and digital contact points, phenomena respectively named e-government and e-commerce. At the same time, mainstream media companies expand their journalistic content on multiple platforms and seek to involve and strengthen their linkages with the audiences in the digital environment.

In post-communist countries, where the press and the Internet are under state control, journalists, de jure professionals, can seldom compete with bloggers, de facto in breaking news, in writing critical stories, and in investigative journalism in the public interest (Gusejnov, 2014; Qiu, 2016). In China, since 2009 a microblog, Sina Weibo, like Twitter, "is often the first place for news to break, and it hosts discussions about breaking news" (Hu, 2012, p. 107). A similar trend towards the enhancement of transparency of those in power (political-economic groups) is occurring in Brazil, India, and South Africa, where activist-bloggers use social media to express their political interests in order to fight for more democratic rules for communication systems and for citizens' rights, or at least to tell the everyday history and the political experience of these countries from different perspectives.

In addition, recent legislative changes in some countries have led to a gradual de-legitimization of the old concept of a media system that included only traditional media – the heritage of churches, political parties, the state, and capital. For example, in Russia the law on bloggers (2014) states that bloggers who have an audience of more than 3,000 users in 24 hours are journalists. Such bloggers are required to register their blogs as media in Roskomnadzor, the Federal Service for Supervision in the Sphere of Telecom, Information Technologies and Mass Communications (Sherstoboeva & Pavlenko, 2015). This new law on bloggers makes the basic law on the mass media (1991) in Russia obsolete in identifying a journalist. However, the decentralization of the production of journalistic content and format coincides with the simultaneous concentration of power of large media groups worldwide.

Among the many factors that impact on journalistic work, the most crucial is digitalization. Today we are all witnesses to how new technology in the field of information and communications disrupts the status quo of the old institution of journalism, as well as its key concepts like journalism, media, and the journalist. Historically, these concepts differed depending on the national interest and the status of journalism in the state in question. For example, the Soviet understanding of the functions of journalism and journalists' roles, oriented to the Communist Party and state service, radically differed from the Western understanding of these, which reflected the needs and values of the market economy. Further, there were cultural differences reflecting the national journalism tradition in the BRICS countries.

The digital era has brought no universal consensus; however, it has given rise to counter-trends from bottom–up and top–down in the revision of the boundaries of these old concepts. The bottom–up trend comes from a society engaged in amateur web-based journalism (blogging, social media, etc.) often integrated with digital citizenship; thus society introduces and maintains grassroots democratization of journalism. The top–down trend goes from the traditional media, which 'outsources' to amateurs (social media) and even contracts influential bloggers as opinion leaders, thus legitimizing openness of their profession as today's standard. The same trend towards the openness of journalism emerges in the field of media regulation. Thus, in 2013, the Organization for Security and Co-operation in Europe published the *Online Media Self-Regulation Guidebook*, which states that there is not and nor should there be a common universal definition of who is a journalist because:

> Everyone is entitled to freedom of expression, the right to seek, receive and impart information regardless of frontiers – which is the basic job description of a journalist. To define, beyond this fundamental right, who qualifies as a 'journalist' and who doesn't is a subjective judgment or merely a description

> of a person's gainful occupation. Basically, it is of no relevance for the exercise of the right to freedom of expression or the production and publication of content on the Internet.
>
> *(Möller, 2013, p. 20)*

Strikingly, in the 1970s, scholars predicted today's fundamental change in journalism by viewing it as a process of de-professionalization or proletarianization. Freidson (1986, p. 110) presented the arguments of authors who stated that the professions of the past with characteristics of high prestige and public trust would be de-professionalized because of changes in the attitudes and behaviour of the public and in the nature of their knowledge (Barber, 1983; Burnham, 1982; Haug, 1973, 1975, 1977; Rothman, 1984). The list of reasons included the rising education of the public, which narrows the gap between the professional's and the client's knowledge, and thus erodes the professional's authority; the standardization and routinization of knowledge; computer technology removing control over practice from the hands of practitioners; and other rising occupations taking over the traditional areas served by the professions, thereby destroying their monopolies.

The prediction is seen today not only in the massive and heterogeneous nature of current journalism and the diversity of journalistic identities and values therein, but also in the arrival of new information technology specialists in the media market, ousting journalists because media production and performance are increasingly dependent on new technologies. To survive in the new media environment, traditional media have merged newsrooms and journalistic labour; as a result, a journalist faces new demands from the employer to combine disparate specializations (multiskilling).

However, a new era of digitalization carries not only the promise of democracy in society, profession, and practice, but also new challenges undermining the former stability and job security of a journalist. The digital innovations in labour are intertwined with the new media economy seeking new business models to pay for the professional work of journalists and editorial costs. Basically, this new media economy is aimed at cost savings leading to a reduction in job opportunities and a call for more intense work encroaching on journalists' private lives, where the boundaries between work and leisure are becoming increasingly blurred (Fraysse & O'Neil, 2015, p. 4). The critical debate in the changing labour (and thus media) profession is represented in such keywords as 'exploitation', 'digital labour', 'virtual work', 'precariousness', 'entrepreneurialism', and 'permatemps' (temporary employees) (Barland, 2013; Hesmondhalgh et al., 2015; Huws & Leys, 2003; Maxwell, 2016; Picard, 2001; Standing, 2011).

In contrast to the West, the BRICS media markets are on the rise and journalism is still a popular profession in these countries, especially among the young, particularly in China and South Africa as well as in India. As recent studies collected in the *Global Journalist* (Weaver & Willnat, 2012) have shown, the popularity of journalism in three BRICS countries – Brazil (Herscovitz, 2012), Russia (Pasti, Chernysh, & Svitich, 2012), and China (Zhang & Su, 2012) – especially among women, is associated with a rapid growth in commercialized media and a growing number of journalism schools. In some countries, for example, Russia, the relatively high status of journalists in the social structure is also a factor; it promises extensive opportunities for professional and social advancement. In China, the profession of journalism is prestigious; "journalists regarded peasants, teachers, and researchers as most respectable, with journalists ranked fourth, while workers, police, business people, nurses and officials came after them in social status" (Zhang & Su, 2012, p. 13). In most of the BRICS countries, journalists belong to the middle class in terms of education, occupation, and income, but, as posited by Bourdieu (Benson & Neveu, 2005), their social position (journalistic field) also locates them in elitist communication environments (political and economic fields) (Pasti, Ramaprasad, & Ndlovu, 2015, p. 222).

However, today journalists are not only seeking employment in the traditional media but are also looking for self-employment (freelancers) or new forms of entrepreneurship (journalistic startups). In the West, this search is due to the consequences of the financial-economic crisis of 2008, which resulted in a decline in jobs in the traditional media, and closed many media outlets (Bruno & Nielsen, 2012). These currently emerging professional practices are considered to be post-industrial journalism, in harmony with the less centralized and decreasingly hierarchical online society and with new production methods (Bell, 2014; Deuze, 2014).

The new practice of journalism does not occur only in the West. In Brazil, the monopoly of the traditional media system coexists with the emergence of new business models and forms of producing information. Blogs and websites considered independent are not always able to achieve significant audiences or viable financial arrangements, but startups – journalistic microenterprises created and directed by small groups of reporters and editors – are currently already paving the way both for diversity in terms of approaches to events and for journalistic practices that are more analytical and creative. Such initiatives have been sustained via financial backing from private companies of various sectors and through investments from public institutions and/or philanthropic foundations, and they tend to target segmented markets and distinct publics (Becker, 2016). Currently, some journalistic startups in Brazil provide content production services for traditional media and establish this kind of partnership with these companies. Other startups in Brazil acquire their financial resources through crowdfunding.

According to the Brazilian Institute of Geography and Statistics (IBGE), the labour market began to suffer a decline in job offers in the private sector (Valor Econômico, 2016; EBC. Agência Brasil, 2016). The decrease in employment and the increase in the number of self-employed workers, with fewer guarantees and lower incomes, is a result of political and economic crises in the country. The political crisis that culminated with the impeachment of the democratically elected President Dilma Roussef had the support of mainstream media. The majority of them were opposed to Dilma's government and biased in the coverage of her impeachment. At the same time, initiatives of more independent journalism have arisen. A journalistic startup, *Agência Pública de Notícias* (Public News Agency) (2016), conducted a survey of independent journalism initiatives and published an interactive map bringing together different work experiences in 2016.

In Russia, emerging new forms of (self-)employment and entrepreneurship among journalists is the only path to professional freedom and independence in conditions of a lack of freedom in the traditional media. In particular, as our study found out, some online journalistic startups arose when journalists, especially the Net generation, which entered journalism in the 2000s, did not want to work in an environment of political censorship. At the same time, they needed to create new means of earning money to live in a reasonable condition in a market characterized by decreasing job opportunities for journalists.

Nonetheless, the entrepreneurial news production business model remains a challenge – not merely in the financial sense, but also in the ethical and professional sense. It does not guarantee a priori that independent news production is always honest and impartial. Online journalists as well as their colleagues in the traditional media control information and web mediation and are able to produce not only cultural diversity and democracy but also conservative alliances and authoritarianism (Curran, 2012; Pasti, 2015). Therefore, it is logical to expect the emergence of new independent self-regulatory journalists' organizations, which would agree on and accept standards of quality journalism and ethical behaviour in cyberspace for new media in the context of growing debates on digital media ethics (Couldry, Madianou, & Pinchevski, 2013; Ess, 2009; Friend & Singer, 2007; Ward, 2010).

The BRICS study

Against this background of a 'power-technology-economy-identity' transformation in journalism, this chapter provides us with answers of journalists to questions about their working conditions, the sources of their (dis)satisfaction, and views about the future of their profession. To elicit their dreams about a better situation, we asked our respondents about what needs to change in the socio-political conditions of their country in order for journalism to fully accomplish its functions and tasks. The goal was to comprehend how the personal situations of journalists have changed, what unites and divides them as they work in the traditional and online news media, and how these changes, localized in the BRICS context, correlate with the global trends in journalism.

Findings

From traditional employment to self-employment

In all the BRICS countries, media organizations have gradually replaced permanent employment contracts with fixed-term or short-term contracts. At the forefront of this trend were new online media. For instance, in Rio de Janeiro only 25 per cent of online journalists and in the provincial city of Vitoria only

42 per cent of online journalists had long-term contracts. In the capital Brasília, part-time work was found only in online media. Some online journalists who did not have a long labour employment contract opened their startups or became partner-founders of journalistic websites, trainees, and collaborators, who usually worked as service providers. Moreover, a few of them took part in the company's profit, becoming owners or shareholders. That is, online journalists in Brazilian cities relied mostly on themselves and one path they could follow was self-employment or entrepreneurship in the profession. On the other hand, traditional media still had the majority of their employees on long-term contracts. This meant that these journalists were officially registered as employees of their companies and had labour cards signed by their employers. An interview with the editor of the independent website *Brazil247* adds some important information about this situation. In particular, Leonardo Attuch[1] noted that press media are losing readers and advertisers, but the Internet still has not discovered an appropriate financing model able to accommodate this immense group of journalists who are leaving traditional editorial offices:

> With this [exodus], in addition to the media companies emerging in the digital field, what has grown is so-called public communications, with an increasing number of journalists being employed by news agencies tied to governments, companies or entities. As I see it, with the weakening of traditional editorial staffs, the production of content will become more decentralised in the following years, with a growing role being played by government agencies and independent websites. Nonetheless, salaries today are less than they were in the past.

In Russia, almost all journalists had a permanent full-time job regardless of where they worked, traditional (88 per cent) or online media (86 per cent). However, Moscow differed from other cities, showing a minimal number of journalists with a permanent job: 67 per cent in old media and 71 per cent in online media. Moreover, a permanent job could actually mean a temporary job held for a long time. As a St. Petersburg journalist said,

> A Moscow correspondent gets 120,000 to 150,000 rubles per month (3,000 to 4,000 euro) net, whereas in St. Petersburg a well-known and experienced TV journalist in the news programme *Vesti* gets 50,000 rubles a month (1,250 euro). But in Moscow there is very tough competition, a big turnover of staff; that is, the job is temporary, perhaps for a long time, but the job is temporary. This is not a career like in a corporation. In journalism, you can only get a steady job for two to three years. On the state-owned TV channel, you can stay put for ten years, but after ten years, everyone will be wondering how to replace you.

A situation similar to Brazil and Russia regarding precarious employment in online media was also found in some Indian cities. In particular, in Hyderabad, a majority of the respondents from traditional media were permanently employed. However, most respondents working in online media were temporary; they were students working part-time or were new employees. Those who started the venture were the only ones who were permanent in these organizations. In Kolkata and Pune, most journalists reported having a permanent job; however, there is a caveat to this. Essentially, permanent in Indian journalism workplaces mostly meant a three-to-five-year contract that was likely to be renewed. There was little indication of journalists shifting from traditional to online media in the samples of these two cities, where independent online establishments were still rare or non-existent. In the capital, Delhi, those working in traditional media changed course or were promoted to the online section in the same organization. Some young journalists directly opted for online web portals. In the words of one male journalist working in Delhi,

> I used to work in print with the *Navbharat Times* in Patna. After working there for two years . . . , I realised I should move to a bigger city like Delhi. At that time, a friend told me that *Dainik Bhaskar* was looking for Hindi reporters and so I applied. I worked there for three years and then got promoted and shifted to their online version called *Daily Bhaskar*. It is only recently that I have shifted to an online medium.

Another online journalist said, "I began my career as a reporter with Zee News (TV). I worked in the organization for close to two years, then I quit. My friends and I from the same organization started this online portal called *Dainik Enews*".

Remarkably, in Communist China, only a fifth of the journalists had a permanent place of work. In the traditional media, these 'lucky ones' amounted to 32 per cent of the respondents, whereas in online media, they accounted for only 5 per cent. The majority of online respondents worked in privately owned news websites, foreign capital news websites, and grassroots online media. Thus, this group of journalists did not belong to the group of official journalists working in state-owned media and enjoying government benefits, "including a form of life-long tenure and government stipends" (Zhang & Su, 2012, p. 11). Moreover, these journalists working for commercial websites "are not granted press cards, . . . which means they cannot conduct interviews or release news. They can only reproduce news from other sources such as newspapers, television, and official news agencies" (Zhang & Su, 2012, p. 10).

In South Africa, the majority of journalists in the old media (76 per cent) and new online media (92 per cent) had permanent full-time jobs. However, the journalists who worked for community media tended to be younger, on internships, and underpaid.

This changing nature of employment from traditional forms of stability (permanent contract) to flexibility (a short-term contract, a temporary contract, a part-time job) and alternative forms of (self-)employment and entrepreneurship was evidence of a growing precariousness of journalistic work and insecurity for journalists. This also created high professional mobility. In Brazil, more than half of the respondents had had between one and four jobs before the current one. In Russia, 86 per cent in the new media and 84 per cent in the old media had such previous experience. In China, these percentages were 34 per cent in online media and 14 per cent in traditional media. In South Africa, 28 per cent in online media and 44 per cent in traditional media held two or more previous jobs. On average, the interviewees had changed jobs two to three times, but all within the field of journalism.

In the Indian megacities of Delhi and Hyderabad, 58 per cent of the journalists had professional experience in both old and new media. From this, it is clear that these journalists did not find it difficult to switch between new and traditional media; many of them were young, working in the field for ten years or less. In the country, almost all newspapers and television channels had their own online versions and most stories that appeared in print or television also appeared in online versions. Most often, it was young journalists who worked in the online section of the traditional media, and later moved from traditional to online media. In Kolkata and Pune, journalists working for online news media were somewhat younger than those who were working for traditional media. Journalists reported considerable job mobility; most of them had started in journalism and changed jobs within journalism, although there were exceptions in both cases.

Second job

A second job was a way to supplement income, hone skills, and increase social capital. It was most popular in Brazil and Russia. The cost of living was high in all Brazilian cities, and journalists were forced to seek additional earnings, for instance in advertising, press relations, translation, or other non-journalistic fields. Nonetheless, even with a second job, they earned less than expected in light of the minimum salary stipulated by the municipal unions of the occupations of the same social status as journalism. Half of the online journalists had a second job; in the traditional media, the share was smaller. A typical explanation, for instance, in the words of one traditional media journalist from Rio de Janeiro, was:

> Rio de Janeiro is an expensive city, so I live always with the rope around my neck: I can't save money, I can't travel. My income is enough for me to have a certain level of comfort, live in the South Zone of the city, go out and do some things, but it's not what I would like.

Journalists who were satisfied with their incomes did not resort to additional employment; nevertheless they faced considerable stress in their newsrooms: "Nowadays, we work with much less; many functions no longer exist"; "[Cuts in] spending [are] reflected in staff cuts in the structure. So a job that was done by ten is done now by two and on a smaller budget"; and "Fewer staff, greater workload . . . generates insecurity in the workplace".

In Russia, there were more online media journalists with a second job (68 per cent) than in traditional media (49 per cent). Interestingly, the provincial cities did not differ much from the metropolises of Moscow and St. Petersburg, in this regard, although the most active in combining jobs were the Moscow online journalists (71 per cent). Like their Brazilian counterparts, they moonlighted in other media or in advertising, or taught journalism at universities, offered individual tutoring for school-leavers, and did other jobs. According to a young female online journalist in Moscow, "Yes, there is moonlighting. The tourism magazine *Where* in Moscow, for them, I occasionally write articles about Moscow. Sometimes [I] shoot photo essays, in particular for *RIA Novosti* (a news agency) and sometimes [I] work as a guide".

In India and South Africa, having a second job was not very popular, and only a few journalists combined their basic job with a second one. In the metropolises of Delhi and Hyderabad, traditional media journalists did not have a second job, citing lack of time and no necessity to do so as reasons. However, most online journalists who had entered journalism by chance had a second job because they were underemployed and perceived journalism as something temporary. For instance, one respondent was the owner of a news portal and wanted to "put his MBA knowledge to use by opening the portal" which "did yield good returns". Another online journalist moonlighted because he wanted to "buy equipment to make films, which is my primary passion. Also, to fund traveling to film festivals, etc." Some who thought that the pay was low in journalism or who did not have a passion for journalism thought of leaving the field. In Kolkata and Pune, most journalists did not have a second job. The few in Kolkata who did take a second job did so either because they wanted extra earnings or because they had a passion for the profession and wanted to continue their journalistic work, one way or another, either by engaging in freelancing as writers/columnists for other media or working as guest lecturers at educational institutions.

In South Africa, only a few journalists had second jobs, the majority reporting that they had "no time" for this. However, those who did have time wanted to supplement their incomes and thus held second jobs. China was in the middle in comparison with the other countries of BRICS; a fifth of the online media respondents and 15 per cent of the traditional media journalists reported having a second job. This group mostly included financial or business reporters and television directors and hosts. They thought their income from the primary job was not enough and they had the extra time for an additional job. In general, they earned extra money by working as financial analysts, copywriters, video makers, hosts, freelancers, or teachers. The greatest number of journalists holding down two jobs was found in the financial capital of the country, Shanghai, and second jobs were held by one in three journalists in online media.

In summary, with regard to job morphing in BRICS journalism, traditional media retained their traditional character by keeping stable workplaces with better salaries, while online media as new and less institutionalized organizations in the market offered short or temporary contracts, preferring to recruit young adults for whom such contracts seemed right at the beginning of their professional careers. The semantic meaning of a permanent job has changed to that of a temporary job that can be extended. Reporters in large cities perceived their frequent job changes to be normal. In comparison with other BRICS countries, Chinese online journalists were the most vulnerable in the labour market in terms of temporary employment and the marginality of their professional status in comparison with official journalists from traditional media.

It was mostly in Brazil, Russia, and China that journalists held a second job and this trend was also apparent in the Indian megapolises among online journalists. Second jobs helped journalists to increase their income and social capital by honing their skills when moonlighting in other media and occupations oriented to journalistic skills and knowledge: public relations, advertising, journalism teaching, and tourism, for example.

In conclusion, the basic reasons for professional mobility were a short or temporary employment contract, an underdeveloped labour market forcing journalists to move from a smaller city to a big city, insufficient income in the media, and a wish for professional career advancement in journalism but also in other occupations. Thus, mobility and holding a second job were due to a growing insecurity among journalists as media workers, but also due to journalists' passion for journalism. These factors forced them to seek new forms of (self-)employment and entrepreneurship. It also somehow had a positive psychological effect on the journalists, providing them with a feeling of autonomy and independence in the labour market in the spirit of a freelancer, fostering a careful attitude to time and their own resources, and accumulating social capital through new contacts in other areas of employment.

Satisfaction

The BRICS journalists had very similar reasons for satisfaction in their work: the high ideals of the profession, freedom, creativity, self-realization, professionalism, serving society, and moral rewards such as acknowledgment by colleagues and gratitude of readers. For instance, Brazilian journalists were happy because they could be useful to society. In Vitória, a journalist said,

> Despite the difficulties, mainly with respect to structural and financial matters, our team remains united. We aren't under the same pressure as profit-based companies. We conduct journalism to serve the people. What satisfies me is to know that my work is useful to society.

Half of the respondents in the capital Brasília and one third in the provincial city of Juiz de Fora said that the ability to write high-quality news stories motivated them. One fourth in Rio de Janeiro derived the greatest pleasure from the opportunity to do creative work and 19 per cent of them claimed that their audiences' gratitude and feedback were their greatest source of satisfaction. Among other reasons for satisfaction were the opportunity to inform and educate people, work in a field they enjoy, have the opportunity to get to know new cultures, work in a decent environment, and enjoy the confidence of their bosses.

Russian journalists most of all valued "the process of creativity itself and the opportunity for creative self-realization as a journalist", "the thanks of the audience and feedback from the audience", "effectiveness of publications", "obtaining new knowledge and meeting new people", and producing "materials of high quality". A young male online journalist in Moscow valued the chance "To do reviews of social media content, seek and invent creative solutions to all sorts of news". For a young male journalist in St. Petersburg, pleasure came from creating text:

> You are proud of the texts you've published. Satisfaction [comes] from finding a unique or the exclusive subject, the way you investigate it, how you write it up and present it. And, finally, from the fact that tens of thousands have read it.

In Petrozavodsk, two journalists mentioned the importance of acknowledgment by the public and colleagues; one specifically said, "When I help people, when I see the real results of my work, the situation changes. When, after publication, I meet these people, and they thank me, 'Thanks, you helped, you wrote'". Another journalist said, "I have an understanding of professional standards. And I have ambition. I don't need external praise or compliments. But the acknowledgment of the professional community is of vital importance to me".

In India, in Delhi and Hyderabad, most of the traditional media journalists were happy in their jobs and cited passion for their jobs and the gratification they received from their audience as being rewarding. One journalist said, "The job itself is the source of satisfaction. I find immense pleasure in the work I do. I love the thrill of going out and chasing stories", while another reported, "I'm not doing it for money; it is for self-respect and passion". And yet another journalist considered it a privilege to "have first-hand access to information", and said, "the sense of gratification from the audience feedback gives the greatest satisfaction". Satisfaction also came from the recognition these journalists received for quality work apart from the money and the promise of a good future in the profession. A journalist from Hyderabad said, "Recognition for journalistic work of high quality makes me happy and proud" and another liked the "openness in the atmosphere". As a journalist in Delhi put it, "[The profession] has a good future, value, and money. It is more about job satisfaction than anything else". A media entrepreneur provided a slightly different angle: "We are not doing it out of goodwill; we expect profits from this as well". Respondents in Kolkata and Pune were particularly pleased when they achieved visibility, for example, when they were published on the front page or when their supervisor or the audience appreciated their stories and discussed them: "When I see people are discussing my special story . . . that is the greatest satisfaction for a reporter". They were pleased as well when their stories contributed to the greater good: "something I can create and society benefits from it". A minority cited satisfaction because of money and opportunities for exclusive stories. Some also mentioned the constant variety in their jobs, including the challenges that kept the job from becoming monotonous.

Chinese journalists were largely satisfied with their jobs for reasons of autonomy, self-fulfilment or sense of achievement, professional recognition, accumulating knowledge and broadening horizons, and maintaining good relationships with colleagues. Professional autonomy first refers to flexible work schedules. As journalists can write or edit news in any place and they often go out for interviews, it is not necessary for them to stay in their offices during work hours. Once journalists have completed the required job in advance, they are free to use the remaining time for their own purposes. For some journalists, autonomy also means the freedom to choose what topics to cover and how to report them. Some respondents emphasized that enlightened leaders in editorial departments played an important role in promoting job autonomy. As one respondent in Shanghai explained, "If you propose a valuable idea, our leaders will provide support and coordinate resources to help you to achieve it". Journalists working in media outlets with low political and economic control were more likely to enjoy this type of professional autonomy, as there was less external influence on journalistic routines in editorial offices. Self-fulfilment and sense of achievement offered Chinese journalists psychological incentives. Some respondents indicated that they were motivated to work hard and stay in this profession if their work could promote social progress and earn public and social recognition.

In South Africa, journalists were particularly satisfied with their jobs per se. Stories that transformed people's lives made them particularly happy. Feedback from communities and audiences also gave them satisfaction, as did the opportunity to be part of history and hold those in public office fully accountable to citizens:

> So it is the work. It is what we do, the people that we meet; like recently, last week, we did a story on *wunga* (South African illegal drug substance) addicts. Even that we actually had to sit there and engage and talk to the people (drug addicts) and realize that they have stories to tell. We worked until some ridiculous hour and none of us was tired because what we got out of it (the story) was worth more than the effort to obtain it.

Dissatisfaction

One set of complaints that journalists from all BRICS countries shared was personal in nature, exposing their vulnerable position in the media, the labour market, and in society: low salaries; irregular and stressful working hours; social inequalities; income disparity; job insecurity; financial limitations on infrastructure, travel, and technological resources; and bad relations in the newsroom. In the words of a traditional media journalist, in Durban:

> I am content, I would probably say. I mean I am not really a quitter, but I do have those thoughts sometimes that 'I can't take this anymore'. You work

super long hours, [with] super little reward, [and] no promise of growth. You just don't know what's gonna happen tomorrow or what's gonna happen next year. I mean in terms of job security you don't know how long you have the job for, you don't know if you are gonna wake up tomorrow and the newspaper is gonna close down. It's tough because these are thoughts that come to you all the time . . . especially when you look at advertising trends in terms of how much you used to spend and how much is being spent now. If you look at 1990 and you look at 2000 and you look at 2010; Oh! What's gonna happen by 2020? The graph is sinking, so you worry about those things.

Another set of complaints related to these journalists' concern for democracy and their anxiety about the quality of journalism and conditions for quality journalism in their countries. In Brazil, an online journalist said that "media companies are always associated with financial power and an ideology that is against the people, and in favour of the elite". Despite Brazil's cultural diversity and territorial size and the fact that the formation of communication system oligopolies is prohibited and the freedom of the press is guaranteed by the Constitution of 1988, media production has been controlled by a limited number of families and media conglomerates. This contradiction is partly explained by the fact that although broadcasting is regulated by the state, the improper use of broadcast licences for political ends and the lack of supervision by the government creates a communications system that is not democratic. As one Brazilian journalist explained,

Brazil desperately needs a media law. . . . The Brazilian press, in theory, follows the principles dictated in its communication vehicles concessions. But these principles are not regulated. So they are disregarded and companies are not penalized for doing that. It is necessary to urgently end the oligopoly of journalism.

The voice of this journalist represents the voices of civil social movements that continually decry the fact that many radio and television channels do not comply with the rules regarding bidding processes. According to the Brazilian Constitution, the private initiative earns the right to operate radio and television channels through concessions of the state due to the limited spectrum of frequency bands. However, there are many irregularities in these processes, such as the formation of oligopolies, the control of a large part of these networks by politicians, the sale of concessions, and non-compliance with rules about the percentage of educational content in programming of media (Bolaño, 2003; Valente, 2008). In addition, in 2016, violence against journalists and press freedom in Brazil increased. The National Federation of journalists (FENAJ) in January 2017 reported that the cases of violence against journalists in the country increased on average 18 per cent in 2016, in comparison with the previous year. They registered 161 cases in which 222 professionals around the country have been subjected to physical or verbal assaults, threats, intimidation, repression through lawsuits, impediments to professional and trade union activity, imprisonment, censorship, attacks, and murders (FENAJ, 2017). For all these reasons, journalists in Brazil demand democratization and the end of the oligopolies of media systems.

Russian journalists worried about the ousting of independent media from the market, their work without results, i.e., the futility of their publications, and poor quality work. In Moscow, a young female online journalist argued, "In Russia there is a crisis of journalism. Good media outlets are few, they are under pressure, editorial staff are being cut, salaries too". In Petrozavodsk, one young male journalist spoke about the 'normalization' of political censorship:

> Recently, I was in the press conference of Galina Širšina, the mayor of Petrozavodsk; she is in confrontation with the Republican authorities [the mayor was a member of the Democratic Party, *Yabloko* (Apple), whereas the Republican authorities belonged to the Kremlin party, *Edinaya Rossia* (United Russia). Then I came back from the press conference, wrote the text, and sent it for proofreading to our curator [preventive political censorship]. We even have curators! We have this craziness now.

In India, in Delhi and Hyderabad, journalists were unhappy owing to "pressure from bosses" and "quality of content". In Kolkata, journalists were unhappy due to an editorial policy that created barriers to reporting the truth, and in Pune, dissatisfaction arose from job insecurity and monotony as well as the lack of a work ethic among colleagues who followed the editors' directives so as to keep their jobs, instead of thinking independently. Women in Pune also mentioned the glass ceiling and the soft topics assigned to them as reasons for dissatisfaction.

Chinese journalists were worried about diminished social prestige, low professionalism among journalists, strict government supervision, and an ineffective performance appraisal system, which in essence failed to increase journalists' intrinsic motivation to work hard and creatively. One traditional journalist said,

> This system doesn't create an atmosphere of competition. Everyone gets the same amount of salary. In addition, our leaders don't force you to work if you don't want to do. I even know some colleagues who earn the salary but never appear in the editorial office.

South African journalists complained about nepotism and racism. Black journalists complained about the slow pace of transformation, while white journalists complained about what amounted to reverse racism when they had to make room for black journalists.

Summarizing the findings on journalists' (dis)satisfaction, the sources of unhappiness of BRICS journalists mainly lay in the institutional conditions and current circumstances in which they had to survive: *economic* (low salary with increasing workload, decreasing staff and funding for work related travel and professional development); *political* (pressure from authorities, business, and owners of media, lack of freedom of media, censorship); *social* (nepotism, racism, inequality in pay), and *professional* (poor quality of work, bad relations in the newsrooms, dangerous profession). But when journalists speculated on the reasons for satisfaction in their work, they referred to their values and high ideals of freedom and justice and love of the profession and the people. That is, the sources of happiness were associated with journalists themselves: personal achievement and self-development in the profession, recognition of colleagues and readers, and the work itself, which was seen as a service to the people and a way to change the situation in society for the better, or to help people. That is, the sources of happiness revealed the values of self-expression, creativity, and passion for the profession, whereas complaints revealed values of survival by testifying about what was wrong and bad in the work, work conditions, and society.

Staying in the profession

The BRICS journalists loved their profession and the majority wanted to stay in journalism, but some thought about leaving it in the future. For instance, in Brazil, in Rio de Janeiro, a few journalists considered journalism to be highly stressful work and wanted to switch jobs in the mid or long term. Some of them had even decided to look for other ways to make a living in the academic and university world.

In Russia, some journalists indicated that they might leave journalism if they found financially better offers or if the situation changed in the future. In Delhi and Hyderabad, some journalists did not want to continue in the profession, mainly due to lack of career advancement resulting in stagnation. One journalist said, "I feel that eventually growth prospects will stop after a point and there will be stagnation in media as this industry does not pay too well". Some said, "There is no creative satisfaction". As most online media journalists were not serious about continuing in the profession, they were clear that journalism was a temporary step: "The thrill of being in the field of journalism is exciting, but my calling is film making. I'll eventually shift . . . to make films". In Kolkata and Pune, a few journalists were concerned about uncertainties surrounding the future of the profession or wanted to start their own businesses. In China, less than 5 per cent of the journalists clearly stated that they would change their profession soon. For example, some journalists planned to find a job in other industries or to seek a higher university degree. Nearly one fifth of the respondents said that their decision was contingent on the situation in the future. As one journalist from traditional media in Shanghai said, "I will stay in the profession unless our newspaper collapses".

The majority of the BRICS journalists were, however, eager to stay in the profession. In Russia, for some, it was a way to change the situation for the better; others practiced journalism as a way of life. As one traditional media male journalist in Petrozavodsk noted, "Well, I think I'll work on this, yes. Journalism is a profession that it is almost not a profession [enjoyment, favourite business]. This is interesting". In Delhi and Hyderabad, respondents said that the profession gave meaning to their lives although the pay was minimal. As one journalist said, "I love my work and it looks as if this is my calling in life". In Kolkata and Pune, the majority of the journalists wanted to stay in the profession because this was their field of interest, one that they were passionate about, and because the profession afforded the opportunity to stay in touch with their communities. As one journalist said, "A career in journalism offers me a multitude of media, and my social network helps me to stay connected with every community". In China, traditional media journalists were significantly more likely to continue in journalism than were online journalists. In South Africa, the majority of journalists wanted to stay in the profession longer. Some presented their views jokingly in terms of "Ja? I am not skilled to do anything else" and "Until my husband allows me to stay at home, yes". Others, however, were serious:

> Um, I still think that there are so many stories to tell about South Africa that are good. I know that sounds very cheesy because everyone wants to tell the bad story, but I think that there is so much about South Africa that people still need to know, and I think that we as journalists are the only voice for people to know the stories. And also, I still want to grow. I have only been here for five months, so I am not even a seasoned journalist yet. So I just want to grow in the field as well. I want to explore all the options and do as much as I can and gain as much experience, and just tell South Africa's beautiful story.

It is surprising that in spite of the difficulties and a growing uncertainty that journalists noted in their interviews, the majority wanted to remain in the profession. This was due to their passion for journalism and perhaps also the young age of the journalists, who were the majority in the BRICS study sample.

Dreaming about better conditions for journalism

The narratives of the BRICS journalists about their satisfaction and dissatisfaction with their current jobs were indirect evidence of the present quality of life and conditions for journalistic work in their respective countries. BRICS journalists' understanding and ideas about the best conditions and the desired type of democracy in order for journalism to fully accomplish its functions and tasks differed between and within countries.

In Brazil, it would include economic independence, the end of corruption, media autonomy, and press freedom. For the improvement of professional practice, the journalists also mentioned the end of media oligopoly, media democratization, and freedom of political expression, which should be more important than the political and economic interests of media companies. In addition, they argued that the quality of news, and not the profits of news companies, should be considered a priority. Journalists were also concerned about the regulation of journalism diplomas and improvement in education. As one journalist explained, "I think there is a lack of an education base capable of awakening the people, the public, and the citizens and making them understand that no means is ideal and impartial".

In Russia, most journalists believed that a broadening of democratic freedoms and practices was needed along with ensuring the economic independence of the media from the state. However, these journalists' perceptions of better conditions were associated with contrasting political values, and their views about democracy referred to various things. In traditional media, in Moscow, some deemed the development of socialism important, but online media journalists advocated the strengthening of liberal approaches. In St. Petersburg, in the traditional media, and in Petrozavodsk in the traditional and online media, journalists believed that nothing should change in the socio-political conditions in the country. This view was also shared by journalists in Yekaterinburg; in the words of one journalist in Yekaterinburg, "Russia with its problems – an ideal country for the development of journalism"; and "no changes were necessary". By this, the journalists did not mean that the country had created favourable conditions for the development of journalism, but that the difficulties forced journalists to be more creative and professional in their approach and in the preparation of their publications. A young, female online journalist reported this:

> I think that any system for journalism is normal. Because here, for example, during the Soviet era there was, of course, strict censorship, but journalists were such a 'thing-in-itself'. They did not write about politics, but they were very perfect in their style; indeed, they wrote true masterpieces that can be compared with literature! Essays and everything else. You are captured by the author's idea, which leads you through the whole text. We have a lot of media now, but whether there are benefits to this abundance of media – that is the question.

In Petrozavodsk, among other opinions, a need was articulated to keep "a balance between *glasnost*[2] and anarchy" as the most suitable social system for the proper functioning of journalism. Other journalists looked at the Scandinavian countries as models.

In the Indian megapolises of Delhi and Hyderabad, almost all journalists echoed that freedom and democracy were primary in their field. "Democracy and freedom where journalists have the right to say what they want with minimum interference from the government" is what most journalists wanted. It was not only freedom from outside agencies, but also within their organization: "More democracy is required inside as well as outside media" and "The key word is freedom. Economic freedom for news media houses is as important as oxygen for humans". But there were some who said that introspection was required among the journalists. As one journalist noted, "It is not the socio-political conditions, but the mindset of journalists that has to change", and "Journalism must become a movement or revolution to set right the socio-political system of the country. Journalists should trigger that change". According to some respondents, journalists should also have a sense of social responsibility along with freedom. Others felt that there should be a change in the people, too, to be "responsible citizens" and to "stop being naive and start prioritising real news". Facebook, etc., were tools to voice their opinions and views, but were not facts. Such social media tools also raised the issue of credibility in the media: "The importance of media changed from being a giver of information to a receiver".

For Kolkata journalists, the seemingly unhealthy relationship with politics plaguing the field, i.e., the "politicised media", was the socio-political condition mentioned repeatedly as preventing journalism from fulfilling its functions and therefore requiring change. Currently politicians are involved in the policies of media houses; the journalists' opinion is that "Political influence should be less on media; it is like a disease". Other socio-political changes journalists would like to see were improved literacy rates and, for a minority of respondents, fewer hazards for journalists on the job and a citizenry responsible for fulfilling its civic duties. For Pune journalists, the lack of literacy and media literacy, i.e., an understanding of how news is produced as well as information about the owner's business connections so that they could critically assess news, were the obstacles. These journalists would also like to see greater penetration of media into "grassroots communities", and suggested that technology such as mobile phones could be leveraged for this.

In China, the respondents highlighted that the government should reduce media regulation and the country should establish the first press law to ensure that journalism could fully perform its functions and tasks:

> A strict control of media may generate unexpected and negative consequences. The public would be inclined to believe that Chinese media outlets were not credible. Thus, they would be more motivated to bypass online censorship to get access to alternative information resources.

A great number of South African journalists pointed out that that they need a more democratic space. There was a general feeling among them that media freedoms won over time were being slowly taken away by political pressure and attacks on independent media. One respondent made the following observation:

> I think that there must not be control from the top. That is the sense that I get, that this desire to portray this one party as the one party that is doing anything in the entire country is coming from the top. Whatever we get from the top we can't question, even my boss can't question, so how can I? If my boss is not allowed to say no, who am I, the journalist, to say no? So I think that from the top down there is political influence there. And they want us to show a specific side to them and if you go against that then you are not a good journalist, and if you go for that then they applaud you and give you a raise, and say come to Joburg and do stories here because you [are] too big for the Eastern Cape, just because you are speaking their stories.

Another said,

> I mean you know that – I read somewhere that with democracy, the ANC over the past couple of years is starting to use the same tactics the past government used to use in order to prevent people from finding out certain things. So the strides that have already been taken, we will see them slowly coming, or going backward, instead of moving forward. In that sense, I think that as journalists we always need to be aware of that, and to the powers that be, we need to be always challenging those conditions as well.

In spite of their peculiar political and professional-cultural contexts, the BRICS journalists dreamed about two basic things: more democracy in their country, which would ensure political and economic independence of the profession, and more democracy at the workplace, in the media outlet where they worked. Only Indian journalists specified an important condition that would contribute to the development of democracy in their country, in particular, the need for citizens to take responsibility for what is happening in their cities and communities.

Foreseeing the future today

The journalists' views on the future were associated with the prevailing situation in the profession and the socio-political situation in their country. Thus, Brazilian journalists argued that journalism would become faster and more informative, with increasingly wide-ranging functions and diverse production models. Journalism would be subjected to greater influence from social networking websites, online media would expand, and journalists would be increasingly required to produce content for diverse media. In the voice of the interviewed editor of the website 247, Leonardo Attuch:

> As I see it, the scenario for the next decade will be increasingly fragmented and therefore more democratic. Journalism will hardly be dominated by large media groups and families, as it was in the past. Since there are no further obstacles to setting up media companies, because graphic printing facilities and vast investments are no longer necessary, the tendency is toward the pulverisation of those who produce content. The greatest challenge is to survive in this jungle.

In his expert interview, the editor of the website *Diário do Centro do Mundo*, Kiko Nogueira,[3] stated that the main future challenge for journalists is the need to reinvent oneself in the digital world: "Traditional media companies, which are just too big, are shrinking and dying out. Journalists will be required to undertake their own businesses".

In Russia, in Yekaterinburg, traditional media journalists predicted total Internetization of the media – Internet newspapers, Internet television – whereas online journalists expected a rise in speed and information that would affect the work of the journalist, who would become a more versatile professional. In Petrozavodsk, in the traditional media, the majority believed that nothing would change in the future. Only in online media did journalists believe that journalism would come faster and provide more information than it does now. Some of them also believed that "journalism will merge with bloggers", "a monopoly of media will be reduced by means of user-generated content, and the audience will become more active in producing journalism", "print media will disappear", and journalism will further divide into fast and slow journalism, into news journalism and analytical journalism. Among other views of the future of journalism were "the journalist will become a universal professional", "[journalism] will descend into entertainment", and "there is a trend towards the reduction of text in favour of video".

In Moscow, journalists' perspectives on the future of the profession and their own personal future were that both were uncertain. This became evident even at the dawn of the new wave of economic crisis, in the beginning and middle of 2014, with uncertainty touching both online and traditional media journalists. It was also unclear what freedoms there would be in the future. According to a male online journalist,

> Today, truly professional journalism has collapsed or is an endangered occupation because it is suppressed by the state in the form of censorship of one kind or another, sometimes an explicit prohibition on the profession. I really hope that in ten years the situation will have changed.

In St. Petersburg, online journalists were more optimistic than their colleagues from newspapers, radio, and television. In the online subgroup, nobody suggested that newspapers would disappear and only one respondent said that "journalism will degrade, disappear" and two journalists thought that nothing would change. In traditional media, the feeling about the future was more pessimistic: at least two out of every ten respondents there did not believe in the survival of their profession.

In the Indian megacities of Delhi and Hyderabad, overall, there was a positive tone about the emerging scene where online media would bring in several changes:

> The future is going to be super exciting with convergence of multiple platforms and faster dissemination of news. I think it will become more democratic eventually as technology becomes cheaper [and cheaper] day by day; the access increases and one doesn't have to go to the traditional media to tell one's story.

There was also a word of caution from some journalists who wanted to wait and watch how the quality of news would be affected in the age of instant news and citizen journalists and bloggers telling their own stories:

> I think there will be more restraint from the media itself and they will be able to deliver quality while the newer medium, Internet, will be flooded with quantity of information. We need to see how this battle of quality vs. quantity plays out in the longer run.

Another journalist said, "I think that the online medium will pick up". One view was that there would be many independent journalist-bloggers, who would sporadically spring up; however, the quality of news would be marred. A few journalists raised concerns about the future of the print media and the effect on the media industry in general: "The task at hand is to keep up the enthusiasm for traditional media, especially print media". One journalist working for a print magazine said, "There are good chances that print media will suffer heavily; [at present] we are only witnessing this decline in the magazine sector . . . ; everything will be shifted to digital platforms" and "I think a lot will change". One traditional media journalist speculated that serious journalism might be affected in the onslaught of technology:

> A lot of genres like development journalism will be rendered useless in the long haul. I am very keen to follow up and see if the monopoly of media will disappear or continue as the industry grows manifold with new technology in the new era.

In Pune and Kolkata, the future of journalism was seen to lie in technology – new media, social media, multimedia online journalism, and smartphones: "I think smartphones have the power to make . . . a difference". Kolkata journalists believed that with technology, the industry would also change, expand, and extend to new places, requiring educated people as the engine behind it. Young people were particularly highlighted as an important part of this change, although some respondents also felt there would not be enough space for newcomers. In Pune, respondents felt that news would be delivered faster to accommodate the audience's need for information and thus result in the decline of print media. In addition, they suggested that the influence of increased global interaction would lead to an increase in global journalism.

In China, respondents estimated that the number of print media outlets would decrease dramatically but that print media would not totally disappear in the short term. There would be a major emigration of traditional journalists due to a lack of opportunities and a decline in the social prestige of this profession. Job mobility would become more common, as the younger generation was more open to future job changes. With the rise of online journalism, more traditional journalists might choose to work in promising online media outlets, or they would take up work in other industries. The journalists also predicted that online journalists would not be excluded from obtaining official press cards from the General Administration of Press and Publication in the future. This prophecy has been fulfilled, as the first group of online journalists received their press cards in early November 2015.

In South Africa, the media system is still dominated by monopolistic traditional media, and will continue to be for a long time. The philosophy of the legislative regime that governs media in general is not going to change radically; it will, however, extend to accommodate digital media developments. These changes would be within the constitutional framework nonetheless. The new digital media-oriented legislative changes will have to guarantee all the freedoms already protected by the South African Constitution: access to the media and freedom of speech/expression. Media organizations are most likely to remain the same in terms of ownership, control, and financing. In the next ten years, very few independent and de-monopolised media will emerge. As media and their environment change, the issue of whether or not it is more prestigious to work in the traditional media or in online media will fade.

South African journalists were concerned about the quality of journalism in the future. One journalist said,

> I think traditional media is actually going down, especially print media. I think young people don't read newspapers. You do not see a young person going to buy a newspaper. They have access to information, like now they have social networks. I think that edgy thing about journalism is slowly fading away; people are just too focused on politics, politics, politics; it's just politics.

To sum up, the BRICS journalists believed in the further digitalization of journalism, which would inevitably lead to its democratization and to a decentralization of the power of mainstream media, the rise of a new identity of a journalist emerging from new economic conditions, and a new technology of journalistic labour.

Conclusion

Journalists, like other professionals, live in an era of downsizing and, according to some forecasts, even in an era of the disappearance of wage labour. According to Beck's (2000/1986) argument from 30 years ago, we stand at the beginning of the counter-industrial process of rationalization that leads not only to the regrouping of the structure of occupations and qualifications, but also to a revision of the principles of previous employment. This revision involves a radical change in all aspects of labour: employment contract, place of work, and working hours. The boundaries between 'on and off the job' are becoming blurred to the extent that wage labour is decentralized because employees may work partially or totally at home on their computers, and a plural form of underemployment emerges. That is, the flexible plural market of partial employment, typical for a society at risk, gradually expands and begins to dominate, and unemployment disappears but reappears generalized in new, risky forms of underemployment. All this points to the beginning of a new dual and contradictory development that includes both benefits and disadvantages, which are inseparably intertwined and whose long-term consequences, primarily for political consciousness and practice, are invisible (Beck, 2000/1986, p. 209).

The personal situations of the BRICS journalists show that they live in a society at risk, where local labour markets and media organizations cannot provide them with the former stability, predictability, and job security. The journalists mostly relied on themselves to survive in the profession. They had both hopes and fears for the future of their profession. On the one hand, they believed that digital technologies already offered opportunities for greater access to and production of information in the virtual environment, and that the influence of digital media on professional journalistic practices was becoming increasingly noteworthy. The web permits collaborative work and greater flexibility in the production and consumption of content. Digital technologies operate in favour of journalism, contributing to business cost reductions and media democratization, as was emphasized in his expert interview by the editor of the website 247, Leonardo Attuch, in Brazil:

> We can list a series of benefits, such as the following: 1) the end of layout and printing costs and news distribution expenses; 2) the end of the need for physical editorial rooms, since reporters and editors can communicate via Google Hangouts, Skype, etc.; 3) the rapidity of obtaining information, thanks to services like Twitter and Facebook, which transform those who are in the news (politicians, artists, etc.) into producers of content; and 4) the engagement of readers with media companies, via platforms for comments and debate on websites.

On the other hand, journalists are worried about the quality of journalism in the context of the growing entertainment genres including digital games and the decline of interest in political news in the young generation, but also growing commercial values among young journalists. The opinion of a journalist from Port Elizabeth, South Africa, was that

> the young ones who are coming into the trade to . . . [chase] fame, . . . mostly now, our journalists . . . are for fame, more than for the craft. If we do not rectify that and nip that in the bud now, we are going to be sitting with celebrity journalists.

Many journalists also feared the devaluation of the profession, concerned that it would become less and less specialized both in terms of training and professional practice, but with lower salaries, little chance of promotion, and no benefits.

As respondents in this study reported, digitalization became the trigger for a complex process of transformation of journalism and undermined the power of the traditional media, traditional forms of employment and payment, and the former status of the media professional. Des Freedman (2014) affirms that the disruption and decentralization of power coincides with an intense and seemingly unbounded concentration of power. While the Internet has certainly facilitated the possibility of broader circulation of marginal voices and the reconstitution of publicness, corporate power, far from disappearing in recent years, is flourishing and has adapted itself to meet the challenges of the digital economy. As Des Freedman (2014, p. 30) puts it, "Media power is both a consequence and an increasingly significant component of continuing, and stratified, processes of social reproduction" in liberal capitalist society.

On the one hand, from the empirical evidence of the BRICS study, it could be suggested that the transformation of journalism is going on along four D vectors: 1) decentralization: de-monopolization of current (political-economic) media systems with the advent of open and accessible digital platforms and sites, including alternatives to government and commercial journalism (journalistic startups, blogs); 2) democratization: de-elitization of the profession with the growth of Internet-facilitated hardware, software, and applications, and venues of communication such as mobile telephony, WhatsApp, and social media enabling the generation, delivery, and receipt of information by citizens; 3) de-monetization: the search for new digital media business models employing voluntary co-creation of information and co-funding of information outlets by Internet users as distinct from business models that are oriented solely towards profit seeking and profit making; and 4) de-professionalization: the advent of new information-providing professions using games and video for example as well as of a new workforce of freelancers from the creative occupations and science fields.

But, on the other hand, we agree with Des Freedman on the complex, controversial, and non-linear processes of the transformation of media and journalism. The ease of dissemination of information on the web and via mobile devices does not guarantee media democratization. The number of clicks tends to be more important than the quality of the news nowadays. False events constructed on the web undermine important debates in society. Non-respectful memes and prejudices, which invent content, tend to produce more hate than clarification, more judgments than explanations, more insecurity than knowledge, more conservative subjectivities than respect for others. Thus, the uses of digital technologies by mainstream media and social networks do not always contribute to a better understanding of the world.

In this context, re-imagining the future of journalism means rethinking the ways of increasing the influence of independent journalism capable of the disclosure of an event's controversies instead of giving priority to balanced neutrality that slants towards maintaining political discourses, values, and guidelines defined a priori by the institutions in which they are produced.

Journalism is not immune to the dilemmas faced by society nowadays. Our analysis of journalistic hopes for the next decade reveals that they are facing various tensions in the daily routines of newsrooms, which arise from social and economic inequalities. And the prediction of Freidson (1986), about the rising education of the public, still has not been confirmed in all BRICS countries.

Certainly, as one Brazilian respondent said, higher education for all the people will make them more critical of media discourses. Our belief is that good journalism has perhaps never been so important to build a just society. Truth of the facts based on the context from variety of perspectives is, perhaps, one of the ways to re-imagine the future of journalism as a form of knowledge and co-creation in the digital media environment.

Notes

1 Leonardo Attuch, editor in chief of independent news website, Brasil247 (www.brasil247.com/), was interviewed for this chapter.
2 *glasnost*: Russian: 'openness', Soviet policy of open discussion of political and social issues; https://global.britannica.com/topic/glasnost.
3 We thank Igor Waltz for his help in the production of the interviews with the editor of the website Brasil247, Leonardo Attuch, and the editor of the website *Diário do Centro do Mundo*, Kiko Nogueira.

References

Agência Pública de Notícias (Public News Agency). (2016). Retrieved from http://apublica.org/mapa-do-jornalismo/#
Barber, B. (1983). *The logic and limits of trust*. New Brunswick, NJ: Rutgers University Press.
Barland, J. (2013). Innovation of new revenue streams in digital media, journalism as customer relationship. *Nordicom Review, 34* (Special Issue), 99–112.
Beck, U. (2000/1986). *Obshchestvo riska. Na puti k drugomu modernu* [Risk society: On the way to another modern]. Moscow: Progress-Tradition; (*Auf Dem Weg In Eine Andere Moderne*. Suhrkamp: Verlag Frankfurt am Main, 1986).
Becker, B. (2016). Doing and thinking journalism in the twenty-first century, a dialogue with Barbie Zelizer. *Journal of Applied Journalism & Media Studies, 5*(1), 3–10, doi: 10.1386/ajms.5.1.3_1
Bell, A. E. (2014, December 3). *Post industrial journalism: Adapting to the present*. Columbia Journalism School: Tow Center for Digital Journalism. Retrieved from http://towcenter.org/research/post-industrial-journalism-adapting-to-the-present-2/
Benson, R., & Neveu, E. (2005). *Bourdieu and the journalistic field*. Cambridge: Polity Press.
Bolaño, C. R. S. (2003). *Políticas de Comunicação e Economia Política das Telecomunicações no Brasil: Convergência, regionalização e reforma* (3rd ed.). Aracaju: UFSE.
Bruno, N., & Nielsen, R. K. (2012). *Survival is success: journalistic online start-ups in Western Europe*. Oxford: University of Oxford, the Reuters Institute for the Study of Journalism.
Burnham, J. C. (1982). American medicine's golden age: What happened to it? *Science, 215* (March 19), 1474–1479.
Couldry, N., Madianou, M., & Pinchevski, A. (2013). *Ethics of media*. London and New York: Palgrave Macmillan.
Curran, J. (2012). Reinterpreting the Internet. In J. Curran, N. Fenton, & D. Freedman (Eds.), *Misunderstanding the Internet* (pp. 3–33). London and New York: Routledge.
Deuze, M. (2014). O Jornalismo, a vida na Mídia e a Sociedade Empreendedora. *Parágrafo, Revista científica de Comunicação Social da FIAM-FAAM, 2*(2). Retrieved from http://revistaseletronicas.fiamfaam.br/index.php/recicofi/article/view/238
EBC. Agência Brasil. (2016). IBGE: mercado de trabalho vive círculo vicioso com perda de emprego e renda [IBGE: The labour market lives vicious circle with loss of employment and

income]. Retrieved from http://agenciabrasil.ebc.com.br/economia/noticia/2016-08/ibge-mercado-de-trabalho-vive-circulo-vicioso-com-perda-de-emprego-e-renda

Ess, C. (2009). *Digital media ethics*. Cambridge: Polity Press.

FENAJ (National Federation of Journalists). (2016). *Relatório 2016. Violência contra jornalistas e liberdade de imprensa no Brasil* [2016 report. Violence against journalists and press freedom in Brazil]. Retrieved from http://fenaj.org.br/wp-content/uploads/2016/06/relatorio_fenaj_2016.pdf

Frayssé, O., & O'Neil, M. (2015). Introduction Hacked in the USA: Prosumption and Digital Labour. In O. Frayssé, & M. O'Neil (Eds.), *Digital labour and prosumer capitalism: The US matrix*. London: Palgrave Macmillan.

Freedman, D. (2014). *The contradictions of media power*. London: Bloomsbury.

Freidson, E. (1986). *Professional powers: A study of the institutionalization of formal knowledge*. Chicago and London: The University of Chicago Press.

Friend, C., & Singer, J. (2007). *Online journalism ethics: Traditions and transitions*. Armonk, NY: M. E. Sharpe.

Gusejnov, G. (2014). Divided by a common web: Some characteristics of the Russian blogosphere. In M. Gorham, I. Lunde, & M. Paulsen (Eds.), *Digital Russia: The language, culture and politics of new media communication* (pp. 57–71). London and New York: Routledge.

Haug, M. R. (1973). Deprofessionalization: An alternative hypothesis for the future. *Sociological Review Monograph, 20*, 195–211.

Haug, M. R. (1975). The deprofessionalization of everybody? *Sociological Focus, 8*(August), 197–213.

Haug, M. R. (1977). Computer technology and the obsolescence of the concept of profession. In M. R. Haug, & J. Dofny (Eds.), *Work and technology* (pp. 215–228). Beverly Hills, CA: Sage.

Herscovitz, H. G. (2012). Brazilian journalists in the 21st century. In D. H. Weaver & L. Willnat (Eds.), *The global journalist in the 21st century* (pp. 365–381). New York: Routledge.

Hesmondhalgh, D., Oakley, K., Lee, D., & Nisbett, M. (2015). *Culture, economics and politics: The case of new labour*. London: Palgrave Macmillan.

Hu, Y. (2012). Spreading the news. *Index on Censorship, 41*(4), 107–111. Retrieved from http://ioc.sagepub.com/content/41/4/107

Huws, U., & Leys, C. (2003). *The making of a cybertariat: Virtual work in a real world*. London: Merlin.

Maxwell, R. (2016). *The Routledge companion to labor and media*. New York: Routledge.

Möller, C. (2013). New forms of journalism. In A. Hulin & M. Stone (Eds.), *The online media self-regulation guidebook* (pp. 20–24). Vienna OSCE Representative on Freedom of the Media. Retrieved from www.osce.org/fom/99560

Pasti, S. (2015). A passion for Robin Hood: A case study of journalistic (in)dependence in Russia. In B. Dobek-Ostrowska & M. Glowacki (Eds.), *Democracy and media in Central and Eastern Europe 25 years on* (pp. 117–136). Frankfurt am Main: Peter Lang.

Pasti, S., Chernysh, M., & Svitich, L. (2012). The Russian journalists and their profession. In D. H. Weaver & L. Willnat (Eds.), *The global journalist in the 21st century* (pp. 267–282). New York: Routledge.

Pasti, S., Ramaprasad, J., & Ndlovu, M. (2015). BRICS journalists in global research. In K. Nordenstreng & D. K. Thussu (Eds.), *Mapping BRICS media* (pp. 205–227). London and New York: Routledge.

Picard, R. (2001). Strategical responses to free distribution daily newspapers. *International Journal on Media Management, 2*(3), 167–171.

Qiu, J. L. (2016). Locating Worker-Generated Content (WGG) in the world's factory. In R. Maxwell (Ed.), *The Routledge companion to labor and media* (pp. 303–314). New York: Routledge.

Rothman, R. A. (1984). Deprofessionalization: The case of law in America. *Work and Occupations, 11*(May), 183–206.

Sherstoboeva, E. A., & Pavlenko, V. Y. (2015). Trends in the regulation of the Russian blogosphere, *Mediascope 4*. Moscow: Moscow State University. Retrieved from www.mediascope.ru/node/2039

Standing, G. (2011). *The precariat: The new dangerous class*. London and New York: Bloomsbury Academic.

Valente, J. (2008). O Uso Indevido das Concessões de TV. *Observatório de Imprensa*. Retrieved from http://observatoriodaimprensa.com.br/imprensa-em-questao/o-uso-indevido-das-concessoes-de-tv/

Valor Econômico. (2016). *IBGE: Perda de emprego com carteira no trimestre foi a maior em 4 anos* [IBGE: Job loss with (work) portfolio in the quarter was the highest in 4 years]. Retrieved from www.valor.com.br/brasil/4543747/ibge-perda-de-emprego-com-carteira-no-trimestre-foi-maior-em-4-anos

Ward, S. J. A. (2010). Ethics for the new mainstream. In P. Benedetti, T. Currie, & K. Kierans (Eds.), *The new journalist: Roles, skills, and critical thinking* (pp. 313–326). Toronto: Emond Montgomery Publications.

Weaver, D. H., & Willnat, L. (Eds.). (2012). *The global journalist in the 21st century*. New York: Routledge.

Zhang, H., & Su, L. (2012). Chinese media and journalists in transition. In D. H. Weaver & L. Willnat (Eds.), *The global journalist in the 21st century* (pp. 9–21). New York: Routledge.

PART II
Two-country comparisons of critical issues

6
TECHNOLOGICAL MANIFESTATIONS IN THE NEWSROOM

India and Brazil

Ravindra Kumar Vemula, Márcio Guerra, Christiane Paschoalino, and Layrha Silva Moura

Introduction

This chapter addresses the concern of journalists within the context of the vast technological changes undertaken recently in the news media of India and Brazil. In this new digital age, in many countries there appeared a sense of uncertainty about media markets, the future of newspapers, and broadcast television (Ram, 2011, p. 1). There is a strong sense that "the news industry is no longer in control of its own future" (Rosenstiel & Mitchell, 2011, p. 3) and that it is technology companies like "Google and the social media that lead the way and are to hegemonize the public space that once belonged to the news media" (Ram, 2011, p. 1). The new digital era has been characterized by instant news to audiences ever hungry for information. Thus, in its effort to satisfy this hunger for news, the media have to keep up to date, whereas journalists need constantly to upgrade their technological skills in order to survive in the profession. According to Franco (2009, p. 5), in order to stay relevant to ever demanding 'news hungry' audiences and to the new generation that is shaping the future, journalists must accept the changes and put themselves at the forefront of the transition. Thus, the implication is that journalists must turn into multiskilled newsmakers but retain power in their profession. Otherwise, news production may be entrusted to droids and IT workers.

There are various opinions about how new technologies influence the profession and practice of journalists and the nature of news. Spyridou et al. (2013) argue that technology has a deterministic impact on the role and working practices of journalists as it is a part of the wider spectrum of human activity. In their opinion, technological determinism is centralized around the idea that social problems can be solved by technological advancement, and this is the way that society moves forward. Other scholars (Kawamoto, 2003; O'Sullivan, 2005) believe that technology has the potential impact of heralding societal functions that serve people by increased accountability and transparency along with dialogue and participatory communication.

There is also the belief that the most prominent impact of technology on journalism is the clear shift in communication control and journalistic practices (Heinonen, 2011; Singer et al., 2011). The traditional form of journalism has given way to convergent journalism that has increased the dynamics of media production. The new technology also gave impetus to the evolution of participatory journalism, in which "the act of a citizen, or group of citizens playing an active role in the process of collecting, reporting, analysing, and disseminating news and information" has become more prominent (Bowman & Willis, 2003, p. 9).

Pondering on changing journalistic practices, Hermans and Vergeer (2009) emphasize the importance of the technical ability of journalists to use new technology but also their cognitive ability to understand the impact of digitalization on their work routines. Journalists have 'cool tools' now. They are filing stories on Blackberries and have cell phone cameras and video. They are also using Twitter and Facebook to track down newsmakers or people who know newsmakers (Lareau, 2010). Lareau (2010) also points to the fact that the journalists are editing video on their desktops; in fact, video is digitized so everyone in the newsroom has all the video on their desktops. Citizen journalism has caused the numbers of reporters and photographers to be smaller. This may not have directly led to layoffs but it has been an enabler of layoffs. The growth in the numbers of amateur columnists and opinion writers is staggering.

By contrast, Kaul (2013) argues that technology just supplements but does not radically change the work styles of the journalists in media organizations. New technology also influences the nature of news. In particular, Reich (2013, p. 417) notes that technology has made news more enigmatic, more fluid, and less observable as "information flows inside and outside the newsrooms". Reich (2013) attributes this to the increase in the number of media platforms. Media managers started owning and cross-promoting between TV, newspaper, and online properties when they started owning properties on all platforms. This phenomenon has led to a decrease in the number for reporters. The same reporter is expected to do stories for all platforms.

In many developing countries, including India and Brazil, printed newspapers and magazines are still prevalent, even with the implementation of new technology in the news media. In both countries, the press is very old, having been in existence for more than two centuries. Its strengths have largely been shaped by its historical experience and, in particular, by its association with the freedom struggle as well as movements for social emancipation, reform, and improvement. In India, the growth trends in circulation and readership are especially strong in regional language news media. The steady rise in literacy rates – from 65 per cent of the population in 2001 to 73 per cent in 2011 – has had unexpected consequences (Subramanian, 2014).

The new middle class is increasingly found in smaller towns in India, and these people prefer to read in their regional languages rather than in English. Meanwhile, major media houses have discovered that English readership is declining or stagnant, and that advertising rates in English-language papers cannot be pushed much higher. Along with an influx of politicians from non-elite backgrounds and the growing importance of regional and state-level politics, these developments have begun to challenge the assumption that English is the lingua franca default medium of Indian public life. By investing more energy in regional languages, the media houses are just adapting to the changing ways of the country (Subramanian, 2014). For instance, while English-language news media form the largest segment, with 40 per cent of advertising revenue, vernacular regional markets follow close behind and account for 30 per cent of advertising revenues in the print media industry, the remainder being spent on Hindi language news media. It is no secret that the print media industry is heavily dependent on advertising revenue because only 30 per cent of its income is from copies sold and the remaining 70 per cent comes from advertising (Sharma, 2012). Regional language newspapers have a strong foothold in the Indian print market and are in a good position to monetize their audience base through both circulation and advertising revenue (FICCI-KPMG, 2016). While in India the reader's interest in the digital medium is increasing, the huge market size offers many opportunities for various media channels to coexist. Although there are very few independent news websites in India, as most traditional media maintain an online presence, journalists are exposed to and also influenced by the technological changes they regularly witness and experience.

In Brazil, the development of digital news media and technology had its first 'boom' in the '90s with the popularization of the Internet. Over the years, the lower than average Internet access costs as well as the more affordable prices of desktops and notebooks made it easier for millions of people to be online. This has profoundly changed the field of journalism in the country as online news media emerged. Traditional media did not fade away, as many scholars predicted. Instead, in an effort to survive in this new digital world, they are adapting themselves to 'media convergence' to retain and increase their audiences. Media houses are trying to create means to survive the ease and swiftness of news disseminated via the Internet. Major players in the sector have encountered difficulties in the model of business management, being obliged to adapt themselves to the new gadgets and apps in order to attract readers' attention. However, most means of communication have failed at some point when trying to reinvent themselves according to the revolution brought about by the Internet, which has caused job losses over the past few years in Brazil (Farah, 2014).

This chapter offers a look at the process of digitalization of newsrooms from within, from the perspective of the journalists themselves, from their personal experiences and opinions about it.

The BRICS study

This chapter presents the voices of journalists narrating *what* technological changes (innovations) have happened in the past few years in the newsroom and *how* these changes have influenced their practices, quality of journalism production, and personal stories. The analysis of their narratives strives to reveal both similarities witnessing the common effects of journalism engineering in both countries, and particularities appearing from personal journalistic experiences within specific local contexts. Journalists in both countries agreed that new technology, including the advent of social media, has indeed brought about revolutionary changes with both positive and negative effects on their current work situation. The chapter discusses three aspects: The impact of technology on journalistic practice, the impact of technology on the quality of journalism production, and the impact of technology on the personal story of a journalist.

Findings

Impact of technology on journalistic practice

Convergence

Journalists in Delhi agreed that there have been rapid technological changes in the media in the past five years: "The world is really changing with the news media". The convergence of technology for gathering, reporting, and disseminating news facilitated journalistic work in traditional and online media alike. A traditional media journalist said, "There is an absolute convergence of media with wires, agencies, and even Twitter as a main source of information".

Although one can see a visible difference in the changes that technology has initiated, there is still much remaining potential, given the vast geographical spectrum of the regional and the national media. As a traditional media journalist in Delhi noted:

> I think we have convergence of media to a very limited extent; it will increase manifold. The change is going to be totally visible sooner or later in the manner of our media consumption patterns with the technology becoming cheaper and access to technology reaching to the remotest corners of the country such as India. Stringers will become more and more important to get the ground perspective.

In the capital Brasília, the majority of traditional media journalists perceived convergence as an important factor in everyday work more often than did online media journalists. For online journalists, convergence was a natural attribute of online journalism. Compared to other cities in Brazil, journalists in Rio in both types of media noted that the main positive impact of new technology was in its facilitation of collecting and processing information. Another positive impact of digitalization was getting feedback from the audience, which was important for journalists not only in the sense of communication with the public, but also for identifying new sources of information. One online journalist saw a positive impact because "the changes brought by technology led to more versatile work for journalists and thus to reaching new audiences". Journalists in Juiz de Fora affirmed that technological changes contributed positively in the way they collected and processed information and how they started to deal with the search for information. Traditional media journalists in Juiz de Fora highlighted that technological changes have led to a possibility of multiplatform convergence, bringing together radio, print, television, magazines, and the Internet.

Social media

Another benefit of technology has been the integration of social media with news media, making the process of sourcing news stories and opinions relatively simple. In Delhi, one journalist indicated, "There is a lot more use of social media networking websites for the purpose of gathering and disseminating the news. It has made the channels of information much faster". A similar opinion about the increasing role of social media in the journalistic work came from another journalist in Delhi:

> Social media reporting has come up in a very big way: information through Twitter is super-fast. Research methodology has greatly changed and the sources of information and access to them have changed. Even the government release system has changed. The news is flashed across online channels instantly.

In Pune, journalists identified both positive and negative impacts of social media on journalism. On the one hand, they acknowledged that social media had not only improved journalists' ability to engage interactively, but had also given them better access to information and provided more promotional opportunities. On the other hand, they indicated that the scope for in-depth reporting had decreased considerably because of the increasing demand for fast content, to the extent that "tweets become stories sometimes".

Smartphones

Many media in India provided their journalists with smart phones with built-in apps to collect and disseminate news. As one journalist in Delhi noted, "It is a changed world; reporters are filing stories from their phones". A majority of people, especially the new generation, access all news through their mobile phones. In the words of one online media journalist, "It is a new age wherein stories are already being done at one tenth of the cost with the help of mobile phones".

In Hyderabad, traditional media dominated; online news media were yet to emerge and grow. As most of the newspapers and television channels had their own websites with hourly news updates, media organizations did not feel the need for independent news portals. However, there were business online websites with a variety of genres like culture, travel, and environment, where one segment could be news. Journalists reported that life had become easier as "news gets around in a matter of a few seconds". For instance, smartphones with 3G/4G connectivity have made professional life very easy for most journalists. Almost all journalists in private media organizations have been provided with a smartphone. However, such was not always the case for the government media. In Hyderabad, one television journalist complained that their government channel was very slow in adapting to technological advances, the income of the journalists was limited, and that as a result the journalists were dissatisfied:

> Our employees want to skip the job and join in some other media outlets; so I can say that it's a negative aspect in Doordarshan [India's national broadcaster]. Moreover, the government owned channel has not recruited for many years, but are taking in people on a fixed-term contract basis. This results in greater dissatisfaction amongst the contract employees. Even the salaries are low for such contract employees.

Impact of technology on the quality of journalism

Losing exclusivity and depth

The world of journalism is moving at breakneck speed with relentless convergence of different media. To cope with requirements for deadlines and multiskilling tasks, a journalist becomes like a robot. A traditional media journalist in Delhi compared the present with the past professional experience:

> Media reach has made work more mechanical and sometimes I feel the personal touch and interaction is lost and with the faster speed sometimes deeper analysis and detailing is lost. This is a significant question as my seniors tell me how they used to report and how we report now. We have luxury. We have to face it. Our background research takes 10–15 minutes. They didn't have that sort of a luxury. We can Google stuff. We have everything right away. They didn't have that. They had to go to the library to pick up news articles and every single thread had to be connected to the story that was filed a decade ago. And now, I can report from my mobile. First thing I do when a vehicle is launched, I take the photograph of the guy launching the car or something. And post it on Twitter from the website. That's it, the news is published.

Almost all the online journalists in Delhi noted that technology was bringing in positive changes, making it much easier to collect and process information. On the other hand, with this flood of information, the journalists felt that there was little or no exclusivity in the stories. One journalist complained about the poor quality of news: "It [technology] has made work much more complicated. Because there are so many channels, there is more diluted news. This need for fast news may have also impaired the quality of work". The online journalists argued that immediacy generated by technology had led to increased work pressures. As one journalist stated, "Technology increases the pressure to perform and have the first mover advantage all the time. Thus, it also increases the chances of making a mistake". One journalist from Pune reported, "I have to write my copy with some risks. I know for a fact that people just read the headlines and the first paragraph". Journalists in Rio de Janeiro stated that journalism had become more superficial, whereas others complained about the new requirement of multi-functionality in work, which has led to an increased workload. In Vitoria, the journalists were concerned about the quality of work in their newsrooms: "They increased the number of employees, but that does not mean quality. Then, the overload of work is the same. Furthermore, although the speed of information increased, the accuracy has to be flawless".

Discovering an explanatory journalism

In India, online journalists expressed the view that technology had rendered it possible to make a story comprehensive with more facts, quotes, and Twitter feeds and by providing hyperlinks to older stories; such news may not be available in traditional media but is prevalent in online media. One of them said, "We can also creatively bring about feature stories about the same topic and bring all the related topics under one branch". In Hyderabad, an online journalist came up with the term 'explanatory journalism', in which,

> We can embed tweets about what someone is saying. So now the whole idea of calling someone, going to a person, and getting his quote is not necessary; you can just embed the person's tweet or hyperlink into older stories related to the person, which makes it all the more credible. For example, get the prime minister himself and put his quote. You can take his tweet and embed it in your story. All these possibilities are there where news becomes more accessible, and the idea that we have of explanatory journalism can happen smoothly.

Becoming a smart ecosystem

Some journalists in India argued that technological advances had bridged the gap between audiences and media. An online media journalist said, "We call ourselves a smart ecosystem that bridges the gap between students, colleges, alumni, institutes, and also companies offering placements. This is solely due to technology. We wouldn't exist without it".

Journalists stated that since the advent of social networks, their relationship with information sources and the public had changed. For them, the possibility of dialogue with the sources and the public was a novelty in the newsroom. A journalist from Delhi said,

> This [technology] has increased the hunger for instant information. There is always this pressure to stay upbeat and on top of the game. In minutes you can lose online audiences; you have to be really fast and synchronized with the info world moving at the most bizarre speed. It certainly gives one the thrill and adventure of being in this ever dynamic and evolving environment but it also adds to the stress levels.

Transforming work styles: online research, competitiveness, and accountability

Many journalists agreed that technology transformed their style of work. They did not have to sit in libraries for research to do a feature story; they could research it online. As a journalist from Hyderabad put it,

> A lot of time is saved. I don't have to spend a day at the library skimming old articles. I can do something else. Today, a journalist can file ten or fifteen stories in a day. That way it is helping. The output is good.

Journalists felt that technology had helped them in upgrading their work styles. Pune journalists reported that, in the past five years, technological changes had impacted media organizations and journalists significantly. Developments in cameras and other equipment, the availability of cloud storage enabling data transfer in minutes and of new software for online journalism, and the presence of social media have all facilitated faster, easier, and more efficient workflows and transformed the ways in which journalists work. Some of these changes, journalists reported, had increased the number of potential sources for stories and made verification across sources easier.

For the younger generation who grew up with the Internet, journalism became a very attractive and easy occupation due to technology. One journalist in India felt this and observed how youngsters are doing their job fast and easily:

> The other day I was covering an event and I saw this guy recording everything that the speaker was saying and it was automatically converted into a Word file and there was nothing much for him to do except maybe editing.

Most respondents in Delhi felt that the advent of technology had brought accountability in jobs. An online media journalist stated, "It is easier to collect information and get instant feedback. [Technology] has reintroduced the element of accountability".

Journalists argued that competition between journalists and media companies increased owing to new technology. Technological upgrading has become the buzzword in the newsroom. A traditional media journalist in India noted the following:

We do upgrade our systems according to the latest technological advances and it does make us more compatible with other counterparts. The work efficiency has really increased and it has become easier to work, and a lot of time is saved. We feel upgraded and competitive as it benefits us in seeking better options for work.

Competition among media organizations has resulted in making the latest software available to journalists. A journalist from Delhi said, "Such software helps in filing stories really quickly and uploading them onto the web portals of news organizations". Competition has led to an increase in OB (Outdoor Broadcast) vans for each organization. This has resulted in an increase in the number of live reports or 'breaking news'. In other words, technology has created a breakneck speed and real competition among journalists in breaking news stories.

In Kolkata, journalists mentioned infrastructure changes as well as changes in editing software, which improved the quality of audiovisual material, images, graphic design, and printing. Technological changes, Kolkata journalists reported, affected their work; these changes increased the pace and pressure that journalists encountered because of increased competition between media houses. Despite this, many journalists described the changes as a convenience; the new technology made it easier to gather information, particularly in the case of foreign news, where correspondents could email their stories and "within a fraction of a second you are getting that report from London".

Impact of technology on a journalist

Re-staffing the newsroom

One of the major challenges that the journalists in India faced due to technological advances was that they had to produce content across multiple formats (print, web, blog, etc.) with a smaller staff. Journalists faced immense pressure to produce more content than ever before due to staff layoffs from budgetary constraints in an uncertain economic environment. A journalist working in a television channel in Hyderabad said, "We are forced to 'work more with fewer people', having layoffs on a daily basis". One consequence of this, according to another journalist in Hyderabad, was that "we have to deal with constant changes in beats and coverage areas. We have to constantly step in for someone else".

In Brazil, the views of journalists were divided: some claimed that digitalization had led to staff reductions in the newsrooms, and many journalists had lost their jobs, while others argued that it had opened up new opportunities for employment. Thus, in the capital Brasília, traditional media journalists talked about how their organizations sought ways to survive. One of them said, "We had a restructuring process in recent years. We reduced the staff in some departments; however, we recruited and prepared other employees to work in other areas of journalism".

Another journalist added, "We did not have a lot of equipment to collect and process the news [in television] and this made it easier for us. And due to the increase in the number of journalists hired, we had a reduction in workload".

One positive result for traditional media was that "today, we are completely digital and all newsrooms are integrated"; that "the volume of information that reaches the newsroom is now very large. This easy access has happened due to technology". On the negative side, journalists saw "a reduction of manpower. People retire and then we keep losing workforce. Investment in this sector is very small. More people were fired than hired".

Even in Rio, the respondents noted a reduction in the number of journalists in their media. One online journalist stated, "Cutting on spending is reflected in staff cuts, in the structure. Then, a job that was done by ten is now done by two and on a smaller budget". Another online media journalist described a similar situation in his media:

> In 2011, the company hired the highest number of journalists, a total of ten. The owners relied on Brazil's potential growth, but in 2012, they stopped hiring and then cut staff. However, they are now considering hiring again. The same staff, increased workload, and insecurity in the workplace.

In Vitoria, traditional media journalists complained about reductions in professional staff and the accumulation of functions. A journalist indicated, "There is variation. I witnessed moments when 50 per cent of the staff was fired due to programming renewal issues and, after two years, most have been hired again". Those working in online media in Vitoria pointed out that "it [digitalization] has influenced everything. I had another job at another company, but because of these changes I resigned to devote more time to the portal, as its potential for growth was clear". In São Paulo, in the traditional media, the situation for journalists was uneasy. One journalist remembered the following:

> We went through a very serious crisis in 2010 and 2011. Many were laid off earlier this year and the newsroom [in São Paulo] was closed. On the other hand, the headquarters in Rio were expanded. I know that in São Paulo about fifty people were fired, but the newspaper is recovering now.

Demand for new digital skills

In India, journalists felt that the new technology was very demanding. Traditional media journalists working either in print or television had to adapt to the new media (Twitter feeds, social networking, etc.). As one journalist in Delhi noted, "The ability to process and filter incoming information efficiently in the 'high volume cacophony' of pitches and press releases is a challenge". Technological changes also fostered professional development; as one journalist in Kolkata noted, "I have to keep myself completely updated". A certain dimensionality was also added to reporting due to increased collaboration with colleagues in other cities via the Internet. In addition, mobile phones allowed journalists to post stories online and to regularly update them. Journalists also no longer depended on a physical office to complete tasks and were even expected to work and send stories from the site. Some journalists felt that there had not been enough technological changes in the past five years: "We need to do more in this field. If you look at Bangladesh, which is also a Bengali based industry like us, they are far more creative than us in terms of technology". Another journalist agreed that editing, visuals, graphics, and animations were not yet evident in the workplace.

Brazilian journalists realized that, having come closer to their audience, they have to use the technology in their favour to perform their job in the best way and to "stay alive" in an increasingly competitive media market. Online journalists in Vitoria felt that advances in technologies had not had any economic impact on their profession. Those working in traditional media had very diverse views on the subject. For some, what happened was just a change in structure. Others said that the change could be identified, for example, only in the a esthetics and visual aspects. Some stated that there was a change in the requirements for journalists, especially those who work online, who now need to know how to deal with the various media platforms. A traditional media journalist from Vitoria noted that the managers and supervisors still do not know how to deal with technological change: "They invested in tangibles but not in staff; therefore, we are overwhelmed and undervalued. The number of professionals in the newsrooms is decreasing".

Need for IT specialists

In Brazil, the traditional media journalists mentioned improvements in equipment purchase, which was not always the solution: "Sometimes the equipment fails and it undermines journalistic production. With technological changes, implementation of new systems, work became faster and requires greater flexibility in the production of news". The majority of journalists argued that their economic situation had changed with the advent of new technologies. One online journalist stated, "New advertisers emerged and there is an increase in revenue. Nowadays we are experiencing a system change; we have to hire computer technicians and have new equipment". The majority of traditional media journalists noted the increased number of employees and they ascribed this to the improvement in equipment availability. Journalists also stated that most of the media organizations were hiring new technical people able to handle new technology. In traditional media, the journalists were concerned about their technical abilities to compete with new online media:

> With technological resources, you have more options. Here [in traditional media], it is precarious. It lacks some of that work with new media. We cannot do live coverage and, due to the cutback in the number of professionals, we are always in a rush.

If technological devices can facilitate information processing in any way, it can also expose or jeopardize it and, therefore, its credibility. A journalist pointed out that

> The changes generated greater equality, but on the other hand they reduced the time and product quality. However, the staff has been reduced. Finally, the company knows how to make money with printed media, but also needs to make money on the Internet and I fear that this will lead to layoffs.

Job insecurity: salary and autonomy

In Brazil, low salaries in both media (traditional and online) were a major concern. The journalists reported that budgetary constraints had limited travel and had restricted personal interviews. One journalist in Vitoria felt that

> Technology could help in news coverage. This would facilitate our work. However, it is the economic issues that discourage us as the wages are stagnant. For now, the increase is only visible in workload; the investments in equipment are higher as they seek to get more sponsorship.

The problems faced by journalists in Brazil were related to editorial interference in their day-to-day work. The online media journalists complained about pressure from the media owners. One respondent said that "big companies can buy media", and another claimed that the person "who has the most money can manage to produce and publish the story". The difficulties of those who worked for online media included lack of accountability to the public, devaluation of small portals in cities, and hostile attitudes to them on the part of other media. In addition, journalists complained that people in general think that the work of a journalist can be done by any other professional from any other field. Some journalists also felt that the lack of professional freedom, a competitive labour market, and biased journalism are roadblocks for journalists to function well in Brazil.

Conclusions

The contemporary journalist is a digital journalist competent in using new technology; working in conditions of convergence of technologies, media platforms, and genres; integrating social media with news; and getting the news story as an outcome of 'multipoint communication' owing to the new technology. This commonality in both countries can be understood as the *technocracy of news*, which is evidence of *new journalistic practice* meeting requirements in the digital era.

Another common attribute in the journalism of both countries is the new *direct relationship* between journalists and their audiences, facilitated by the new technology, which provides easier ways for journalists to connect with their public. Some journalists considered this greater interactivity with the public to be a positive aspect of the new technologies. The emergence of social networks and their interface with journalism, whether in content production, in the search for assignments, or in the feedback and repercussions that it generates, has brought a new reality to the profession. On the one hand, it has created a certain enchantment, but on the other, it has led to a concern about a certain loss of the 'power' of the journalist, as the boundary between professionals and non-professionals is eroding.

Another concern with the advent of new technologies in the work is increasing pressure on journalists to produce content across various multiple media formats such as print, TV, web, etc. The pressure to produce more content is also caused by staff cuts and severe budgetary constraints. Thus, journalists did experience stress in their work, both owing to economizing efforts in their newsrooms, fewer workers, more workload, and advanced technology to collect and process information at a brisk rate.

In both countries, journalists felt a lack of professional freedom as their media promoted the business and political interests of their owners, and journalists produced biased publications. Most journalists also agreed that there was a lack of in-depth reporting, and a focus on investigative journalism was missing. They experienced job insecurity and weak protection from their professional associations in conditions of increasing market competition, reduction of journalistic positions in newsrooms, and the opening of new positions for IT professionals in journalism.

In India, journalists were more concerned about bringing accountability into their journalistic work. Brazilian journalists expressed concerns about the declining quality of journalism and the lack of in-depth reporting. It is also clear from the findings that media companies should invest more in personnel and salaries. Brazilian as well as Indian journalism appears to be going through a transition where many doubts about the future remain. One thing that is certain from the interviews is that a journalist's profile is not the same as it was earlier. The professional who should be educated in universities to face the labour market, in traditional or online media, now has to be a journalist who is able to work on multiple functions and platforms. It is an undeniable fact that technology has caused a revolution and has created media convergence, which can be perceived as positive. Thus, faced with this new reality, with leaner newsrooms, and a requirement for multitasking, journalists were definitely rethinking the process of 'reinventing' themselves in this process. This perhaps predicts that there will be less and less news, just more sources of the same news and lots of opinions.

References

Bowman, S., & Willis, C. (2003). *We media: How audiences are shaping the future of news and information*. The Media Center at the American Press Institute. Retrieved from www.hypergene.net/wemedia/

Farah, A. G. V. (2014). *The print media industry in Brazil*. Retrieved from http://thebrazilbusiness.com/article/print-media-industry-in-brazil

FICCI-KPMG. (2016). *The future now streaming: Indian media and entertainment industry report.* Retrieved from https://home.kpmg.com/content/dam/kpmg/in/pdf/2016/12/The-Future-now-streaming.pdf

Franco, G. (2009). *The impact of digital technology on journalism and democracy in Latin America and the Caribbean.* Austin: Knight Centre.

Heinonen, A. (2011). The journalist's relationship with users. In J. B. Singer, A. Hermida, D. Domingo, A. Heinonen, S. Paulussen, T. Quandt, Z. Reich, & M. Vujnovic (Eds.), *Participatory journalism: Guarding open gates at online newspapers* (pp. 34–55). Oxford, UK: Wiley-Blackwell.

Hermans, L., & Vergeer, M. (2009). Internet in the daily life of journalists: Explaining the use of the internet by work-related characteristics and professional opinions. *Journal of Computer-Mediated Communication, 15*(1), 138–157.

Kaul, V. (2013). Journalism in the age of digital technology. *Online Journal of Communication and Media Technologies, 3*(1), 125–143.

Kawamoto, K. (Ed.). (2003). *Digital journalism: Emerging media and the changing horizons of journalism.* Lanham, MD: Rowman & Littlefield Publishers.

Lareau, L. (2010). The impact of digital technology on media workers: Life has completely changed. *Ephemera: Theory & Politics in Organization, 10*(3–4), 522–525.

O'Sullivan, J. (2005). Delivering Ireland: Journalism's search for a role online. *Gazette, 67*(1), 45–68.

Ram, N. (2011, December). *The changing role of the news media in contemporary India.* Lecture delivered at the Indian History Congress at Punjab University, Patiala.

Reich, Z. (2013). The impact of technology on news reporting: A longitudinal perspective. *Journalism & Mass Communication Quarterly, 90*(3), 417–434.

Rosenstiel, T., & Mitchell, A. (2011). *The state of the news media 2011: Overview.* Pew Research Center's Project for Excellence in Journalism. Retrieved from http://stateofthemedia.org/2011/overview-2

Sharma, A. D. (2012). *In fine print: Growth of print media in India.* IBEF Blogs Perspectives on India. Retrieved from www.ibef.org/blogs/in-fine-print

Singer, J. B., Hermida, A., Domingo, D., Heinonen, A., Paulussen, S., Quandt, T., Reich, Z., & Vujnovic, M. (2011). Participatory journalism: Guarding open gates at online newspapers. Boston, MA: Wiley-Blackwell.

Spyridou, L. P., Matsiola, M., Veglis, A., Kalliris, G., & Dimoulas, C. (2013). Journalism in a state of flux: Journalists as agents of technology innovation and emerging news practices. *International Communication Gazette, 75*(1), 76–98.

Subramanian, S. (2014, June 9). India After English? *The New York Review of Books.* Retrieved from http://www.nybooks.com/daily/2014/06/09/india-newspapers-after-english/

7
JOURNALISTS AND PROTEST
Russia and China

Dmitry Gavra, Dmitry Strovsky, and Dieer Liao

Defining political protests: theory and practice

The term 'political protest' is far from new, given the history of its investigation in political science. Some scholars (Jenkins & Klandermans, 1995) consider such protest as a form of collective action intended to change the system of representative and/or executive power, the policy of the state as such, or the relations between citizens and the state. Others (Porta & Tarrow, 2012; Tarrow, 1994) define protests as destructive action aimed at political institutions, elites, and other groups to achieve the collective goals and claims of protesters.

To better understand protests, a few clarifications to the above definitions are in order. First, political protests do not necessarily and inherently lead to system change. In some situations, they stimulate a more careful observation of the existing political hierarchy but this observation does not always result in system transformation. Second, political protests are not characterized solely by destructive intent; they can be implemented peacefully and, therefore, can gradually evolve towards a positive outcome, without causing any serious disruptions.

In general, political protests are many-sided social phenomena. They may assume many different forms: conventional or non-conventional, destructive or non-destructive, violent or non-violent, etc. They can have different goals and trends. Further, political protests may be initiated by individuals but more often by social groups that seem to be unable to resolve their problems on the basis of existing legislation or through routine procedures such as elections, referendums, parliamentary discussions, and so on. Political protests may assume active and passive forms. In their active form, protests are expressed through mass meetings and picketing, whereas in their passive form, they are defined by a specific social behaviour, absenteeism.

Inherently, political protests develop from one of two basic types of contradictions: 1) those between the powerful and society (or, at least, a segment of society) and 2) those arising inside society. Acting political institutions, including mass communication, may be unable to overcome these contradictions, with the consequent risk of sparking protests and creating an unmanageable situation (Podyachev, 2012). In one way or another, the situation leads to a protest; this protest can be interpreted as a form of citizen participation to compensate for the lack of a legal, official solution to the contradiction. As Cohen and Arato (1992) noted, an individual's claims about the desecration of his basic rights will never be heard unless they are supported by public discussions and meetings or in some cases by public movements exercising civil disobedience.

Opp (2009) suggested that political protests are stimulated by two basic factors: growing political discontent and the personal influence of individuals capable of inciting passions and, perhaps, motivating the masses to achieve certain results. Both of these are necessary for the successful evolution of protests. Opp also highlighted two other aspects of political protests: a moral incentive for the people to participate in the conflict, and consequences which might arise if the political protest fails, including repercussions that may be very tough and likely repression imposed by the government against protesters (Opp, 2009).

Thus, political protests are a complex social phenomenon affecting, to a great extent, the traditional relationship between the powerful and the rest of society. They are influenced by uncertainties serving as the imperfections of everyday life, which take actors away, sometimes gradually but more often speedily, from 'prescribed borders' to initiate their own scenarios for resolving situations, scenarios which do not match habitual political priorities and therefore provoke conflict. The most important aspect of political protests is not their activities or the publicity they provoke, but their repercussions affecting political institutions and governmental policy.

For the purposes of this chapter, political protests are defined as being focused on bringing about some change and as being addressed to power institutions, elites, and other actors who have authority. Further, the chapter considers protesters to be motivated not only by political but also by economic, social, and cultural conditions.

Protests in Russia and China from 1990 to 2015: history, structure, and main trends

Russia

According to some scholars (Petrushina, 2012; Podyachev, 2012; Shkel & Sabitov, 2012), protest movements in post-Soviet Russia have traversed five stages. The *first stage* (1989–1991) began to develop as early as before the dissolution of the USSR and was initiated by the long strike of miners that occurred in different parts of the country. Millions of people protested, not only against low salaries but also about the 'insufficient democracy' that evolved under the decrepit Communist rule. These activities in the last period of Gorbachev's perestroika still remain as the most large-scale protest actions in modern Russian history. They took place in European Russia as well as in the Baltics, Caucasus, and Middle Asia, all territorial parts of the Soviet Union. Although the slogans during these actions differed from region to region and tackled both political and economic ideas, it was clear that ordinary people saw discrepancies between Gorbachev's promises on the one hand and the everyday practice of his government on the other (Davies, 1989; Hoskins, 1990; Korotich, 1991; Remnick, 1994; Stepankov & Lisov, 1992).

The *second stage* (1992–1993) was initiated by left-wing political forces, which protested against the political and economic reforms promoted by Russian president Boris Yeltsin and his regime (Reddaway & Glinski, 2001). In October 1993, this brought the nation to a harsh confrontation over domestic social and economic policies between Yeltsin and his political supporters on the one hand and the Supreme Soviet (the Russian Parliament, led at that time by the Communist Party) on the other. The protest, known as the October *putsch*, was short, compared to the preceding miners' strikes, but it brought the country close to complete political collapse. The sharp and violent confrontation in October 1993 between the presidential and legislative branches resulted in President Yeltsin's order to use tanks and open fire on the building of the Russian Parliament where his Communist opponents were located. The armed violence escalated the political crisis in Russian society and threatened to provoke a civil war. The number of those killed in the protests remains unknown. In December 1993, a new constitution was adopted; it gave the president more power, including the ability to appoint high-ranking officials. The events that took place in October 1993 secured the domination of the executive branch over the legislative and judicial branches, effectively prohibiting the country from being a parliamentary republic (Kolesnichenko, 2013).

The *third stage* of the protest movement in the country also occurred under President Yeltsin and lasted for five years (1994–1999) (Klingemann, Fuchs, & Zielonka, 2006). The main reasons for the protests were rapid inflation and low salaries that did not keep up with the soaring prices for essential commodities.

The government of President Yeltsin failed to solve the economic problems between 1994 and 1999, but the next president, Vladimir Putin, was more successful. Therefore, Putin's first term in office (2000–2004) was marked by a sharp decline in Russian protest activity. Due to increasing prices of natural resources, Russia started to gradually overcome the negative economic and living conditions of the 1990s. The global market was conducive to the growth of Russia's GNP and this in turn led to higher living standards for most of the population. As a result, social discontent rapidly subsided in Russia.

The *fourth stage* of the Russian protest movement dates from 2005–2011 and was characterized by street protests not only in metropolitan cities such as Moscow and St. Petersburg but also in the provinces. This new wave of protests concerned a 'monetization of benefits', wherein the government replaced in-kind benefits with cash payments, which turned out to be insufficient to cover the expenses of old-age pensioners. The pensioners perceived this change as a rude attack on their home budgets (Myers, 2005). In terms of geographical scope, duration, and the determination of the protesters, this protest was different from those of the past. It was characterized by road closures and other radical actions (Rabinovich, 2005). If earlier protests were mostly explained by economic problems, then the noticeable street rallies during 2005–2011 were inspired by a much wider context, including fighting for human rights, for economic and ecological issues, and so on.

A similar rejection of the Russian social and economic priorities was seen in the protests against the government's declared intention in spring 2005 to issue a law that would ban right-wheel cars in Russia (Feklyunina & White, 2013). Motorists who owned such cars from an early 1990s massive import from Japan, especially to the Asian regions of the country, protested against this declaration. Another protest that took place in Vladivostok in December 2008 (*Sputnik*, 2009) for the same reason was marked by police action to brutally disperse the protesters. After a while, however, the government stopped its attempts to forbid right-wheel cars. What was remarkable about these protests was the eagerness of the protesters not to limit themselves only to the 'car issue', but also to express their anger against the violation of their civil rights. Numerous banners deployed during the protest actions confirmed that people were worried about the corruption that was penetrating into a number of the state institutions and resulting in loss of protection of citizens from the state bureaucracy.

In this 2005–2011 fourth period of protests, social discontent adopted a more fundamental political context based on blaming state institutions for their inefficiency as exemplified by the case of Kaliningrad during the period 2009–2010. Kaliningrad, formerly the East Prussian capital of Königsberg, became part of Russia as a result of World War II. The entire Kaliningrad region is located apart from the rest of Russian territory and is surrounded by European Union countries. The Kaliningrad protests were among the most noticeable in modern Russia. The rally that took place on January 30, 2010, gathered a record number of about 10,000 protesters who loudly demanded the resignation of both the regional governor and the federal government (Harding, 2010; Pan, 2010).

Environmental issues were another reason for social discontent in that period. Some of the most significant actions of the time were the rallies to protect the Khimki forest on the outskirts of Moscow and the struggle against the construction of an oil pipeline near Lake Baikal. The environmentalists were supported by urban citizens who opposed the idea of new dwellings too close to their houses (Evans, 2012).

Several mass actions occurring in many Russian cities were connected to yet another issue, that of an ethnic minority. The violent conflict between the local population and migrants from the Caucasus in the city of Kondopoga, in the Republic of Karelia, in 2006, was the first noteworthy incident of this nature for Russia.

Another dimension of the protests in this period was workers' strikes. Some of the most noteworthy were the strike at the Ford assembly plant in Vsevologsk, in the Leningrad region, occurring on various dates in the years 2006, 2007, and 2009, and the meetings at the AVTOVAZ corporation in Togliatti, in 2008, in the

Samara region (Berdnikova, Kuznetsov, & Grout, 2007; Petrov, 2007). The workers in both cases demanded higher salaries and 'more democracy'. The capture of the city office and the forcible closure of federal highways initiated by workers in the town of Pikalevo in the Leningrad region in 2008 (Feklyunina & White, 2013) and the protests of miners in Mezhdurechensk in the Kemerovo region in Siberia, in 2010, after the explosion at the mine 'Raspadskaya' (Kueppers, 2010), were further confirmation of the uneasy situation in the economic and social spheres.

The *fifth stage* of the modern Russian protests dates from December 2011 to the end of 2012. These protests were caused by the overwhelming distrust, on the part of the urban population, of the official results of the State Duma (Russian Parliament) elections in December 2011. The day after the results were announced, thousands of Moscovites and St. Petersburgers gathered in the streets to give vent to their emotions about the massive electoral fraud that occurred during the elections. This reaction was generated by posts, which circulated intensively on the Internet, about numerous violations of the election law. Within a week, the demands calling for 'fair elections' had spread to other large Russian cities. More than 30,000 people pledged their virtual support for the opposition on Facebook, and the street-based protests attracted a diverse range of discontented citizens (Koesel & Bunce, 2012). Among these citizens were very different groups, including pensioners, students, university professors, urban professionals, office managers, and intellectuals. The political spectrum supporting these actions was also very broad; communists, monarchists, liberals, and nationalists joined the rallies.

According to the estimates of the Russian police, 25,000 people joined the demonstrations, but opposition leaders reported that participants actually numbered 150,000 (Amos & Sawer, 2011). This action was one of the largest after the collapse of the Soviet Union (Koesel & Bunce, 2012). Demonstrators and picketers tied small white ribbons to their clothes, thereby proclaiming their allegiance to the 'colour revolutions' in Europe and Northern Africa against traditional regimes there. The protest leaders and activists largely used social networking to coordinate their activity; they put instructions, addresses of meetings, and slogans on these networks. On one day, Moscow was occupied by a chain of protesting city dwellers. Some of them marched silently with tape covering their mouths to indicate they had 'no voice'. There were also those who held up posters that said that 'United Russia' is the 'party of crooks and thieves' (*Partiya zhulikov i vorov*) (Ilyichev, 2012).

One of the biggest rallies took place on Sakharov Avenue on December 24, 2011. According to the Levada Research Center (2012), 73 per cent of the protesters linked the situation to discontent regarding the state of affairs in the country and government policy. The All-Russian Center for the Study of Public Opinion (VTsIOM) surveyed 800 protesters on Bolotnaya Square in Moscow on February 4, 2012. More than 70 per cent of the protesters were male and younger than 45 years old, more than 50 per cent had a university degree, and 85 per cent were identified as those who had middle or high incomes (VTsIOM, 2012).

The *sixth stage* of the protest movement, 2012–2013, was characterized by little public activity. Koesel and Bunce (2012) suggest that the reasons for the lack of major activity were lack of unity among democratic and liberal forces in today's Russia, the absence of a single leader capable of taking over the reins of management in the elaboration of the protest movement, the complexity of undertaking a unified programme of actions for heterogeneous political forces, lack of an effective organizational structure that would ensure the participation of all organizations and initiative groups in the coordination of the protest, and the isolation of sophisticated and wealthy people living in big cities from the mass protest groups.

In the past few years, the government has taken a number of effective legislative measures to pay off, or at least reduce, unconventional protests. It tightened its control over the Internet and adopted a few amendments to the Law on Counteraction to Extremism (Federal'nyi Zakon, 2002), which made the state of the Russian media even more feeble. Along with this, Russian NGOs were put under strict political control (Federal'nyi Zakon, 2012), and those funded from abroad were prohibited from operating. Simultaneously, a great part of Russian society consolidated itself with the government and with President Putin. This consolidation became even more evident after Russia's operations in the Crimea in 2014 and in Syria in 2015, and with the economic sanctions against Russia imposed by the US and other western European countries. The "conflict with the West" around the Crimea and Syria strengthened the political prestige of Putin himself as a "defender of the national interests" of his country, which in turn weakened the positions of the protest movement (*RBK*, 2014). The political protests that took place in 2011–2013 are now in decline. In the meantime, the reasons that provoked this situation remain unresolved.

Thus, Russian protests over the last two decades were different in nature, in semantic orientation, and in their objectives. It is difficult to provide a definite number of protests but just within the last six years, from 2010 onwards, there have been 1,573 cases of labour protests, not to mention the protests initiated for political and other reasons (*Solidarnost*, 2014). In the current political situation caused by the confrontation between Russia and the West, the number of protests is predicted to be even greater than before. People's spirit in contemporary Russia continues to confront the precarious status quo between the state and society; many people live with a feeling of uncertainty and anxiety.

China

China has witnessed an increase in both the number and scale of social movements and collective action during recent decades. Structurally speaking, the cause of collective action lies in the contestation and conflict between different stakeholders. In China, collective action resulted from individual grievances, community appeals, and organizations working towards certain economic, social, or political purposes. China has become a 'risk society'. The German sociologist Beck (1992) defined a risk society as society marked by "hazards and insecurities induced and introduced by modernization itself" (p. 21). Two characteristics make China a risk society. First, China has witnessed frequent and large political protests and collective actions, which keep escalating at an unprecedented rate. From 1993 to 2009, the number of collective actions in China soared from 8,709 to almost 90,000 annually, and the number of participants rose from 700,000 to more than 3 million per year (Yu, 2010). Second, the number of social incidents and disastrous accidents detrimental to public security and stability has continued to rise, such as the coal mine disaster, the SARS epidemic, drug abuse, and so on. The social structure, social mechanisms, and social relationships of China are undergoing a process of transition that is both complicated and full of conflicts.

Other contributors, actual and potential, to China as a risk society also exist. After 1989, China pushed forward its reform and opening-up policy, which stimulated its rapid economic growth and social development. In the meantime, a series of social dilemmas emerged, such as the wealth gap, the urban–rural divide, poverty, and inequality. Despite the substantial economic growth achieved in the 1990s and the considerable improvement in living and working conditions, the uneven distribution of wealth undermines social stability in China and its sustainable development. Chinese society is stratified into different groups, and the group that has not benefited from social development is an important factor in social conflict. The elite group represented by political leaders and business tycoons, on the other hand, has gradually established a relatively stable ruling class and obtained the privilege to make use of social resources to the fullest. This economic, political, and cultural divide underpins Chinese social instability, leading to various political protests and demonstrations.

In recent years, the deteriorating environment and heavy pollution in China have awakened the public's awareness and concern about ecological issues, and this has become one of the most common motives for protests and demonstrations. Ecological issues such as PM2.5 contaminations, excessive mining, chemical plant construction, and nuclear infrastructure all serve as triggers for many protests and demonstrations. Besides, religious and ethnic issues have become another significant factor impacting political protests in China. China boasts about its diversity in ethnicity and religion, and has a policy of minority self-governance and freedom of religious belief. However, for historical and geographical reasons, there is still some estrangement of minorities and misunderstanding concerning religious and ethnic disputes in China, particularly in certain autonomous regions like Tibet and Xinjiang, which may breed social instability and protest.

According to earlier research, this amalgam of political protests and social movements in China can be primarily classified into four main historical stages, featuring different social backgrounds and a periodical character (Yu, 2010; Zhao, 2012).

The *first stage* (1989–1994) is commonly perceived as an idiosyncratic political period in China's contemporary history. The Tiananmen Square incident of

1989 is considered the climax of the liberalism trend among the masses since the end of the Cultural Revolution (1966–1976) in China. The Tiananmen Square protests were sparked by the death of a prominent national leader on April 15, 1989: Hu Yaobang, party chair from 1981 to 1982, and general secretary of the Communist Party from 1982 to 1987. By the evening of Hu's state funeral, some 100,000 students had gathered in Tiananmen Square to observe the funeral; however, no leaders addressed them. The movement lasted from Hu's death on April 15 until tanks rolled into Tiananmen Square on June 4, 1989. In Beijing, the military response by the Chinese government to the protest left many civilians in charge of clearing the square of the dead and severely injured. The exact number of casualties is not known and many different estimates exist. After the incident, the Chinese central government implemented stringent social regulations and carried out mass arrests and punishments, which led to a reduction in collective political actions in the following several years. Since the Tiananmen Square incident of 1989, political protests in contemporary China have been rather contentious and sensitive.

Collective action during the *second stage* (1995–1998) experienced a conspicuous shift from the political to the economic arena. After 1989, the Chinese government pushed forward marketization-oriented economic reform successfully but did not choose to carry out a political overhaul such as that in eastern European countries. While the achievement of economic reform considerably improved people's working and living conditions, this unprecedented social transformation also brought with it a series of social problems, including official corruption, social inequality, laying off workers in state-owned enterprises, etc. Compared with the previous phase, collective actions during this period were smaller in scale and mostly economy-oriented. Most of the demonstrations were not aimed against the central government but against local officials or company managers. During the late 1990s, a large number of demonstrations were held, led by laid-off workers, farmers pleading for tax reductions, and businesspeople making appeals to maintain market order.

The *third stage* (1999–2006) of protests continued the trend of localizing and de-politicizing, as the central government generally refused to intervene in the resolution of local political protests. However, the Chinese government attached great importance to the construction and optimization of the administrative petition procedure, endeavouring to resolve and alleviate social tensions in a lawful and systematic way. Owing to this, the organizational capability of social collective actions was severely paralyzed, which was reflected in the decreasing number and smaller scale of political protests after 1999, especially those occurring locally. Different from other stages, this historical period witnessed several major political protests stemming from disputes in international politics and relations. Also, these demonstrations manifested the extremist nature of the nationalism epidemic in China during that period. On May 7, 1999, during the NATO air raid over Yugoslavia, five US JDAM-guided bombs hit the

Chinese Embassy in New Belgrade, killing three Chinese reporters and outraging the Chinese public. Large demonstrations erupted at the consular offices of the United States and other NATO countries in China in reaction to the news of the bombing. The protests continued for several days, during which tens of thousands of rock-throwing protesters kept US Ambassador James Sasser and other staff trapped in the Beijing embassy. The residence of the US Consul in Chengdu was damaged by fire, and protestors tried to burn the consulate in Guangzhou. In 2003, more than 50,000 college students marched on the streets of Xi'an for three days to protest several Japanese students' improper behaviour on campus. In spring 2005, anti-Japan protests over Japanese history textbooks also erupted in several Chinese cities.

The latest changes in collective actions in China, the *fourth stage* (2007–present), has the following characteristics. As economic reform and the opening-up of China are moving forward, public consciousness of civil rights is rising to a higher level, reflected in a series of protests by people defending their interests concerning medical care, education, food safety, environment, housing, etc. In the meantime, an array of non-governmental organizations has sprung up and developed rapidly in China, some of which cooperate with local authorities quite successfully in resolving social conflicts. During this period, ecological and environmental issues have become the core concern for several major collective actions in China. The first massive demonstration took place in Xiamen, the capital city of Fujian Province, in southern China. Tens of thousands of protestors rallied over a proposed paraxylene (PX) plant in one of the first large displays of citizen disgruntlement with the deteriorating environment. Similar protests have since occurred in the northeastern city of Dalian and the southwestern city of Anning. Since 2010, China has been the world's largest PX producer and consumer, going through 16 million tons of the product in 2013. In 2014, demonstrations against a petrochemical plant reverberated throughout cities in China's southeastern Guangdong province, at times becoming riotous. The unrest began on March 30, when 1,000 protestors assembled outside government buildings in Maoming, a city in southern China's industrial heartland. They objected to long-standing plans for a 3.5 billion yuan PX plant, a joint venture between the local government and Sinopec, a state-owned oil and gas company. After several days of protest in Maoming, by April 4, smaller demonstrations had broken out in the cities of Shenzhen and Guangzhou.

According to the statistics released by the Chinese Academy of Social Sciences (2014), from 2000 to 2013 (statistics before 2000 were barely recorded or described by any official body), there were 871 collective actions (each with more than 100 participants) altogether in mainland China. As far as the geographical distribution of the protests is concerned, South China was ranked first with 319 cases, with Guangdong Province making up 30.7 per cent of the total number. East China ranked second with 189 cases, while Southwestern China ranked third with 118 cases.

News media and protest in Russia and China: 1990–2015

Russia

In 1992, the position of the media in Russia was contradictory. The time between 1992 and 1993 was marked by an increased confrontation between the executive and legislative power branches. Media were split and supported opposing parties. Some of them supported Yeltsin's decisions to continue political reforms and others sided with the Parliament (at the time the Supreme Council) controlled by Communist conservatives. The media from both sides fuelled the conflict by dispersing *kompromat* (compromising material) and constantly violating ethical standards.

The national media were privatized during the third stage of protests (1994–1999) and were owned by proprietors who held different views on politics. The two most influential tycoons, Boris Berezovsky and Vladimir Gusinsky, belonging to competing political and business groups, vigorously confronted and played off against each other in their media. Consequently, the positions of the media were also irreconcilable. Journalists were mostly reporting on protests from the point of view of their media partisanship. This competitive situation enabled the public to be better informed about the protest actions and rallies in the country.

Since 2005 and the start of the fourth period of the protest movements in the country, the social benefits monetization reform has been the specific topic of media coverage. Unlike all the preceding situations, the media have widely informed the public about the protests taking place in different cities and even supported them, giving rise to public indignation about the Ministry for Health and Social Policy by blaming it for professional incompetence and bureaucratic adherence. In other words, the journalists were emotionally engaged with protesters, as the risk of reduction of social benefits was a concern of practically every family.

In the period 2005–2011, given their focus on different protests, especially those concerning economic issues, the media provided more factual than analytical information. Most publications were only informative and did not discuss the reasons or the pros and cons of the protests. Therefore, it was almost impossible to see clashes of different views in the media. The Russian media thereby looked at the situation from the outside, without taking a definite political position. It became evident that the media deliberately refrained from comments that could undermine the reputation of the government.

What became obvious during the Russian media coverage of social and political protests from 2005 to 2011 was the dubious position of journalists. Although the media could not ignore the conflicts and seemed to provide the audience with necessary details, the information itself was very far from being complete. To a very large extent, this is likely explained by the state of journalistic freedoms in the country. As early as 2004, Reporters without Borders (RWB, 2005) ranked Russia in 140th place among 167 countries with regard to press freedom. Russia was followed by Sudan, Kazakhstan, and Uzbekistan, which are not states that guarantee free dissemination of information. Over the next few years, the standard of freedoms in Russia became even worse. For example, in a memorandum published by RWB in May 2010, Russia was mentioned among 40 states (along with Belarus, Libya, Cuba, Iran, and others) where press freedom was being actively suppressed, resulting in limiting the right of citizens to receive reliable information. The Russian president Putin was named as an enemy of the free press (RWB, 2010). The media were gradually becoming more dependent on certain political and economic interests and thus subscribing less to ideas of objectivity and non-partisanship. This situation undoubtedly affected journalists' motivations as they covered protests. Due to these factors, the information the media supplied could not be unbiased.

If the previous protests were mainly local and for social or economic reasons, in the 2010s, discontent was much more widespread and united different people protesting against the announced 2011 parliamentary election results regarded by the opposition as falsified in some regions. The period from late 2011 to the first half of 2012 was the first in the history of contemporary Russia when mass protests took place for purely political reasons. Journalists as members of urban civil society, not just as media professionals, were also involved in the protest actions.

The attitude of the media to the situation differed based on allegiance. While the outlets and main TV channels that were close to the Kremlin were reluctant to have wide discussions about the political situation in Russia, a few liberal media, including the radio station *Ekho Moskvy*, the newspaper *Novaya Gazeta*, and some others, were much more reflective about the conflict and repeatedly confronted the official position of the authorities. The media, especially those that were liberally oriented, became an arena of political debates for the clarification of the situation.

China

Although the Chinese media system has been constantly criticized for strict government scrutiny and censorship, there is no denying that the media are playing an increasingly important role in the dynamics of political protests in China. As the media, sponsored and operated by the government, constitute a majority in China, political protests and demonstrations during the early periods of the protest history have been barely exposed in newspapers or television programmes.

In the early 1990s, when traditional media still prevailed around China, most collective actions were largely ignored by mainstream media as journalists who intended to report sensitive issues had to obtain approval from their editors in chief and accept their recommendations. Under these circumstances, Chinese media failed to fulfil the role of engagement with the construction of public opinion during political protests or social turmoil. Therefore, most Chinese could only resort to rumours when media chose not to cover, or partially cover, collective actions taking place around them, which created a huge barrier for the public to access facts about the incidents.

The robust development of the Internet and personal computers since the beginning of the 21st century has provided more objective and instant sources for the Chinese public to acquire information about political protests. The birth and evolution of social media obscured geographical limits and established an interactional platform to help people engage more in collective actions. Activists devised numerous ways to use these new technologies for mobilizing, realizing new political opportunities, and shaping the language in which movements are discussed (Garrett, 2006). The mainstream media also adjusted their strategies and norms concerning political protest coverage accordingly. Recent years have witnessed more media in China playing the role of a 'mediator' between the authorities and the public, particularly in environmental disputes that of late occur frequently. The latest shift in the media's role has accelerated the proper resolution of social problems and helped rebuild the government's credibility.

The BRICS study

Given the interplay between protests and media coverage, journalists in the BRICS study were asked about their attitude to protests. It was expected that attitudes would differ on these factors: personal (political values, professional education), media (ownership and type of media), and geographical-urbanization (region and type of city).

Findings

Journalists' attitudes to protests

Russia

In Russia, interviews were carried out between December 2012 and January 2015. Responding to the question "What is your attitude to protests in your city, country?" many journalists recollected recent mass protests against the electoral fraud of 2011 and the mass protest meetings of May 2012 in Moscow and other cities.

General attitude

Respondents were almost evenly divided in their attitudes to protest: one half (47 per cent) supported the protest; the other (53 per cent) did not. Journalists explained their position. The supporters associated protests with the process of democratization and the civil society movement. For instance, a St. Petersburg respondent liked the fact that people had started to get out of their flats and speak up. Although, in her opinion, only a few members of the public were coming out to participate, the number was increasing: "I believe that there is a boiling point, and we are approaching it. Now the process has only begun to gurgle but it will undoubtedly go ahead".

A Moscow correspondent from an online portal considered that it was necessary for individuals to express their opinions without hesitation: "There are so many reasons for protests in contemporary Russia. How is it possible to be silent in the situations that have to be resolved? It is more than justifiable to go ahead and fight for positive solutions for ourselves". An editor of a quality magazine in Moscow argued that protests are necessary because they are part and parcel of social life. According to his opinion, protests are drivers for social change: "Without protests, life never can be considered as being complete. Protests stimulate the development of society". A journalist from a Petrozavodsk television company agreed, "Protests are the only method to defend human rights in the modern political situation in Russia. People cannot express their views differently because the government seems to be totally lukewarm to their needs".

Negative attitudes to protests were associated with their ineffectiveness and the lack of clear objectives and of questions important in the lives of respondents, but also with a lack of responsibility for the consequences of the protest. For instance, a senior editor from Moscow argued that

> [Protests] are not effective in our country and only lead to provocations. . . . Those who protest demonstrate the principle of collective irresponsibility. Instead of marching along the streets, these people could better start making small steps in their everyday life and make their life more effective.

An online journalist from St. Petersburg was of the opinion that political protests as such are useless in Russia because the powers will easily suppress them: "I would prefer to protest for local initiatives, which seem to be much more productive. There exists a chance in this regard that the situation will change". A reporter from a state TV company in Petrozavodsk shared this position, saying that she had lost hope that "protests can change the current political situation in Russia. If we lived in a normal country, protests could be supported by trade unions, but in Russia these organisations are useless also".

And further, a deputy editor of a newspaper from Yekaterinburg saw no sense in protests:

> People who go out to express their views often turn out to be motivated emotionally, without a clear understanding of what exactly has to be done for changing the situation. Emotions are a bad assistant in this regard. Not protests, but more likely negotiations with the powers can be salutary.

Although half of respondents had negative attitude to the protests, their critical evaluations included some positive consequences of these actions, such as the revitalization of public opinion and the formation of certain types of feedback with the authorities.

Differences by geographical-urban dimension

Journalists in the capital cities Moscow and St. Petersburg, although divided in their opinions, were more inclined to support protests and to treat them with sympathy or, at least, with understanding and even to participate in these actions. Journalists from the provincial cities were much more critical of protests. Some of them saw protesters as "detrimental for the state system", "undermining the existing status quo" between society and the authorities, and "violating the balance of interests" in the country. Moscow had the highest support for protests (on average, 69 per cent). St. Petersburg and Petrozavodsk had almost the same number of journalists supporting protests (on average, 42 per cent and 39 per cent respectively). Yekaterinburg had the smallest number of journalists with a positive attitude to the protests (on average, 22 per cent).

Reasons for these differences should be sought in the peculiarities of the local contexts. Moscow in late 2011 and early 2012 became the epicentre of protest actions. Most marches and meetings took place in December 2011 on the Manezhnaya and Bolotnaya squares. In May 2012, more than 100,000 people participated in the Moscow march following violent confrontations between the police and the demonstrators. The police were not lenient, and many protesters were arrested. Some of them were even prosecuted for organizing of mass disorder. In the meantime, the march itself excited the Moscow media, and many respondent journalists participated in it as citizens, without their press cards. Therefore, it is not surprising that among the 48 Moscow interviewees, every fourth one (on average, 26 per cent) participated in the protest actions and meetings either as an ordinary citizen or as a journalist.

In St. Petersburg, as in Moscow, there were also clashes between the police and protesters following the detention of the latter. A few journalists were also taken into police custody. In Petrozavodsk, protests arose after the December 2011 elections to the State Duma (Parliament). They were preceded by long resistance by enthusiasts including journalists against the policy of the regional authorities, which had led to the exacerbation of environmental problems. As a result, the first decade of the 2000s became the stimulus for the oppositional spirit of journalists. Some groups of protesters defended historical monuments, including the island of Kizhi, a World Heritage site, which was abandoned by the regional authorities. This struggle left traces in the consciousness of both the elite and the masses long before the political protests of late 2011. Regional journalists supported the protest activity of citizens with their publications and their participation in the protests. The Karelian Union of Journalists has earned a reputation as an independent union, able to defend journalists in difficult situations including trials.

It is important to note that the Republic of Karelia, with the capital Petrozavodsk, borders on the EU (Finland); it experienced a long history of Western influence due to its proximity to and the resulting regular contact with the West. This territory is thus very different from the regions of Russia far from the Western borders.

Moreover, Petrozavodsk and St. Petersburg are closely connected geographically, politically, and economically. Both are located in the north-west of Russia, only five hours' journey from each other. Politically, both are the main supporters in the country of the democratic party, 'Yabloko' (Apple), in the post-Soviet period. Recently, Yabloko's candidates again became members of the local parliaments in the elections of 2016, whereas in other cities this party failed. New governors to rule Karelia come from St. Petersburg and the Leningrad region. Economically, St. Petersburg is an attractive labour market for residents of Petrozavodsk and Karelia, including journalists, and trade between St. Petersburg and Karelia is firmly established. Karelia is also a favourite holiday destination for St. Petersburg's residents. Briefly, these factors determine the close relationship of the cities and, in this context, the similarity of approach on part of the journalists from these two cities to the protests of late 2011 and early 2012 is not surprising. A few Petrozavodsk journalists participated and even became organizers of local protest actions.

As distinct from the three other sample cities, in Yekaterinburg, the capital of the Sverdlovsk region and the main industrial and cultural centre of the Ural Federal District, only every fifth journalist (on average, 22 per cent) was positively disposed to protests, making it the city with the most conservative attitude to political protests among journalists. The reason for such modest support for protests lies in the city's stable economic situation for many years, due to the high level of employment and good wages. This rendered massive protests in Yekaterinburg impossible. In 2011–2012, in a city with a population of about 1.4 million, only a few people, no more than 5,000, expressed their dissatisfaction with the falsification of the parliamentary elections in Russia. There were three meetings in the city centre. However, journalists did not want to come to these meetings, even out of curiosity. Only a small number of journalists took part in these actions. Thus, a good economic situation on the one hand, and a lack of a tradition of mass protest in the post-Soviet history of Yekaterinburg on the other, explained the fact that this city had the smallest number of journalists positively oriented to protests.

The opinions of journalists in the provincial cities reflected greater caution about the consequences. For instance, a correspondent of one news website from Yekaterinburg agreed that Russia has to be an open country, but this journalist was also concerned that criticism "is becoming risky because a real journalist becomes alien to the Russian authorities". An editor in chief of a radio station, also from Yekaterinburg, believed that journalists "always carry an increased responsibility, especially if they represent federal media". Responsibility was a very important word in the reflections of these respondents. One of them, a correspondent of one Petrozavodsk television channel, was confident that a journalist "has to be attentive to pros and cons in the coverage of any situation due to his public responsibility towards the audience". An older correspondent of a regional newspaper in Petrozavodsk noted that a journalist has to think about the risks "before he starts dealing with a political situation in his texts. Otherwise, the result can be dangerous".

Differences by type of media

In traditional media, journalists were somewhat less supportive of protests (47 per cent) than journalists of online media (53 per cent), perhaps because most traditional media are impacted by their close (and very often financially supportive) relationship with governmental structures of the state hierarchy. This dependence on the institutions of authority has been a historical tradition in Russia, and the current situation derives its support from the past. The connection between the government and journalists in these media develops both formally and informally, and this affects the political position of journalists. Online journalists position themselves, formally at least, as independent of the state agenda and have many fewer contacts with governmental structures, which in turn influences their political position.

Moscow is undoubtedly a leader in the number of online media journalists who supported the last mass protests in Russia (83 per cent). St. Petersburg and Petrozavodsk had about half such journalists (48 per cent) and (45 per cent) respectively, and Yekaterinburg lagged behind on this indicator (13 per cent). Journalists' position in this matter could depend on social factors such as income, level of financial dependence on the authorities and owners, and the 'quality' of the professional environment. In this regard, the positions of journalists of the three cities seem to be less stable than for their colleagues in Moscow, who are more protected in terms of self-sufficiency.

Differences by ownership

There is a noticeable difference in the evaluation of political protests between journalists working at the editorial offices subsidized and owned by state institutions, and colleagues contributing to private media. Editors and reporters of state-owned media were more intolerant of the protests (60 per cent) than were those in private media (49 per cent). These positions are greatly affected by money. State media are most likely to be financed by governmental structures, which regularly instruct their journalists on how and what to write, whereas journalists working in private media are not subordinated to such an extent by the state structures.

Still, even those who do not directly subordinate themselves to the state system seem to be cautious in evaluating the situation. Having learned Soviet history at universities and remembering family stories, most journalists know how unfriendly the political system's response has been to those who attempted to disagree with it. Therefore, they are not eager to be at risk of receiving negative feedback from the state, especially under the contemporary political circumstances in Russia. Journalists, even those very independent in their thinking, are afraid about a probable negative reaction from state institutions against them.

China

General attitude

The positions of Chinese journalists with regard to protests can be mainly divided into two types: support and lack thereof. Not surprisingly, Chinese journalists had mostly negative attitudes to political protests; a majority of the respondents (91 per cent) referred to political protests with aversion, denial, or condemnation. The following quotations selectively chosen are identical to many others received during the interviews; they provide a view of attitudes to protests in the Chinese journalistic community.

Among the positive opinions were those of a journalist in Beijing who said that protests and demonstrations can be deemed one of the vehicles through which people can vent their emotions, acting as a buffer for social controversy. He added that if these are conducted under proper guidance, protests should be treated as a "normal phenomenon". Likewise, a journalist in Guangzhou said, "personally speaking, I think protests are quite reasonable for today's society and I choose to support them depending on specific motives and occasions". A journalist in Shanghai argued that "protests amid the masses are quite normal as people are endowed with the right to express their points of view concerning social issues". However, she objected to those protests and demonstrations that disrupt social order or damage social stability. A journalist in Wuhan supported protests that are non-violent and in line with the law; he considered protests as very necessary in public expression: "The problem now is that we are quite lacking in ways of expression in China. Therefore, protests can be seen as one type of expression".

Among the negative opinions about protests were those of a journalist from Beijing who argued that there are far better ways of expression than protests or demonstrations like the National People's Congress and the Chinese People's Political Consultative Conference, operating the right of administrative review and the law of executive accusation, etc.: "It is high time that the public be educated and informed of the above-mentioned ways of expression; such mechanisms should also be improved". A journalist in Guangzhou said, "I don't support collective actions like protests or demonstrations because I think individuals might become rather irrational in a certain group with a specific purpose, which may lead to some bad consequences in society".

A journalist in Shanghai did not support protests. From his point of view, protests are not a proper way to solve problems, as people should resort to more reasonable ways: "What I also need to emphasise is that people's deeds should be restricted within the law, which is the bottom line". Another journalist in Wuhan said, "I don't support protests because I think people should be more reasonable and the government should also enhance guidance and management in social disputes. Most of the protests may lead to some extreme and dangerous actions for society".

Differences by geographical-urban dimension

Naturally, the overwhelming majority (91 per cent) of overall negative attitudes among the Chinese respondent journalists to protests of all forms and purposes was reflected in the data for cities. Although journalists in the metropolitan cities of Beijing and Shanghai were slightly more positive about political protests than were their counterparts in the provincial cities of Guangzhou and Wuhan, the percentage of respondents supporting political protests made up a comparatively small portion (13 per cent) of the total.

Interestingly, Beijing, as the national capital and political centre, had the largest percentage (18 per cent) of journalists with positive attitudes towards protests. Shanghai, as the largest city and metropolis in east China, ranked second in terms of the percentage of support (8 per cent). Guangzhou and Wuhan, the provincial cities, had the lowest percentage (4 per cent) of protest supporters.

Journalists who supported political protests claimed that collective actions such as demonstrations and sit-ins may be viewed as proof that China has experienced social enlightenment and development in terms of individual expression and freedom of speech. Moreover, some respondents considered political protests as 'self-therapy' in this special historical phase caught within the forces of social transition and political turmoil. In turn, journalists who opposed political protests shared the opinion that protests had a negative impact on society.

A journalist in Beijing said, "Protests are a reflection of the immaturity of Chinese society because I think a developed or improved social mechanism will harbour more and better ways for people to express their opinions". A journalist in Shanghai, the other metropolis, argued, "If a protest breaks out, someone or a group of people must be facing agony or a need to make an appeal; we should listen to their voices". From provincial cities, a journalist in Guangzhou advocated that "people's rights of expression and attending protests should be guaranteed by law; they are supposed to do it in a right and lawful way". However, a journalist in Wuhan believed that most of the protests and demonstrations in China are irrational: "I think the concept of a harmonious society should be highly valued". It is apparent that provincial journalists were more cautious and thus possibly self-regulated their political reporting more than their metropolitan colleagues did.

Differences by type of media

Only 19 per cent of respondents from traditional media and 29 per cent from online media supported protest activities. In Shanghai, only 4 per cent of journalists from online media held a positive stance towards political protests. In Wuhan, only journalists from traditional media expressed a positive view on protests; none working in online media responded to this issue positively. Even Guangzhou, which, compared with these three cities, enjoys a relatively more open journalistic environment, had only one online journalist with a positive attitude towards protests.

Differences by ownership

Respondent journalists working in private media had a more positive attitude to political protests (14 per cent) than those who worked in state owned or state subsidized media (7 per cent).

Conclusion

Both Russian and Chinese journalists were divided in their attitudes to political protest. The Russian journalists were much more divided on this issue than were Chinese journalists; the overwhelming majority of Chinese journalists were opposed to protests. From our viewpoint, this situation can be explained by different levels of political activity in the countries. Compared to China, Russia in the last few years has been much more exposed to political and economic instability. This is due to the ongoing transformation of the country from 'traditional socialism' to a market system as well as due to serious social problems, which to this day are caused by this transition. The journalists from the very beginning were actively involved in this process but due to many social contradictions turned out to evaluate it differently. Many of those who support protest actions have inherited their positions from the years of Gorbachev's perestroika, with its more open discussions on main issues of the day. Russian journalists who supported protests admitted that they tried to think more independently than their counterparts who expressed negative attitudes about these actions.

Attitudes of both Russian and Chinese journalists towards protests were similar in terms of the territorial factor and the types of media. The type of region (metropolitan vs provincial) did affect the journalists' attitudes to protests. Journalists living in metropolitan cities in both cases had more positive attitudes and were more personally involved in protests than were their colleagues living in provincial cities. This can be explained, to some extent, by the broader worldview of journalists affiliated with bigger and more influential media and the access of these people to alternative sources of information, unlike their provincial colleagues, who are usually not so involved in this. The information sphere that exists in big cities, as confirmed by our survey, makes the mentality of journalists if not freer, then at least more receptive to new ideas. Respondent journalists willingly spoke about human rights, rights and obligations of journalists in the modern world, freedom of information, etc., and attempted to try to relate these matters to national political realities. Protests create unstandarized situations and thus stimulate new thinking and perhaps a more multidimensional understanding of these situations among metropolitan journalists who are ready for such a reaction. However, provincial journalists were equally concerned about the negative consequences of protests that could threaten either the individual or the social order. In both China and Russia, they stressed the importance of awareness of the social responsibility of the journalist as a no less important virtue than the right.

Along with this, Russian and Chinese online journalists were more interested in the coverage of protests than their counterparts in traditional media who had a lukewarm attitude to protests. The traditional media journalists usually had a much more stable connection with authorities and therefore considered protests as detrimental to fundamental principles. Likewise, those working for state-owned news media seemed to be more cautious about expressing their political views than journalists working in private media were. The personal involvement of state media journalists in the activities of state organs, as part of their professional engagement, likely made them more cautious in their behaviour and in expressing their views. At the same time, while Russian journalists' attitudes also differed by type of media ownership (state vs. private), this was not the case for Chinese journalists.

The lack of influence of ownership on Chinese journalists' attitudes to protests may be explained by the dominance of a particular political perspective in Chinese society. Unlike Russia, where the situation is 'mixed' in terms of the political, economic, cultural, and other spheres of consciousness, China serves as an example of a much more monolithic society headed by the Communist Party and centrally managed. The media in this country are part and parcel of the political system, and serve the idea of socializing the public into certain ideological priorities.

Such factors as political generation and professional education were not important for either the Russian or the Chinese journalistic community with regard to their attitudes to political protests. The sample included journalists with a very good level of formal education, some of whom did not approve of political protests and especially the participation of journalists in this activity, while others favoured protests.

It may be surmised that work in new online media makes individuals more critical about traditional values, albeit not always. Metropolitan cities also likely stimulate a more critical position of journalists towards traditional priorities and thus influence in particular their attitudes to protests. In smaller places, it is much more difficult to become 'irrational' and to think independently from social and especially professional communities; therefore, it is not surprising that provincial cities and small-circulation news media stimulate in the consciousness of journalists an idea that political protests destroy traditional values and make a situation more unpredictable and unstable. In fact, these journalists are much more scared of change than their counterparts in larger cities are, although they often cannot clearly explain the reasons for these fears. Younger journalists working in large cities and having sufficient skills to manage information through new technologies were less restrained in expressing their views.

In sum, the main predictors of support for political protests were: a) working in online media; b) working in private media; and c) living and working in a metropolitan city. The main predictors of a negative attitude to political protests were the opposite conditions of working in the traditional media and in state-owned/subsidized media, and living and working in the provinces. However, as shown by our study, as well as by the review of the protests in both countries, the province can be the heart of protests and journalists in the provinces could be in solidarity with the protesters.

References

Amos, H., & Sawer, P. (2011). *Russian protests: 10 December as it happened.* Retrieved from www.telegraph.co.uk/news/worldnews/europe/russia/8947840/Russian-protests-live.html

Beck, U. (1992). *Risk society, towards a new modernity.* London: Sage Publications.

Berdnikova, S., Kuznetsov, A., & Grout, D. (2007). *Ford workers in Russia strike.* Retrieved from www.cbsnews.com/news/ford-workers-in-russia-strike/

Chinese Academy of Social Sciences. (2014). *Annual report on China's rule of law, 12.* Beijing: Social Sciences Academy Press.

Cohen, J. L., & Arato, A. (1992). *Civil society and political theory.* Cambridge, MA and London: MIT Press.

Davies, R. W. (1989). *Soviet history in the Gorbachev revolution.* Bloomington: Indiana University Press.

Evans, A. B. (2012). Protests and civil society in Russia: The struggle for the Khimki Forest. *Communist and Post-Communist Studies, 45*(3/4), 233–242.

Federal'nyi Zakon. (2002). *O protivodeistvii ekstremistskoi deyatel'nosti* [Federal Law 'On countering extremist activity']. Retrieved from www.referent.ru/1/95895/context

Federal'nyi Zakon. (2012). *O vnesenii izmenenii v otdel'nye zakonodatel'nye akty Rossiiskoi Federatsii v chasti uregulirovaniya deyatel'nosti nekommercheskikh organizatsiy, vypolnyajushchikh funktsii inostrannogo agenta* [Federal law 'On the involvement of the changes into separate legislative acts of the Russian Federation on the regulation of activity of non-commercial organizations fulfilling the functions of a foreign agent']. Retrieved from http://rg.ru/2012/07/23/nko-dok.html

Feklyunina, V., & White, S, (2013). Discourses of 'krizis': Economic crisis in Russia and regime legitimacy. In V. Feklyunina & S. White (Eds.), *The international economic crisis and the post-Soviet states* (pp. 143–156). London: Routledge.

Garrett, R. K. (2006). Protest in an information society: A review of literature on social movements and new ICTs. *Information, Communication & Society, 9*(2), 202–224.

Harding, L. (2010, February 2). Kremlin shocked as Kaliningrad stages huge anti-government protest. *The Guardian.* Retrieved from www.theguardian.com/world/2010/feb/02/russia-anti-government-protest-kaliningrad

Hoskins, G. (1990). *The awakening of the Soviet Union.* Cambridge, MA: Harvard University Press.

Ilyichev, G. (2012, January 11). *Dekabristy-2011. Sotsiologi izmerili kachestvo protestnogo dvizheniya* [Decembrists-2011: Sociologists have measured quality of the protest movement]. Retrieved from www.novayagazeta.ru/politics/50325.html

Jenkins, J. C., & Klandermans, B. (1995). The politics of social protest. In J. C. Jenkins & B. Klandermans (Eds.), *The politics of social protest: Comparative perspectives on states and social movements* (pp. 3–13). Minneapolis, MI: University of Minnesota Press.

Klingemann, H. D., Fuchs, D., & Zielonka, J. (2006). *Democracy and political culture in Eastern Europe.* London: Routledge.

Koesel, K. J., & Bunce, V. J. (2012). Putin, popular protests, and political trajectories in Russia: A comparative perspective. *Post-Soviet Affairs, 28*(4), 403–423. Retrieved from http://dx.doi.org/10.2747/1060-586X.28.4.403

Kolesnichenko, A. (2013, October 3). How October 1993 led to President Putin. *Russia Beyond Headlines.* Retrieved from http://rbth.com/politics/2013/10/03/how_october_1993_led_to_president_putin_30489.html

Korotich, V. (1991). *Zal ozhidaniya* [The waiting room]. New York: Liberty.

Kueppers, A. (2010, May 15). Russia coal miners protest after deadly blasts. *Reuters: Morning Briefing*. Retrieved from www.reuters.com/article/us-russia-coal-protest-idUSTRE64E1RM20100515

Levada Research Center. (2012, December 27). *Protestnaya aktivnost' rossiyan: Protsess po delu na Bolotnoi ploshchadi* [Protest activity of the Russians: The process on the case of Bolotnaya Square]. Retrieved from www.levada.ru/27-12-2012/protestnaya-aktivnost-rossiyan-protsess-po-delu-na-

Myers, S. L. (2005, January 16). Putin reforms greeted by street protests. *The New York Times*. Retrieved from www.nytimes.com/2005/01/16/world/europe/putin-reforms-greeted-by-street-protests.html?_r=2

Opp, K. D. (2009). *Theories of political protest and social movements: A multidisciplinary introduction, critique, and synthesis*. Abingdon: Routledge.

Pan, P. P. (2010, March 20). Russian exclave of Kaliningrad at forefront of a nationwide protest movement. *The Washington Post*. Retrieved from www.washingtonpost.com/wp-dyn/content/article/2010/03/19/ar2010031904767.html

Petrov, A. (2007, December 4). Russia: Key strike at the Ford Plant in Leningrad (St. Petersburg). *Defence of Marxism*. Retrieved from www.marxist.com/russia-strike-ford-petersburg121207.htm

Petrushina, A. (2012). *Diskurs politicheskogo protesta v soobshcheniyakh novostnykh internet-saytov* [Discourse of the political protest in the information of news websites]. Retrieved from http://psibook.com/philosophy/diskurs-politicheskogo-protesta-v-soobscheniyah-novostnyh-internet-saytov.html

Podyachev, K. V. (2012). Protestnoe dvizhenie "nulevykh": Genezis i spetsifika [Protest movement of the 2000th: Origin and specifics]. *Vestnik Instituta Sotsiologii [Sociology institute messenger]*, 5, 146–163.

Porta, D., & Tarrow, S. (2012). Interactive diffusion: The coevolution of police and protest behavior with an application to transnational contention. *Comparative Political Studies*, 20, 1–34.

Rabinovich, S. (2005, October 2). Russian benefit monetisation protests. *The Russian Reader*. Retrieved from https://therussianreader.wordpress.com/tag/russian-benefit-monetization-protests-2005/

RBK. (2014, April 17). *Vladimir Putin vsyo simpatichnee. Blagodarya prisoedineniyu Kryima ego reiting priblizilsya k pikovym znacheniyam* [Vladimir Putin is becoming more sympathetic: Owing to the annexation of the Crimea his rating has approached the peak rates]. Retrieved from www.rbc.ru/newspaper/2014/04/17/56beeafc9a7947299f72d227

Reddaway, P., & Glinski, D. (2001). *The tragedy of Russia's reforms: Market Bolshevism against democracy*. Washington, DC: US Institute of Peace Press.

Remnick, D. (1994). *Lenin's tomb: The last days of the Soviet Empire*. New York: Vintage Books.

RWB (Reporters without Borders). (2005). *The 2004 global press freedom world tour*. Paris: Reporters Without Borders.

RWB (Reporters without Borders). (2010, May 4). *Reporteryi bez granits nazvali Putina i Kadyrova glavnyimi vragami svobodnoy pressyi* [Reporters without Borders called Putin and Kadyrov as the main enemies of a free press]. Retrieved from http://ma-zaika.ru/post125792087

Shkel, S., & Sabitov, M. (2012). Massovyi politicheskiy protest v sovremennoi Rossii: dinamika i spetsifika razvitiya [The mass political protest in modern Russia: Dynamics and specifics of development]. *Pravo i politika. Nauchnyi juridicheskiy zhurnal [Law and Politics: Scientific Law Journal]*, 10, 1669–1675.

Solidarnost (Central trade union newspaper). (2014, October 1). *Nedovol'stvo, protesty i statistika; Tsentr sotsial'no-trudovykh prav predstavil doklad o trudovykh protestakh v Rossii* [Dissatisfaction, protests and statistics: The Center for Social and Labor Rights represented a paper about labor protests in Russia]. Retrieved from www.solidarnost.org/articles/articles_4477.html

Sputnik. (2009, October 24). *Russian motorists in Far East protest new rules, taxes*. Retrieved from http://sputniknews.com/russia/20091024/156575034.html

Stepankov, V., & Lisov, Y. (1992). *Kremlevskiy zagovor* [The Kremlin plot]. Moscow: Ogonek.

Tarrow, S. (1994). *Power in movement: Social movements, collective action and mass politics in the modern state*. Cambridge: Cambridge University Press.

VTsIOM. (2012, February 15). *Miting 4 fevralya na Bolotnoy Ploshchadi: Rezul'taty oprosa uchastnikov* [Meeting of February 4 at Bolotnaya square: Survey of participants]. Retrieved from http://old.wciom.ru/novosti/press-vypuski/press-vypusk/single/112492.html

Yu, J. R. (2010). *Contentious politics: Fundamental issues in Chinese political sociology*. Beijing: People's Press.

Zhao, D. X. (2012). *Social and political movements* (2nd ed.). Beijing: Social Sciences Academic Press.

8

COMMUNITY RADIO FOR THE RIGHT TO COMMUNICATE

Brazil and South Africa

Tanja Bosch, Raquel Paiva, and João Paulo Malerba

Introduction

Established in 1947 by a Catholic priest for broadcasts to his parish, Radio Sutatenza in Colombia is often considered to be the first ever community radio station (Àlvarez, 2004). The original broadcasts were made through a homemade transmitter and had the objective of bringing education to the rural people of Sutatenza, Colombia (Fraser & Restrepo-Estrada, 1998). The Bolivian miners' radio stations established in 1948 are also an early example of the use of alternative radio, in this case for political struggles (O'Connor, 1990). The first of these Bolivian stations began in 1948 as Radio Sucre in Radio Nuevos Horizontes; by the 1960s, 23 radio stations covering all the mining centres were operating as a credible source of news and information and a platform for local debate (Buckley, 2000). Community radio stations were simultaneously emerging organically in the Caribbean, Asia, Australia, Europe, and Africa, and these early examples of radio paved the way for what we today understand as community radio.

Community radio advocates criticized the mainstream mass media for giving priority to narratives and agendas which were not relevant to the citizens of developing countries, and instead drew on scholars like Freire (1970, 1985) for inspiration in the creation of participatory communication initiatives, which have included not only community radio, but also print and video initiatives around the world.

The key principles of community radio include access, participation, and self-management (Lewis, 1993). Community radio stations are non-profit institutions; they foreground the widespread participation of ordinary people in production, decision making, and management, and they emphasize programming designed to meet the interests of local communities – especially social, ethnic, sexual, or religious minorities – so that they finally feel represented in the media through their own voices. While there is a diversity of community radio stations, "what allows us to define a medium as 'community' is not its capacity to provide a service but its intention, its clear aim to mobilise as connected to exercising citizenship" (Paiva, 1998, p. 160). There is thus a strong focus on the notion of 'community', which sometimes refers to geographic location, but may also refer to groups with specific cultural, religious, or ethnic affiliations.

In the newly formed BRICS association of five emerging national economies, Brazil and South Africa are the two countries with the strongest tradition of community radio. This chapter provides a description of the evolution and current state of community radio in Brazil and South Africa, highlighting strengths and current trends, similarities and differences, and also challenges despite its continued success in these countries.

The BRICS study

The BRICS study did not specifically speak to community radio, but journalists often spoke about community radio in response to other questions. While this chapter draws on other sources, it also includes voices of the BRICS study respondent journalists, reflecting their experiences and beliefs.

Findings

History of community radio

Brazil

In Latin America, community radio has played a key role in the liberation struggles against dictatorships and, more recently, in preserving indigenous languages at risk of becoming extinct.[1] The first decades of the emergence of radio in Brazil were marked by a vision that this new vehicle would be a powerful tool for social transformation and democratization.

Radio stations that were less politically oriented, but instead had aesthetic and libertarian motives, were also set up by many Brazilian broadcasters. Producing radio was easy and thus attracted the attention of young people and socially or culturally marginal groups. In fact, they were inspired by the so-called pirate radio stations, which invaded the European dials with their irregular and unplanned programmes in an attempt to totally deconstruct notions of competence and specialization associated with the traditional mainstream broadcasters. Thus, the 1980s saw the growth of the free radio stations (equivalent to the pirate stations in Europe): immigrants, gays, the homeless, prostitutes, non-professional groups, etc., providing exposure to a multiplicity of voices. The majority of these groups were not linked to any political party or movement, but challenged the concentration of ownership and orthodoxy in the Brazilian media scenario (Machado, Magri, & Masagão, 1987).

Community radio was also important in the process of re-democratization in Brazil, after 20 years of military dictatorship. In spite of its social importance, it was only in 1998 that the federal government added the category of community radio to its regulatory responsibilities. Today, Brazil's community radio stations are low-power stations, with a maximum broadcast range of one kilometre, and are formally operated by local civic groups such as neighbourhood associations (Boas & Hildago, 2011). Brazilian community radio's reach is mostly in rural areas and small villages, where residents often cannot tune in to the commercial or state broadcasters; thus, in such locations community radio is very important. In Brazil, many low-power stations have appeared, some linked to a more progressive wing of the Roman Catholic Church, others to grassroots social movements (mainly rural unions) and/or left-wing political parties. These stations were created with a more defined political profile and with the clearly targeted objective of democratizing the channels of communication in order to democratize society and promote human rights.

South Africa

In South Africa, community radio emerged after the country's first democratic elections in 1994; it was central to the repositioning of the media landscape in the 'new' South Africa. The emergence of community radio was within the context of the flourishing alternative press of the 1980s, which acted as a catalyst for the liberation struggle and popularized anti-apartheid discourse (Teer-Tomaselli, Tomaselli, & Muller, 1989). Community radio was intended to give marginalized communities access to the means of production, as well as provide them with a vehicle for the expression of their own ideas, in their own voices. While some stations and radio projects in Cape Town attempted illegal broadcasts during the early 1990s, it was only in 1994, after the first democratic elections, that legal provision was made for community radio. In South Africa, community radio stations are defined as those run, owned, and controlled by community members or organizations, for their own communities, and funded by grants, sponsorships, donations, and advertising, with profits ploughed back into the community (Mtimde, 2000). There are currently around 200 licensed community radio stations operating in South Africa.

Regulatory framework of community radio

Brazil

In Brazil, the 1980s marked the consolidation of a national and international movement for the organization and support of community radio. The majority of Latin American countries including Brazil had no regulatory provisions related to any spectrum reserve for non-commercial or non-state, low-power broadcasting. As a result, unauthorized radio stations were systematically closed down, often through the use of police violence and a violation of people's rights, a trend that continues today due to the slow process of granting licences after community radio was legalized. However, more positive events also occurred. On the international level, the World Association of Community Radio Broadcasters (AMARC) was formed in 1983. At the national level, in Brazil, a Cooperative of Radio Lovers was created in São Paulo in 1985 "to help with the construction of transmitters and show solidarity in case of oppression" (Machado, Magri, & Masagão, 1987, p. 43). In 1995, an AMARC branch was formed, followed in 1996 by the formation of the Brazilian Association of Community Radios; ABRAÇO, its acronym, means 'hug' in Portuguese.

These developments culminated in the legalization of community radio stations in February 1998, during the time of a neo-liberal government and as the result of a congress comprising many members who were owners of commercial radio and TV stations. As Paiva (1998) states, "the media can accept the existence of another model, as long as it doesn't mean sharing the same technical conditions" (p. 169). Today, there are 4,702 such stations in the country.[2]

Brazilian community radio law 9612 (1998) limits full development of the licensed community radio. Malerba (2012) indicated that in South America, Brazil has the most restrictive community broadcasting laws with respect to the legal definition of community radio, power and transmission reach, spectrum reserve, potential for sustainability, and licence length. In establishing that the station is restricted to "serving a determined community in a neighbourhood and/or 'vila'", Brazilian law only provides for geographical communities, excluding so-called interest communities, which are recognised with similar laws in neighbouring countries such as Argentina, Ecuador, and Uruguay. This restriction is reinforced by the limit placed on transmission power at 25 watts and in FM (the typical modulation or local transmissions). Thus, in Brazil, ethno-linguistic communities (indigenous, quilombola, migrants, etc.), which do not conform to these geographic communities, are prevented from constructing their own electronic means of communication. This "supposition that the individuals should be in the same territory, sharing the same physical space" in order to form a community, has been questioned (Paiva, 1998, p. 56); "nowadays, a broadening of the concept [that ties community to territorial space] can be conceived, mainly by way of a communication network" (p. 187).

In addition, the state's elevated levels of bureaucracy and inefficiency in granting licences 'makes' many radio stations illegal. Research by NGO Article 19 revealed that, from 2008 to 2011, the Ministry of Communication had accumulated 11,842 cases that were pending analysis, having managed to process only 30 per cent of them (5,322 out of a total of 17,164) (ARTIGO 19, AMARC, & MNRC, 2013). As such, the wait for a licence can take up to ten years or more. This has led to the permanent closure of radio stations without licences and the punishment of their broadcasters; the number of these closures and punished broadcasters is larger than the number of licences granted (ARTIGO 19, AMARC, & MNRC, 2013). According to data from the National Agency for Telecommunications (Anatel), in

2010, 940 radio stations without licences were taken off the air, an average of more than 2.5 stations per day. The following year, the Federal Police and Anatel closed more than 698 stations, almost two stations per day.[3] Despite this hostile landscape, Brazilian community radio stations continue to be effective in the fight for human rights in general and for the right to communicate in particular.

South Africa

South Africa is often cited as the African country with the most progressive broadcasting regulation with regard to community radio. Internationally, community radio stations often operate on commercial radio licences, whereas in South Africa the situation is different. In 1993, during the process of political transformation, the government formed an Independent Broadcasting Authority (IBA) as a regulatory body. The role of the IBA as set out in Section Two of the IBA Act (153 of 1993) was to open up the broadcast media environment. Section 2 of the act lists several objectives: to encourage historically disadvantaged ownership, to diversify ownership and programming, and to encourage local programming (Duncan & Seleoane, 1998). The IBA was to democratize the airwaves, to ensure the reception of broadcasts free of government interference, and to encourage ownership and control of broadcasts by previously disadvantaged groups (Mtimde, 2000). The IBA approved community and commercial broadcast licences, and was also tasked with enforcing local content quotas, dealing with audience complaints through its Monitoring and Complaints Committee, and issuing licences to the first community radio stations.

The IBA issued more than 100 12-month licences between 1994 and 1997, with 82 stations going on air. In 1997, the IBA issued a position paper and called for applications for four-year licences (Tacchi, 2002). The formation of the IBA was particularly crucial to the transformation of broadcasting in South Africa and for the licensing of community radio (Barnett, 1999).

In 2000, the IBA merged with the South African Telecommunications Authority (SATRA) to form the Independent Communications Authority of South Africa (ICASA), the current regulatory authority. Shortly thereafter, the Media Development and Diversity Agency (MDDA) was set up by Parliamentary Act 14 of 2002 to enable more widespread access, ownership, and control of the media by previously disadvantaged groups. The MDDA funds community media and small commercial media, and is funded by the government, together with contributions from commercial media.

Podcasts, online radio, and social media

Developments that have affected community radio considerably in recent times are the development of podcasts, the digitalization of radio/online radio, and social networking sites.

Young people today tend to consume recorded programmes on web-connected platforms (computers, tablets, smartphones) instead of engaging in linear consumption of traditional TV and radio programmes. Loyalty to one particular channel has been replaced by access to a multiplicity of channels. Audiences often know specific programmes well, but do not often know the original channel that carries their favourite programmes; they have become more interested in programmes rather than channels.

On the radio, this process is happening by way of the podcast, an on-demand mode of radio broadcasting (broadcaster and receiver do not simultaneously share broadcast and reception). These podcasts are radio programmes of varying types (journalistic, artistic, musical, scientific, etc.), usually recorded in MP3 format for easy download from the Internet and heard on MP3 players, mobile phones, or even computers.

It is worth noting that a large number of human rights–themed podcasts are found on the Internet today. The majority of podcasts deal with individual or activist initiatives (or rather, non-community initiatives, in the commonly accepted use of the term), but community radio stations, both FM and online, also make parts of their programming available in this format.

Online radio is an audio transmission service via the Internet using streaming technology, generating audio in real time. Like FM radio, the listeners are presented with continuous programming (not being able to pause or replay), which differentiates online radio from podcasting (which involves downloading and not streaming). It is live transmission, synchronized, worldwide, and available through any form of Internet connection. As it does not require a licence, online radio is a viable alternative for a number of social entities that feel excluded from the media scene and that have difficulty in obtaining broadcasting licences legally.

Regarding journalism on community radio stations in the digital era, social networking sites like Facebook and the microblogging service Twitter are increasingly intersecting with traditional mainstream news outlets, resulting in more participatory news production. Social networking sites could be seen as the latest generation of mediated publics (Fenton, 2012) or as a networked public sphere. Peripheral involvement on social media has been likened to radio listening, a process that occurs in most online spaces. Crawford (2009) argues that posting, commenting, and direct interaction are not the only significant forms of participation, and that listening participants can feel a deep sense of connection in online spaces. The ongoing social media news feed and listeners who simply scan through this feed engage in a type of background listening, similar to what happens when they listen to the radio. When listeners also engage with their favourite radio stations via social media (together with listening on the airwaves), social media can become a natural extension of the listening experience. In some ways, it expands the listening experience, adding another dimension and making radio less of a flat, one-dimensional medium. Being able to instantly get responses on Twitter, or seeing photographs of in-studio activities on Facebook, accentuates the experience of radio listening as compared with only hearing a presenter's voice. The growth of social media and its intersection with radio thus provides many new possibilities for community radio stations to connect even more with their audiences.

With digitalization and the irreversible trend towards media hybridization and convergence, today community radio is undergoing an interesting process of reinventing techniques and broadening its potential, while also facing new challenges. These developments create interesting tensions in the classical understanding of what community radio is, at the same time as community radio demonstrates a dynamic ability to keep social innovation moving along with technological innovation.

Brazil

In Brazil, Radiotube (www.radiotube.org.br), a social network for sharing information – mainly podcast audio – exclusively related to citizenship, attracts thousands of activists, students, community radio members, and teachers, among others, from all over Brazil and the Portuguese-speaking world, via the Internet (Malerba, 2009).

According to Malerba (2012, 2009), there is currently a series of restrictions in Brazilian law, which among other things, make it difficult for interest communities and even extensive geographical communities to access broadcasts. In this hostile environment, online radio provides a viable alternative.

One example is the Santa Marta community radio station, situated in the Santa Marta favela, in the South Zone of Rio de Janeiro. Since its inception in 2010, Radio Santa Marta has used conventional radio and the Internet for its transmissions. During the process of creating the station, which involved individuals (principally cultural and political leaders from the Santa Marta favela) and local organizations (mostly NGOs), fortnightly meetings were held to encourage participation and to discuss the programming. Democratic decision making was used to decide how the station would be run. As a collective, the group decided to put the station on air before the licence from the Ministry of Communication was granted. This resulted in the radio station being shut down and the equipment confiscated by the state on May 3, 2011. After this, the members of the radio group decided to continue the station only on the Internet while they waited for the result of the licence application. According to Custódio (2011), online transmissions helped to bring external agents together to develop new networks for articulation, mobilization, and action with the local actors within the Santa Marta favela. But the engagement of the local population declined significantly after the decision to keep only the online station going. There was a decline in interest in maintaining the programming due to the fact that the ideal audience – the local population – was not used to listening to the radio over the Internet.

The digitalization of radio affords opportunities, but also entails many risks for Brazilian community radio stations. With better use made of the dial, the limited space reserved today for community stations (Brazilian law only reserves one FM frequency per community station per region, or rather, about 2 per cent of the total) could be opened up without the excuse of lack of space on the spectrum. On the other hand, as William (2013) states,

> As there is no permission for local commerce advertising and no public funding for financing the stations, the community stations don't have the money to digitalize. Transmission equipment is expensive and, with no mechanism of support, the technological migration would be impossible for these stations.

Also, the tests for radio digitalization being carried out by the Ministry of Communication do not consider the current legal restrictions on community radio. As previously mentioned, Law 9612 limits stations to 25 watts, and "as digital power is much lower than in analogue, urban noise could cause a real 'black-out' of community radio stations that already operate on very low-power analogue transmissions" (William, 2013).

Research still underway on community radio stations throughout Brazil has confirmed the intersection in Brazil between traditional media and social media.[4] Still, in recent years, community communication in Brazil has been synonymous with community radio stations. This is the case even though some stations have migrated to the Internet, like the station Bicuda, based in the city of Rio de Janeiro, which, after violent persecution and being shut down by the police at the end of the 1990s, abandoned the station and migrated to a website, intensifying the environmental sustainability agenda which had already become their focal point. Community TV stations hardly exist at all; some examples of such stations are Tevê Ovo, in Santa Maria, and Rio Grande do Sul, in the south of the country, which survives by projecting programs in public spaces using volunteers. Community printed press is rarer still; the newspaper *O Cidadão* stands out, produced by residents of the favela of Maré, Rio de Janeiro. This is a monthly periodical that has managed to sustain its printed format for more than ten years before migrating solely to blog and social network formats.

South Africa

Despite the challenges arising from the digital divide in developing countries, in South Africa, there has been a steady increase in Internet-based radio stations. There are around 30 online radio stations currently operating in South Africa and broadcasting exclusively online, but there is no clear data on the listenership of these stations. Online radio is currently unregulated in South Africa.

Examples of South African online radio include former radio and television celebrity Gareth Cliff's CliffCentral.com, branded as "uncensored, unscripted, *unradio*", with all content podcast for later download, moving away from the traditional practice of live broadcasting. Similarly, a well-known media celebrity and former Primedia radio host runs The Taxi, which broadcasts online at www.thetaxi.co.za. 2oceansvibe Radio claims a listenership of 25,000, peaking at 4,000 unique listeners per day, higher than several FM stations.[5] 2oceansvibe Radio also has a Facebook and Twitter presence. Community journalists frequently use social media, engaging in forms of meta-journalism by rating, commenting, and re-posting material (Bosch, 2013). As one respondent journalist said:

> When you go do a story, you obviously have SABC online, you hashtag whatever story you are at so that people who are outside of where you are can know exactly what's happening by just looking at that; if there is a protest, if there is a car crash . . . So you never actually stop. Even when you leave work, when you drive past a place and you see that there is a gang fight or something, you are allowed to take pictures, tweet it, and literally send your script online, and can have your story play on air in an hour. That's the advantage of social media.

Social media raises the potential agenda-building role of community media, and simultaneously enhances one of the basic functions of community radio by engaging with audience members in participatory and collaborative ways in the creation of news content.

In South Africa, many mainstream and community outlets have parallel online spaces such as blogs and websites, but with the growth of social networking sites, community radio has become very active in that space. Internet access in South Africa is still relatively low, but the growth of the mobile Internet in South Africa has meant that more people, youth in particular, use their mobile phones to go online (Donner & Gitau, 2009). While nearly all mainstream South African radio stations stream online, fewer community stations do so, and listening to these in real time requires a high-speed Internet connection. Social networking sites thus become an easy way for radio stations to enhance their broadcast content and interact with audience members, particularly as audiences already use these sites in large numbers. Radio has always been considered a 'blind' medium in that it comprises only noise and silence (Crisell, 1994). In the 1950s, this was considered a primary disadvantage in the competition with television. The introduction of picture and text has reduced the anonymity of the radio host and started to close the gap between presenter and audience.

While many benefits of social media are evident, one BRICS study journalist mentioned limitations of social media:

> I think [social media journalism is] about strengthening and extending democracy, and I think that journalists play an important role in putting information in the hands of citizens. And I understand that social media for example is important for citizens to be able to access information themselves, but I think that journalists still have a role to provide information which is trustworthy, which has been tested in some way, using the kind of professional tools that come with their work, so that the public can rely on that.

Challenges to community radio

Brazil

In Brazil, the independence of community radio has been challenged by the ability of municipal politicians to gain government approval for community radio stations, which they have then used to influence future electoral campaigns. Boas and Hildago (2011) demonstrate that control of communication media is an important mechanism for perpetuating local political power in Brazil, showing that in cases where there was a licensed radio station with ties to a candidate, it raised their share of the votes by 17 per cent and the probability of winning by 28 per cent. After Brazil's transition from authoritarian rule in 1985, during the late 1980s, political criteria were used to award broadcasting licences, with commercial radio and television concessions often given directly to politicians as payment for votes on key legislation (Boas & Hildago, 2011).

In Brazil, citizen participation on community radio often takes the form of giving listeners the opportunity to phone in to programmes, rather than involving them in the actual conceptualization and production of programmes (Torres, 2011). The issue of community participation is difficult to define, and there are no guidelines provided in the legislation, which merely calls for broad-based community participation. While community radio is often associated with the principles of an open and accessible public sphere for audience members, it is ironic that practices often contradict this theoretical notion. Community broadcasting organizations regulate access to the airwaves and their media assets via formal and informal structures. Not all audience members have the opportunity to participate in the creation of content and not everyone is given access to the airwaves. Stations usually have formal procedures in which very few volunteers eventually gain access to training and their own radio shows. Informally, station premises limit access to members and staff, with policies around access in turn limiting membership and participation. As Van Vuuren (2006) explains:

> To be accepted as a legitimate alternative voice in a wider mainstream public sphere, a process of exclusion ensures that access to broadcasting is limited to those individuals and groups whose points of view best represent a station's purpose and thus preserve its value and purpose.
>
> (p. 380)

Financial sustainability is also a major threat to community radio. In view of the legal difficulties impeding financial sustainability, use of the Internet as a news source has shown itself to be a viable alternative for community radio stations. The lack of funds has made it impossible for stations to invest in technology or pay personnel dedicated to producing local information. In the words of Nilson José dos Santos[6]: "Money is a problem, we can't survive on what the station brings in. For me to do a report in the countryside, for example, it costs time and money on transport". This is one more example of how the current restrictive legislation has impeded the complete development of community radio stations in Brazil and inhibited them from carrying out their mission to the fullest extent possible.

South Africa

The key challenges currently facing the community radio sector in South Africa, as identified by community radio stakeholders themselves, are the production of quality content, issues of governance and community participation, and the ability to achieve financial sustainability. As one respondent journalist from the BRICS study reflected:

> It is not easy working for a community television station. Soweto TV has been up and running for five years now . . . , but we still have those financial constraints. We still feel like . . . firstly we could expand our newsroom a bit more. We have zeal to cover bigger stories and to cover many stories but, at the moment, [we] get like one journalist out in the field as opposed to getting two or three, which impacts sometimes on the number of stories we can get, and maybe even the quality of stories.

Maintaining independence from advertisers and government is an additional challenge. In the words of a BRICS study respondent journalist:

> In our last meeting as the Association of Independent Publishers, there are some who reported that there are some politicians who are bullying them, especially those who are in government positions. [These politicians] say "if you continue writing in this manner, we are going to cut off your advertising from the municipality". [This] was discussed at length. . . . There are certain municipalities that are no longer advertising with us. You can go and pitch whatever you want, they will not advertise. I think it is because of the articles that we put in the newspaper.

Despite a range of policies governing the operation of community radio, a challenge for stations is that these policies identify broad areas without providing specific guidelines to stations about how they should comply. The quality of content varies widely across community radio in South Africa, with fewer and fewer stations producing researched documentaries, and many following commercial formats of talk and predominantly foreign popular music, in an attempt to compete for advertising with mainstream stations. With respect to governance and community participation, the policy of local community involvement and participation is intended to facilitate citizens' access to the station's airwaves. However, many stations interpret community participation differently, particularly as national broadcasting policy makes no provision for how this should be realized in practice. In some stations, participation is understood to be the provision for volunteers from the target community to present programmes at the station, while in other stations, it is perceived as the community members' ability to participate in governance structures by serving as board members or attending the Annual General Meetings (Bosch, 2010).

Financial sustainability is an ongoing challenge for South African community radio stations. Because stations originally had to apply for renewal of their licences after one year, they faced challenges in sustainability. Without the certainty of renewal, it was hard for stations to secure long-term advertising contracts, and the process of reapplying was time-consuming and expensive. In South Africa, community radio stations are registered as Section 21 companies, i.e., non-profit companies, with boards of directors. However, despite the formation of the Media Development and Diversity Agency (MDDA) to fund community and small commercial radio, most community radio stations see financial sustainability as the greatest threat to their continued existence. While the MDDA has government funding, it does not have sufficient funding to service all the community radio stations that apply to them for funding. Scholars have previously argued that in order to become financially sustainable, stations must engender a sense of participation and ownership by audiences (Bosch, 2010), which is often hard given the diversity within the geographic communities that stations serve.

Conclusions

Community radio has existed for decades in both Brazil and South Africa, but what reasons justify the continued existence of a community vehicle today? One could argue that community radio is a key part of the global media landscape, and remains at the centre of democratization in both countries today. With the increased centralization of media ownership and the growth of commercial music radio, community radio remains a key vehicle for alternative voices and for deliberative talk and dialogue, and also a space for the rise of civic journalism and a move away from the dominant normative notions of journalism. This type of community communication constitutes a counter-hegemonic force in the field of communication.

Community radio continues to be a tool of education and development, both in rural and urban areas. Moreover, community radio stations demystify media by potentially turning media consumers into media producers, and training them to produce radio programmes, working towards a polyphony of voices, and breaking down barriers between message producers and consumers. The continued existence of community radio implies possibilities for subaltern counter-publics (Fraser, 1990), where subordinated social groups can create and circulate counter discourses. As subaltern counter-publics, community radio stations have great potential to increase diversity in the media landscape of both Brazil and South Africa, and to drive agendas that are not influenced by government or commercial imperatives. Through the use of new communications technologies, in particular the Internet and social media, community radio stations have an opportunity to grow, to strengthen relationships with their audiences, and to build communities in ways that are not bound by geography.

Notes

1. www.amarceurope.eu/community-radio-latin-america-the-reference/
2. Data obtained from NGO Clause 19, based on the recently approved *Lei de Acesso à Informação* (Law for Access to Information). Retrieved from http://artigo19.org/centro/esferas/detail/251
3. Data obtained from NGO Clause 19, based on the recently approved *Lei de Acesso à Informação* (Law for Access to Information). Retrieved from http://artigo19.org/centro/esferas/detail/251
4. Reference is to the doctoral research by Paulo Malerba entitled "Rádios comunitárias no limite" (Community radio stations at their limits), supervised by Dr Raquel Paiva, which covers a quantitative study of 100 stations and another qualitative study of ten community radio stations, involving a process of immersion into the daily lives of radio stations.
5. www.2oceansviberadio.com/about/
6. Nilson José dos Santos, journalist of the community radio Esperança FM, a quilombo station in the town of Queimada Nova in the desert region of Piauí, North-West Brazil, was interviewed for this chapter on September 22, 2015.

References

Àlvarez, P. (2004). As rádios da esperança [Radios of hope]. *Infosolidaria.org*. Retrieved from www.infosolidaria.org/verarticulo.php?idarticulo=524&idautor=41&idversion=0&ididioma=1

ARTIGO 19, Associação Mundial de Rádios Comunitárias (AMARC Brasil), & Movimento Nacional De Rádios Comunitárias (MNRC). (2013). *Situação das rádios comunitárias no Brasil* [Overview of Brazilian community radios]. Retrieved from http://artigo19.org/wp-content/uploads/2013/03/CIDH-RadCom-Documento-final-3.pdf

Barnett, C. (1999). Broadcasting the rainbow nation: Media, democracy and nation-building in South Africa. *Antipode*, *31*(3), 274–303.

Boas, T., & Hildago, F. (2011). Controlling the airwaves: Incumbency advantage and community radio in Brazil. *American Journal of Political Science*, *55*(4), 869–885.

Bosch, T. (2010). Community radio in South Africa 15 years after democracy. In N. Hyde-Clarke (Ed.), *The citizen in communication* (pp. 139–154). Johannesburg: Unisa Press.

Bosch, T. (2013). Social media and community radio in South Africa. *Digital Journalism*, *2*(1), 29–43.

Brazilian Community Radio Law 9612. (1998). On establishing the community broadcast service and other measures. Retrieved from http://www.planalto.gov.br/ccivil_03/leis/L9612.htm

Buckley, S. (2000). *Community radio the new tree of speech*. Imfundo Background Paper. Retrieved from http://ncsi-net-ncsi.iisc.ernet.in/cybersoace/societal-issues/235/imfundo.pdf

Crawford, K. (2009). Following you: Disciplines of listening in social media. *Continuum: Journal of Media & Cultural Studies*, *23*(4), 525–535.

Crisell, A. (1994). *Understanding radio*. London and New York: Routledge.

Custódio, L. (2011). They still matter! The importance of print and analogue media for youth civic participation in the digital age. Paper presented at the International Association for Media and Communication Research (IAMCR) conference, Istanbul.

Donner, J., & Gitau, S. (2009). New paths: Exploring mobile-centric internet use in South Africa. Paper presented at Mobile 2.0: Beyond Voice? Pre-conference workshop at the International Communication Association (ICA) conference, Chicago, IL.

Duncan, J., & Seleoane, M. (1998). *Media and democracy in South Africa*. South Africa: Human Sciences Research Council and Freedom of Expression Institute.

Fenton, N. (2012). Internet and social networking. In J. Curran, N. Fenton, & D. Freedman (Eds.), *Misunderstanding the Internet* (pp. 123–148). London and New York: Routledge.

Fraser, C., & Restrepo-Estrada, S. (1998). *Communicating for development: Human change for survival*. London and New York: I. B. Tauris.

Fraser, N. (1990). Rethinking the public sphere: A contribution to the critique of actually existing democracy. *Social Text, 25*(26), 56–80.

Freire, P. (1970). *Pedagogy of the oppressed*. New York: Continuum.

Freire, P. (1985). *The politics of education: Power, culture and liberation*. South Hadley, MA: Bergin and Garvey.

Lewis, P. (1993). *Alternative media: Linking global and local*. Paris: UNESCO Publishing.

Machado, A., Magri, C., & Masagão, M. (1987). *Rádios livres a reforma agrária no ar*. São Paulo: Editora Brasiliense.

Malerba, J. (2009). *Rádios comunitárias 2.0: Propostas éticopolíticas de uma rede de redes* [Community radios 2.0: Ethical-political propositions of a network of networks]. Dissertation, Federal University of Rio de Janeiro (UFRJ), Rio de Janeiro.

Malerba, J. (2012). *Rádios comunitárias: Panorama da situação legal na América Sul* [Community radios: Overview of the legal situation in South America]. *Observatório da Imprensa, edição, 712*. Retrieved from www.observatoriodaimprensa.com.br/news/view/_ed712_panorama_da_situacao_legal_na_america_sul

Mtimde, L. (2000). Radio broadcasting in South Africa: An overview. *International Journal of Cultural Studies, 3*(2), 173–179.

O'Connor, A. (1990). The miners' radio stations in Bolivia: A culture of resistance. *Journal of Communication, 40*(1), 102–110.

Paiva, R. (1998). *Espírito Comum: comunidade, mídia e globalismo*. Petrópolis: Vozes.

Tacchi, J. (2002). Transforming the mediascape in South Africa: The continuing struggle to develop community radio. *Media International Australia, 103*, 68–77. Retrieved from http://eprints.qut.edu.au

Teer-Tomaselli, R., Tomaselli, K. G., & Muller, J. (Eds.). (1989). *Broadcasting in South Africa*. Vol. 2. Johannesburg: Currey.

Torres, B. (2011). Community radio stations in Brazil. *Journal of Radio & Audio Media, 18*(2), 347–357.

Van Vuuren, K. (2006). Community broadcasting and the enclosure of the public sphere. *Media, Culture and Society, 28*(3), 379–392.

William, A. (2013). *Rádio Digital: Padrão será escolhido no Brasil em 2013*. Retrieved from http://amarcbrasil.org/radio-digital-padrao-sera-escolhido-no-brasil-em-2013/

APPENDIX A

Data collection protocols

NOTE

Two slightly different versions, but covering the same questions directly or in probes, were used to conduct the study. Both are included here.

QUESTIONNAIRE: Brazil, Russia, and China

Translated into Portuguese, Russian, and Chinese

A1 Respondent's name and name of medium and type (newspaper, magazines, radio, television, online media)
Interviewer code/name: _____
A2 Classify the respondent's rank according to the following categories:
Senior manager (editor in chief, managing editor)   1
Junior manager (desk head, department head, senior editor)   2
Non-management staff (reporter, news writer)   3
A3 Date of interview: _____ (format: dd.mm.yy)
A4 Start and end time of interview: _____ (format: hh:mm, 24hrs)
A5 Respondent's location: Office 1   Home 2   Other 3
A6 Respondent's contacts (phone, email) for the possibility of feedback:
_____

Start of interview

1. **Background** (19 questions)
    1. Sex (male, female)
    2. Pseudonym of respondent
    3. Age (year of birth)
    4. Marital status
    5. Education (journalism or not? If not, what institute and faculty?) (*Here we want to know if a respondent has a professional journalism education or came into the journalism profession from another profession.*)
    6. Who are your parents? (What is your parents' education? Where do they work? Where did you grow up?)
    7. Year of beginning work in journalism
    8. Motivation: Why did you become a journalist? (*Here we want to clarify for what reasons and how the respondent came into the profession.*)
    9. Briefly, places of work from the beginning of working career
    10. Ownership (state, private, mixed as state-private)
    11. Who is the owner of your media?
    12. Size of your media organization (How many employees? How many journalists?)
    13. Specialty (present) (which beat or area do you usually work on?)
    14. Form of employment (On staff or not? Working full time or not? Salaried or hourly wage worker?)
    15. Do you have a second job?
    16. How often do you work a second job? Why do you work a second job?
    17. Income monthly (size of your income)
    18. Is your monthly income enough or not?
    19. Influence of gender on the profession:
        What are your views about how the gender of the journalist influences reactions in the organization in terms of pay, assignments, opportunities, etc.?
        Does it help or hinder your work and career?
2. **Job conditions: changes** (10 questions)
    2.1. **New technology and economy impact**
        2.1.a. *What* technological changes (innovations) have happened in the past years in your media organization?
        2.1.b. *What* economic changes (innovations) have happened in the past years in your media organization?
        2.1.c. *How* have these changes influenced the profession?
        2.1.d. *How* has journalism changed owing to the new technology and the new economic politics (workload has increased, 'economic or profit emphasis) in your media?

2.2. Outcomes of job
1) About job satisfaction or dissatisfaction
2.2.a. What gives you the greatest satisfaction in your job?
2.2.b. Why?
2.2.c. What causes you the greatest dissatisfaction in your job?
2.2.d. Why?
2) About commitment
2.2.e. Do you want to stay in the profession?
2.2.f. Why or why not?

3. Journalists and democracy (9 questions)
3.1. Citizen participation in and through media
3.1.a. Are ordinary people's voices and opinions represented in your media?
3.1.b. If yes, how are they represented? By what topics and rubrics?
3.1.c. What is your opinion about social media?
3.1.d. How do you use social media in your professional work?
3.1.e. How do you use social media in your private life?

3.2. Freedom of speech
3.2.a. Do you agree that "journalists should not cover subjects that play into the hands of our country's enemies"?
3.2.b. "It is sometimes necessary to block access to the Internet. For example, to prevent the spread of pornography. But control of the Internet may also be necessary in other cases – since the Internet is a source not only of political information but also of disinformation." Do you agree with this statement? Explain your position.
3.2.c. Is there a need to control the content of political materials in media?
3.2.d. Is there a need to control the content of entertainment in media?

4. Professionalism and ethics (32 questions)
4.1. Perceptions on professionalism
4.1.a. Who is a professional in journalism?
4.1.b. Do you consider yourself a professional? Explain
4.1.c. What do you consider to be the most unprofessional qualities of a journalist?
4.1.d. What do you consider should be the functions of journalism?
4.1.e. How are you and the journalists of your media different from the journalists working in the traditional/new online media?
4.1.f. Is it more prestigious to work in the traditional media or in new online media?

4.2. Political independence and self-regulation
4.2.a. Are you a member of an association or union of journalists?
4.2.b. Why yes or no?

- 4.2.c. Is there a primary organization of a professional association/union in your media outlet?
- 4.2.d. If not, why?
- 4.2.e. Are you a member of some other professional organization?
- 4.2.f. Should journalists have their own trade union?
- 4.2.g. Why?
- 4.2.h. What are the barriers to establishing a trade union?
- 4.2.i. What is the hierarchy in your newsroom/media?
- 4.2.j. How does the hierarchy help or complicate your work?
- 4.2.k. What is the nature of the relationship between you and your boss? (*Here we would like to clarify the work atmosphere – is it friendly and creative or more formal and hierarchical?*)
- 4.2.l. What factors impede solidarity of journalists?

4.3. Corruption
- 4.3.a. How is the widespread practice of writing articles for money connected with the notion of professionalism? Could they be combined?
- 4.3.b. What is your opinion about this journalistic practice of writing articles for money or services?
- 4.3.c. During the past 12 months, have you produced articles for money or services?
- 4.3.d. Have you experienced ethical dilemmas (difficult moral choices) in your professional work? Give examples.
- 4.3.e. Are there unwritten rules in your journalistic community? What are these rules?

4.4. Present status and future of the profession
- 4.4.a. What is your opinion about the profession of a journalist today?
- 4.4.b. What will the profession be like after ten years?
- 4.4.c. What needs to change in the social–political conditions of the country in order for journalism to fully comply with its functions and tasks?
- 4.4.d. Is a journalist an important/influential person in your city?
- 4.4.e. Are you a member of a political party?
- 4.4.f. Are you a member of a voluntary organization?
- 4.4.g. What is your attitude to protests in your city, country?
- 4.4.h. What *should be* the three most important roles of journalists?
- 4.4.i. What are the roles journalists actually perform?

QUESTIONNAIRE: India and South Africa
Translated into Bengali, Marathi, Hindi, Telugu, and Urdu in India

A. Technical information *(to be completed by the interviewer)*
    T0. Interviewer name: _____
    T1. Respondent code: _____ and phone number: _____
    T2. Date of interview: _____
    T3. Start time of interview: _____
    T4. End time of interview: _____
    T5. Interview conducted in: Office 1   Home 2
          Other 3: _____
    T6. Type of medium: Newspaper 1   Magazine 2   Radio 3
          TV 4   Online 5
    T7. Name of outlet: _____
    T8. Ownership of outlet: State 1   Private 2   Mixed state–private 3
          Other 4: _____

Get following from reliable source such as reports, top brass, etc.
    T9. Owner of outlet?   _____
    T10. Size of outlet (number of journalists):   _____

Begin interview

B. Background and job details of respondent
    B1. Gender: Male 1 Female 2
    B2. Year of birth: _____
    B3. Marital status: Married 1   Single 2   Other 3: _____
    B4. Education: High school 1   Some college 2   Bachelor's 3
          Master's 4   Other 5
    B5. *If education is more than some college:* Is your degree in journalism?
          Yes 1 No 2
    B6. *If No,* What subject/institute/faculty did you study (in)?
          _____
    B7. Who are your parents? (Your parents' education, workplace, etc.)
    B8. Briefly, where did you work from the beginning of your working career?
    B9. Year of beginning work in journalism: _____
    B10. Current job title (e.g., reporter, editor, photojournalist, managing editor, etc.): _____
    B11. *Interviewer should classify the respondent's rank according to the following categories:*
          Senior manager (editor in chief, managing editor)   1
          Junior manager (desk head, department head, senior editor)   2
          Non-management staff (reporter, news writer)   3

B12. Which beat or area do you usually work on?_____
B13. Permanence of employment:
Permanent 1   Long-term contract (3–5 years) 2   Short-term contract (< 3 years) 3   Temporary (no contract) 4
B14. Form of employment: Salaried 1   Hourly wage worker 2   Other 3 (please specify): _____
B15. Monthly income from your primary journalism job:
   1   Up to Rs 10,000   2   Rs 10,001 to Rs 20,000
   3   Rs 20,001 to Rs 30,000   4   Rs 30,001 to Rs 40,000
   5   Rs 40,001 to Rs 50,000   6   Rs 50,001 to Rs 60,000
   7   Rs 60,001 to Rs 70,000   8   Rs 70,001 to Rs 80,000
   9   Rs 80,001 to Rs 90,000   10   Greater than Rs 90,000
B16. Is this monthly income sufficient?
B17. Do you have a second job?   Yes 1   No 2
B18. *If yes*, is your second job in: Journalism 1   PR 2   Advertising 3   Other 4: _____
B19. *If yes*, how often do you work a second job?
B20. *If yes*, why do you work a second job?
B21. Total monthly income from all jobs: _____
B22. Are you a member of an association or union of journalists?   Yes 1   No 2
B23. *Probe*: Why yes or no?
B24. Is there a primary organization of a professional association/union in your media outlet?   Yes 1   No 2
B25. *If No, probe*: Why?
B26. *If Yes, probe*: Name? Your involvement? Benefits? Management view of it? Etc.
B27. Should journalists have their own trade union?   Yes 1   No 2
B28. *Probe*: Why yes or no?
B29. What are the barriers to establishing a trade union?
B30. Are you a member of a political party?   Yes 1   No 2
B31. Are you a member of a voluntary organization?   Yes 1   No 2

C. Job satisfaction

C1. How satisfied are you with your job?
   A lot 4   Somewhat 3   Little 2   Not at all 1
C2. *If answer is 4 or 3*: What gives you the greatest satisfaction in your job?
C3. *Probe*: Why?
C4. *If answer is 2 or 1*: What causes you the greatest dissatisfaction in your job?
C5. *Probe*: Why?
C6. Do you want to stay in the profession of journalism?   Yes 1   No 2
C7. *Probe*: Why or why not?

D. Influences on job/profession

D1. Has the ratio of male to female journalists changed in your media outlet in the past five to ten years?   Yes 1   No 2

D2. *If yes*, in what way?

D3. *If yes, probe:* How has the change influenced pay, assignments, opportunities, etc., in your organization?

D4. *If yes, probe:* Has the change influenced your work and career?   Yes 1   No 2

D5. *If yes, probe*: How?

D6. What technological changes (innovations) have happened in the past five years in your media organization?

D7. How have these changes transformed your work?

D8. *Probe:* Do you use social media in your journalistic work?   Yes 1   No 2

D9. *Probe:* Why or why not?

D10. *If yes, probe:* How has this use of social media influenced your work?

D11. Do you use social media in your personal life?   Yes 1   No 2

D12. *If yes, probe*: Does your use of social media in your personal life play into your journalistic work?   Yes 1   No 2

D13. *If yes, probe*: How?

D14. What economic and budgetary changes have occurred in the past five years in your media organization?

D15. How have these changes influenced your work?

D16. *Probe*: Staff reduction? Increased workload? No travel funds for stories in other towns/places? Emphasis on profit? Etc.

D17. What changes have you seen in ownership patterns of media organizations? (*e.g., media concentration, increased independent ownership, etc.*)

D18. *If changes observed*: What is the influence of these changes (*probe changes one by one*) on:
a. Your work?
b. The profession of journalism? *Probe*: In terms of editorial plurality, democratic voices, market orientation, etc.?

D19. What is the hierarchy in your newsroom (*i.e., relationship between different levels of staff, nature of newsroom culture – democratic, formal, etc.*)?

D20. How does the hierarchy influence your work?

D21. What is the nature of the relationship between you and your boss?

D22. How does this relationship influence your work?

D23. What are the sources you and your colleagues use for your journalistic work?

D24. In what kind of stories are ordinary citizens used as sources?

D25. In your most recent story, how many sources were ordinary citizens?

D26. *Probe:* Why or why not?

E. Freedom of speech

- E1. Do you think there are certain cases in which the country is justified in controlling the news media? Yes 1 No 2
- E2. Why or why not?
- E3. Should the government control the Internet? Yes 1 No 2
- E4. Why or why not?
- E5. Should the government control access to mobile telephones?
  Yes 1   No 2
- E6. Why or why not?
- E7. Should the government track use of mobile telephones?
  Yes 1   No 2
- E8. Why or why not?
- E9. Should the government control political affairs content in media?
  Yes 1   No 2
- E10. Should the government control entertainment content in media?
  Yes 1   No 2
- E11. Are there subjects that should not be covered by journalists?
  Yes 1   No 2
- E12. Why or why not?
- E13. *If yes*: What are these subjects (*national security/interest, pornography*)?
- E14. What is your attitude to protests in your city, country?

F. Professionalism

- F1. What are the characteristics of a professional journalist?
- F2. Do you consider yourself a professional journalist?
- F3. Why or why not?
- F4. Why did you become a journalist?
- F5. Who are your role models?
- F6. In the past year, have you produced news articles for money or services?   Yes 1   No 2
- F7. *If yes*: Why?
- F8. Is the practice of paid news prevalent in [country]?
- F9. How does this practice of paid news relate to professionalism in journalism?
- F10. Have you experienced ethical dilemmas (difficult moral choices) in your professional work? Give examples.
- F11. Is there solidarity among journalists in India [country], i.e., a feeling of a professional community that sticks together?
  Yes 1   No 2   Not Sure 3
- F12. Why or why not?
- F13. What factors impede or facilitate solidarity among journalists?
- F14. What are the main functions of journalism?
- F15. *Probe*: What is the role of the news media in the public sphere?
- F16. *Probe*: What is your opinion about the watchdog role of the news media?

F17. What needs to change in the social–political conditions of the country in order for journalism to fully comply with its functions?

F18. Is a journalist an important/influential person in your city?

G. Miscellaneous

G1. Is it more prestigious to work in the traditional media or in new online media?

In the following question, use the words 'traditional/online' as appropriate to the interviewee's workplace.

G2. How are journalists of your media different from the journalists working in the traditional/new online media?

G3. What is the current state of the journalism profession in India?

G4. What is the future (next five years) of the journalism profession in India?

APPENDIX B

Data collection and processing teams

The interviews were organized, conducted, and processed by the following researchers and students

Brazil

Brasília, Rio de Janeiro, Juiz de Fora, and *Vitória:* Raquel Paiva, Márcio Guerra, Christiane Paschoalino; and students from the Federal University of Juiz de Fora: Layrha Silva Moura, Yuri Fernandes, and Vanessa Ferreira.

Russia

Moscow: Maria Anikina, Svetlana Pasti; and Ph.D. students from Lomonosov Moscow State University: Kristina Zuykina, Anastasia Obraztsova, Daria Sokolova, Maria Nedyuk, and Venera Oganova.

St. Petersburg: Dmitry Gavra, Svetlana Pasti; and from St. Petersburg State University faculty: Dmitry Shishkin and Alyona Savitskaya; and master's students: Ekaterina Akimovitch, Anna Nenasheva, Zalina Barkhinkhoeva, and Emilia Sinitsyna.

Yekaterinburg: Dmitry Strovsky, Svetlana Pasti; founder and director of the research centre 'Analyst', Andrei Mozolin; and master's students from Ural Federal University.

Petrozavodsk: Svetlana Pasti; interview organizers from the Union of Journalists, Karelia: Natalia Meshkova and Anastasia Ermashova; and master's student from St. Petersburg State University: Ekaterina Akimovitch.

India

Delhi: Nagamallika Gudipaty and Ravindra Kumar Vemula; and master's students from the Jamia Millia Islamia University: Remya Muralidharan and Palak Malik.

Hyderabad: Nagamallika Gudipaty and Ravindra Kumar Vemula; master's students from the English and Foreign Languages University: Uma Pranathi Narayan, Spandana Arpula, D. V. S. Raja, and Nazish Hussain; and freelance journalist Dake Vijaya Sekhar Raja.

Kolkata: Jyotika Ramaprasad; Bridgette Colaco, assistant professor, Troy University, USA; Sheeva Dubey and other students from the School of Communication, University of Miami, USA; students from the Department of Journalism & Mass Communication, Surendranath College for Women, Kolkata, India; and students from the Department of Journalism and Mass Communication, the University of Calcutta, Kolkata, India.

Pune: Jyotika Ramaprasad; Sheeva Dubey and other students from the School of Communication, University of Miami, USA; and students from the Department of Journalism and Mass Communication, MES Abasaheb Garware College, Pune, India.

China

Beijing: Xianzhi Li; and student from the Capital University of Economics and Business: Hongxuan Mu.

Shanghai: Ruiming Zhou.

Guangzhou: Ruiming Zhou and Yu Xu.

Wuhan: Ruiming Zhou and Yu Xu.

South Africa

Cape Town and *Durban:* Musawenkosi Ndlovu.

Johannesburg: Musawenkosi Ndlovu; and post-graduate student from Wits University: Robyn Evan.

Port Elizabeth: Musawenkosi Ndlovu; and post-graduate student from Rhodes University: Mvuzo Ponono.

APPENDIX C
Tables for Brazil

TABLE C.1 Sample of Brazilian news media

City and number of respondents	Press/news agency (Traditional)	Radio/TV (Traditional)	Online
Brasília: 48	*Brasil Econômico*	Rádio Senado	Câmara Legislativa
	Jornal de Brasília	Rádio Jovem Pan AM	Agência Brasil
Traditional: 24	*Jornal da Comunidade*	Rádio Cultura	Portal Costume
Online: 24	*Correio Braziliense*	TV Brasil	Clica Brasília
		TV Justiça	Portal em Pauta
		TV Globo Brasília	Acontece Brasília
		TV Brasília	Correio Web
		SBT Brasília	Vírus Planetário
		TV Globo Rio	Blog Edson Sombra
		Rede Record	Blog do Cafezinho
			Começo, meio e fim
			Blog Eixo Capital
			Blog da Denise

City and number of respondents	Press/news agency (Traditional)	Radio/TV (Traditional)	Online
Rio de Janeiro: 48	*Jornal O Globo*	Rádio CBN	Purepeople
	Jornal O Dia	Rádio Globo	R7
Traditional: 24	*Extra*	Rádio em Revista	Popline
Online: 24		Rádio Roquette Pinto	Sopa Cultural
		Esporte Interativo	Manchete Online
		Globo News	Portal Comunique-se
		SporTV	Portal Terra
		TV Brasil	Reuters Thomson
			Goal.com
			Agencia EFE
			Meu olhar
			Blog do Rio de Janeiro
			A Boa do Rio
			Caos Carioca
			Blog da Mariah
Vitória: 24		*Rádio Espírito Santo*	*Folha Vitória*
		TV Educativa	*Folha Diária*
Traditional: 12		*TV Capixaba*	*ES Hoje*
Online: 12		*TV Gazeta*	*Século Diário*
		TV Vitória	*Gazeta Online*
		TV Tribuna	*Blog Juliana Morgado*
Juiz de Fora: 24	*Folha JF*	Rádio Solar	Acessa.com
	Tribuna de Minas	Rádio Itatiaia	Toque de Bola
Traditional: 12		TVE	E-Caderno
Online: 12		TV Integração	Notícias Fora do Ar
			O Estandarte
			Blog Vinnicius de Moraes
			Blog Rumo Certo

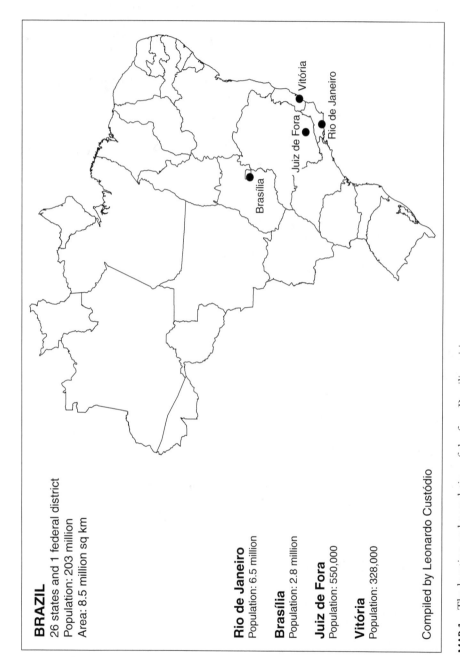

MAP 1 The location and population of the four Brazilian cities

Source: Brazilian Institute of Geography and Statistics, 2014

TABLE C.2 Demographic background and other variables in number of respondents (percentages in brackets)

City	Brasília		Rio de Janeiro		Juiz de Fora		Vitória		All	
Media	Traditional	Online	Traditional	Online	Traditional	Online	Traditional	Online	Traditional	Online
Number of respondents	24	24	24	24	12	12	12	12	72	72
Age: 18–29	4 (17)	12 (50)	17 (71)	14 (58)	7 (58)	5 (41)	6 (50)	5 (41)	34 (47)	36 (50)
Gender: Female	15 (62)	13 (54)	10 (42)	16 (66)	2 (16)	4 (33)	9 (75)	8 (67)	36 (50)	41 (57)
Influence of gender: None	19 (79)	16 (67)	13 (54)	17 (71)	8 (67)	11 (92)	9 (75)	11 (92)	49 (68)	55 (76)
Degree: College	22 (91)	22 (91)	20 (83)	24 (100)	11 (91)	10 (83)	12 (100)	8 (67)	65 (90)	64 (89)
Major: Journalism	20 (83)	14 (58)	20 (83)	16 (67)	11 (91)	6 (50)	12 (100)	7 (66)	63 (87)	43 (60)
Social class: Professional	14 (58)	12 (50)	17 (71)	9 (37)	6 (50)	5 (41)	9 (75)	7 (58)	46 (64)	33 (46)
Year of entering journalism: Since 2001	6 (25)	16 (66)	17 (71)	16 (66)	10 (83)	9 (75)	8 (66)	7 (58)	41 (57)	48 (66)
Marital status: Married	11 (46)	6 (25)	6 (25)	9 (37)	5 (41)	4 (33)	5 (41)	6 (50)	28 (39)	25 (35)
Number of previous jobs: Two and more	21 (87)	20 (83)	22 (91)	19 (79)	9 (75)	11 (91)	12 (100)	9 (91)	64 (89)	59 (82)
Form of employment: Salaried	20 (83)	14 (58)	22 (91)	15 (62)	12 (100)	4 (33)	12 (100)	10 (83)	66 (91)	43 (60)
Type of employment: Permanent, full time	24 (100)	9 (37)	15 (62)	20 (83)	11 (91)	8 (67)	10 (83)	5 (42)	60 (83)	42 (58)
Second job: Yes	3 (12)	12 (50)	8 (33)	13 (54)	7 (58)	8 (67)	0 (0)	6 (50)	18 (25)	39 (54)
Total monthly income: Sufficient	19 (79)	13 (54)	14 (58)	13 (54)	5 (42)	9 (75)	8 (67)	7 (58)	46 (64)	42 (58)
Union membership: Yes	9 (37)	4 (16)	5 (21)	3 (12)	4 (33)	0 (0)	2 (16)	2 (16)	20 (28)	9 (12)
Party membership: Yes	2 (8.3)	0 (0)	0 (0)	2 (8)	0 (0)	0 (0)	0 (0)	0 (0)	2 (3)	2 (3)
NGO membership: Yes	11 (46)	14 (58)	4 (16)	8 (33)	1 (8)	6 (50)	1 (8)	2 (16)	17 (23)	30 (41)

TABLE C.3 Three most frequently mentioned reasons for journalists' job satisfaction

	Reason 1	Reason 2	Reason 3
Brasília: Traditional	High-quality journalistic material	The gratefulness and feedback from the audience	Recognition at the work environment
Brasília: Online	High-quality journalistic material	The gratefulness and feedback from the audience	Material's effectivity
Rio de Janeiro: Traditional	The gratefulness and feedback from the audience	Material's effectivity	The creative process and the creative self-fulfilment Recognition at the work environment
Rio de Janeiro: Online	The creative process and the creative self-fulfilment	High-quality journalistic material and the gratefulness and feedback from the audience	Material's effectivity and recognition at the work environment
Juiz de Fora: Traditional	High-quality journalistic material	The gratefulness and feedback from the audience	Recognition at the work environment
Juiz de Fora: Online	High-quality journalistic material	The gratefulness and feedback from the audience	Recognition at the work environment
Vitória: Traditionalz	The gratefulness and feedback from the audience	High-quality journalistic material	Material's effectivity
Vitória: Online	The gratefulness and feedback from the audience	The creative process and the creative self-fulfilment	High-quality journalistic material

TABLE C.4 Three most important social media apps for journalists

	Social media apps 1	Social media apps 2	Social media apps 3
Brasília: Traditional	Facebook	Twitter	Instagram
Brasília: Online	Facebook	Twitter	Instagram
Rio de Janeiro: Traditional	Facebook	Twitter	Instagram
Rio de Janeiro: Online	Facebook	Twitter	Instagram
Juiz de Fora: Traditional	Facebook	Twitter	Instagram
Juiz de Fora: Online	Facebook	Twitter	Instagram
Vitória: Traditional	Facebook	Twitter	Instagram
Vitória: Online	Facebook	Twitter	Instagram

TABLE C.5 Professional orientation in number of respondents (percentages in brackets)

City	Brasília		Rio de Janeiro		Vitória		Juiz de Fora		All	
Media	Traditional	Online	Traditional	Online	Traditional	Online	Traditional	Online	Traditional	Online
Number of respondents	24	24	24	24	12	12	12	12	72	72
To stay in profession: Yes	23 (96)	22 (92)	21 (88)	16 (66)	12 (100)	12 (100)	12 (100)	12 (100)	68 (94)	62 (86)
Journalists should not cover subjects that play into the hands of our country's enemies: Yes	20 (41)	20 (41)	20 (41)	21 (44)	8 (66)	6 (50)	10 (83)	10 (83)	58 (80)	57 (79)
Sometimes it is necessary to block Internet access: No, in no circumstance	14 (58)	16 (66)	15 (62)	13 (54)	7 (58)	8 (66)	6 (50)	7 (58)	42 (87)	44 (91)
Need to control political affairs content: No	16 (66)	14 (58)	16 (66)	17 (71)	9 (75)	8 (66)	6 (50)	10 (83)	47 (65)	49 (68)
Need to control entertainment content: No	14 (58)	10 (41)	17 (71)	17 (71)	6 (50)	10 (83)	8 (66)	9 (75)	45 (62)	46 (64)
Approach to corruption in journalism: Negative	13 (54)	17 (71)	11 (46)	18 (75)	9 (75)	5 (41)	10 (83)	5 (41)	43 (60)	45 (62)
Have you produced articles for money or services in past 12 months? Yes	5 (21)	2 (8)	4 (16)	7 (29)	1 (8)	3 (25)	2 (16)	6 (50)	12 (16)	20 (28)
Attitude to protests in your city, country: Positive	22 (91)	24 (100)	18 (75)	21 (44)	10 (83)	12 (100)	9 (75)	11 (91)	59 (82)	68 (94)

TABLE C.6 Three core qualities of professional journalists

	Quality 1	Quality 2	Quality 3
Brasília: Traditional	Honest, sincere	Competent, knowledge on subjects	Independent/not speculative
Brasília: Online	Honest, sincere	Independent	No prejudices
Rio de Janeiro: Traditional	Honest, sincere/ good writing and technical skills	Competent, knowledge on the subject/general and professional ethics/ multitasking	Independent, no prejudices, not corrupt
Rio de Janeiro: Online	Honest, sincere/ independent, no prejudices, and not corrupt	Competent, knowledge of the subject	Courageous, stubbornness
Juiz de Fora: Traditional	Honest, sincere	Competent, knowledge on subjects	Good writing skills
Juiz de Fora: Online	Honest, sincere	Good writing skills	Ethical behaviour
Vitória: Traditional	Competent, knowledge on subjects	Honest, sincere	Good writing skills, ethical behaviour
Vitória: Online	Honest, sincere	Competent, knowledge on subjects	Good writing skills

TABLE C.7 Three key functions that journalism should fill

	Function 1	Function 1	Function 1
Brasília: Traditional	Informing with objectivity	Educating/generating critical consciousness	Serving society
Brasília: Online	Informing with objectivity	Investigating	Serving society, raising public debates
Rio de Janeiro: Traditional	Informing with objectivity	Educating	Defending social interests
Rio de Janeiro: Online	Informing with objectivity	Educating	Entertaining
Juiz de Fora: Traditional	Informing with objectivity	Educating	Serving society, investigating
Juiz de Fora: Online	Informing with objectivity	Serving society	Educating
Vitória: Traditional	Informing with objectivity	Being impartial	Educating
Vitória: Online	Informing with objectivity	Serving society	Entertaining, raising public debates

TABLE C.8 Three key roles that journalists should perform

	Role 1	Role 2	Role 3
Brasília: Traditional	Report objectively	Educate/raise awareness	Provide service to society
Brasília: Online	Report objectively	Investigate and ascertain	Provide service to society
Rio de Janeiro: Traditional	Report objectively	Educate/raise awareness	Educate
Rio de Janeiro: Online	Report objectively	Educate/raise awareness	Provide service to society
Juiz de Fora: Traditional	Report objectively	Educate	Provide service to society
Juiz de Fora: Online	Report objectively	Educate	Provide service to society
Vitória: Traditional	Report objectively	Be impartial	Educate
Vitória: Online	Report objectively	Provide service to society	Raise awareness/entertain

TABLE C.9 Three key differences between traditional and online news media journalists

	Difference 1	Difference 2	Difference 3
Brasília: Traditional	Speed	Quality of journalism procedure	No differences
Brasília: Online	Speed	Quality of journalism procedure	No differences
Rio de Janeiro: Traditional	Degree of responsibility	Speed	Quality of journalism procedure
Rio de Janeiro: Online	Speed	No differences	Quality of journalism procedure
Juiz de Fora: Traditional	Speed	Quality of journalism procedure	Degree of responsibility
Juiz de Fora: Online	Speed	Quality of journalism procedure	
Vitória: Traditional	Speed	No differences	Quality of analysis
Vitória: Online	Speed	Quality of journalism procedure	

TABLE C.10 Three most important social–political changes needed in your country for journalism to perform its functions

	Change needed 1	*Change needed 2*	*Change needed 3*
Brasília: Traditional	Ensure media and economic independence	Reform legislation	End corruption
Brasília: Online	Ensure media and economic independence	Reform legislation	End corruption
Rio de Janeiro: Traditional	Ensure media and economic independence	Reform legislation	End of oligopoly
Rio de Janeiro: Online	Ensure media and economic independence	Reform legislation	End of oligopoly
Juiz de Fora: Traditional	Ensure media and economic independence	Obligation of the diploma	Greater appreciation of the professional
Juiz de Fora: Online	Ensure media and economic independence	Obligation of the diploma	Greater appreciation of the professional
Vitória: Traditional	Ensure media and economic independence	Reform legislation	End corruption
Vitória: Online	Ensure media and economic independence	Reform legislation	End corruption

APPENDIX D

Tables for Russia

TABLE D.1 Sample of Russian news media

City and number of respondents	Press/news agency (Traditional)	Radio/TV (Traditional)	Online
Moscow: 48 Traditional: 24 Online: 24	Newspapers: *Rossiyskaya gazeta* *Komsomolskaya pravda* *Vechernyaya Moskva* *Sport-ekspress* Magazines: *Bolshoj gorod* *Russkiy reporter*	Siti FM Radio Rossii Ekho Moskvy TV Moskva 24 TV Tsentr TV Rossiya 24	Chastnyi korrespondent Ezhednevnyi zhurnal Gazeta.ru Newsru.com Lenta.ru LifeNews Rbc.ru Journalistic startups: Colta.ru TV Dozhd Look at Me Slon.ru The Village

(Continued)

TABLE D.1 (Continued)

City and number of respondents	Press/news agency (Traditional)	Radio/TV (Traditional)	Online
St. Petersburg: 49 Traditional: 26 Online: 23	Newspapers: *Nevskoe Vremya* *Komsomolskaya pravda* *RBK* Magazines: *Darya* *Ekspert Severo-Zapad* *Gorod 812*	Radio Zenit Radio Baltika Radio Svoboda Radio Rossiya TV-Pyatyi Kanal LOT TV Sankt-Peterburg TV	Firstnews.ru Lenizdat.ru Peterburgskiy dnevnik Rbc.ru Zaks.ru Journalistic startups: Bumaga.ru TV Dozhd Fontanka.ru Karpovka.net Obshchestvennyi control Politgramota.ru V kurse
Yekaterinburg: 24 Traditional: 12 Online: 12	Newspapers: *Oblastnaya gazeta* Magazines: *Biznes i zhizn* *Ekspert Urala*	Ekho Moskvy–Yekaterinburg Chetvertyi Kanal TV Studia 41 TV	EAN Internet TV Malina Just media Novyi region Journalistic startups: Ura.ru Znak.com
Petrozavodsk: 23 Traditional: 12 Online: 11	Newspapers: *Karelia* *Moi Petrozavodsk* *TVR Panorama*	GTRK Karelia (Radio) GTRK Karelia (TV) Nika TV Sampo TV	Respublika Karelia Stolitsa na Onego Vedomosti Karelii Vesti Karelii Journalistic startups: Internet zhurnal Litsei politika.karelia.ru

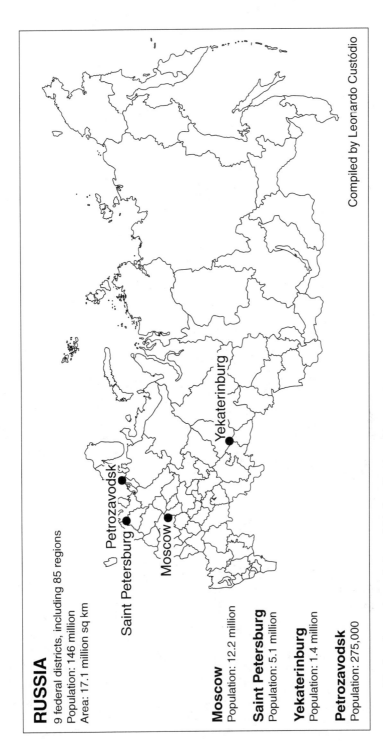

MAP 2   The location and population of the four Russian cities

Source: Russian Federal State Statistics Service (Rosstat), 2015

TABLE D.2 Demographic background and other variables in number of respondents (percentages in brackets)

City	Moscow		St. Petersburg		Yekaterinburg		Petrozavodsk		All	
Media	Traditional	Online	Traditional	Online	Traditional	Online	Traditional	Online	Traditional	Online
Number of respondents	24	24	26	23	12	12	12	11	74	70
Age: 18–29	12 (50)	12 (50)	10 (38)	18 (76)	6 (50)	9 (75)	5 (42)	3 (27)	33 (44)	41 (58)
Gender: Female	15 (63)	17 (71)	11 (42)	10 (43)	6 (50)	5 (42)	9 (75)	6 (55)	42 (57)	37 (53)
Influence of gender: None	13 (54)	16 (67)	14 (54)	10 (43)	9 (75)	11 (92)	8 (67)	10 (91)	44 (59)	48 (68)
Degree: College	23 (96)	22 (92)	25 (96)	21 (91)	12 (100)	12 (100)	12 (100)	11 (100)	72 (97)	66 (94)
Major: Journalism	14 (58)	13 (54)	9 (35)	15 (65)	9 (75)	8 (67)	1 (8)	2 (18)	33 (44)	27 (53)
Social class: Professional	15 (64)	13 (54)	22 (85)	22 (96)	8 (67)	5 (42)	8 (67)	8 (73)	53 (72)	48 (68)
Year of entering journalism: Since 2001	14 (58)	17 (71)	6 (23)	19 (82)	5 (42)	7 (58)	7 (58)	5 (45)	33 (44)	48 (68)
Marital status: Married	11 (46)	12 (50)	20 (77)	8 (34)	7 (58)	3 (25)	8 (67)	5 (45)	8 (62)	28 (40)
Number of previous jobs: Two and more	15 (63)	17 (71)	24 (92)	22 (96)	11 (92)	11 (92)	12 (100)	10 (91)	62 (84)	60 (86)
Form of employment: Salaried	18 (75)	22 (92)	26 (100)	23 (100)	12 (100)	12 (100)	12 (100)	11 (100)	68 (92)	68 (97)
Type of employment: Permanent, full time	16 (67)	17 (71)	26 (100)	22 (96)	11 (92)	12 (100)	12 (100)	10 (91)	65 (88)	60 (86)
Second job: Yes	8 (33)	17 (71)	17 (65)	15 (65)	7 (58)	5 (42)	5 (42)	9 (82)	36 (49)	60 (68)
Total monthly income: Sufficient	17 (71)	14 (58)	7 (27)	8 (34)	1 (8)	9 (75)	7 (58)	4 (36)	33 (44)	37 (53)
Union membership: Yes	5 (21)	1 (4)	8 (31)	4 (17)	2 (16)	1 (8)	8 (67)	6 (55)	24 (32)	13 (18)
Party membership: Yes	0 (0)	1 (4)	0 (0)	0 (0)	0 (0)	0 (0)	0 (0)	0 (0)	0 (0)	1 (1)
NGO membership: Yes	1 (<4)	1 (4)	5 (19)	4 (17)	2 (16)	0 (0)	2 (16)	3 (27)	9 (12)	8 (11)

TABLE D.3 Three most frequently mentioned reasons for journalists' job satisfaction

	Reason 1	*Reason 2*	*Reason 3*
Moscow: Traditional	Creative work and new knowledge	Communication with people	Effectiveness of materials and gratitude from the audience
Moscow: Online	Creative work and process of work	Awareness of well-done work	Feedback from the audience, 'likes' of users
St. Petersburg: Traditional	Creative work and self-realization	Gratitude and feedback from the audience and interaction with them	Materials of high quality
St. Petersburg: Online	Gratitude and feedback from the audience and interaction with them	Creative work and self-realization	Respect and acknowledgment from colleagues
Yekaterinburg: Traditional	Creative work and self-realization	Gratitude and feedback from the audience and interaction with them	New knowledge and new people
Yekaterinburg: Online	Creative work and self-realization	Gratitude and feedback from the audience and interaction with them	Effectiveness of materials and new knowledge, people
Petrozavodsk: Traditional	Gratitude and feedback from audience and interaction with them	Materials of high quality	Creative work and self-realization
Petrozavodsk: Online	Creative work and self-realization	Materials of high quality	Gratitude and feedback from audience and interaction with them

TABLE D.4 Three most important social media apps for journalists

	Social media apps 1	*Social media apps 2*	*Social media apps 3*
Moscow: Traditional	Facebook	Twitter	VKontakte
Moscow: Online	Facebook	Twitter	VKontakte
St. Petersburg: Traditional	VKontakte	Facebook	Twitter
St. Petersburg: Online	VKontakte	Facebook	Twitter
Yekaterinburg: Traditional	Facebook	VKontakte	LiveJournal
Yekaterinburg: Online	Facebook	VKontakte	Twitter
Petrozavodsk: Traditional	VKontakte	Facebook	Twitter
Petrozavodsk: Online	VKontakte	Twitter	Facebook

TABLE D.5 Professional orientation and related variables in number of respondents (percentages in brackets)

City	Moscow		St. Petersburg		Yekaterinburg		Petrozavodsk		All	
Media	Traditional	Online	Traditional	Online	Traditional	Online	Traditional	Online	Traditional	Online
Number of respondents	24	24	26	23	12	12	12	11	74	70
To stay in profession: Yes	3 (13)	23 (96)	18 (69)	16 (61)	11 (91)	11 (91)	11 (92)	6 (55)	43 (58)	54 (77)
Journalists should not cover subjects that play into the hands of our country's enemies: Yes	3 (13)	2 (8)	4 (15)	2 (8)	4 (33)	2 (16)	1 (8)	1 (9)	12 (16)	6 (9)
Sometimes it is necessary to block access to the Internet: No, in no circumstance	15 (63)	21 (88)	4 (15)	12 (48)	9 (75)	7 (58)	2 (17)	2 (18)	30 (41)	40 (57)
Need to control political affairs content: No	14 (58)	21 (88)	17 (66)	16 (61)	7 (58)	5 (42)	2 (17)	5 (45)	41 (55)	46 (65)
Need to control entertainment content: No	4 (17)	19 (79)	9 (34)	12 (52)	9 (75)	6 (50)	7 (58)	4 (36)	29 (39)	40 (58)
Approach to corruption in journalism: Negative	16 (67)	17 (71)	13 (50)	7 (30)	7 (58)	2 (16)	3 (25)	7 (64)	39 (53)	35 (47)
Have you produced articles for money or services in past 12 months? Yes	4 (17)	1 (4)	3 (11)	4 (18)	4 (33)	8 (63)	3 (25)	5 (45)	14 (19)	19 (25)
Attitude to protests in your city, country: Positive	13 (54)	20 (83)	9 (35)	11 (48)	4 (33)	2 (16)	4 (33)	5 (45)	30 (41)	38 (51)

TABLE D.6 Three core qualities of professional journalists

	Quality 1	Quality 2	Quality 3
Moscow: Traditional	Skills in gathering and analysing information	Ethical conduct	Generally erudite and scholarly
Moscow: Online	Experience in profession	Objectivity and honesty	Communicative and managerial skills
St. Petersburg: Traditional	Generally erudite and scholarly	Competence about subject	Ethical conduct
St. Petersburg: Online	Skills in writing and using technology	Generally erudite and scholarly	Honest, sincere
Yekaterinburg: Traditional	Skills in gathering and analysing information	Honest, sincere	Ethical conduct
Yekaterinburg: Online	Generally erudite and scholarly	Ethical conduct	Skills in gathering and analysing information
Petrozavodsk: Traditional	Skills in writing and using technology	Generally erudite and scholarly	Honest, sincere
Petrozavodsk: Online	Competence about subject	Generally erudite and scholarly	Skills in writing and using technology

TABLE D.7 Three key functions that journalism should fulfil

	Function 1	Function 2	Function 3
Moscow: Traditional	Provide information	Educate and enlighten	Entertain
Moscow: Online	Provide information	Educate and enlighten	Entertain
St. Petersburg: Traditional	Provide information	Enlighten	Entertain
St. Petersburg: Online	Provide information	Entertain	Make audience think
Yekaterinburg: Traditional	Provide information	Entertain	Promote objectivity
Yekaterinburg: Online	Provide information	Enlighten	Educate
Petrozavodsk: Traditional	Provide information	Entertain	Form opinions
Petrozavodsk: Online	Provide information	Entertain	Form opinions

TABLE D.8 Three key roles that journalists should perform

	Role 1	Role 2	Role 3
Moscow: Traditional	Report news	Enlighten	Entertain
Moscow: Online	Report news	To provide communication between society and power, to be moderator	Enlighten
St. Petersburg: Traditional	Report news	Enlighten	Help people
St. Petersburg: Online	Report news	Provide analysis	Entertain
Yekaterinburg: Traditional	Report news	Enlighten	Help people
Yekaterinburg: Online	Report news	Provide analysis	Teach
Petrozavodsk: Traditional	Report news	Report objectively	Entertain
Petrozavodsk: Online	Report news	Enlighten	Help people

TABLE D.9 Three key differences between traditional and online news media journalists

	Difference 1	Difference 2	Difference 3
Moscow: Traditional	No principal differences	We have good experience and a serious school of journalistic profession	Quality of journalism is higher here
Moscow: Online	Speed	Universality of online journalists and reduction of online media staff	Work with information and amount of information in online media
St. Petersburg: Traditional	Speed	Quality of analysis	Level of responsibility
St. Petersburg: Online	Speed	Quality of analysis	Quality of journalism
Yekaterinburg: Traditional	Speed	Approaches to work	Quality of journalism
Yekaterinburg: Online	Speed	Quality of analysis	Approaches to work
Petrozavodsk: Traditional	Speed	Quality of analysis	Quality of journalism
Petrozavodsk: Online	Speed	Quality of analysis	Quality of journalism

TABLE D.10 Three most important social–political changes needed in your country for journalism to perform its functions

	Change needed 1	Change needed 2	Change needed 3
Moscow: Traditional	Have more democracy	Socialism	Developed and civilized society
Moscow: Online	Have more democracy	Liberal values	Deliberate society with developed culture of mutual respect
St. Petersburg: Traditional	Ensure media and economic independence	Nothing to change	Have more democracy
St. Petersburg: Online	Have more democracy	Ensure media and economic independence	Increase political competition, compliance with the laws in the country, the openness of the authorities
Yekaterinburg: Traditional	Have more democracy	Russia with its problems is ideal country	Nothing to change
Yekaterinburg: Online	Russia with its problems is the ideal country for journalism	Ensure media and economic independence	Have more democracy
Petrozavodsk: Traditional	Have more democracy	Nothing to change	Ensure media and economic independence
Petrozavodsk: Online	Have more democracy	Nothing to change	Ensure media and economic independence

APPENDIX E
Tables for India

TABLE E.1 Sample of Indian news media

City and number of respondents	Press/news agency (Traditional)	Radio/TV (Traditional)	Online
Delhi: 48	*Asian Age,*	Aaj Tak	BBC Media Action
	Business Standard	Aaj Tak (Hindi news)	Beyond Headlines
Traditional: 38	*Dainik Bhaskar*	BBC News	Cogenics
Online: 10	*Deccan Herald*	CNBC TV	Daily Bhaskar Digital
	Hindustan Times	CNN IBN	Dainik enews
	Indian Express	P7	First Post
	Navbharat Times	ET Now	NDTV Convergence
	The Hindu	Headlines Today	TOI Digital
	The Pioneer	Hindi Hindustan	
	Amar Ujala	IBN7	
	India Today	India News	
	Matrubhumi	India Times	
	Sakal	NDTV 24x7	
	Veer Arjun	NDTV Hindi	
	World Wide Media	NDTV Prime	
		New Express	
		News X	

(Continued)

TABLE E.1 (Continued)

City and number of respondents	Press/news agency (Traditional)	Radio/TV (Traditional)	Online
Hyderabad: 48	The Hindu,	ABN Andhra Jyothi	And Beyond.com
	The Times of India	CVR News	Serndipity.com
Traditional: 42	Eenadu	CVR English	Telugu TV.com
Online: 6	Andhra Jyothi	ETV	
	Andhra Bhoomi	Mahaa News	
	Andhra Prabha	NTV	
	Deccan Chronicle	Sakshi	
	Metro India	T News	
	Namaste Telangana	TV9	
	Sakshi	TV5	
	Hans India		
	Vishwas Daily		
Kolkata: 24	8	Radio: 1	Newspaper: 2
	(privately owned)	(state owned)	(privately owned)
Traditional: 19		TV: 10	Radio: 1
Online: 5		(8 privately owned; 2 mixed ownership, i.e., government subsidized)	(state owned)
			Online Outlet: 2 (privately owned)
Pune: 25	11	Radio: 2	Online Outlet: 6
	(privately owned)	(state owned)	(privately owned)
Traditional: 19		TV: 6	
Online: 6		(privately owned)	

Note: For Kolkata and Pune, only numbers of sample media outlets are provided; names of sample media outlets are not provided because journalists were promised this confidentiality. Online could be portals or online versions of offline outlets.

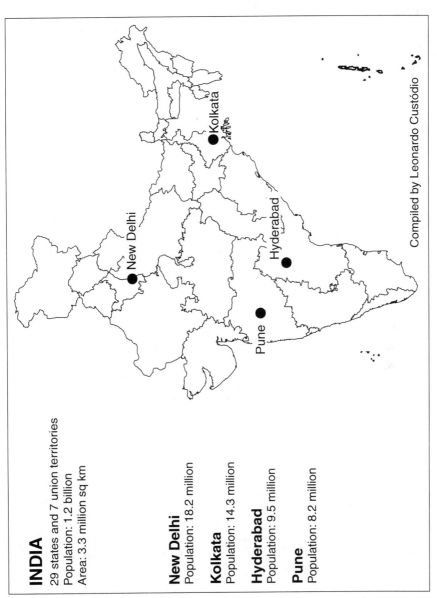

MAP 3 The location and population of the four Indian cities

Source for Map: http://image40.com/state-map/state-map-of-india-outline/
Source for population figures: Census of India, 2011. http://image40.com/state-map/state-map-of-india-outline/

TABLE E.2 Demographic background and other variables in number of respondents (percentages in brackets)

City	Delhi		Hyderabad		Kolkata		Pune		All	
Media	Traditional	Online	Traditional	Online	Traditional	Online	Traditional	Online	Traditional	Online
Number of respondents	38	10	42	6	19	5	19	6	118	27
Age: 18–29	27 (71)	9 (90)	22 (54)	5 (83)	6 (32)	3 (60)	6 (32)	0 (0)	61 (52)	17 (63)
Gender: Female	12 (32)	4 (40)	14 (33)	2 (33)	5 (26)	1 (20)	7 (37)	0 (0)	38 (32)	7 (26)
Influence of gender: None	31 (82)	4 (40)	8 (19)	2 (33)	6 (32)	2 (40)	7 (37)	3 (50)	52 (44)	11 (41)
Degree: College	35 (92)	9 (90)	40 (95)	4 (67)	19 (100)	5 (100)	18 (95)	6 (100)	112 (95)	24 (89)
Major: Journalism	28 (74)	9 (90)	25 (60)	4 (67)	11 (58)	3 (60)	16 (84)	5 (83)	80 (68)	21 (78)
Social class: Professional	15 (40)	4 (40)	11 (24)	2 (33)	NA	NA	NA	NA	26 (33)	6 (38)
Year of entering journalism: Since 2001	34 (90)	10 (100)	37 (89)	5 (84)	12 (63)	5 (100)	12 (63)	5 (83)	95 (81)	25 (93)
Marital status: Married	8 (21)	1 (10)	28 (67)	2 (34)	9 (47)	2 (40)	12 (63)	4 (67)	57 (48)	9 (33)
Number of previous jobs: Two and more	32 (84)	10 (100)	26 (62)	5 (84)	NA	NA	NA	NA	58 (73)	15 (94)
Form of employment: Salaried	38 (100)	10 (100)	42 (100)	6 (100)	6 (32)	5 (100)	16 (84)	6 (100)	102 (86)	27 (100)
Type of employment: Permanent, full time	31 (82)	8 (80)	29 (69)	0 (0)	9 (47)	4 (21)	11 (58)	4 (67)	80 (68)	16 (59)
Second job: Yes	3 (8)	2 (20)	2 (05)	3 (50)	5 (26)	0 (0)	0 (0)	1 (17)	10 (8)	6 (22)
Total monthly income: Sufficient	27 (71)	7 (70)	27 (64)	4 (67)	8 (42)	4 (80)	8 (42)	2 (33)	70 (59)	17 (63)
Union membership: Yes	8 (21)	1 (10)	17 (41)	4 (67)	6 (32)	1 (20)	12 (63)	3 (50)	43 (36)	9 (33)
Party membership: Yes	1 (3)	0 (0)	1 (2)	0 (0)	2 (11)	0 (0)	0 (0)	1 (17)	4 (3)	1 (4)
NGO membership: Yes	34 (90)	10 (100)	7 (17)	1 (17)	7 (37)	0 (0)	2 (11)	1 (17)	50 (42)	12 (44)

TABLE E.3 Three most frequently mentioned reasons for journalists' job satisfaction

	Reason 1	*Reason 2*	*Reason 3*
Delhi: Traditional	Unbiased	Honest and sincere	Competent, knowledge about subject
Delhi: Online	Honest and sincere	Independent	Good writer
Hyderabad: Traditional	Honest and sincere	Good writer	Competent, knowledge about subject
Hyderabad: Online	Unbiased, engages in ethical conduct, courageous	Educated	Honest and sincere, competent, knowledge about subject
Kolkata: Traditional	Power/achievement/ doing great news	Interaction with people	Story impact
Kolkata: Online	Passion	Achievement/exclusive stories	Involvement/dedication
Pune: Traditional	Impact	Freedom	Appreciation/ recognition
Pune: Online	Freedom	Various reasons	

TABLE E.4 Three most important social media apps for journalists

	Social media app 1	*Social media app 2*	*Social media app 3*
Delhi: Traditional	Facebook	WhatsApp	Twitter
Delhi: Online	Facebook	Twitter	WhatsApp
Hyderabad: Traditional	Facebook	Twitter	LinkedIn
Hyderabad: Online	Facebook	Twitter	WhatsApp
Kolkata: Traditional	Facebook	Twitter	WhatsApp
Kolkata: Online	Facebook	Twitter	WhatsApp
Pune: Traditional	Facebook	WhatsApp	Twitter
Pune: Online	Facebook	Twitter	WhatsApp

TABLE E.5 Professional orientation and related variables in number of respondents (percentages in brackets)

City	Delhi		Hyderabad		Kolkata		Pune		All	
Media	Traditional	Online	Traditional	Online	Traditional	Online	Traditional	Online	Traditional	Online
Number of respondents	38	10	42	6	19	5	19	6	118	27
Stay in profession: Yes	27 (71)	8 (80)	28 (67)	4 (67)	18 (95)	5 (100)	18 (95)	4 (67)	91 (77)	21 (78)
Journalists should not cover subjects that play into the hands of our country's enemies: Yes	16 (42)	3 (30)	18 (45)	2 (33)	NA	NA	NA	NA	34 (43)	5 (31)
Should government control the Internet? No, in no circumstance	32 (87)	9 (90)	23 (57)	6 (100)	10 (53)	1 (20)	6 (32)	5 (83)	71 (60)	21 (78)
Should government control political affairs content? No, in no circumstance	35 (92)	8 (80)	18 (45)	3 (50)	18 (95)	4 (80)	15 (79)	5 (83)	86 (73)	20 (74)
Should government control entertainment content? No, in no circumstance	7 (18)	2 (20)	12 (26)	1 (17)	15 (79)	2 (40)	12 (63)	5 (83)	46 (39)	10 (37)
Approach to corruption in journalism: Negative	NA	NA	NA	NA	NA	NA	NA	NA	NA	NA
Have you produced articles for money or services in past 12 months: Yes	3 (8)	2 (20)	12 (26)	1 (17)	1 (5)	0 (0)	0 (0)	0 (0)	16 (14)	3 (11)
Attitude to protests in your city, country: Positive	27 (71)	7 (70)	15 (36)	2 (33)	NA	NA	NA	NA	42 (53)	9 (56)

TABLE E.6 Three core qualities of professional journalists

	Quality 1	Quality 2	Quality 3
Delhi: Traditional	Unbiased	Honest and sincere	Competent, knowledge about subject
Delhi: Online	Honest and sincere	Independent	Good writer
Hyderabad: Traditional	Honest and sincere	Good writer	Competent, knowledge about subject
Hyderabad: Online	Unbiased, engages in ethical conduct, courageous	Educated	Honest, sincere, competent about subject
Kolkata: Traditional	Truthful/honest	Hardworking/dedicated/committed	News oriented
Kolkata: Online	Truthful/honest	Impartial	Various characteristics
Pune: Traditional	Balanced/unbiased/ethical	Empathetic/sensitive	Integrity
Pune: Online	Honest/truthful	Various characteristics	

TABLE E.7 Three key functions that journalism should fulfil

	Function 1	Function 2	Function 3
Delhi: Traditional	Enable communication between people and institutions	Inform	Educate and enlighten
Delhi: Online	Provide cognitive fodder for people	Inform	Promote objectivity
Hyderabad: Traditional	Educate	Enlighten	Inform
Hyderabad: Online	Regulate for societal order; Regulate to enable communication between people and institutions	Educate/promote objectivity/build people's mindset	Help to form opinion
Kolkata: Traditional	Collect and deliver news/provide right information	Be honest/tell the truth	Various functions
Kolkata: Online	Provide right information	Punctuality	Various functions
Pune: Traditional	Engage in activism (empower, work on social justice, etc.)	Inform	Educate
Pune: Online	Inform	Engage in activism	Provide truth

TABLE E.8 Three key roles that journalists should perform

	Role 1	Role 2	Role 3
Delhi: Traditional	Report news	Provide information	Educate and enlighten
Delhi: Online	Report news	Provide information	Promote objectivity
Hyderabad: Traditional	Educate and enlighten	Educate and enlighten	Provide information
Hyderabad: Online	Educate and enlighten/protect people and society	Regulate for societal order/build people's mindset	Help to form opinion
Kolkata: Traditional	Provide news	Be the fourth estate	Impact public opinion
Kolkata: Online	Work towards social justice	Various roles	
Pune: Traditional	Watchdog	Engage in activism (empower, work on social justice, etc.)	Impact public opinion
Pune: Online	Watchdog	Inform	Various roles

TABLE E.9 Three key differences between traditional and online news media journalists

	Difference 1	Difference 2	Difference 3
Delhi: Traditional	Speed	Quality of journalism	Quality of analysis
Delhi: Online	Speed	Quality of journalism	Quality of analysis
Hyderabad: Traditional	Quality of journalism	Quality of analysis	Speed
Hyderabad: Online	Speed	Quality of journalism	Quality of analysis
Kolkata: Traditional	Different time constraints/online faster, clued in	No difference	Various differences
Kolkata: Online	Online faster		
Pune: Traditional	Online faster, more immediate	No difference	Traditional is more of a watchdog, has more perspective, is more analytic
Pune: Online	Online faster, more immediate	Various differences	

TABLE E.10 Three most important social–political changes needed in your country for journalism to perform its functions

	Change needed 1	Change needed 2	Change needed 3
Delhi: Traditional	Independence of the media, including economic independence	Have more democracy	Increase political competition
Delhi: Online	Have more democracy	Independence of the media, including economic independence	Increase political competition
Hyderabad: Traditional	Have more democracy	Independence of the media, including economic independence	Independence of the media, including economic independence
Hyderabad: Online	Have more democracy	Independence of the media, including economic independence	Increase political competition
Kolkata: Traditional	Politicians should not interfere with news/political influence should decrease	Society/people should be more responsible and engage in civic duties	Various changes
Kolkata: Online	Politicians should not interfere with news/political influence should decrease	Various changes	
Pune: Traditional	News media	Literacy rate should increase	Politicians/government should not interfere with news media
Pune: Online	People should support media when media raise issues that will assist them to solve issues with government	Literacy rate should increase	Access to government/other information should be available

APPENDIX F

Tables for China

TABLE F.1 Sample of Chinese news media

City and number of respondents	Press/news agency (Traditional)	Radio/TV (Traditional)	Online
Beijing: 50 Traditional: 33 Online: 17	Party newspapers: *Economic Daily* *People's Daily* *Worker's Daily* *China Industry News* *Ta Kung Pao* Metropolitan newspapers: *The Beijing News* Specialized newspapers: *Beijing Business Today* Magazines: *Bizfriends* *Disability in China* *Beijing Review* News Agency: *China News Service* *Xinhua News Agency*	China National Radio Radio Beijing Corporation BTV CCTV MASTV-Beijing China News Service Xinhua News Agency	State-owned news websites: BRTN Private-owned news websites: Sina BitAuto Ifeng.com NetEase Commercial Vehicle News China Road Machinery Online Mixed-owned news websites: Takungpao.com Foreign capital news website: SELF Grassroots media: Socialmouths Youyouluming99

City and number of respondents	Press/news agency (Traditional)	Radio/TV (Traditional)	Online
Shanghai: 48 Traditional: 24 Online: 24	Party newspapers: *Jiefang Daily* *Wenhui Daily* Metropolitan newspapers: *Shanghai Morning Post* *Oriental Morning Post* *Shanghai Times* Specialized newspapers: *The Economic Observer* *Financial Times* Magazines: *Xinmin Weekly* *CBN Weekly*	Shanghai Radio Television CaixingZhizuo	State-owned news websites: Thepaper.cn Shanghai Observer BesTV Eastday.com Yuduxian Private-owned news websites: Q Daily Lanjinger.com China30s Mixed-owned news websites: Caixin Media Jiemian.com Grassroots media: TCWeekly Futeetee Anonymous Wemedia
Guangzhou: 24 Traditional: 12 Online: 12	Party newspapers: *Southern Daily* *Guangzhou Daily* Metropolitan newspapers: *Yangcheng Evening News* *Southern Weekend* Magazines: *Nanfengchuang*	Guangdong Television Station	State-owned news websites: Southern News Dayang News Private-owned news websites: Sohu Focus – Guangzhou Sina – Guangdong 3G.cn Grassroots media: Trigger Trend www.my1510.cn

(*Continued*)

TABLE F.1 (Continued)

City and number of respondents	Press/news agency (Traditional)	Radio/TV (Traditional)	Online
Wuhan: 24 Traditional: 12 Online: 12	Party newspapers: *Hubei Daily* *Changjiang Daily* Metropolitan newspapers: *Chutian Metropolis Daily* Magazines: *Zhiyin*	Hubei Radio and Television Station Wuhan Radio and Television Station	State-owned news websites: Jingchu News People's Daily Online – Hubei Private-owned news websites: Focus.cn - Wuhan House.sina.com.cn – Wuhan Mixed-owned news websites: Tencent – Hubei Grassroots media: Goodqq27 Point Break

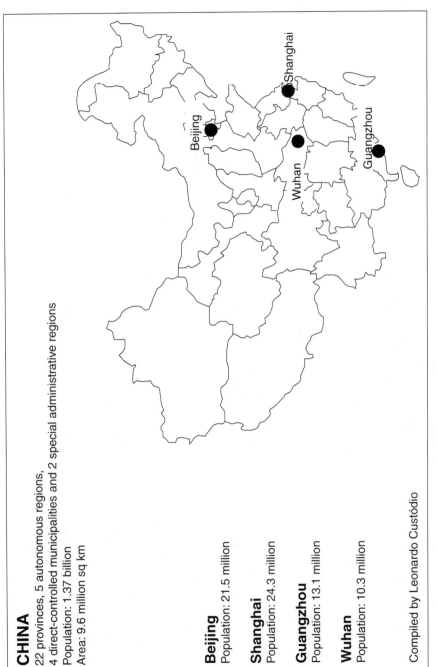

MAP 4 The location and population of the four Chinese cities

Source: National Bureau of Statistics of China, 2014

TABLE F.2 Demographic background and other variables in number of respondents (percentages in brackets)

City	Beijing		Shanghai		Guangzhou		Wuhan		All	
Media	Traditional	Online	Traditional	Online	Traditional	Online	Traditional	Online	Traditional	Online
Number of respondents	33	17	24	24	12	12	12	12	81	65
Age: 18–29	23 (70)	14 (82)	15 (63)	19 (79)	8 (67)	6 (50)	10 (83)	7 (58)	56 (69)	46 (71)
Gender: Female	17 (52)	7 (41)	12 (50)	13 (54)	5 (42)	6 (50)	7 (58)	7 (58)	41 (51)	33 (51)
Influence of gender: None	13 (39)	8 (47)	13 (54)	14 (58)	6 (50)	9 (75)	3 (25)	6 (50)	35 (43)	37 (57)
Degree: College	33 (100)	17 (100)	24 (100)	24 (100)	12 (100)	12 (100)	12 (100)	12 (100)	81 (100)	65 (100)
Major: Journalism	22 (67)	7 (41)	21 (88)	14 (58)	7 (58)	7 (58)	4 (33)	4 (33)	54 (67)	32 (49)
Social class: Professional	29 (88)	7 (41)	7 (29)	9 (38)	9 (75)	5 (42)	8 (67)	6 (50)	53 (65)	27 (42)
Year of entering journalism: Since 2001	30 (91)	16 (94)	24 (100)	24 (100)	11 (92)	11 (92)	11 (92)	11 (92)	76 (94)	62 (95)
Marital status: Married	12 (36)	5 (29)	9 (38)	7 (29)	5 (42)	8 (67)	4 (33)	5 (42)	30 (37)	25 (38)
Number of previous jobs: Two and more	3 (9)	7 (41)	3 (13)	4 (17)	3 (25)	6 (50)	2 (17)	5 (42)	11 (14)	22 (34)
Form of employment: Salaried	33 (100)	17 (100)	24 (100)	24 (100)	12 (100)	12 (100)	12 (100)	12 (100)	81 (100)	65 (100)
Type of employment: Permanent, full time	11 (33)	0 (0)	6 (25)	0 (0)	6 (50)	3 (25)	3 (25)	0 (0)	26 (32)	3 (5)
Second job: Yes	5 (15)	1 (6)	4 (17)	8 (33)	1 (8)	2 (17)	2 (17)	2 (17)	12 (15)	13 (20)
Total monthly income: Sufficient	26 (79)	13 (76)	22 (92)	15 (63)	8 (67)	4 (36)	11 (92)	7 (58)	67 (83)	39 (60)
Union membership: Yes	25 (76)	1 (6)	9 (38)	5 (21)	8 (67)	2 (17)	6 (50)	3 (25)	49 (60)	11 (17)
Party membership: Yes	22 (67)	7 (41)	18 (75)	10 (42)	10 (83)	1 (8)	9 (75)	5 (42)	59 (73)	23 (35)
NGO membership: Yes	8 (24)	6 (35)	9 (37)	4 (17)	3 (25)	3 (25)	2 (17)	2 (17)	22 (27)	15 (23)

TABLE F.3 Three most frequently mentioned reasons for journalists' job satisfaction

	Reason 1	*Reason 2*	*Reason 3*
Beijing: Traditional	Accumulating knowledge and broadening horizons/ expanding social networks	The process of creativity and creative self-realization	Effectiveness of materials/job autonomy
Beijing: Online	Accumulating knowledge and broadening horizons	The process of creativity and creative self-realization	Compatible with one's own interests
Shanghai: Traditional	Job autonomy/maintaining a good relationship with colleagues	Recognition in a professional environment	The process of creativity and creative self-realization
Shanghai: Online	Job autonomy/maintaining a good relationship with colleagues/future prospect of the media organization	Recognition in a professional environment	The process of creativity and creative self-realization/ effectiveness of materials
Guangzhou: Traditional	Job autonomy	The process of creativity and creative self-realization	A sense of achievement
Guangzhou: Online	Job autonomy	The process of creativity and creative self-realization	Recognition in a professional environment
Wuhan: Traditional	Job autonomy/accumulating knowledge and broadening horizons	The process of creativity and creative self-realization	Recognition in a professional environment
Wuhan: Online	Enhancing professional skills	The process of creativity and creative self-realization	Recognition in a professional environment

TABLE F.4 Three most important social media apps for journalists

	Social media app 1	*Social media app 2*	*Social media app 3*
Beijing: Traditional	Wechat	Weibo	QQ
Beijing: Online	Wechat	Weibo	Facebook
Shanghai: Traditional	Wechat	Weibo	Instagram
Shanghai: Online	Wechat	Weibo	Instagram
Guangzhou: Traditional	Wechat	Weibo	Twitter
Guangzhou: Online	Wechat	Weibo	Renren/Twitter/ Facebook/LinkedIn
Wuhan: Traditional	Wechat/Weibo	Renren/Facebook/Douban	Twitter/Instagram
Wuhan: Online	Wechat/Weibo	Instagram	Renren

TABLE F.5 Professional orientation and related variables in number of respondents (percentages in brackets)

City	Beijing		Shanghai		Guangzhou		Wuhan		All	
Media	Traditional	Online	Traditional	Online	Traditional	Online	Traditional	Online	Traditional	Online
Number of respondents	33	17	24	24	12	12	12	12	81	65
To stay in profession: Yes	29 (88)	11 (65)	19 (79)	14 (58)	9 (75)	8 (67)	11 (92)	10 (83)	68 (84)	43 (66)
Journalists should not cover subjects that play into the hands of our country's enemies: Yes	10 (30)	5 (29)	3 (13)	6 (25)	4 (33)	1 (8)	4 (33)	5 (42)	21 (26)	17 (26)
Sometimes it is necessary to block access to the Internet: No, in no circumstance	3 (9)	4 (24)	10 (42)	6 (25)	2 (17)	4 (33)	5 (42)	3 (25)	20 (25)	17 (26)
Need to control political affairs content: No	3 (9)	4 (24)	5 (21)	7 (29)	3 (25)	7 (58)	4 (33)	4 (33)	15 (18)	22 (34)
Need to control entertainment content: No	12 (36)	12 (71)	6 (25)	8 (33)	6 (50)	9 (75)	7 (58)	4 (33)	31 (38)	33 (51)
Approach to corruption in journalism: Negative	18 (55)	7 (41)	9 (38)	4 (17)	7 (58)	4 (33)	4 (33)	2 (17)	38 (47)	17 (26)
Have you produced articles for money or services in past 12 months? Yes	12 (36)	11 (65)	17 (71)	13 (54)	4 (33)	7 (58)	8 (67)	10 (83)	41 (51)	41 (63)
Attitude to protests in your city, country: Positive	4 (12)	5 (29)	2 (8)	2 (8)	0 (0)	1 (8)	1 (8)	0 (0)	6 (8)	8 (12)

TABLE F.6 Three core qualities of professional journalists

	Quality 1	Quality 2	Quality 3
Beijing: Traditional	Good writer	Engages in ethical conduct in general and in profession	Is objective
Beijing: Online	Is objective	Engages in ethical conduct in general and in profession	Competent/knowledgeable about subject
Shanghai: Traditional	Curiosity	Good writer	Generally erudite and scholarly/is objective
Shanghai: Online	Curiosity	Competent/knowledgeable about subject/good writer/unbiased/engages in ethical conduct in general and in profession/is objective	Independent
Guangzhou: Traditional	Competent/knowledgeable about subject	Engages in ethical conduct in general and in profession	Independent
Guangzhou: Online	Competent/knowledgeable about subject	Is objective	Unbiased/engages in ethical conduct in general and in profession/courageous/has grit/rational
Wuhan: Traditional	The ability to judge news value/social interaction ability/interview skills	Engages in ethical conduct in general and in profession	Good writer/unbiased/is objective
Wuhan: Online	The ability to judge news value/social interaction ability/interview skills	Engages in ethical conduct in general and in profession	Generally erudite and scholarly/competent/knowledgeable about subject/good writer

TABLE F.7 Three key functions that journalism should fulfil

	Function 1	Function 2	Function 3
Beijing: Traditional	Provide information	Guide opinion	Social supervision
Beijing: Online	Provide information	Promote objectivity	Protect people/society
Shanghai: Traditional	Provide information	Guide opinion	Provide a picture of the world/day
Shanghai: Online	Provide information	Interpret issues such as new laws, societal problems, etc.	Help form groups' opinions
Guangzhou: Traditional	Provide information	Educate	Enlighten/search for solutions (constructive criticism)
Guangzhou: Online	Provide information	Search for solutions (constructive criticism)	Educate
Wuhan: Traditional	Provide information/help people/society	Search for solutions (constructive criticism)	Entertain/interpret issues such as new laws, societal problems, etc.
Wuhan: Online	Provide information	Provide a picture of the world/day	Guide opinion

TABLE F.8 Three key roles that journalists should perform

	Role 1	Role 2	Role 3
Beijing: Traditional	Information disseminator	Supervisor	Social observer/rational thinker
Beijing: Online	Information disseminator	Objective information recorder	A bridge between the government and the public
Shanghai: Traditional	Neutral information disseminator	Public opinion guider	Social progress promoter
Shanghai: Online	Neutral information disseminator	Public opinion guider	Social progress promoter
Guangzhou: Traditional	Information disseminator	Supervisor	A bridge between the government and the public
Guangzhou: Online	Information disseminator	Social progress promoter	Information recorder
Wuhan: Traditional	Neutral information disseminator	Supervisor	Social order maintainer
Wuhan: Online	Neutral information disseminator	Public opinion guider	Opinion expresser

TABLE F.9 Three key differences between traditional and online news media journalists

	Difference 1	Difference 2	Difference 3
Beijing: Traditional	Speed	Quality of journalism produced	Thinking pattern
Beijing: Online	Speed	Thinking pattern	Quality of journalism produced
Shanghai: Traditional	Functions they perform	Speed	Quality of journalism produced
Shanghai: Online	Functions they perform	Speed	Quality of journalism produced
Guangzhou: Traditional	Functions they perform	Quality of journalism produced	Speed/professional quality/regulation from the party-state
Guangzhou: Online	Quality of journalism produced	Functions they perform	Speed
Wuhan: Traditional	Functions they perform	Speed	Quality of journalism produced
Wuhan: Online	Functions they perform	Speed	Quality of journalism produced

TABLE F.10 Three most important social–political changes needed in your country for journalism to perform its functions

	Change needed 1	Change needed 2	Change needed 3
Beijing: Traditional	Relax media regulation	Strengthen legislation	Marketization
Beijing: Online	Relax media regulation	Strengthen legislation	Protect the rights of journalists
Shanghai: Traditional	Relax media regulation	Ensure the independence of the media, including economic independence	NA
Shanghai: Online	Relax media regulation	Have more democracy	Ensure the independence of the media, including economic independence
Guangzhou: Traditional	Have more democracy	Relax media regulation	Strengthen legislation
Guangzhou: Online	Relax media regulation	Ensure the independence of the media, including economic independence	Increase political competition
Wuhan: Traditional	Relax media regulation	Ensure media and economic independence	Have more democracy
Wuhan: Online	Relax media regulation	Ensure media and economic independence	Have more democracy

APPENDIX G

Tables for South Africa

TABLE G.1 Sample of South African news media

City and number of respondents	Press/news agency (Traditional)	Radio/TV (Traditional)	Online
Johannesburg: 50 Traditional: 41 Online: 9	City Press Mail Guardian The Sunday Times The Times live The Daily Vox Khanyisa The Mail Forbes magazine Stuff Magazine	SABC PowerFM Mpower Emalahleni FM e.TV Soweto TV	Daily Maverick Money web ENCA Politicsweb

City and number of respondents	Press/news agency (Traditional)	Radio/TV (Traditional)	Online
	Mail Guardian	SABC (Radio)	Media24
Cape Town: 50	City Press	SABC (Radio)	
	The Sunday Times	UCT Radio	
Traditional: 45	Beeld	SABC (TV)	
Online: 5	Reuters	ENCA	
	Rapport	Cape TV	
	Business day		
	The New Age		
	AFP		
	SAPA		
	Cape Times		
	Cape Argus		
	Saturday Independent		
	Die Burger		
	Bloomberg		
	Sunday Times	SABC (Radio)	
Durban: 25	Sunday Independent	Vuma	
	The Zululand Observer	InandaFM	
Traditional: 25	The Mercury	e.TV	
	The Post	SABC (TV)	
	Isolezwe	KZN TV	
	Ilanga		
	The Witness		
	Daily Dispatch	SABC	
Port Elizabeth: 25	The Herald		
	The Grottis Mail		
Traditional: 25			

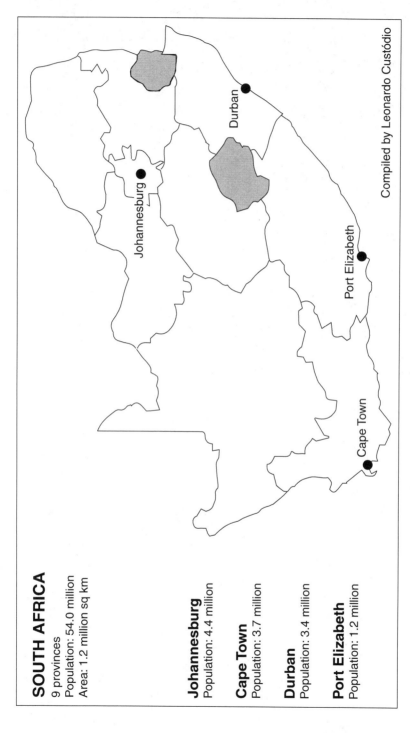

MAP 5   The location and population of the four South African cities
Source: Census data 2011

TABLE G.2 Demographic background and other variables in number of respondents (percentages in brackets)

City	Johannesburg		Cape Town		Durban		Port Elizabeth		All	
Media	Traditional	Online	Traditional	Online	Traditional	Online	Traditional	Online	Traditional	Online
Number of respondents	41	9	45	5	25	0	25	0	136	14
Age: 18–29	17 (51)	6 (66)	9 (18)	2 (40)	10 (40)	0 (0)	12 (48)	0 (0)	48 (35)	8 (57)
Gender: Female	21 (51)	4 (44)	21 (48)	4 (80)	10 (40)	0 (0)	11 (44)	0 (0)	59 (44)	8 (57)
Influence of gender: None	33 (82)	8 (88)	36 (80)	5 (100)	21 (84)	0 (0)	18 (72)	0 (0)	108 (80)	13 (92)
Degree: College	33 (82)	8 (88)	40 (90)	5 (100)	24 (96)	0 (0)	24 (96)	0 (0)	121 (91)	13 (92)
Major: Journalism	30 (74)	8 (88)	36 (80)	4 (80)	23 (92)	0 (0)	21 (84)	0 (0)	110 (83)	12 (85)
Social class: Professional	NA	NA	NA	NA	NA	0 (0)	NA	0 (0)	NA	NA
Year of entering journalism: Since 2001	12 (32)	8 (88)	28 (64)	4 (80)	17 (68)	0 (0)	19 (76)	0 (0)	76 (60)	12 (85)
Marital status: Married	12 (32)	2 (22)	16 (36)	2 (40)	6 (24)	0 (0)	4 (16)	0 (0)	38 (27)	4 (28)
Number of previous jobs: Two and more	12 (32)	2 (22)	15 (34)	2 (40)	15 (60)	0 (0)	12 (48)	0 (0)	54 (44)	4 (28)
Form of employed: Salaried	28 (72)	8 (88)	44 (98)	5 (100)	18 (72)	0 (0)	22 (88)	0 (0)	112 (86)	13 (92)
Type of employment: Permanent, full time	23 (56)	8 (88)	39 (88)	5 (100)	18 (72)	0 (0)	22 (88)	0 (0)	102 (76)	13 (92)
Second job: Yes	4 (12)	0 (0)	1 (2)	0 (0)	1 (4)	0 (0)	4 (16)	0 (0)	9 (7)	0 (0)
Total monthly income: Sufficient	NA	NA	NA	NA	NA	0 (0)	NA	0 (0)	NA	NA
Union membership: Yes	10 (20)	0 (0)	2 (4)	0 (0)	7 (28)	0 (0)	2 (8)	0 (0)	21 (15)	0 (0)
Party membership: Yes	0 (0)	0 (0)	0 (0)	0 (0)	0 (0)	0 (0)	0 (0)	0 (0)	0 (0)	0 (0)
NGO membership: Yes	0 (0)	0 (0)	0 (0)	0 (0)	0 (0)	0 (0)	0 (0)	0 (0)	0 (0)	0 (0)

TABLE G.3 Three most frequently mentioned reasons for journalists' job satisfaction

	Reason 1	Reason 2	Reason 3
Johannesburg: Traditional	Gratitude from the audience and feedback	Job security	Creative work and self-realization
Johannesburg: Online	Gratitude from the audience and feedback	Job security	Good working conditions
Cape Town: Traditional	Gratitude from the audience and feedback	Job security/ making change in people's lives	Creative work and self-realization
Cape Town: Online	Gratitude from the audience and feedback		
Durban: Traditional	Gratitude from the audience and feedback	Job security	Creative work and self-realization
Port Elizabeth: Traditional	Gratitude from the audience and feedback	Good working conditions	Making change in people's lives

TABLE G.4 Three most important social media apps for journalists

	Social media app 1	Social media app 2	Social media app 3
Johannesburg: Traditional	Twitter	Facebook	Instagram
Johannesburg: Online	Twitter	Facebook	
Cape Town: Traditional	Twitter	Facebook	
Cape Town: Online	Twitter	Facebook	
Durban: Traditional	Twitter	Facebook	Instagram
Port Elizabeth: Traditional	Twitter	Facebook	

TABLE G.5 Professional orientation and related variables in number of respondents (percentages in brackets)

City	Johannesburg		Cape Town		Durban		Port Elizabeth		All	
Media	Traditional	Online	Traditional	Online	Traditional	Online	Traditional	Online	Traditional	Online
Number of respondents	41	9	45	5	25	0	25	0	136	14
To stay in profession: Yes	NA	NA	NA	NA	NA	NA	NA	NA	NA	NA
Journalists should not cover subjects that play into the hands of our country's enemies: Yes	0 (0)	0 (0)	0 (0)	0 (0)	0 (0)	0 (0)	0 (0)	0 (0)	0 (0)	0 (0)
Sometimes it is necessary to block access to the Internet: No, in no circumstance	30 (74)	9 (100)	40 (90)	5 (100)	24 (96)	0 (0)	19 (76)	0 (0)	113 (84)	14 (100)
Need to control political affairs content: No	32 (80)	9 (100)	40 (90)	5 (100)	24 (96)	0 (0)	20 (80)	0 (0)	116 (87)	14 (100)
Need to control entertainment content: No	27 (68)	9 (100)	40 (90)	5 (100)	24 (96)	0 (0)	22 (88)	0 (0)	113 (86)	14 (100)
Approach to corruption in journalism: Negative	33 (82)	9 (100)	40 (90)	5 (100)	25 (100)	0 (0)	25 (100)	0 (0)	123 (93)	14 (100)
Have you produced articles for money or services in past 12 months? Yes	NA	NA	NA	NA	NA	NA	NA	NA	NA	NA
Attitude to protests in your city, country: Positive				0 (0)		0 (0)	13 (52)	0 (0)	13 (10)	0 (0)

TABLE G.6 Three core qualities of professional journalists

	Quality 1	Quality 2	Quality 3
Johannesburg: Traditional	Independence	Unbiased	Non-corruption
Johannesburg: Online	Independence	Unbiased	Non-corruption
Cape Town: Traditional	Independence	Unbiased	Non-corruption
Cape Town: Online	Independence	Unbiased	Non-corruption
Durban: Traditional	Independence	Unbiased	Non-corruption
Port Elizabeth: Traditional	Independence	Unbiased	Non-corruption

TABLE G.7 Three key functions that journalism should fulfil

	Function 1	Function 2	Function 3
Johannesburg: Traditional	Inform the public	Entertain	Empower community
Johannesburg: Online	Inform the public	Educate	Empower community
Cape Town: Traditional	Inform the public	Investigate stories	Empower community
Cape Town: Online	Inform the public	Educate	Empower community
Durban: Traditional	Inform the public	Investigate stories	Empower community
Port Elizabeth: Traditional	Inform the public	Investigate stories	Empower community

TABLE G.8 Three key roles that journalists should perform

	Role 1	Role 2	Role 3
Johannesburg: Traditional	Inform the public	Entertain	Empower community
Johannesburg: Online	Inform the public	Educate	Empower community
Cape Town: Traditional	Inform the public	Investigate stories	Empower community
Cape Town: Online	Inform the public	Educate	Empower community
Durban: Traditional	Inform the public	Investigate stories	Empower community
Port Elizabeth: Traditional	Inform the public	Investigate stories	Empower community

TABLE G.9 Three key differences between traditional and online news media journalists

	Difference 1	Difference 2	Difference 3
Johannesburg: Traditional	Speed		
Johannesburg: Online	Speed		
Cape Town: Traditional	Speed		
Cape Town: Online	Speed		
Durban: Traditional	Speed		
Port Elizabeth: Traditional	Speed		

TABLE G.10 Three most important socio-political changes needed in your country for journalism to perform its functions

	Change needed 1	*Change needed 2*	*Change needed 3*
Johannesburg: Traditional	Ensure media and economic independence	Have more democracy	
Johannesburg: Online	Ensure media and economic independence	Have more democracy	
Cape Town: Traditional	Ensure media and economic independence	Have more democracy	
Cape Town: Online	Ensure media and economic independence	Have more democracy	
Durban: Traditional	Ensure media and economic independence	Have more democracy	
Port Elizabeth: Traditional		Have more democracy	

INDEX

2oceansvibe Radio 204
60 Minutes 27

African Journalism Studies (AJS) (Pasti and Ramaprasad) 1
African National Congress (ANC) 42
Agência Pública de Notícias 52, 53, 133–134
agenda setting 51
Al Jazeera Media Network 8
All China Journalists Association 77
All-India Newspaper Editors' Conference, Code of Ethics of 76
All India Radio 76, 106
All-Russian Center for the Study of Public Opinion (VTsIOM) 177
Andrade, S. L. 54
Anti Unfair Competition Law of the People's Republic of China (AUCL) 74
Apple 49
Apple News 49
Arato, A. 174
Arquembourg, J. 50
association memberships 41–43
Attuch, L. 148, 152
audiences, as publics 50–51
Azevedo, J. A. 104

Banga Mahila (Bengali magazine) 106
Banyard, K. 125
Beam, R. A. 25
Beck, U. 151–152, 179
Berezovsky, B. 182
Blackberries 160

Bloomberg 3
Boas, T. 205
Brazil: better conditions for journalism in 145–146; codes of ethics in 75; community radio in 196–208 (*see also* community radio for right to communicate); convergence of media in 162–163; corruption defined in 73; decreasing number of male journalists in 122; digital technology and newsmaking in 52–54; ethical dilemmas in 89–90; female journalists in 104–105, 108; future of journalism as profession/practice in 148; gendered journalistic roles in 116, 117–118, 119; government control and journalists in 60; journalism professionalism in 26; journalism quality in, impact of technology on 164–167; journalism's functions in 38; journalists in, impact of technology on 167–170; map of 224; market logic and deregulation in 78; paid news in 81–82; pay/career advancement opportunities in 123; power of profession in 33; press freedom in 51; reporting structures in, hierarchy and 65–66; second jobs in 137; self-appraisal in 29–30; social media as journalism tool in 57; staying in journalism profession in 144; tables for 223–230; technological changes in (*see* technological changes in India and Brazil); traditional to self-employment journalism in 134–135, 137; union/

association memberships in 41; women as assets to journalism profession in 121; work dissatisfaction in 142–143; work satisfaction in 139–140
Brazil, Russia, India, China, and South Africa (BRICS nations) *see* BRICS nations (Brazil, Russia, India, China, and South Africa)
Brazil247 (independent website) 135, 148
Brazilian Association of Community Radios 199
Brazilian Information Access Law 73
Brazilian Institute of Geography and Statistics (IBGE) 133
Brazilian journalists' code 75
Brazilian Law Against Corruption 73
Brazilian Telecommunication Code 78
Bretton-Woods system 6
BRICS Communication Ministers Meeting 9
BRICS Contingent Reserve Arrangement 6–7
BRICS Credit Rating Agency 7
BRICS journalism: committee approach to implement study research 14–15; comparative approach to study's findings 13–14; introduction to 1–16; study method used 12–13, 211–221; study of, impetus for 10–12
BRICS Media Summit 9
BRICS nations (Brazil, Russia, India, China, and South Africa) 1; clarifying 2–10; codes of ethics in 75–77; contextual/multifaceted understanding of journalistic ethics in 93–100; corruption in, defining 73–75; as disciplines specialization type 4–5; economic/cooperative action initiatives 6–8; economic strength of 3–4; gender in journalism 112–124; international communication initiatives 8–9; market logic and deregulation in 77–80; media initiatives 9–10; multidimensional nature of 2–6; political dimension of 4; press freedom in 51; Russia-China as forerunner to 4; Western press accounts of 5
Broadcasting Complaints Commission (BCCSA) 77
Broadcasting Content Complaints Council (BCCC) 76
brown envelope journalism 88
"Building Responsive, Inclusive and Collective Solutions" 7

Bunce, V. J. 178
Byerly, C. M. 107

Cable Television Networks (Regulation) Act 76–77
Central Board of Film Certification (CBFC) 62
Chaudhurani, H. K. 106
Chernysh, M. 125
China: better conditions for journalism in 147; bribery forms in 74; codes of ethics in 77; corruption defined in 74; digital technology and newsmaking in 55; ethical dilemmas in 92; female journalists in 106, 108–109, 114; future of journalism as profession/practice in 150; gendered journalistic roles in 117, 118; glass ceiling for females in 114–115, 116; government control and journalists in 64–65; journalism professionalism in 27; journalism's functions in 39–40; journalists' attitudes to protests in 189–191; map of 251; market logic and deregulation in 79; news media and political protests in 183–184; paid news in 86–88; pay/career advancement opportunities in 123; political protests in 178–181; power of profession in 35–36; press freedom in 51; reporting structures in, hierarchy and 68; as risk society 178–179; second jobs in 138; self-appraisal in 31–32; social media as journalism tool in 59; staying in journalism profession in 144, 145; tables for 249–257; traditional to self-employment journalism in 136, 137; union/association memberships in 42; women as assets to journalism profession in 122; work dissatisfaction in 143; work satisfaction in 141; World Media Summits (WMS) 8
Chinese Academy of Social Sciences 181
Chinese journalists' attitudes to protests 189–191; general attitude 189; by geographical-urban dimension 190; by media type 190; by ownership type 191
Chinese Universities Media Alliance 108–109
citizen journalism 160
Cliff, G. 203
CliffCentral.com 203
CNN 50
Code of Ethics of a Russian Journalist 75–76

Code of Professional Ethics for Chinese Media Workers 77
codes of ethics in BRICS countries 75–77
Cohen, J. L. 174
Coletivo Mariachi 52, 53, 54
Coletivo Papo Reto 53–54
commercial bribery 74
commercial journalism 50
committee approach 14
Committee to Protect Journalists (CPJ) 30, 51
community radio for right to communicate 196–208; challenges to, in Brazil 205–206; challenges to, in South Africa 206–207; developments affecting 200–202; digitalization of radio/online radio in Brazil 202–203; digitalization of radio/online radio in South Africa 203–204; history of, in Brazil 197–198; history of, in South Africa 198; introduction to 196–197; podcasts in Brazil 202; principles of 196; regulatory framework of, in Brazil 198–200; regulatory framework of, in South Africa 200; social media in Brazil 202; social media in South Africa 204; study findings 207–208
comScore 54
convergent journalism 160, 162–163
Cooperative of Radio Lovers 199
corruption in BRICS countries, defining 73–75
Council on Foreign and Defense Policy of the Russian Federation 5
Crawford, K. 201
Criminal Law of the People's Republic of China 74
critical issues, two-country comparisons of; *see also individual issues*: community radio in Brazil and Africa 196–208; political protests in Russia and China 173–192; technological changes in India and Brazil 159–171
Custódio, L. 202

Daily Maverick, The 56
Dainik Enews 136
Daniels, G. 111
da Silva, C. 105
decentralization of journalism 153
democratization of journalism 153
de-monetization of journalism 153
de-professionalization of journalism 153
deregulation in BRICS countries, market logic and 77–80

Deuze, M. 25, 28–29, 45
Diário do Centro do Mundo (blog) 54, 148
digital technologies: as factor in feminization of journalism 109; newsmaking practices and 52–56
Doordarshan 76
dos Santos, N. J. 205–206
Drum (magazine) 28
Dutt, P. 106
dzhinsa (paid article) 97

Eapen, K. E. 27
economic/cooperative action initiatives 6–8
economic dissatisfaction 143
Ekaterina II (empress of Russia) 105
Ekho Moskvy (Russian radio station) 183
ethical dilemmas 89–93; in Brazil 89–90; in China 92; in India 91–92; in Russia 90–91; in South Africa 92–93
ethics in journalism 72–100; BRICS study findings 80–93; codes of 75–77; contextual/multifaceted understanding of 93–100; corruption, defining 73–75; ethical dilemmas and 89–93; introduction to 72–73; market logic and deregulation, advent of 77–80; paid news and 80–89
Evetts, J. 28, 44
explanatory journalism 165

Facebook 53, 54, 58, 59, 160, 177, 201
factoid 50
femininity features 109
feminization of journalism 104; *see also* gender in journalism
feuilleton (critical, analytic, in-depth articles) 26
Financial Times 3
Flipboard 49
Folha de São Paulo 9, 60
Fora do Eixo 53
Ford Foundation 53
Franco, G. 159
Freedman, D. 152–153
Freedom House 8, 51
Freidson, E. 24, 132, 153
Freire, P. 196
Fridman, L. 105
Future Focus Brazil 2015 54

Gallagher, M. 110
Galvão, P. 105
gendered roles in journalism 116–119
gendered women in journalism 111–112
gender equality: in journalism, lack of 109–111; UNESCO terming of 124

gender in journalism 104–126; BRICS study findings 112–126; current situation 107–109; digitization as factor in feminization 109; equality and, lack of 109–111; female journalists, number of 113–114; gendered roles 116–119; gendered women 111–112; glass ceiling 114–116; historical parallels in BRICS 104–107; men leaving profession and, concerns over 122–123; pay/career advancement opportunities and 123–124; sexist attitudes 120–121; women as assets to profession and 121–122

General Administration of Press and Publication 150

Getúlio Vargas Foundation (FGV) 53

glass ceiling in journalism 114–116

Glasser, T. L. 25, 28, 29

Global Journalist for the 21st Century, The (Weaver and Willnat) 11, 107, 132

Goldman Sachs 3, 4

Gonzalez, A. M. 111

government control, newsmaking practices and 60–65

Groundup 56

Gusinsky, V. 182

Hallin, D. 78

Hanitzsch, T. 11–12

Haraway, D. 109

Hermans, L. 160

hierarchy in reporting structures: in Brazil 65–66; in China 68; in India 66–68; in South Africa 68–69

Hildago, F. 205

Hindu, The 27

Hongbao 87–88, 98

Hughes, E. C. 24

Hu Y. 180

ideology: defined 25; elements of 25

Independent Broadcasting Authority (IBA) 200

Independent Communications Authority of South Africa (ICASA) 200

India: better conditions for journalism in 146–147; BRICS Joint Working Group on Counter Terrorism 7; "Building Responsive, Inclusive and Collective Solutions" 7; codes of ethics in 76–77; convergence of media in 162; corruption defined in 74; digital technology and newsmaking in 55; English *vs.* Hindi language news in 160–161; ethical dilemmas in 91–92; female journalists in 106, 108, 113–114; future of journalism as profession/practice in 149–150; gendered journalistic roles in 117, 118, 119; glass ceiling for females in 114; government control and journalists in 62–63; journalism professionalism in 27; journalism quality in, impact of technology on 164–167; journalism's functions in 38–39; journalists in, impact of technology on 167–170; map of 241; market logic and deregulation in 79; paid news in 84–86; pay/career advancement opportunities in 123; power of profession in 34–35; press freedom in 51; reporting structures in, hierarchy and 66–68; second jobs in 138; self-appraisal in 30–31; smartphone use in 163–164; social media as journalism tool in 58–59, 163; staying in journalism profession in 144–145; tables for 240–247; technological changes in (*see* technological changes in India and Brazil); traditional to self-employment journalism in 135–136, 137; union/association memberships in 41–42; women as assets to journalism profession in 121–122; work dissatisfaction in 143; work satisfaction in 140–141

Indian Broadcasting Foundation (IBF) 76

Indian Penal Code 74

informal intermediaries 94

international communication initiatives 8–9

International Federation of Journalists (IFJ) 108

International Monetary Fund (IMF) 6

International Women's Media Foundation (IWMF) 107, 109–110, 124

Joseph, A. 125

journalism as profession and practice 130–154; better working conditions and 145–148; BRICS study findings 134–154; future of 148–151; introduction to 130–134; second jobs and 137–139; staying in profession and 144–145; traditional to self-employment 134–137; work dissatisfaction and 141–144; work satisfaction and 139–141

journalism professionalism 23–46; in BRICS, historical view of 26–28; BRICS study findings 43–46; critical 'power' approach to 32–37; described 24–25; functions of 37–41; moral dimension to 43; self-appraisal and 29–32, 37; term

use of 23–24; understanding, as concept 28–29; union/association memberships and 41–43
journalism's functions 37–41
journalistic ethics, contextual/multifaceted understanding of 93–100

Kaul, V. 160
Koesel, K. J. 178

Landingo, L. C. 54
Lareau, L. 160
Larson, M. S. 23, 24
Law of The Russian Federation No. 2124-1 on Mass Media 62
law on bloggers 55, 131
Levada Research Center 177
Li, C. 9
Lima, S. 108
Lin, G. C. 108
Lukin, A. 5–6
Lukyanov, F. 5, 6, 7

Made, P. 109
Malerba, J. 199, 202
Mancini, P. 78
market logic and deregulation in BRICS countries 77–80
masterstvo 26
Media Appeals Tribunal 56, 65
Media Development and Diversity Agency (MDDA) 200, 207
media initiatives 9–10
Miami Herald, The 111
Mick, J. 108
Mídia Ninja 52, 53
Mingzhao, C, 10
Moody's 7
Morna, C. L. 109
Moscow Charter of Journalists 75
Mouillaud, M. 50
Mukherjee, P. 74
multiskilling 132
Murdoch, R. 72
Muzarte, Z. L. 104

Narayanan, N. 96–97
National Agency for Telecommunications (Anatel) 199–200
National Association of Broadcasters (NAB) 77
National Federation of Journalists (FENAJ) 41, 142–143
Neves, M. A. 110

New Development Bank (NDB) 6–7
News24 56
News Broadcasters Association 77
News Broadcasting Standards Authority 77
newsmaking practices 49–70; BRICS study findings 56–69; digital technologies and 52–56; government control and 60–65; introduction to 49–51; press freedom and 51; reporting structures and 65–69; social media and 57–60
news media and political protests: in China 183–184; in Russia 182–183
News of the World 72
news.xinhuanet.com 77
New York Times, The 50, 53
Nogueira, K. 148
Novaya Gazeta (newspaper) 183

O Cidadão (newspaper) 203
October *putsch* 175
official bribery 74
O Globo 60
Olimpieva, I. 94
Omidyar Network 53
O'Neil, J. 3–4
Online Media Self-Regulation Guidebook 131–132
Open Society Foundations 53
opinion journalism 50
Opp, K. D. 174
Organization for Security and Co-operation in Europe 131–132

Pachenkov, O. 94
paid news: advertorials in Russia as 81; in Brazil 81–82; in China 86–88; ethics in journalism and 80–89; extortion to hide story as 81; in India 84–86; Press Council of India definition of 80; in Russia 82–84; in South Africa 88–89; writing favourable articles as 81
Paiva, R. 199
Parsons, T. 24
participatory journalism, 160
Pasti, S. 125
Patarra, J. 105
pay/career advancement opportunities in journalism 123–124
Peter the Great (Tsar) 105
Petrobras Journalism Award 53
pink journalism 125
political dissatisfaction 143–144
political protests 173–192; in China 178–181; contradiction types in

173–174; defining 173–174; journalists' attitudes to, in China 189–191; journalists' attitudes to, in Russia 184–188; news media and, in China 183–184; news media and, in Russia 182–183; in Russia 174–178; study findings 191–192
post-bipolar world 2–3; power shifts leading to 3
power approach: to journalism professionalism 25, 32–37; to professions 23, 24
Pragmatismo Político (blog) 54
Press Council of India (PCI) Code of Ethics 76
Press Trust of India 9
Prevention and Combating of Corrupt Activities Act, South Africa 74–75
Prevention of Corruption Act, India 74
Primakov, Y. 2–3, 4
Primakov's Triangle 4
professional dissatisfaction 144
professionalism; *see also* journalism professionalism: as a concept 28–29; definition of 23; term use of 23
professionalization 24
professions: critical 'power' approach to 23, 24; functionalist approach to 24; traits approach to 23–24
Protection of State Information Bill 56, 65
publicism 50
publics, audiences as 50–51
publitsistika, defined 26
Putin, V. 175, 183

Rabe, L. 111
Radio Sucre in Radio Nuevos Horizontes 196
Radio Sutatenza, Colombia 196
Radiotube 202
Rai, U. 106
Ramos, R. H. P. 105
Rand Daily Mail 56
Randolph, L. M. 109
red package/envelope 87
Reform Movement of 1898 106
Reich, Z. 160
Reporters Sans Frontières 51; Reporters Without Borders 8, 182–183
reporting structures, newsmaking practices and 65–69
Resnyanskaya, L. 94
Reuters Digital News Report 52
Revista Fórum (magazine) 54
Revista Maçaneta (online magazine) 54

Rio Grande do Sul (community TV station) 203
risk society, defined 179
Rodny-Gumede, Y. 119, 125
Rodrigues, N. 104
Roskomnadzor 55
Rossouw, R. 106–107
Roussef, D. 133
Russia: better conditions for journalism in 146; BRICS Communication Ministers Meetings 9; Civic Forum BRICS 8; codes of ethics in 75–76; corruption defined in 74; decreasing number of male journalists in 123; digital technology and newsmaking in 54–55; ethical dilemmas in 90–91; female journalists in 105, 113; future of journalism as profession/practice in 148–149; gendered journalistic roles in 117; glass ceiling for females in 114, 115–116; government control and journalists in 61–62; journalism professionalism in 26–27; journalism's functions in 38; journalists' attitudes to protests in 184–188; law on bloggers 55, 131; map of 233; market logic and deregulation in 78–79; news media and political protests in 182–183; paid news in 82–84; political protests in 174–178; power of profession in 33–34; press freedom in 51; reporting structures in, relationships and 66; second jobs in 138; self-appraisal in 30; sexist attitudes in 120; social media as journalism tool in 57–58; staying in journalism profession in 144; tables for 232–238; traditional to self-employment journalism in 135, 137; union/association memberships in 41; urbanization in, gender structure of journalists and 108; women as assets to journalism profession in 121; work dissatisfaction in 143; work satisfaction in 140
Russia, India, and China (RIC) 4
Russian federal law (No. 273) *On Combating Corruption* 74
Russian journalists' attitudes to protests 184–188; general attitude 184–185; by geographical-urban dimension 186–187; by media type 188; by ownership type 188

Sakwa, R. 4, 6
Santa Marta community radio station 202
Sasser, J. 181

Scoop 49
second jobs 137–139
self-appraisal, journalistic professionalism and 29–32, 37
Self-discipline Convention, China's Internet Industry 77
Self-discipline Convention for Mobile Phone Media, China 77
Severo, C. 54
sexist attitudes in journalism 120–121
Shaer, M. 53
Sina Corporation 55
Sina Weibo 55, 59, 130
smart phones 163–164
Sobesednik Liubitelei Rossiiskogo Slova (magazine) 105
social dissatisfaction 144
social media: as feedback mechanism 58; newsmaking practices and 57–60, 163; technological changes in India/Brazil and 163
social media as journalism tool: in Brazil 57; in China 59; in India 58–59, 163; in Russia 57–58; in South Africa 59–60
South Africa: better conditions for journalism in 147–148; codes of ethics in 77; community radio in 196–208 (*see also* community radio for right to communicate); corruption defined in 74–75; digital technology and newsmaking in 55–56; ethical dilemmas in 92–93; female journalists in 106–107, 109, 114; future of journalism as profession/practice in 151; gendered journalistic roles in 116, 118–119; glass ceiling for females in 115, 116; government control and journalists in 65; journalism professionalism in 28; journalism's functions in 40; map of 258; market logic and deregulation in 79–80; paid news in 88–89; pay/career advancement opportunities in 123–124; 'please call me' service in 52; power of profession in 36; press freedom in 51; reporting structures in, hierarchy and 68–69; second jobs in 138; self-appraisal in 32; sexist attitudes in 120–121; social media as journalism tool in 59–60; staying in journalism profession in 145; tables for 259–265; traditional to self-employment journalism in 136; union/association memberships in 42; women as assets to journalism profession in 122; work dissatisfaction in 143; work satisfaction in 141

South African Broadcasting Corporation (SABC) 9, 69
South African Freelancers Association (Safrea) 42
South African National Editors' Forum (SANEF) 111
South African Press Council Code of Ethics and Conduct for South African Print and Online Media 77
South African Telecommunications Authority (SATRA) 200
Southern Metropolis Daily 40
Soviet Union *see* Russia
Spyridou, L. P. 159
Standard & Poor's 7
Stuenkel, O. 6
Sugrahini (Hindi magazine) 106
Svitich, L. 125

Taxi, The (online radio show) 203–204
technocracy of news 170
technological changes in India and Brazil 159–171; convergence and 162–163; exclusivity/depth, losing 164–165; explanatory journalism and 165; impact of, on journalism quality 164–167; impact of, on journalistic practice 162–164; impact of, on journalists 167–170; introduction to 159–161; IT specialists, need for 169–170; job insecurity and 170; new digital skills and 168–169; newsroom re-staffing and 167–168; scholarly opinions on influence of 159–160; as smart ecosystem 165–166; smart phones and 163–164; social media and 163; study findings 170–171; work styles and, transforming 166–167
Tencent company 55
Tevê Ovo (community TV station) 203
Tiananmen Square protests 179–180
TICKS (Taiwan, India, China, and South Korea) 3
Toloraya, G. 4, 5
traits approach: to journalism professionalism 24–25, 29–32; to professions 23–24
Turner, T. 50
Twitter 55, 58–59, 130, 160

union/association memberships 41–43
Union of Russian Journalists 108

Van Vuuren, K. 205
Vedomosti (Russian newspaper) 105

Vergeer, M. 160
Vigil, L. H. 112, 125
von Euler, M. 110
Vsiakaiavsiachina (magazine) 105
Vyarawallah, H. 106

Weaver, D. H. 11, 72–73, 107
WeChat 55, 59
Weibo *see* Sina Weibo
Western credit rating agencies 7
WhatsApp 58, 153
Wilhoit, G. C. 72–73
William, A. 203
Willnat, L. 11, 107
witness 51
women in news media: as assets to profession 121–122; current situation for 107–109; historical parallels in BRICS for 104–107

working conditions, journalists' views on 145–148
World Association of Community Radio Broadcasters (AMARC) 199
World Audit 8
World Bank 6
World Media Summits (WMS) 8
Worlds of Journalism Study (Hanitzsch et al.) 11–12

Xinhua News Agency 9, 10

Yeltsin, B. 175, 182

Zakaria, F. 3
zakazuha (ordered publications) 97
Zee News (TV) 136
Zhang, J. J. 108
Zhang, Z. A. 108